Beyond Gated Politics

University of Minnesota Press
Minneapolis • London

# Beyond Gated Politics

Reflections for the Possibility of Democracy

Romand Coles

Published by the University of Minnesota Press
111 Third Avenue South, Suite 290
Minneapolis, MN 55401-2520
http://www.upress.umn.edu


Library of Congress Cataloging-in-Publication Data

Coles, Romand, 1959-
  Beyond gated politics : reflections for the possibility of democracy /
Romand Coles.
    p.   cm.
  Includes bibliographical references and index.
  ISBN 0-8166-4689-9 (hc : alk. paper) — ISBN 0-8166-4690-2 (pb : alk.
paper)
  1. Democracy. 2. Democracy—United States. I. Title.
  JC423.C6474 2005
  320.973'09'0511—dc22
                                                              2005007869


Printed in the United States of America on acid-free paper

The University of Minnesota is an equal-opportunity educator and employer.


12  11  10  09  08  07  06  05            10  9  8  7  6  5  4  3  2  1

# Contents

# Acknowledgments

THIS BOOK IS INDEBTED to a series of enthusiastic dialogues over the past several years, and it is hard for me to stay calm about them. Without numerous conversational and political contexts at Duke University and in Durham, North Carolina, these reflections would have been unimaginable. Let me limit myself to acknowledging several.

During the past four years, a vibrant bunch of scholars from across the university has gathered monthly in a working group we call "Dialogical Ethics and Critical Cosmopolitanism," sponsored by Duke's Center for Globalization and the Humanities and co-convened by Walter Mignolo and myself. I have presented chapters from this book to this group, and I have been inspired by and learned a great deal from its many regular participants, including Walter Mignolo, Wahneema Lubiano, Leo Ching, Nelson Maldonado-Torres, Teresa Berger, William Hart, Ibrahim Moosa, Ashwini Chhatre, Craig Borowiak, and Roberto Dianotto, among others. I have also learned from and been profoundly shaped by conversations I have had over the years with faculty and graduate students in the Department of Religion and the Duke Divinity School, including Stanley Hauerwas, Mary McClintock Fulkerson, Peter Dula, Joe Winters, Joel Shuman, Alex Sider, Chris Huebner, Charlie Collier, Jonathan Tran, Jeff McCurry, and others. I have been blessed by an incredible group of graduate students in political theory; Craig Borowiak, Laura Grattan, Troy Dostert, P. J. Brendese, Stefan Dolgert, Tania Roy, Alisa Kessel, and David McIvor have all commented insightfully on significant portions of this work, and daily I learn a great deal from their own productions. Upon completing his PhD, Troy Dostert fully coauthored the last chapter of this book. My political theory colleagues Peter Euben, Kimberley Curtis, Tom Spragens, Ruth Grant, Michael Gillespie, Evan Charney, and Elizabeth Kiss constitute an important field of insights and tensions in which I continue to grow. Jason Frank, Melissa Orlie, and Jeffrey Lomonaco carefully reviewed the entire manuscript for the University of Minnesota and each offered suggestions that were immensely helpful and have found their way in to the final version.

During the past seven years I've been active with many scores of people in a grassroots democracy organizing project in Durham called Durham CAN. The myriad dialogues, struggles, and actions we perform together feed my imagination, thought, and judgment day in and day out. Thinking for me is impossible without hope. Without those who are daily bringing democracy to life in this small southern city I would muster little of either.

# Introduction

Is DEMOCRACY SAILING INTO A "PERFECT STORM"? Is it about to plunge beneath mounting waves of transnational corporate and financial power, myriad fundamentalisms, neofascist megastates, gargantuan media conglomerates, ruthless neocolonial power, bloody state and nonstate terrorism, and environmental catastrophe? Perhaps the most formidable challenge today comes from new modes of power that weave tightly together several of the above in political articulations capable of penetrating social life ever more deeply, thoroughly, relentlessly, flexibly, and resiliently.[1] Although each new move to consolidate power meets democratic resistance, these new articulations thus far show a striking capacity to legitimate and intensify their development with reference to one or more of the other "waves" said to threaten the polity. In the face of these claims, many of the established, more democratic contenders begin to adopt significant aspects of the language, rationality, policies, and modes of operating of those they would challenge. Hence—thinking now of the United States—even as elections continue to go back and forth between Republicans and Democrats, many antidemocratic trends of recent decades continue generally unabated, at best moving a little more slowly at times, pausing in certain domains, or sneaking in a bit of humanity here and there.

The administration of George W. Bush in the early years of the new millennium takes antidemocratic tendencies to new depths, with policy-making circles of super-elites who no longer even pretend to consult the broader spectrum of opinion and interest; the increasing Republicanization of corporate lobbyists; the blatant profiteering from government contracts by corporate giants like Halliburton; the increasing fusion of public and private operations of surveillance, pedagogy, policing, and punishment; the Clear Channelization of the megamedia public sphere; the crystallization of foreign and domestic "antiterrorism" policy through a constellation of preemptive strike doctrine, unrelenting deceit, periodic "alerts," and a culture of deafness to the rest of the world and all who dissent; the proliferation of international political economic institutions that lubricate corporate power and diminish established and emergent democratic institutions as "unfair barriers to trade"; a domestic economic policy that promotes a "race to the bottom"; the effort to mount religious war against homosexuals and all who threaten "our way of life"; the uncontrolled devastation of the earth; and so forth. The Democratic resistance to many of these efforts has generally not been very successful at articulating alternative discourses or policies, so even if they succeed in winning an election here and there, it is unclear whether they will have much ability or will to significantly alter the current course of things.

We live—and I write—in the face of tremendous political dangers.

Yet insurgent democratic mobilizations are developing new networks, modes of organizing, powers, and grassroots experimental practices in cities and rural areas around the world, as well as visions that promise serious resistance, prefigure brighter days, and, in the words of an old punk rocker, offer some "reasons to be cheerful."[2]

Hope lies in hyperactive efforts to invent arts of receptive democratic engagement across differences, through which alternative collective powers might gather the strength to actually make another world possible. This book is written from and seeks in modest ways to inform and nourish the wellsprings of this hope in the face of the dangers mentioned above. This book is borne by the radical democratic efforts (in which I am active) to deepen democracy and justice in Durham, North Carolina, and in scores of cities across the United States. It is borne by other grassroots efforts at the World Social Forum by organizations that coalesce annually from around the world, aiming toward a different globalization. Hence, this is a book written in the midst of specific dangers and hopes, in an effort to nurture a democratic wisdom that might have some broader import. It is a series of reflections and provocations concerning some of the conditions—both theoretical and practical—that might enhance democratic struggles and might even help them flourish. And it seeks to envision what a more radically democratic flourishing might look like in a heterogeneous world.

My wager is that the future of democracy hinges significantly upon moving beyond the dominant forms of disengaged liberal democracy with which many in Western nations are familiar. The above challenges to current democratic institutions and practices will probably require major *democratizing* innovations if democracy is to survive in any meaningful sense. The preservation of the better elements of democratic traditions around the world now requires experimenting with more-radical modes of democratic practice to create viable terrains of culture, habit, and knowledge—modes of receptivity, engagement, and coalition that can engender sources of power that both resist and provide alternatives to both long-standing and mounting antidemocratic forces.

We live in very dangerous times, but when has democracy *not* been seriously endangered and even nonexistent for many? Democracy has never been a safe, transparent possession; rather, it has been a practice largely in search of itself, struggling beyond pasts and presents in which it was unrealized (both for many people and across many domains of life) and in the face of futures threatening to retrench its achievements and aspirations. Democracy happens primarily as a generative activity in which people seek to reinvent it in challenges and contestations concerning the question of what it might become. Democracy is *democratization*. And when it has been brought to life historically (by abolitionists, feminists, antiwar activists, populists in the nineteenth century, the civil rights movement, Native American rights activists, grassroots community activists, and so on), it has always hinged upon those who sensed, in their myriad insurgent, inventive, and receptive capacities, that democracy was, is, and will be significantly beyond democracy as "we" "know" it in its dominant forms: beyond the arbitrary exclusions, subjugations, and dangers that accompany every democratic "we" and their "knowing" and disclose complacency toward present practices as a sham. Democratization has always depended upon those who embark beyond democracy's dominant forms to invent greater equality, freedom, and receptive generosity toward others.

Surely great and small struggles of vast importance have been waged to defend what were already widely recognized democratic institutions, practices, and faiths of the day (against totalitarianism, McCarthyism, racist backlash, and the like)—to defend "democracy as we know it." Democracies must continually mobilize these sorts of deeply admirable struggles in the face of antidemocratic powers that mobilize and begin to undermine advances won in earlier struggles. Yet even here, the defense of widely recognized existing democratic institutions, practices, and values must often be entwined with initiatives that move beyond democracy's dominant modes, as movements to preserve what is presently valued find themselves drawn to invent or (re)discover practices, values, virtues, virtus (in Machiavelli's sense), and enthusiasms not yet widely recognized in order to cultivate the requisite power. And often people become enamored of and transfigured by these inventions and (re)discoveries.

There is, moreover, another related way in which democratization is entwined with a sense of moving beyond democracy in its dominant forms. People struggling with and beyond the established faiths of an order often become aware of something that seems very hard for many theorists to grasp. As their struggles rearticulate "history," they gain a sense that their own capacities for judgment and action are deeply indebted to a multitude of transformative past acts that were *unwonted* at the time of their invention.[3] Hence, for example, feminists of color become aware of their agonistic indebtedness to white feminist struggles of a hundred years before and to early struggles against racism—both of which were surprising in their own day with respect to their vision, intensity, and modes of political practice. Thus inspired, feminists of color gradually gain a deeper appreciation for and generosity toward political initiatives that move unwontedly beyond various historical presents. Furthermore, as they contend with the enormous contestability of judgment and action in the present, many begin to embrace and cultivate a sense that *their* deeds will and must be implicated in and transcended by significantly unanticipatable regenerative movements of radical democracy in the future. They gradually come to recognize that the promise of democratizing action and judgment hinges very profoundly on people's _knowing not to know democracy too well._ They begin to be moved not only beyond the sensibilities and faiths of the given order but toward a sense that at the heart of the democratic promise is the wisdom to sense the limits of our own vision, even as we vigorously pursue it. This recognition that our own finite efforts unwittingly engender damage better enables insurgent democrats to infuse their judgment and action with a greater degree of suppleness, receptivity, and open-endedness, without which democracy quickly loses its distinction. At the heart of the democratic promise is the idea that democracy is always significantly beyond democracy as we know it. My sense is that democratic action across a variety of struggles is increasingly engendering this awareness and that many involved are seeking actively to cultivate it. I see it frequently in grassroots democratic efforts to build community power in Durham and elsewhere, in the writings of feminists of color, in postcolonial movements and theories, in the coalition of progressive black pastors and conservative whites in Charlotte, North Carolina, in the writing of deconstructionist feminists like Judith Butler, in queer activists and theorists like Shane Phelan, in environmentalists in the Pacific

Northwest seeking to form coalitions across lines of race and class, in people involved in the work of the Mennonite Central Committee, and many others.

To emphasize this receptive sensibility toward the unwonted is not to ignore the fact that efforts to transcend the present must questioningly draw upon the traditions of judgment they inherit for wisdom if they are to resist being singularly overwhelmed by such a dizzying relationship to the new that they risk aiding a "return of the worst," as Jacques Derrida put it. Thus, I seek to explore modes of radical democratic judgment and action at the enlivening discordant edge between democracy as we know it and democratic possibilities beyond the borders of extant political topographies. I seek, with insurgent democrats across time, to bring an edgy political world into being.

Working "in between" different impulses and insights that are in tension with one another is vital to the practice of radical democracy being explored in this book—vital to the possibility of cultivating powerful alternatives to the antidemocratic challenges mentioned above. I seek a democratic ethos that cultivates *tension-dwelling* as a most promising mode for exercising judgment and engaging in democratic action. I am particularly interested in the tensions between cultivating what appears to be the best of the received wisdom of a tradition and cultivating a readiness for reformation in the face of others and new circumstances. In the stretching that occurs when we are discrepantly drawn by different considerations, concerns, insights, and bodily locations, our receptive capacities can acquire a depth, multidimensionality, and supple mobility without which we tend to do poorly in our relations with others. Hence, the tension-dwelling affirmed and developed here stems from a strong sense that we ought to relish certain tensions—difficult though they are—as a source of democratic ethical and political generativity. Though the insights on either side of the tensions cultivated in the following chapters are extremely important in their own right, I locate the strongest wellspring of ethical and political hope in how the tensions themselves might work our collective practices, our spirit, and our flesh toward greater receptive generosity toward plurality.

In the foreground of the present inquiry are those tensions that concern our various inheritances—particularly our relations with traditions of democratic struggle and dialogical practice that orient, animate, provoke, and disturb us. The Latin root of "tradition" is *traditio*. The fact that *traditio* is also the Latin root of "treason" suggests that there is a vital and enduring agon at the heart of our relation to what history passes on to us. Indeed, *traditio* means "to pass on," "to hand over," and both of these tropes have a similar double valence. "To pass on" can evoke a sense of bestowing something. In this sense, something passed *on* (or handed over, in the sense of "handed down") is given across time to some other(s) who receive it and in so doing (re)establish a certain continuity, a legacy, a tradition that somehow orients us. Yet "to *pass* on" can also mean to refuse: to refuse to pass something forward in time—to refuse to hand it down or over, or to refuse to receive what is thus given. To *pass* on thus establishes a rupture, a break with the past and with those who wish to see its legacy continue in an unbroken stream. And this rupture is often viewed by the latter as treasonous, as "handing over" in the sense of treacherous betrayal, a rebellious attack against the generally recognized highest gifts and givers (for example, that which is sovereign) and all those associated with them.

This contradiction sheltered in the Latin *traditio,* this polysemy harbored in tropes like "to pass on" and "to hand over," gestures toward an indeterminacy that so often lurks within our discrepant ethical and political judgments. (Which ones are continuing what is most promising and least dangerous in our legacies? Which are betraying these aspects of our legacies?) Of course, claims that "we" uphold the deepest wisdom of a tradition, along with accusations that the others betray it, are frequently duplicitous. Yet they often also reveal an essential contestability at the heart of our relation to history. They reveal an indeterminacy *at the heart of traditions themselves,* each tradition of which is always already constituted through endless responses in which those who came before us, and those who came before them, leaped toward judgments and actions with and beyond the finite yet indeterminate traditions they inherited. Tradition, even at its democratically most promising, is imbued at each moment of its history with indeterminacies concerning whether and how an inheritance and the related responses to it move toward democracy and justice or somehow betray these aims. Our finitude suggests that even our best efforts will unwittingly harbor elements of blindness and violence.

Gloria Anzaldúa articulates a proximate theme with the term *nepantla* (Aztec for "to be between" or "torn between ways"), and she seeks to embrace the work of creative judgment and action that locates itself in these tensions by cultivating a nepantilist state of mind and being. As a borderland Chicana, feminist, and lesbian, with roots in the struggles of farmworkers, she writes in the midst of numerous traditions of struggle, each of which harbors potent insights and damaging blindness. The work of living well, she argues, involves culling through these various inheritances in an effort to pass *on* what is valuable from each and to *pass* on what is violent. The task is to work history in this way in an effort creatively to forge better modes of coexistence while resisting those tendencies and forces that would congeal into a new, tensionless, unreceptive totality.

The tensions and indeterminacies evoked by terms like *traditio* and *nepantla* have, I think, great ethical and political significance. They suggest that at the heart of democratic aspirations we must recognize and embrace a constitutive tension between teleological and ateleological responsibilities. We have teleological responsibilities to dialectically listen to and cultivate the knowledge and practices we inherit in order to help orient further efforts to deepen democracy, for these contain—among other things—potent sedimentations of other such judgments and struggles. We must search our inheritance for the wisdom that might be found there and work it immanently in an effort to discern as well the damages and dangers that also reside within it—and within us. Such dialectical responsibilities are integral to the ethical and political efforts of the finite historical beings we are. At the same time, beyond the limits of our teleological efforts to critically extend the traditions we inherit, the indeterminacies and finitude of our condition call us to recognize how crucial are our ateleological receptive responsibilities to be radically open to and opened by others and new events beyond "our traditions." Why? Because every determination of what is "within" a tradition—and what is not—is made with a finite leap that is virtually assured of carrying forward unreflective blindness and of imposing damages that are grasped poorly—if at all. At any point in time we grasp the complexity, entanglements, history of others, dangers, and humiliations of our situation only in very limited ways. Think, for example, of today, of the vertiginous complexity and unexpected consequences attending questions of political economy and freedom, or questions of democracy around public-private distinctions, or questions at the heated intersection of deep cultural difference, or questions of radical dependence and care, or questions concerning our relations to the nonhuman. Think too about how all such questions are invested and overdetermined by deep structures of power and interest that disproportionately determine how they are resolved. And yet human societies decide historically, and these decisions—along with everything those societies did not see or hear or care about—often sediment into affective responses, widespread habits, capacities and incapacities, assumed worldviews, institutions, principles, closures, and the like. Hence, insofar as democracy is entwined with ideas of moving dialogical relations, judgment, and action, we, working toward democracy, must *also* endlessly renew our radical efforts to generously receive inputs from those beyond the directions and limits of our traditions of making democratic sense. These efforts toward radical receptivity must reach all the way down—even concerning the character and meaning of democratic dialogue itself.

Thus we have a double responsibility: to cultivate dialectically the teleological traditions of making sense that we inherit, on the one hand, and to genealogically interrogate these traditions and cultivate a radically ateleological receptivity to what lies beyond this sense, on the other. To the extent that each task denies the other, it becomes increasingly irresponsible and risks the worst. We must, then, learn and invent arts of juxtaposing these tensional responsibilities, interrogating each with the other, fluctuating our modes of responsiveness, like the blinking of our eyes that is so integral to our vision. Such, at any rate, is the stance I shall try to support in the chapters that follow.

These juxtapositions, polysemous tensions, and fluctuations are often difficult to evoke and articulate theoretically. Yet I believe (and will try to show) that the demands of everyday existence—stretched as many people are between multiple imperatives, concerns, identities, impulses, legacies, languages, roles, spaces, and responsibilities—tend to draw out and develop these capacities, as feminists of color, postcolonial writers, and myriad insurgent radical democrats have experienced and argued repeatedly. If we theorists must struggle mightily to articulate the tensional quality of democratic life and responsibility, perhaps this has more to do with the discursive impoverishment of a legacy of theorizing that too often aims to expunge these qualities of ethical and political life. Theorists often pride themselves on articulating genealogies, subtleties, and paradoxes often missed in the flows of everyday life. Just as often, I suspect, we theorists miss subtlety, critiques of power, and paradoxes painfully obvious to many and carefully negotiated by far more people than we recognize.

Contemporary antidemocratic challenges have provoked various theoretical responses, four of which I mention here in an effort to situate the tension-laden project I pursue in this book. One familiar response is to articulate a basic framework of fundamental principles that will regulate and limit unequal accumulations of wealth and power, as well as the contestations among differences, in ways said to secure the conditions of liberal democracy. The idea here is to protect, orient, and limit ourselves by theorizing and tenaciously defending the deepest commitments of mainstream democratic traditions. Political liberalism is the most familiar school of political theory associated with this effort to step beyond politics to construct a cosmopolitan bedrock for politics for everyone—or at least everyone in liberal societies.

A second response is to strive to resist as much as possible working according to dominant pseudo-cosmopolitan ideologies and practices—whether those of the market, of bureaucratic rationality, or of "neutral" liberal reason—by focusing on cultivating *specific* traditions; communities of deliberation; social, economic, and political practice; virtues; visions of the good or of God; and so on. Here the focus is on embracing inherited traditions of faith and judgment that articulate ways of coexisting deemed preferable to the dominant practices. Often there is a cosmopolitan*izing* aspect to these projects, but they refuse to seize the "neutral" cosmopolitan podium and instead see the processes of transformation, reformation, and possible conversion of the surrounding world in terms of local, long-term, and risky dialogical engagements among differences that are all situated on a provincial plane. (Traditionalists like Alasdair MacIntyre and Mennonite theologian John Howard Yoder are among those who have most compellingly pursued variants of this project.)

A third response, construed variously in different streams of genealogy, deconstruction, and postmodernism, is to theorize a vital moment of democracy beyond all foundational principles or substantive traditions of inquiry, vision, and struggle—beyond any dialectical development of these principles or traditions, in future events where unwonted otherness might be encountered. Here, in radical resistance to what are viewed as essentializing, power-saturated, and endlessly recolonizing interpretations and practices of democracy oriented by principles or specific histories, the accent is on the flow of becoming in democratic encounters that always remains significantly "not yet." When democracy is rendered *wholly* in this vein (and in the most compelling versions of genealogy, deconstruction, and the like, it is not; rather, the "not yet" is agonistically juxtaposed with dialectical judgment), in order to move beyond all the traps mobilized in democracy's name, we are to eschew all substantial aims: the advent of encounter becomes the end itself. Jean-Luc Nancy, in his reflections on *mestizaje,* and very occasionally Derrida, in some of his most vertiginous writing, exemplify this response.

A fourth response to the dangers threatening democracy is to urge a retreat from the academic amalgam of debates concerning the precise articulations of first principles, theoretical questioning without determinate resolution, deep critique, experiments at the limit of political possibility, futural evocations, and so on in favor of moves toward "pragmatic," "relevant," and "engaged" modes of inquiry. The sense often articulated here is that by focusing on differences, genealogies of micropower, esoteric cultural critique, far-ranging utopic possibilities, and the like, intellectuals distance themselves from "real world" engagements and concrete political initiatives, as well as from "everyday" people with whom we might align ourselves. Often this response calls us to re-embrace and coalesce around the basic ends of social democracy (as in the work of Todd Gitlin or Richard Rorty) in ways that would discipline more-radical theoretical efforts of various stripes.[4]

I work here in relations of resonance and critical tension with each of these contending projects in order to suggest a more hopeful direction for democracy and open a more receptive and generous space for political thinking and practice. Below I broadly situate my project in relation to the above responses, beginning with the fourth response, namely, the turn to engagement, pragmatics, relevance.

I find many prominent articulations of the turn to pragmatic engagement to be problematic when they are insufficiently cognizant of new modes of power[5] that render increasingly improbable the success of projects to simply reaffirm progressive democracy as practices in social-democratic Western democracies. They are equally problematic insofar as they tend to greatly underplay the insights and struggles in recent decades (concerning race, nation, secularism, urban suffering, gender, sexuality, class, coloniality, ecology, and so on) that complicate our understanding of power, freedom, difference, democracy, self, bodies, and history. These solicit radical reformations of dominant modes of progressive democratic politics. The insistence that theory become pragmatic and relevant is too often a thinly veiled effort to discipline political theory and practice in ways that I think normatively and strategically undesirable. Finally, these articulations are frequently unreflective about how their own positions and modes of politics might be implicated in the growing disaffection many mainstream people feel toward "progressives" and are thus unhelpful for formulating responses to this problem.[6] Nevertheless, there are important concerns in some of the claims put forward here, to which I think radical democratic theorists must respond and which I think they must even strive to further articulate.

A substantial portion of left-leaning theory operates too often and too comfortably in a universe of abstract hermetic discursive currency, rarely seeking to listen to or address textured political struggles or broader publics. The problem here does not lie essentially in abstraction, demanding and specialized concepts, inquiries beyond the limits of "common sense," explorations of utopic possibility for audiences that do not necessarily exist yet, or the like. All these are features of important work that can enhance our critical relation to the world and our sense of alternatives to it.[7] Rather, the problem lies in the extent to which many of these publics have become increasingly hermetic, the extent to which those who work within them rarely venture out to read, write, speak, and listen in other different or broader public venues. I embrace theoretical projects oriented toward far-reaching "strangeness, risk, and world-making,"[8] and I engage a number of them in the chapters that follow. Yet I think that the task of radical democratic scholarship is most insightful and hopeful when it *experiments at moving between different public venues:* exploring utopic projects here, addressing more-urgent immediate problems and pragmatic possibilities there; deepening genealogies of power that push the limits of intelligibility here, working on specific struggles for reform that are unable to reach as deeply there; or probing abstract (even ethereal) concepts and paradoxes here, engaging the tensions and practices of everyday political life there.

In other words, we ought to cultivate more multidimensional modes of public engagement when it comes to time horizons, depths of criticism, range of visions for political possibility and transformation, narrowness and breadth of publics, and so forth.

I seek to do this here by ranging, for example, between Derridean philosophy concerning the far-ranging and paradoxical nature of the democratic promise, on the one hand, and concrete engagements with radical democratic work involving the way practices of listening, movement across neighborhoods, and pragmatic responses to immediate issues are developing in Durham, on the other; deep theological reflections on Jesus and the church's historical hermeneutic of peoplehood by Yoder, on the one hand, and concrete questions of how radical democrats might begin to engage fundamentalist Christians in Tennessee, on the other. I think we need to learn better modes of fluctuating to and fro between different idioms and spaces and to cultivate the difficult translation arts these alternations require. We need to invent arts of moving and mixing democratic efforts, public spaces, and temporalities. We need to pursue these activities, not in order to discipline the multiplicity of important endeavors from the vantage point of one privileged modality but in order to infiltrate each space with vital questions and insights that unsettle the narrow complacencies that arise as each space becomes comfortable with its range of vision, genre, norms, places, concerns, and habitual movements. Of course, each public has its pressures and constraints that enable and disable our reflective capacities. The aim is not simply to slacken these constraints—though often we surely must—but also to employ them critically against each other in order to *invent* new possibilities for more democratic and just vision and action in the synergy, friction, and heat that ensues.

These movements help enliven the tensions and receptive modes of inquiry that are a basic condition for the enduring liveliness and intelligence of each arena. By moving to and fro in these ways we are drawn into practices of tension-dwelling without which radical democracy withers. On the whole, theorizing agon, logics of hegemony, difference, the incompleteness of democracy, and the like tends to become stale, empty, and increasingly blind when removed from attentive interrogative engagements with embodied social movements, actual others' speaking, writing, listening, and struggling from the margins in specific idioms, and so forth. Similarly, struggles on the ground are vitiated when they are cut off from publics engaged in reflection that has greater temporal extension and critical historical depth. In chapters 7 and 8 I explore possibilities of thinking in ways that are attentive to theories and practices that are emerging in urban radical democratic struggles. Attentiveness to such practices is integral to our ability to re-imagine radical democracy.

I now turn to situate my project in relation to political liberal efforts to defend and extend liberal democracy by establishing a foundation of principles and discursive practices to orient and limit political life. My book strikes a largely critical stance toward some of the fundamental political sensibilities, ideals, and practices professed by political liberals. Yet I do not think that the political liberal ideas of society as a system of fair cooperation between free and equal persons, or the difference principle (affirming only those inequalities that are advantageous for the least well-off), or the abstention from using coercive power to force doctrinal conformity are bad things. Far from it: at a general level, these ideas support aspects of the liberal democratic tradition with which I am largely sympathetic, and they can even be used to push in desirable directions well beyond the limits of established liberal democracies.

Political liberalism is neither the dominant ideology today nor the dominant political economic practice (though it is one of the leading paradigms of political theory). Rather, as I have suggested, I think an increasingly antidemocratic right wing is gaining ascendancy in ways that threaten many institutions, practices, values, and aspirations that I and most radical democrats share with political liberals. A world in which political liberalism gained ascendancy over this assault on democracy and freedom would be, despite all the criticisms I would have of it, so much better than our current situation and the directions in which many powerful forces would push present conditions. My critique occurs in an agonistic zone cognizant of this fact, and I recognize both many points of contact between radical democrats and political liberals, around which I hope enduring political coalitions will form, and many differences that may—from my vantage point if not theirs—be fruitful.

And yet I see serious problems with the way political liberalism frames the task of theory, depoliticizes its own political interventions, and imagines political life. These problems are related to broader political tendencies—of which political liberalism is (partly) one expression (among many)[9]—which in important ways diminish the power of democratic resistance to antidemocratic assaults, dissuade emerging political alternatives that I find hopeful, and foment resentment on the part of many people who find themselves either beyond the charmed circle of public reason or the objects of professionals seeking to manage them according to arrogantly held knowledge and practice that comes from elsewhere. By offering a vision of politics with a vitiated sense of political contestation and engagement, political liberalism articulates a position from which democratic political power is difficult to sustain or cultivate. By marginalizing as it does important political contestations inspired by visions of flourishing, it drains sources of political motivation, vision, and creativity in ways that would put undue pressure on resistance and emergent alternatives. By morally excluding comprehensive doctrines that exceed public reason from political life while tacitly packing in its own vision of coexistence as relatively uncontestable, political liberalism cultivates an immodesty—and sometimes even arrogance—that foments resentment. By claiming possession of a political knowledge in light of which the polity is to be governed—or managed—it performs at a metalevel (and provides a meta-image of) a politics that reinforces the presumptuous stance of many in the professional managerial class who seek, from on high, to implement political policies on others, whom that managerial class objectifies. In all these ways and in spite of itself, political liberalism risks a politics that is weak, provokes backlash, and is ethically and politically insufficiently democratic and receptive. Because political liberalism is one of the most dominant contemporary political theories, because it resonates with broader social and political tendencies that I find problematic, and because many with whom I share some important political aspirations find it compelling, I devote the first two chapters of this book to a close critical engagement with several of political liberalism's leading proponents. Though much of my reading critically explores ethical-political themes, no small part of my motivation also concerns (related) strategic-political questions. Put simply, I think that political liberalism—though often embraced by many "progressives"—is an ineffective position (and increasingly so) for supporting democratic life: It is too disengaged; it seeks to stand above heterogeneity when the task is to build coalitional power by bridging differences through more receptive engagements "in the fray." Without this patient political work across myriad local differences, I suspect that most visions of democracy and freedom will come to naught.

In the more ethical political registers, one of my basic contentions with political liberalism boils down to this: Although formulating a broad direction and limits for democratic political life—what I understand as teleology in the broadest sense of this term—is a crucial task for those engaged in democratic theory, judgment, and action (without which we become increasingly blind and prone to unreflective complicity in violence), I see this as only one pole of our ethical and political responsibility. When the project of establishing fundamentals *establishes itself as fundamental,* as the single most important task of political thought and action, it begins to undermine its highest aspirations from within. It becomes systematically blind to its own finitude, to the concealments and damages of its own orders, and to others who bring forth alternative ethical and political visions. It slides into the activity of stridently insisting on itself and dismissing others in expressions that repeat "reasonable" several times per sentence, until the word begins to look and sound like a whip. In the overtones of certain formulations of freedom, equality, and tolerance, one can hear a certain kind of fundamentalism unaware of and nonresistant to itself. Much of my critical effort in chapters 1 and 2 seeks to examine these operations and effects in the rhetorical practices of some political liberal texts as well as in their theoretical formulations of principles and politics.

Though radical democrats must endlessly work to discern directions and limits for ethical and political life, that is, to put it somewhat crudely, only about half of our responsibility. The other part (usually entwined with the former in relations of both sustenance and disruption) consists in cultivating modes of receptivity toward those who name different histories and who struggle toward futures that exceed the horizons we bring to our encounters with them. This task is harder to formulate and must be ceaselessly reinvented in both theory and practice. Yet its importance is second to none.

Ironically, some of those who eschew cosmopolitan public reason and instead situate themselves explicitly in provincial histories of vision and practice understand this better than the political liberals who dismiss them as sectarian purveyors of politicized "comprehensive doctrines." In the second section of the book, in chapters 3 and 4, I examine the textures of political vision and receptivity in the work of two who explicitly cultivate their roots within specific traditions: Alasdair MacIntyre (a neo-Thomist) and John Howard Yoder (a Mennonite). I try to show how these very different articulations of traditioning judgment (I use the verbal form "traditioning" here to emphasize the dynamic interrogative quality that is otherwise often overlooked) and practice — so often mischaracterized as sectarian withdrawals from the larger world—provide important theoretical insights for those aiming to proliferate challenges that are more radically democratic and dialogical challenges to the dominant order of things (even though "radically democratic" is not an accurate characterization of MacIntyre's own project). Moreover, they both provide compelling accounts of how the finitude and specificity of their own loci of enunciation must call those in the traditions they affirm toward receptive and vulnerable engagements with those from beyond their traditions. I find in each of these efforts an affirmation of dialogical plurality that in some important ways exceeds many versions of liberalism and selectively informs my own project. Radical democrats can learn from MacIntyre's and Yoder's sharp attentiveness to specific historical practices that engage numerous registers of life, as well as from the way they strive to combine affirmative vision and commitment with a responsiveness to others that must proceed by inventing difficult and risky arts of reciprocal translation.

Yet I take leave of many traditionalist projects because they give the task of pursuing the teleologies of their particular traditions priority over the task of rendering themselves receptive in engagements with others. My sense—extensively argued in critical relation to MacIntyre in chapter 3—is that many advocates of tradition overemphasize the teleological dimension of ethical and political work in ways that threaten to undermine the receptive ateleological responsibilities they also seek to affirm. This in turn risks bringing into play some of the dangers that political liberals (among others) identify. In a way that is not without resonances with political liberal "tolerance," vulnerability to other traditions can become a mantra that reinforces an increasing sense of the superiority of one's own "vulnerable" tradition over all the others' traditions (which aren't vulnerable). When this happens, a certain overconfidence can undermine responsiveness and generate fortress-like defenses within which it is very difficult to hear the others one is called to engage.

Yet perhaps situating oneself with a strong faith in a particular tradition of theology, inquiry, and practice need not have this consequence. The work of Yoder serves as a haunting possibility that might mobilize itself in modes of expression and practice that exceed other radical democrats' accomplishments in relation to many of the aspirations and responsibilities I strive to advance in this project. This remains to be seen.

Mine is a haunted book, yet I place my wager on resolute efforts to dwell on a more discordant edge between teleological and ateleological ethical-political modes, working with and against the other. My efforts draw upon Derrida's work, which often pursues a proximate project with great insight. More often than not, I read genealogists (like Michel Foucault), critical theorists (like Theodor Adorno), and existential phenomenologists (like Maurice Merleau-Ponty) as working (albeit in significantly different ways) toward a tensional ethics and politics of "questioning the limits" of what is given as natural and necessary in ways that are consonant with and inspire my work in this book. Often they are misread and dismissed as advocating an utterly nonsensical and empty politics of "the new." As I read Derrida, however (and others elsewhere), a substantial portion of his work gives philosophically profound expression to what he in *The Other Heading* calls a "double contradictory responsibility": to dialectically develop the dialogical traditions one inherits, on the one hand, and to "anticipate the unanticipatable" (become more hospitable to and be opened by unwonted otherness beyond the horizons one recognizes as one's own), on the other hand. Either task alone tends to engender blindness and violence, and hence Derrida calls us to cultivate ethical and political judgment and to experiment with political action on the discordant interrogative edge between the two. At his best, Derrida theorizes tensions and aporias of ethical and political responsibility in ways that exemplify how we might dwell with some intelligence along the difficult edge between tradition and treason, sense and nonsense, dialectic and deconstruction, the good sense of legacies we call our own and vulnerability to what seems uncanny to us about the others. In a world where negotiating unexpected differences is absolutely crucial to building democratic relationships and power, I think Derrida offers invaluable lessons for political judgment and for encountering others across time. Too often these are eclipsed by efforts that either seek to subsume our responsibilities within a broadly "inclusive" teleology unaware of its own tragic finitude or fall into vacuous celebrations of difference that are, variously, politically dangerous and impotent.

However, I depart from Derrida (and Jean-Luc Nancy, in chapter 6) in a number of respects. First, too often he accents the ateleological character of our encounters in ways that seem to rip free from the tensions of reciprocal interrogation with our teleological orientations. This move risks incapacitating ethical and political responsibility in ways that I think are deleterious (and Derrida elsewhere gives us good reasons to think so). Second, he overplays the "contradictory" character of the teleological/ateleological antagonism. In contrast, I think there is much to support a view of these twin responsibilities as related not only in contradictory manners but also in manners that might nurture one another. Some teleologies nurture receptive generosity toward otherness far more than do other teleologies. The development of some lines of action, authority, and power can, in part, enhance practices of radical hospitality—as I suggest shortly, for example, in relation to urban social movements. Traditions of rights and respect for strangers, dialogical problem solving, and democratic associative dispositions and freedoms contribute significantly to the possibility of responsiveness to others. Similarly, ateleological encounters often enrich and deepen the democratic sensibilities and teleologies that preceded them, even as they transfigure them. Encountering others who, after a long struggle, come to be recognized as having made vital and unexpected contributions to a political history can in some ways extend teleologies—sensibilities, pedagogies, practices, institutions—that are fashioned with an eye toward the importance of encountering and being transfigured by those beyond extant borders. Although Derrida is absolutely right that there is ineliminable discord and paradox in the relationship between these two responsibilities, reducing that discord and paradox to contradiction conceals important aspects of political hope and possibility. Finally, however insightfully the bulk of Derrida's work addresses "the other," it does so in a manner that remains too wedded to a philosophical project that almost never ventures into nor is marked by engagements with "others" beyond European philosophical horizons. The few times he does engage such others (for example, in *Monolingualism of the Other; or, Prosthesis of the Origin, Works of Mourning*), one gets the sense that they are being absorbed into his philosophical project rather than participating in its development in more substantive ways. His textual practice in this regard falls short of his most compelling theoretical calls to engage the "other headings."

For these reasons, though greatly indebted to Derrida, I seek to move beyond him in the chapters that follow. With feminists of color, I seek to develop ethical and political possibilities that are often suggested but too often occluded or undeveloped in Derrida's writing. We find a richer sense of ethical and political generativity in much of the work written by women living on several borders of nationality, race, sexuality, gender, class, and so forth. We also find a powerful articulation of what I earlier referred to as an ethics and politics of *traditio*, in ways that more often sustains the hopeful tensions I seek to articulate. They also bring a desirable attention to *specificity* that contributes in ongoing transformative ways to both the theoretical insights and the rhetorical styles one finds in many of their texts.

Extending this effort to work receptively with the textures of specific sensibilities, ideas, and practices, struggling at the margins of democracy as it is officially articulated and recognized, I turn in the fourth section to engage insurgent democratic organizing efforts in urban areas around the United States. I argue that such engagements have much to contribute to a dynamic theory of democratic judgment and practice. It is not just that a turn to these political practices of what I call "moving democracy" helps explicate in more detail the theoretical efforts that precede it. Just as important, the turn to engage these everyday efforts of blacks, Hispanics, whites, and others, opens up *new* ways of imaging the democratic promise. These efforts bring a receptivity to the fore that is corporeal, material, and geographic. My hope, in turn, is that giving theoretical articulation to these practices can help draw them even more explicitly into the foreground of grassroots organizing and discussion, for they are easily misrecognized and weakened when activists themselves interpret them through dominant democratic lenses that make them difficult to witness.

It is important to stress at the outset that though my discussion of this political work comes in the final section of this book, my engagement with it is in a sense profoundly prior to every chapter and infused in each. For the past ten years I have been involved in a variety of local political efforts that have, in the most textured of ways, imbued my

sense of receptivity and democratic practice and power. The questions
I bring to each theorist I discuss here, the problems I see, the unexpected openings they reveal, the ways I develop their arguments, the
places I push where they do not want to go—all this is inseparable
from my experiences of surprise, transformation, rediscovered humility, exuberance, frustration, unexpected lessons of the profoundest sort
in the living rooms, churches, community centers, city hall, cafés, and
streets of Durham with people who are inventing capillaries of democracy yet who, for the most part, have little interest in theoretical scholarship. I am profoundly indebted to more theorists than I can name,
yet in this book I sense that my debts to nontheorists and our political work and movement may be even greater—certainly greater than
I can fully grasp.

I have important reasons for offering a glimpse of this political work
here at the outset. First, because it informs the sensibility with which
I engage every thinker who follows. Second, because a sketch of some
of the concrete political activity I think is entwined with the theoretical work I do in the next several chapters will give readers a sense of
some of the political stakes involved. A brief discussion of this politics now will allow readers to critically engage my work throughout
the book in registers they would otherwise be denied until the last fifty
pages. Third, I think this political work is a crucial "number"—if you
will—in the political combination necessary to unlock the ascendancy
of antidemocratic forces that I discussed at the beginning of this introduction. I do not think it is sufficient, but it is a necessary *part* of what
I think is involved in defending and cultivating the democratic promise
today—and it may have lessons for other important tasks as well. When
I say, for example, that political liberalism is politically relatively unen-
gaged, too limited in the range of differences it will morally tolerate,
and looking for a politics that is too much "above the fray," my critique here is significantly indebted to engagements with theorists like
MacIntyre, Yoder, Derrida, Chicana feminists, and others. Yet many
of the concrete kinds of alternatives I have in mind come from or are
inspired by urban organizing practices that are developing across the
United States and around the world. My sense is that the modes of
receptive politics being developed in these diverse settings are crucial
to engaging a broader spectrum of people in building radical democratic power that bridges difficult political divides. Without such developments, democratic visions—no matter how appealing—will probably
succumb to the forces I mentioned at the beginning of this introduction. The point is not that democracy must be primarily a local affair

but that local politics provides a crucial learning ground for political work on many other scales and, moreover, that analogous modes of receptivity will have to be invented at these larger scales if democratic efforts are better able to avoid problems of political disengagement, bureaucratic professionalization, and so forth. Some of the recent developments in the World Social Forum that accent more regional forums in diverse locales strike me as promising in this regard.

It is commonplace in contemporary theory to envision democracy through the lens of rational measured deliberation. Often—as argued in numerous critiques—theories of deliberation contain biases that operate in unacknowledged ways to marginalize many who are disempowered along lines of race, class, gender, and culture. Moreover, they often share with many other versions of democratic theory an accent on voice, paying little attention to patient listening or to practices of receptivity that are more corporeal.[10] Yet in dozens of cities, modes of democratic engagement are developing beyond this relatively constrained picture.

It is not that deliberation is lacking from our efforts. Far from it. In virtually all such efforts, a large portion of the political engagement is deliberative in numerous senses: We deliberate among ourselves about what issues to tackle, what alternatives to advocate, how power operates in our cities, who the key players are and how we should seek to engage them, what strategies might work best, and so on. And we spend countless hours deliberating in situations of inequality with public officials and private powers—negotiating how to address problems. These deliberations intertwine normative, pragmatic, and strategic modes. Yet this important work takes place amid a host of other activities without which grassroots democratic organizing would be unlikely either to develop for long, to flourish to the extent that it is beginning to in many places, or to provide such inspiring alternative visions and practices of more ethical relationships in our cities.

For our world is densely penetrated by antidemocratic powers that cripple our imaginations of the possible; impede our encounters with heterogeneous people and circumstances by gating our geographies and engendering habits of conceptual, emotional, and perceptual oblivion; and vitiate our capacities for active democratic political engagement. Deliberation alone is insufficient for transforming this situation, in which "it's not dark yet, but it's gettin' there."[11] Hence, grassroots organizing efforts have begun to develop strategies that accent listening, engage people in receptive traveling across the lines of our gated world, solicit people into enduring democratic work, and wildly inspire our sense of the possible. Let me briefly sketch a few of these practices that I think are most crucial to further developing a politics of receptive generosity—each of which I will discuss at length in the last section of this book.

First, although these organizing efforts do a great deal to empower the *voices* of those so often marginalized from power, the organizing culture actually emphasizes the arts of *listening* as integral to developing receptive relationships that can bridge divides and enhance democratic power. Hence, one of the most basic practices—and one that is considered by many organizers to be the most radical aspects of their work—is the "one-on-one relational meeting." Where grassroots organizing is vital, thousands of these meetings take place, meetings in which those engaged get together with each other as well as with those who are currently inactive. The aim of these meetings is not to "sell" an organization but to listen carefully to others' angers, dreams, passions, sense of a city's specific problems and possibilities, their local knowledges, and so on. One could even say that one of the key aims of such meetings—and the most difficult—is to *learn better how to listen, to generously receive others, to create a counterculture that develops power through the practice of these arts.*

Yet in a world as gated as is ours, listening is not sufficient. Democratic engagement requires that we literally travel about our urban spaces with some frequency, venturing in heterogeneous groups into neighborhoods, religious institutions, schools, community centers, and streets we would never otherwise visit. The aim of this traveling is to engage receptively situations different from our own, stories told about the problems and hopes of this street, dreams that emerge from the walls of this small church, angers that emerge from living next to run-down houses abandoned by slumlords, in areas where city government entirely ignores the infrastructure. We gather issues for our political work in this process, but, equally important, we also gradually learn the arts of receptive witness to situations that dominant modes of power would have many people ignore. There is an affective element in this engaged witness that is far more transforming than most deliberation. For the same reason, we consciously move our meetings around to various institutions and neighborhoods, working to gain each time a better sense of the shape of the different worlds we inhabit and from which we aspire. The tables of democracy must move if we are to cultivate a more generous counterculture and power. As we move, the members of each host institution gain a sense that their/our spaces—so often neglected by the official hall and established table—are worthy sites for generating democratic experience and power. And each of us gains a sense of democracy as it is differently inflected in this particular space, this history of hope and suffering, the sound of this choir, these worn chairs.

We also engage in practices concerned to actively engage not so much the differences of those on the other side of myriad barriers as, more, the worlds of radical democratic possibility (or is the name for this the beloved community possibility? there are many words that gesture toward proximate possibilities) beyond the official parameters of "the possible and the impossible" that would box us all in. Here we open ourselves to and are actively opened by Dionysian events that we stage in order to feel and inspire our way beyond the overbearing powers, damages, and constraints of the present. In Durham, this often takes the form of tremendous speakers, ecstatic call and response, frenzied evocations of the infinite power of love and justice—all rendered with a thunder that can rattle the bones, steal the breath and then fill the lungs, and instill in the flesh a sense that another world *is* possible and that we are helping to make it so. At these moments we are thrown toward our dreams in directions only vaguely suggested by the teleologies we variously embrace. Yet we get thrown so far out and are so dizzyingly together in our obvious differences that we are left to receive this place as much as an inspiring question as a determinate soliciting response to our current aspirations and problems. We are opened by the *possibility of a different future* that so much in the present would deny.

Each of these practices—deliberation, pragmatic work, receptive traveling, ecstatic conjuring of utopic possibility, and many others—is integral, I think, to a vision of radical democracy more worthy of our aspirations and more hopeful in its prospects in the face of current powers. Democracy requires a tensional ecology of practices that gradually work beyond the limits of the present toward a more generous and receptive justice.

Very briefly, here is an overview of the chapters that follow.

In chapter 1, "Tragedy's Tragedy: Political Liberalism and Its Others," I critically interrogate ways in which political liberalism seeks to establish its position as the fundamental bedrock of politics. Rawlsians, by constructing a tragic narrative that significantly incapacitates critical reflection on the limits of their own project, close off more-receptive democratic engagements and unintentionally weaken their ability to address inequality. Tragedy shifts, in the hands of many political liberals, away from being a sensibility that nurtures critical self-interrogation and becomes instead largely a discourse of defensive fortification. "Tragedy's tragedy" is thus a trope that refers equally both to the tragedy that befalls tragedy in the hands of political liberals and to the tragedy that occurs when this strange tragic narrative undermines the best aspirations of political liberalism—and thereby, the important aspirations of many who would contest it.

In chapter 2, "Contesting Cosmopolitan Currency," I further develop a critique of political liberals by critically examining their efforts to formulate a cosmopolitan "currency" that consists of agreed-upon terms for the orientation and limitation of global politics. I situate the currency rhetoric of such cosmopolitanism in the context of John Locke's story of the emergence and implications of money. Then I critically sketch the way the currency trope frames the politically dangerous and unhelpful antinomies of political liberal (neocolonialist) cosmopolitanisms. Following this, I introduce an alternative position that I call "nepantilist generosity" (elaborated in chapter 6), which is, I argue, not only normatively preferable but also linked with a number of historical, global developments that promise certain practical possibilities in relation to many of those struggling against neocolonialism. *Nepantla* informs the tensional sensibility that runs throughout this book and suggests a radically different vision of democratic globalization.

In chapter 3, "MacIntyre and the Confidence Trickster of Rivalish Tradition," I suggest that a nepantilist politics of receptive generosity has much to learn from this theorist of tradition. In contrast to many of his defenders and critics, I read MacIntyre as offering a theory that seeks to cultivate a version of dialogical enlightenment in the context of contingency, conflict, difference, and heterogeneous traditions. He does so in a manner that illuminates much that many liberal versions of enlightenment conceal. MacIntyre not only insightfully illuminates teleological development but also makes a powerful case for how teleological horizons themselves must nurture a vulnerability to ateleological aspects of human historicity. Nevertheless, MacIntyre's project nurtures an "(over)confidence trickster" that vitiates some of what I take to be his most admirable aims. His strong accent on teleological cultivation ultimately hampers his capacity to vulnerably and receptively engage other positions—a weakness that shows up in his reading of post-Nietzschean theorists. Although ultimately my sense of weaknesses in MacIntyre's project leads me in alternative directions, the path I take beyond his work remains significantly indebted to him. He is profoundly at work in my attention to ethical and political practices in later chapters.

In chapter 4, "The Wild Patience of John Howard Yoder," I explore a Mennonite reading of Christianity. I find in Yoder's writings a vision of dialogical communities that brings forth very particular and powerful practices of generous solidarity precisely *through* creative uses of conflict and a vulnerable receptivity toward the "least of these" within the church and outside it. Yoder offers strong counterpoints to the teleological overconfidence of MacIntyre's project by construing tradition as a vine that must be repeatedly cut back so the roots can be given a chance to generate new and radically reformed life in a tradition that is always "peccable in fact."[12] Yoder interprets the binding lordship of Christ as the opening of dialogical relations between the church and the world in which giving and receiving is probable in many directions. Vulnerable relations with outsiders are integral to the church's capacity to discern its own otherness, and when this understanding of *caritas* is unpracticed and forgotten, the church tends to assimilate to the violence of the world. When Christians cease to engage outsiders with receptive generosity, they cease to "let the church be the church." They lose sight of Jesus, who not only guides but is discerned through such engagements.

There are few offering positions so radically different from my own (which harbors no faith that Jesus is Lord or that Christianity identifies the "grain of the universe") who haunt me as much as Yoder does. It is not clear to me that Yoder (or Yoderians) might not cultivate something akin to receptive generosity that exceeds projects I more fully embrace. We will need a wild patience with which to witness the works and expressions of these efforts, as they respectively stumble here, come to fruition there, fail in other places, form unexpected alliances — unexpected struggles. It is quite likely that rivalry will be in many cases an inappropriate lens for discerning the comparative possibilities and dangers of these alternative modes, their myriad paths of development and perhaps even syncretism. I sense that there might be a nonmerging or nonconverting syncretism at work in both the way I read Yoder and the way his spirit profoundly infiltrates this book.

Yet I imagine that my own project is inflected less by Christianity and more by a struggling faith in a *traditio* of discontinuous and discrepant insurgent struggles of radical democracy. And the mode I seek to cultivate is not confessional — or, better, it is not *only* confessional — but, rather, tensional, in the senses indicated by terms like *traditio, nepantla,* and *torn.* In chapter 5, "Derrida and the Promise of Democracy," I draw heavily on Derrida's work on tradition, teleology, intersubjectivity, ideality, ethics, responsibility, alterity, and democracy to show how (the democratic promise must be stretched between teleological and ateleological responsibilities and to show what this might mean for political thought, judgment, and practice.)I think that Derrida offers one of the most compelling philosophical and political accounts of the ways in which all teleologies of sense and reason as such harbor inexpugnable aspects of contingency, concealment, unintelligibility, otherness, arbitrary construal—an ineliminable darkness that haunts the realm of ideality, rationality, and faith where proponents claim there is only light. Whereas MacIntyre would acknowledge some of this but significantly underestimate its importance as he develops his larger project, Derrida develops these themes with a depth of insight and power that maintains them in the foreground of our pursuit of judgment, ethics, and politics, where most would rather not have to face them. Derrida provides a convincing case that facing and responding to these "ghosts" is central to our ethical and political responsibility, not a secondary matter we can adequately attend to with tepid pronouncements about "fallibility." Derrida incites and energizes this sensibility. Yet he comes to it *through* a serious and penetrating discussion of teleology, intersubjectivity, tradition, ideality, and so forth. In so doing, he simultaneously provides one of the strongest arguments for how and why it is that we must also bear responsibility for the *teleological* elaboration of sense, judgment, and practice. Ultimately, what is most profound about Derrida's work is the way he interweaves these two tensional responsibilities and articulates the implications of doing so. In chapter 5 I also pursue some of the ways MacIntyre's and Derrida's positions bring critical pressure to bear upon each other. As I read the encounter I stage here, Derrida gets the upper hand. Yet a certain *spirit* of MacIntyre reemerges in the interrogative energy that leads me to read Derrida against himself to illuminate problems with the way Derrida sometimes articulates his project.

Chapter 6, "Feminists of Color and the Torn Virtues of Democratic Engagement," fleshes out a vision of nepantilist generosity by juxtaposing it to the liberalism of Arthur Schlesinger Jr. and the postmodernism of Jean-Luc Nancy. Writing from the underside of power configurations of race, gender, nationality, sexuality, and class, those I engage in this chapter articulate a nepantilist vision of ethics and politics that has numerous resonances with Derrida's position. Yet they also offer important criticisms of some postmodernists, who articulate an ethics and politics that becomes so ethereal and futural (in the name of avoiding "essentialism") that the specificity of people's traditions and struggles is again rendered taboo. The writers I engage here argue for an ethics and politics torn (or at least stretched) between the often (though not always) discordant tasks of constructing ethical-political frameworks for engaging others *and* cultivating an awareness that political relations also call us to the difficult task of heightened receptivity to those beyond the orientations of our ethical and political horizon. Many feminists of color express provocative democratic visions that evoke and sustain the vitality of this tension. One of the things that distinguishes the mode in which these theorists frequently articulate democratic sensibilities of broad significance is that their arguments are almost always developed in response to problems and possibilities of their particular histories. These specificities—for example, living as a working-class Chicana lesbian on the border between the United States and Mexico—are explicitly woven into the fabric of their more general aims. This gives their ethical vantage points a vernacular mode of expression and substance that inflects and informs questions of difference and solidarity in ways that often significantly shape their contributions to broader debates. It also gives their work a kind of energy that draws questions of affect and corporeality to the fore of their interventions. Finally, in the best of these works, the "marked" character of their discourse tends to engender a heightened awareness that they are not the last cosmopolitan word, and this finds expression in more open-ended and inviting textual practices. All this lends to much of their work a heightened sense of democratic possibility.

In chapter 7, "Moving Democracy: The Political Arts of Listening, Traveling, and Tabling," in an effort to further discern the possible textured practices of radical democracy, I offer a reading of insurgent democratic organizing developing in urban areas across the United States. Yet, again, I am not primarily looking to discover an "example" that fleshes out the meaning of what I already knew before my inquiry began. In fact, as I have discussed above, my aspirations are quite otherwise. Although in academic contexts I have occasionally labeled my involvement with this group "participant observer," this term misses the affective dimensions of my involvement, and (related to this, no doubt) it misses the way my engagement has shaped my mode of seeing and listening and the questions I ask—not to mention my very sense of democracy. In some ways I can trace and in some I cannot, my experiences working with people every day bridging lines of religiosity, race, class, nationality—reinventing democracy in as-yet modest but pregnant modes—mark every chapter in this book. I did not anticipate what I now see I needed most.[13] My discussion in chapter 7 is organized around the receptive political arts I discussed briefly above. I draw together and develop ways in which dwelling upon these insights might significantly alter a fundamental metaphor that underpins many democratic theories. Hence I am led to ask: If listening and receptivity are given more-prominent places as we theorize democracy, how might we be pushed to re-envision the space-time of democratic engagement? It turns out that a thick description of some IAF spaces of democratic engagement once again suggests some fruitful directions: Those spaces gesture toward a critical discussion of the limits of the imaginary of the solid democratic table that guides a lot of democratic theory (that of Hannah Arendt and many others), and they suggest that democratic theorists begin to work more with an imaginary of democracy as *tabling*. On this reading, democracy should be reconceptualized more as an activity in which the tables of engagement and governing must be repeatedly altered through practices in which they are *moved and multiplied*.[14] In the conclusion I reflect upon some of the difficulties and challenges facing this type of democratic politics.

Chapter 8, "Reconsidering the Politics of Education" (coauthored with Troy Dostert), discusses democratic *traditio* in relation to a group of people whose differences greatly challenge radical democracy, namely, the Christian fundamentalist parents in Hawkins County, Tennessee, who objected to the public school reading curriculum on the grounds that it threatened their ability to teach their children the proper way of life. The court case that ensued, *Mozert v. Hawkins County,* has been widely discussed by liberals of various stripes. Considering several political liberals as well as William Galston's liberal pluralism through the lens of their divergent responses to the *Mozert* case, we argue that although they evaluate the outcome of the case differently, both political liberalism and liberal pluralism assume a hegemonic theoretical stance for addressing the issues involved. This leads each to avoid bringing—or allowing others to bring—the contestability of liberal presuppositions to the fore. Both approaches thus avoid fully engaging the challenges posed by the *Mozert* families, and this raises questions about the adequacy of their attempts to come to terms with the way radical plurality affects social and political life.

After criticizing each of these approaches, we draw on both the theology of Yoder and the politics of nepantilist generosity to defend a response to these challenges that, in its greater desire to vulnerably engage otherness, is not only better able to respond to the challenges of the *Mozert* case and others like it but also furnishes us with a more compelling approach to the numerous challenges of plurality and public life we currently confront. We sketch more-promising political engagements in which the cultivation of unwonted *relationships* and a politics of *moving* democracy (working significantly in bodily, geographical registers of our political imaginations) might open political possibilities that are closed to more-dominant projects. Rather than a politics of moralizing from on high, we suggest a transfigurative politics of rhizomatic relationship building. These, I argue, harbor greater promise for resisting the dark ages that threaten us all.

# 1

# Tragedy's Tragedy: Political Liberalism and Its Others

POLITICAL LIBERALISM FAMOUSLY SEEKS TO FORMULATE a "public reason" that will orient and limit the terms and also the *modes* of democratic engagement. It has an impact on the latter partly through explicit formulations of how we are to act in political life but even more through the ways in which its texts conceptually engender an existential stance toward politics and performatively enact an attitude that has significant implications for political encounters. This posture, I shall argue, informs and inflects the terms of political discourse that it prescribes—equality, liberty, reciprocity, tolerance, fairness—in ways that have great influence. I examine ways in which political liberalism's formulations of public reason, its existential stance toward finitude and tragedy, and its textual performances interweave to produce a politics that tends to be politically ineffective and far stingier than its professed ideals would lead us to believe. Many of the themes introduced here receive much more detailed elaboration in other chapters in relation to other political positions and practices. In short, I am interested in how it is that political liberalism tends, in spite of itself, to be relatively unreceptive to difference and to generate a politics with only weak capacities for addressing inequality (this latter point is argued more fully in the chapter 6).

As I have already noted in the introduction, it is not because I think political liberalism is the theoretical articulation of our dominant political and economic order that I criticize it here. In fact, this seems to be less and less the case, and in my view a world that abided more by several political liberal principles would be much better than the present one. And yet I see serious problems with the way political liberalism frames the task of theory, depoliticizes its own political interventions, and imagines political life. These problems are related to broader political tendencies that in important ways diminish the power of democratic resistance to antidemocratic assaults, dissuade emerging political alternatives that I find both more generous and more hopeful, and foment resentment on the part of many people who find themselves beyond the charmed circle of public reason or who are the objects of professionals seeking to manage them according to arrogantly held knowledge and practice that comes from elsewhere. With a more strategic-political focus, though political liberalism is often embraced by "progressives," it is an increasingly ineffective position for supporting democratic life: It is too disengaged; it seeks to stand above heterogeneity when the task is to build coalitional power by bridging differences through more receptive engagements in the fray.

In this chapter, I seek to illuminate a certain tragedy that befalls political liberalism's efforts to establish a political order in which tolerance, equality, respect, and so forth are maximized in the relations among different constituencies. As the title of this chapter suggests, I am also, and relatedly, interested in the tragedy that befalls *tragedy* in the hands of political liberalism. My claim is that "tragedy" is employed in this discourse in ways that betray some of what is most profound in the best contemporary efforts to theorize it (as well as the dramatic practices of many tragedians). I understand a tragic sensibility to be one that stretches its listeners between calls to the importance of articulating, mediating, and striving toward the highest values of a community, on the one hand, and painful evocations of the unacknowledged suffering often wrought by a community's ideals (or constitutive failure in light of them) and the inextinguishable need to be transformed through receptive engagements with those a community marginalizes and subjugates, on the other. Tragedy thus *informs and energizes* political judgment and action by situating us at the crux of this tension. Political liberalism, in contrast, misconstrues the tragic in ways that exaggerate our self-assurance, reinforce certain closures in public discourse, and de-energize political practice. This self-assurance is entwined with an insistence that political liberalism is "above the political fray," a stance often sustained by retreating to a level of abstraction that is at once insufficiently textured to give critical expression to—let alone resist—many kinds of suffering and too unreceptive to engage contending traditions and emergent idioms that might do better. Tragedy's tragedy is thus the misconstrual of the tragic aspects of our situation in ways that vitiate rather than vivify our capacities to respond to them.

Below I first discuss how political liberalism (especially as articulated by John Rawls) misunderstands tragedy in ways that diminish its capacity to provoke critical political self-interrogation. Rather, it renders tragedy through the lens of violent doctrinal conflict in ways that generate and secure the orientation and limits of public reason. Next I examine how its construal of the ubiquity of tragic encroachment persistently diminishes the significance of its imposition upon those positions that would exceed these limits (looking particularly at Rawls's and Donald Moon's admirable efforts to expand the capaciousness of liberalism). Following this, I discuss the ways in which the particular tragic sensibility cultivated by political liberalism is woven into what I call the disciplines of (un)reflective equilibrium that would push people along a path toward a pseudo-clarity that marginalizes many of the most important ethical and political questions. In the fourth section, "Clarity's Concealments: Bringing Political Liberalism's Borders into Question," I explore ways in which the questions raised by political liberal Kent Greenawalt both challenge—more profoundly than he recognizes—much of the scenario depicted thus far and suggest a markedly different account of tragedy and political discourse and engagement. In the final section, "Concluding Reflections," I reconsider the dangers identified by political liberal discourse and rework a minimalist and hybridizing notion of political currency that might help identify some of the greatest political dangers. I introduce themes of radical participatory democracy across wide-ranging differences that are developed more fully in the chapters that follow.

Political liberalism leads to tragic effects, I shall argue, by dismissing worthy political visions and practices that might begin to address significant problems and by deflecting critical examination of its own complicity with dangerous aspects of the contemporary order. Thus, for example, it contributes to a flattened culture of political disengagement by disqualifying a priori diverse advocates of more-radical democracy as proponents of "comprehensive doctrines" while insisting that its own "common currency" of principles must alone determine the fundamental direction and limits of political discourse and power. This stance not only constitutes an a priori disqualification of contending visions nurtured in various minority communities but also conceals the extent to which its own position might be marked by historical finitude in ways that would require "views from elsewhere" to illuminate. Relatedly, its diminished sense of its own historical specificity tends to deflect its critical attention away from inquiry into ways its own stance might be entwined with modes of historical power (as I discuss in relation to colonialism in chapter 2, and embodiment and inequality in chapter 6) in vicious circles of indebtedness and reinforcement. At the deepest levels, this concealment of power occurs in the way political liberalism utilizes tropes like "comprehensive doctrines" and "sectarian ways of life" to gesture toward the dangers with which we should be most concerned. This frames power and danger in a way that tends to veil the extent to which ideas and dispositions are constituted profoundly and with comprehensive effects by micro-practices of production, consumption, discipline, intimacy, urban design, and so forth that constitute the dominant way of life. Hence, where it discerns no particular doctrines or ways of life at work, political liberalism tends to assume a situation of political discourse that is relatively free and equal. Yet many dominant modes of power shape our political imaginations and operate precisely insofar as they are unrecognized as such—a process that this construal of power and its concealments tends to aid even as it undermines some of political liberalism's own aspirations.

Hence, for instance, many political liberals support vast economic inequalities as necessary "incentives" to improve the conditions of the least well-off, assured that investors and innovators require such incentives to be productive. Yet it is precisely individuals whose sense of self, equality, fairness, and liberty have been greatly influenced by radically inegalitarian modes of capitalism—practices of production oriented primarily toward a myopic notion of profit, practices of insatiable material consumption, a culture that undermines alternative modes of solidarity and intimacy that might engender sensibilities and practices of resistance to high levels of inequality, and the like—who require vast inequality to be thus made productive. Such selves, if persuaded to inhabit the "original position" (which many will anyhow resist), will bring with them the dominant yet largely unrecognized assumptions of their world and likely (re)authorize many of the inequalities through which they were engendered. They will, of course, raise questions that create more fairness than, say, a libertarian might find compelling, but their challenges are likely not to go very far. More critical challenges will usually rely upon visions and dispositions associated with minority traditions and struggles (such as theological, radical democratic, genealogical, socialist, borderland, indigenous, commonwealth, postcolonial) that, whatever their merits or dangers, are disqualified at the outset, for they are obviously not a part of the public reason "we all share."[Here, public reason, in the name of tolerance, tends to generate closures to political-economic contestation that secure terms animated and construed through practices whose effects are largely unrecognized (and, again, at odds with more admirable currents in political liberalism).]

One could generate a long list of ways in which political liberalism engenders a lack of receptivity to a variety of critical expressions and struggles concerning fundamental problems of our age. For example, many political liberals are oblivious to radical environmentalists who make claims about human obligations to nonhuman beings from a variety of pagan, theistic, and atheistic traditions of faith; to movements for complete global debt forgiveness for poor countries and massive redistribution of resources significantly rooted in the biblical practice of jubilee or in radically democratic socialist visions and histories of struggle; to movements that are significantly shaped by atheistic, theistic, borderland, or postsecular visions of generosity or forgiveness that seek to radically transform practices of punishment; to similarly inspired movements to dismantle war machines and open borders. Thus, tragedy's tragedy in the hands of political liberalism is entwined with political liberalism's perpetuation of tragic suffering and tragic a priori invulnerability to those who would contest it from beyond its own horizon.

*Of course, it would be absurd to propose that there is a tragic sensibility that could exempt itself from tragedy. Absurd to hold up a "pure" sense and practice of the tragic with which to judge all other imperfect efforts. Tragedy's tragedy, on my reading, must always be an expropriation—a displacement, a misreading—that is partly inherent, or at least in some way anticipated, in a tragic sensibility itself. Yet even if there is no sense of tragedy exempt from tragedy's tragedy, no tragedy that would escape itself and establish a "perfect" set of tensions between striving toward our visions and receptively opening to that which challenges us from elsewhere, my claim is that we can do better than political liberalism's current efforts to figure the tragic. Both the lived tragedies of our world and the tension-laden sense of the tragic itself call us to do better.*

Because this chapter is devoted primarily to a critique of political liberalism, the sensibility—both tragic and exuberant—that calls us beyond liberalism's limits will remain largely unformulated until later. Yet a brief sketch of the philosophical perspective that orients the paths of questioning below is helpful at the outset.

Foucault's genealogy, Adorno's critical theory, Derrida's deconstruction, Merleau-Ponty's existential phenomenology, the borderland ethos of Chicana feminists, and the Mennonite theology of Yoder are vastly different from one another. Yet at their profoundest moments, they each cultivate political judgment and sensibility in the tensions between selves' and communities' pursuit of particular visions of justice and goods, on the one hand, and a deep awareness of the often tragic blindness that generally clings to our efforts, on the other. In very different ways, they formulate ethical modes of learning how to live that are stretched between the need for teleological directness (in the most general sense, so that here political liberalism too is a teleology, as many now acknowledge) and ateleological receptivity to the otherness beyond the horizons of our teleologies (or eschatologies). Enlivened by a sense of unnecessary suffering and richer possibilities beyond the present, each burns with a searching and transformative ethical-political flame that is sparked in the friction between these agonistic responsibilities.

Peter Euben, in *The Tragedy of Political Theory*, offers a vision of tragedy that is often proximate with the one I am suggesting here. Tragedy, he argues, was an integral part of the Athenian democratic tradition and "presented to a popular audience the need for distance from one's own."[1] Sometimes this distance was ultimately affirmative, illustrating the highest aspirations of the polis even as it illuminated the expanse between these ideals and current practices. Sometimes this distance was more genealogical, exposing deafness, violence, and contingency in Athenian ideals that citizens would rather ignore. At its most successful, tragedy both constituted and challenged the democratic tradition—constituted it significantly *through* challenge. Stretched between binding and loosening, it deepened a sense of the dangers of both impiety and piety (*Tragedy*, 35). At the same time as it deconstructed the simple romanticization of otherness, in it, "assured demarcations are confounded, confidence in what one knows and how one knows it is eroded . . . reason loses its hold and foresight its reliability" (36). Its power emerged from the way it stretched its readers between these two sensibilities to enliven the idea that "justice must be continually rewon and reconstituted" (39). "Showing people learning to change, tragedy helped its audience see the need to do the same" (58).

In the present context I am interested in the ways a tragic sensibility unsettles assurances, solicits renewed and farther-reaching receptivity, and instigates explorations of alternative, more generous ethical-political possibilities. Although integral to political wisdom, this sensibility is weakened in political liberal discourse and practice.

Yet political liberalism, some say, is oriented by a very deep sense of tragedy. Indeed, it is animated by nothing so much as the desire to constitute a just polity in which our ineliminable finitude, erring, and tendencies toward tragic conflict are contained within a framework that reduces violence to a minimum and maximizes respectful tolerance among those who in many other contexts might subjugate and even kill one another. All orders contain exclusions, but political liberalism is more capacious than any other, and thus its ideals and limits must be vigorously defended.

## Born/e by Tragedy of Absolute Depth

Rawls claims to "complete and extend the movement of thought that began three centuries ago" and is exemplified by Locke's *Letter on Toleration*.[2] "Extend" suggests Rawls's sense of being at the cutting edge of a historical direction; "complete" suggests a certain limit. At the heart of the liberal democratic tradition, he claims, is a general agreement—tacit if not explicit—concerning fundamental questions of political justice. Both the direction and the limit of this agreement are said to arise and be sustained in an ever-renewed relation to a set of tragic events and possibilities.

Yet, as is often noted, when one looks at contemporary liberal democracies, it is very difficult to discern a broad consensus on the directions and limits sketched by Rawls's "justice as fairness" and tolerance governed by "public reason." Rawls too suggests this when he writes, "our public political culture may be of two minds at a *very deep* level" (*Political Liberalism*, 9, my emphasis). Liberty, equality, and the meaning of tolerance appear more often as sites of contestation than as sites of consensus. This "very deep" disagreement "suggests that if we are to succeed in finding a basis for public agreement, we must find a way of organizing familiar ideas and principles into a conception of political justice that expresses those ideas and principles in a somewhat different way than before" (ibid.). → *eg "Hebrew Bible" not OT or Tanakhot*

To understand Rawls's strategy here it is important to recall the two "fundamental questions" he seeks to answer in *Political Liberalism*. The first is "about political justice in a democratic society, namely what is the most appropriate conception . . . for specifying fair terms of social cooperation between citizens regarded as free and equal." The second concerns the nature and grounds of toleration (3–4). These questions are deeply entwined. Without securing the latter, "no reasonable political conception of justice is possible" (xxviii); freedom and equality will be violated at the start as some people's intolerant, comprehensive doctrine(s) gain constraining power over other people. Likewise, unless we can establish agreement on the "freestanding" grounds

*four terms of social cooperation*
*nature/ grounds for toleration*

of political justice, it will be impossible to establish the direction and limits of public discourse and governance without relying arbitrarily upon some comprehensive doctrines rather than others, thereby eroding tolerance. Yet our ideas of tolerance and fairness have a deep fragility, given the extent of our "deeply contested ideas" of justice (4).

Thus, Rawls seeks to re-present our basic ideas by offering a "deeper self-understanding" with which "we can attain wider agreement" (*Political Liberalism*, 26). Yet what could get "deeper" than this already very deep contestation, which so often appears implicated in our very notions and measurements of *depth itself?* Vital to Rawls's response is remembering a tragic conflict near the birth of our modernity. By repeatedly recalling the "wars of religion," Rawls believes he gets beneath our current conflicts: He recalls the tragic possibility that might fundamentally inform, orient, and limit our understanding of what is desirable in politics. In the face of this death—"mortal conflict" over comprehensive doctrines with "transcendent elements not admitting of compromise"—political liberalism discovers a certain resolution and resoluteness (xxviii).

"Political liberalism starts by taking to heart the absolute depth of that irreconcilable latent conflict" (*Political Liberalism*, xxviii). These words express the profound role that tragic sensibility plays in Rawlsian liberalism. With tropes like "by taking to heart" (the organ that pumps the life blood that renews the body and a metaphor for the deepest place) and with expressions like "absolute depth," Rawls seeks to transcend the very deep contestations he acknowledges. Political liberalism's vitality will thus require that we repeatedly remember such mortal and never-too-distant conflict. Moreover, it requires cultivation of a sense that conflict lurks not just in religious conflicts over what is right and pleasing to God but in far more disagreements than we often realize. To avoid sliding toward this abyss, we would have to reach a very deep agreement on the limits of public reason that establish the necessary moral exclusions and barriers.

Tragic doctrinal conflict functions as a pivotal conceptual and inspirational resource, not only in the crucial framing discussion of mortal conflicts in Rawls's *Political Liberalism* but also in his "Idea of Public Reason Revisited." In response to critical questions about whether the limits of public reason are too narrowly framed and unnecessary in societies no longer nearly as riven by violent conflicts or potentially violent hostilities, Rawls again insists that we take to heart the absolute and ever-latent depth of tragic finitude. Unless we ban this finitude (manifest in our fallible efforts to shape our public lives in light of truths about meaning, being, and the good) from public forums when it exceeds the limits of public reason concerning questions of basic justice, "divisions and hostilities between doctrines are bound in time to assert themselves."[3] Insofar as societies now have less conflict, it is significantly *because* of the exclusions of public reason, without which, we "easily fall into bitterness and resentment" ("Idea of Public Reason Revisited," 175). Rawls does not argue this point. Rather, in response to those who have carefully analyzed the ways this may or may not be entailed, his text *conjures* it, deploys the phantom of an easy slide toward a tragic abyss in order to reassure the choir and deflect the critics. So public reason must be absolutely sovereign over the borders of legitimate public discourse and define the principles that are to govern liberal public territory: It must not be altered in agonistic relations with contending doctrines, or it will quickly become ineffective and meaningless—and we will "easily fall" into the abyss.

To better grasp Rawls's understanding of the sovereignty of "public reason") in relation to his tragic narrative, it is helpful to sketch briefly his understanding of public reason before continuing with his tragic narrative. On Rawls's account, the term "comprehensive doctrine" refers to all those religious, philosophical, and moral frameworks concerning fundamental questions of being, knowledge, the good, and so forth. Whether or not they make claims that obviously involve "transcendent elements," they are all transcendent in the sense that these questions and answers transcend the capacities of human reason to secure agreement. Thus, "the diversity of reasonable comprehensive . . . doctrines found in modern democratic societies is not a mere historical condition that may soon pass away; it is a permanent feature of the public culture of democracy" (*Political Liberalism*, 36). This "fact of reasonable pluralism" is due to inexpugnable "burdens of judgment" (such as evidence that is very complex and hard to assess, disagreements concerning how to weigh different considerations, conceptual indeterminacy, difficult-to-recognize effects of our life experiences, diverse and conflicting normative considerations, and social space that is too limited to affirm all values and thus necessitates hard choices with no clear answers (56–57). Reasonable people must acknowledge these ambiguities and recognize that consensus on comprehensive doctrines (as well as political decisions fundamentally based on them) can only be maintained by oppressive force under which some reasonable people will find themselves arbitrarily constrained. This "fact of oppression" leads reasonable citizens to refrain from using political power "to repress comprehensive views that are not unreasonable, though different from their own" (60). Rawls construes this repression broadly, to include not only direct violations of the liberties of conscience and thought but also any use—or public advocacy of such use—of state power to decide "constitutional essentials or basic questions of justice in light of comprehensive doctrines" (62). The phrase "basic questions of justice" is important here, for Rawls's public reason is not limited to a "constitutional consensus" that would "cover only certain fundamental procedural political principles for the constitution" (149).[4] Rawls's "overlapping consensus" is deeper and broader and applies to the whole basic structure of social cooperation.

Rawls's articulations of the limits (moral, not legal) of legitimate "public reason" are somewhat ambiguous and have shifted over time. Rawls first leaned toward what he calls the "exclusive view" of these limits, which maintains that "reasons given explicitly in terms of comprehensive doctrines are never to be introduced into public reason" (*Political Liberalism,* 247). In *Political Liberalism,* he moves toward the "inclusive view," which "allow[s] citizens, in certain situations, to present what they regard as the basis of political values rooted in their comprehensive doctrine, provided they do this in ways that strengthen the ideal of public reason itself" (247). In the "Introduction to the Paperback Edition," Rawls opens public discourse even further and now affirms "the wide view" with a "proviso": "Reasonable [comprehensive] doctrines may be introduced in public reasons at any time, provided that in due course public reasons . . . are presented sufficient to support whatever the comprehensive doctrines are introduced to support" (li–lii). In his most recent discussion, "The Idea of Public Reason Revisited," Rawls maintains this stance, but he now emphasizes the great value of people introducing their comprehensive doctrines when these are "reasonable"—that is, when they exemplify shared values across differences—and emphasizes the way diverse doctrines contribute to the vitality of these values, thus strengthening civic friendship (section 4).

These shifts illustrate how Rawls aims to accommodate the concerns of his critics. Yet the basic structure of his thinking changed little, and it is this foundation I seek to question.[5] What is always crucial for Rawls is that the ideal of public reason must exclude as illegitimate all political contributions inspired by "doctrinal" differences that are at odds with or exceed the overlapping consensus (concerning liberty and equality) framed by political liberal justice. (This idea of public reason is proximate to those articulated by most political liberals, most of whom fall somewhere along the spectrum traced by Rawls's theoretical movements over time.)[6] The "or exceed" is important to note here: One must not introduce beliefs that go beyond what public reasons alone are *sufficient to support.*" "At odds with or exceed" is thus redundant in relation to Rawls:[To exceed political liberalism's general scope and direction is a priori defined as being at odds with it.]The range of our voices and our efforts to hear must stop here. Violate this limit, and we begin down the tragic slippery slope toward the absolute depths of conflict."

Given the centrality of these limits to Rawlsian political theory, we will have to look much more carefully at exactly how political liberalism attempts to achieve and defend public reason as an ideal and limit. We must also trace the theoretical and practical effects of this "reasonableness." Yet because the enactment of public reason is driven by a certain reading of the tragic, we must first discuss another dimension of the latter, namely, political liberalism's sense of its relations to those who and that which exceed its limits.

## Political Liberalism's (Not So) Tragic Impositions

Like other political liberals,[7] Rawls reads Isaiah Berlin as articulating a sense of the imposition and loss that is an inexorable aspect of all social arrangements. Indeed, this reading is central to the orientation, energy, and limits—as well as to the textual and political practices—of Rawlsian liberalism. Following an analysis of how Rawls's reading of Berlin functions in political liberalism, I return to Berlin in order to initiate questions concerning both Rawls's reading and political liberalism itself.

Rawls, claiming to follow Berlin, acknowledges a tragic aspect that political liberalism can never entirely expunge, even if it might escape the most tragic possibilities by focusing on and responding to the absolute depths of mortal conflict over comprehensive doctrines. Working in tandem with the way Rawls's rendering of these depths orients his project, his rendering of loss and lamentation works to assure and legitimate this orientation and to resist the most difficult questions.

In Rawls's words: "No society can include within itself all forms of life. We may indeed lament the limited space . . . of social worlds, and of ours in particular; and we may regret some of the inevitable effects of our culture and social structure. . . . there is no social world without loss: that is, no social world which does not exclude some ways of life that realize in special ways certain fundamental values. But those social necessities are not to be taken for arbitrary bias or injustice" (*Political Liberalism,* 197). Because the scarcity of social space is universal (that is, because "values clash and the full range . . . is too extensive to fit in any one social world"; ibid.), there will always be loss and lamentation. Political liberalism cannot exempt itself from this tragic calculus. Yet Rawls immediately deploys the idea that imposition is universal in order to comfort us and dull our receptivity to those impassioned aspects of grief, sensibility, and vision that might—with determinacy or a more haunting indeterminacy—raise questions about whether the losses imposed are really necessary, just, or desirable.

I say determinacy *or* indeterminacy because lamentations of imposition can draw an order into question in at least two ways. More-determinate modes of lamentation identify injustices or other problems in light of alternative visions of ethical and political life that appear preferable to the political liberal order. Yet there are other cries that are just as impassioned but that are less certain of their direction. Here an overwhelming grief at loss is voiced, but along with it is voiced a sense of ethical or material complexity or inchoateness, a sense that we have not yet worked out alternatives. Nevertheless, the cries split our ears and hearts. They say to us: There *must* be a better way, even if we currently only grope toward the smallest and most inadequate first steps—even if we cannot yet say what these may be. In the fissures of these splits, animated by those cries, an intensity of questioning, new efforts to listen, and experimentation are born. For increasing numbers of people, the deepest ethical questions concerning our violent impact upon the nonhuman world, the encroachment of liberal societies upon different modes of social being, the responsibilities of citizens to welcome the vast (sometimes overwhelming) numbers of people who seek to transgress a polity's border laws—all partake of this indeterminacy.

But Rawls stifles both kinds of challenges to the limits of political liberalism with his narrative of the universality and necessity of tragic imposition. He rarely seriously engages the determinate force of liberalism's more radical critics (a textual practice that embodies the oblivious aspects of his theory) and consistently exorcises its more indeterminate ghosts. Rawls's account of tragedy contributes to a readiness to legitimate the moral exclusion both of expressions of suffering and of possibilities that exceed political liberalism's limits: They are simply "social necessities" that "are not to be taken for arbitrary bias or injustices." He deflects more-indeterminate challenges by foregrounding a presumption of inevitable imposition in a way that places the entire burden of questioning upon those excluded. Displaying (and engendering) an attitude of calm reticence to engage challenges, Rawls writes, "Without further exploration, it would not appear unfair to them, for social influences favoring some doctrines over others cannot be avoided by any view of political justice" (*Political Liberalism*, 197). Assimilating his others, he writes, "There is no criterion for what counts as sufficient space except that of a reasonable and defensible conception of justice itself. The idea of sufficient space is metaphorical and has no meaning beyond that shown in the range of comprehensive doctrines that the principles of such a conception permit and that citizens can affirm as worthy of their full allegiance. The objection might still be that the political conception fails to identify the right space, but this is simply the question of which is the most reasonable political conception" (198). In other words, Rawls cultivates a (not so) tragic disposition that will be troubled by and listen seriously to only those lamentations and challenges that are very determinately framed. Regarding the challenges, he will engage only questions concerning whether a more reasonable political liberalism is being proposed.

I am not dismissing the importance of Rawls's demands for determinate calculations of losses and gains. I am, however, questioning Rawls's fundamental presumptuousness in relation to political liberalism's others and asking whether justice might not require more-agitated and self-critical reflections *and attitudes,* more-active and open-ended questioning that explores and risks transformations and reformations, more-receptive generosity toward those who would draw us into question. I am questioning whether Rawlsian justice—or any position—ought to predetermine the space for criticizing its impositions with such exaggerated self-confidence. Might not justice be eroded—even undermined— from within by Rawls's claims, sensibilities, and textual practices?

Ironically, such hubris is unwittingly called into question by Rawls himself. Is not Rawls's claim that "these necessities are not to be taken for arbitrary bias or injustice" greatly at odds with his acknowledgment—in his discussion of (burdens of judgment) and again referring to Berlin—that in making decisions among competing values in limited social space, "we face great difficulties in setting priorities and making adjustments? Many hard decisions may seem to have no clear answer" (*Political Liberalism,* 57). This passage appears to say that it is precisely at the zones of imposition that we often find our judgment, vision, and hearing most impaired and in doubt. *If* such zones (and are they not widespread?) combine encroachment and exclusion with lack of clarity, and *if* we cannot dispel the important effects that this entwinement of encroachment and murkiness *as such* has in our lives (while we may gain insight into specific types of exclusion or confusion), *then* would not wisdom and justice demand humility, receptivity to political liberalism's others, and more-searching self-critical inquiries? Although a reticence to impose upon others under such burdened conditions would importantly *involve* some of the self-restraints of public reason, it would call into question the way public reason hardens "tolerance" into dogmatic exclusions that enhance and conceal imposition. A wisdom and justice born of *this* tragic sensibility would work hard to remember that it is almost certainly engaged in unnecessary injustices of which it is only dimly aware. Such a wisdom and justice would avoid at all costs insinuations that it had risen wholly beyond the arbitrary in its measures and practices.

Berlin leans much more in these directions than does Rawls. His liberal vision is less comforting and consolidated, more open-ended, more specific, and (in some ways) more generous in spirit. Berlin offers an account of moral and political life as inexorably entangled in "incommensurable visions" and "incompatible values" that are often "objective" (in the sense that they are "different ends that men may seek and be fully rational, fully men, capable of understanding each other and sympathizing and deriving light from each other"). Proponents of different modes of life may "admire and respect" each other, but they may be incapable of fitting their differences harmoniously within one social horizon.[8] There will always be loss and elements of discord, and people in disagreement over "What is to be done?" will frequently have to face up to the fact that "there is . . . no clear reply" (*Crooked Timber of Humanity,* 17). Throughout his writing he recommends the softening of collisions, balance, negotiation, a sense that "the concrete situation is almost everything" (18). He draws hope from the yearning to prevent harm that he believes is affirmed across diverse cultures, and he seeks to provide room for the pursuit of different ends by establishing robust protections for negative liberties.

Berlin cultivates a sense that politics is always about forging an "uneasy equilibrium, which is constantly threatened and in constant need of repair," negotiated between different visions or values that are in tension within any mode of life (*Crooked Timber of Humanity,* 19). We are "doomed to choose" (13) without clarity because the scales and methods for measuring and assessing many losses are themselves implicated in the contestations they would evaluate. Moreover, each political initiative "creates a new situation which breeds its own new needs and problems, new demands . . . and so on, forever and unpredictably" (14). Even *within* liberal societies, our efforts to mediate between different values often has a tragic aspect, and there is in principle no "reason" that will clarify and harmonize all our dilemmas.[9] Though risks are unavoidable, we can often do better or worse, depending upon whether or not we exercise "humility" and are attuned to our predicament. Berlin emphasizes that in murky political contestations, "placing human beings in contact with persons dissimilar to themselves" is one of the primary sources of knowledge (*Crooked Timber of Humanity*, 90). He is a strong proponent of tolerance, and for him this means not an absolute ban on different doctrines in politics but a cultivated reticence to impose violently upon others, combined with the willingness to undertake difficult conversations and negotiations among those of differing forms of life in situations where some imposition is unavoidable.

Berlin's modesty and sense of the tragic might have developed even further if he had not unwittingly accepted certain ideas commonplace in his day. For example, his reliance on Giambattista Vico and Johann Gottfried von Herder for temporally and geographically distanced examples of cultural difference tends to underestimate the great extent to which cultural identity is often at a very deep level constituted by and entwined with the suppression of cultural difference at its borders and within.[10] Reformulations taking account of such facts would primarily serve to increase the substantial pressure that Berlin's own elaboration of the concepts of incommensurability and loss places upon Rawls's efforts to assimilate Berlin to a defense of the moral exclusions of political liberalism. In Rawls, Berlin's more nuanced tragic argument for humility, forbearance, and the importance of negative liberty hardens into a more dogmatic liberalism than Berlin affirms. It is hard to imagine Berlin thoroughly exempting his own liberalism from his observation that "to force people into the neat uniforms demanded by dogmatically believed-in schemes is almost always the road to inhumanity" (*Crooked Timber of Humanity*, 19). By exempting political liberalism from this insight, Rawls risks magnifying the extent to which it embodies this tragic truth.

J. Donald Moon, in his pursuit of a defense of political liberalism is more insightfully resonant with Berlinian themes than is Rawls: "Political liberalism . . . strives to be deeply attuned to its own inadequacies and to the necessarily partial character of any account of how we should structure our relationships to others or understand their identities. It seeks to remain open to the ways its own constructions may exclude some voices even as a result of its effort to be inclusive. It acknowledges that the principles and structures it advances may stand in deep tension to the values with which it begins" (*Constructing*

*Community,* ix). Yet though I admire much in Moon's writing,[11] his rendering of the meaning and implications of a tragic sensibility often "stands in deep tension" with the spirit of inadequacy, openness, and contradictions with which it is repeatedly reintroduced. Animated by a respect for persons and an ideal of political community governed by principles all can freely accept, Moon, with other political liberals, argues for a limited public sphere guided by a "constrained discourse." A sense of tragic conflict makes Moon uncomfortable with liberal hubris and modulates his articulation of ideals of public reason and their place in political life. Still, there are weaknesses in his discussion of tragic imposition that are related to his allegiance to Rawls's strategy of bracketing differences and the continuing presence of associated problems.

Moon is critical of neo-Aristotelian efforts to guide politics according to a vision of flourishing, arguing that agreement is not to be expected on questions of final ends and that thus "this strategy is an invitation to a conflict in which there are likely to be winners and losers" (*Constructing Community,* 35). Rather, we should pursue agreements that "all can share" without a consensus on ultimate questions, by "seek[ing] to 'bracket' differences . . . in search for common values and principles on the basis of which their interchange of giving and taking can be regulated in a manner that is fully acceptable to each" (8).

On Moon's reading, when we abstract from our disagreements we discover a widely shared and significant sense of ourselves as "agents": "Our freedom also consists in the fact that we cannot tell ahead of time what particular features of everyone's identities will be seen to be alterable or unalterable. This is a key insight. . . . Because we can call into question our goals, . . . and thereby alter ourselves . . . we should not take a particular system of aims and purposes . . . as the basis for an ideal . . . political order. . . . We must abstract [from these and] . . . base our political lives on our capacity for agency. To do otherwise is . . . not only to exclude those who do not share the particular ideals in question, but it also limits the moral autonomy of everyone" (50–51). Hence, with Rawls, Moon thinks that public discourse over basics should exclude particular doctrines and aim to ensure agency.

Yet Moon insightfully recognizes a circularity in all models of constrained discourse, a circularity that harbors the possibility of tragic imposition upon those who do not share those models' aspirations. For  the constraints imposed as conditions of achieving consensual norms "necessarily presuppose a particular set of norms or values, or at least delimit the range of positions which can be effectively articulated."

Some will be silenced or burdened by the requirements and limits of a public discourse in which "it is difficult to articulate their experiences and needs" (*Constructing Community*, 96). Moon argues that such imposition is ineliminable, for the alternative (mythical) unconstrained discourse can coercively impinge too—for example, upon the privacy and integrity of citizens—in perhaps even worse ways. Yet he is critical of political liberals such as Charles Larmore (and others) for being "too sanguine in his expectations for this strategy, in part because he exaggerates the 'neutrality' of his justification of neutrality" (61). He is concerned not only about Larmore's righteousness toward "fanatics and would-be martyrs" but also about the possibility that such liberalism overlooks the way strategies of abstracting to shared beliefs often greatly privilege those for whom the commonality is central over those for whom it is a marginal or instrumental value (for example, consider the greater value Rawls places on economic efficiency, compared to the Amish).

To tame the potentially vicious circularity of liberal oblivion and the asymmetrical burdens that public reason places upon its others, Moon proposes a "two-stage process" that is "open but not unconstrained." Political liberal citizens will endorse the constraints of public reason, but they will do so in a manner that recognizes the particular historical context of those constraints, acknowledges their partiality, and allows them to be called into question. Moon is sketchy about what this might mean practically or institutionally, but the spirit of his argument is clear: "Each 'we' must remain alive to the possibility that what 'we' consider reasonable may be experienced by others as . . . imposition. But such possibilities can only be canvassed in a particular discursive context, framed by a specific structure of constraints, one in which dissenting voices will have to struggle to make themselves heard precisely because their demands will involve a violation of the established framework of rights" (*Constructing Community*, 60).

Moon seems to urge us to cultivate a space—present but largely undeveloped in Rawls—between the ideality and the legality of public discourse. Rawls notes that whereas citizens *ideally* ought to affirm the limits of public reason, liberalism *legally* protects a much greater space for political expression and listening. Moon sees this discrepancy as crucial for nurturing political liberalism's capacity to best negotiate the tragic opacities and impositions of our condition. In contrast to Larmore's righteousness and to Rawls's rendering of imposition in ways that sedate us and resist critique, Moon calls us both to strongly affirm public reason and to listen to legally protected voices that exceed liberal ideals, in order to discern aspects of previously unrecognized, unnecessary, and undesirable unreason in liberal reason. Because the overwhelming task of liberal citizens is to uphold the constraints of public reason, "this approach obviously disadvantages certain perspectives, but its aim is to secure a reasonable balance between the scope of discourse at any particular point in time and the need for openness" (*Constructing Community*, 60).

Moved by a sense of the inexpugnable tragic aspects of human life, Moon pushes beyond Rawls's limits to listening. And Moon is right, I think, to point out that there is no "unconstrained" mode of discourse that one could offer that would be free of closures and impositions. Thus, at a formal level, Moon theorizes in a space I suggest is ethically and politically vital: the space between the need to affirm a direction and set of limits for politics and the need to listen to those who would move in other directions. Admittedly, in Moon's scheme, these others must "struggle," perhaps mightily, to get a "hearing," but I see no political path that could move wholly beyond this problem and achieve some sort of absolute—egalitarian in every direction—welcoming. Furthermore, I do not think this would be desirable even if it could be achieved.

My criticism of Moon, then, will focus on his articulation of "reasonable balance," for it does not seem quite reasonable to me. Or, for reasons I give below, concerning more-radical challenges to the sovereignty of "reason," perhaps it is *too* reasonable and we should seek a more unreasonable balance—which is not to say one without reason.

Though Moon's work on the tragic goes beyond Rawls's, it remains entangled in some of the latter's problems. We can begin to see this when Moon, in an a priori manner, effectively ranks degrees of tragedy or degrees to which tragedy is troubling. Some impositions (for example, constraints upon those who are randomly violent) are not tragic. "More troubling" are liberal conflicts with and impositions upon those who hold other comprehensive doctrines in dogmatic, nonnegotiable fashion—others whom we recognize as morally, if erroneously, motivated. Yet "it is only when the liberal strategy suppresses voices to which [it] itself seeks to remain open that we encounter its tragic dimension in its full form" (*Constructing Community*, 10). Here, even if all are good political liberals, we may recognize "inner contradictions" and "irreconcilable values" that can only be resolved by means of some imposing upon others (see, for example, abortion). This, he writes, is the highest form of tragedy.

Moon seems to adopt a posture of having significantly assimilated and conquered tragedy by claiming to have seized its measure (or rendered contending measures trivial). Political liberalism thus postures as *the* mode of political theory and practice that best recognizes the tragic—and its degrees—and gives it its due in the form of rights, bases, orientations, and limits to public discourse that minimize the most tragic of conflicts. Hence, liberalism best assimilates tragedy by assimilating itself *to* tragedy, by recognizing and allowing tragedy to work upon liberalism in ways that might diminish its probability.

I think hopeful efforts to respond to the tragic aspect of the human condition must partake of this strategy, allowing our sense of tragic finitude to shape theory and practice and evaluating our efforts partly (not wholly) by how well we think it has informed our striving toward justice, freedom, generosity, and so on. We should try to minimize tragedy by partially shaping and governing ourselves in light of a recognition of finitude. This partly implies developing an orientation to tragedy that involves a certain evaluative stance toward other such efforts. Thus far I am not far from Moon.

Yet Moon renders the assimilation of tragedy in exaggerated terms, such that the influence of our relation to tragic possibility risks undergoing a dangerous reversal. Whereas a tragic sensibility at its deepest evokes a powerful awareness of the weakness of our capacity to acknowledge tragedy in ways that would allow us to adequately respond to many who question our political directions, in Moon's account, tragedy is assimilated in ways that often tend to fortify and secure more than unsettle and call to question. Certainly he illuminates a dimension of tragic imposition that we probably never surpass. But the disturbing effects here are significantly vitiated by his sense that liberalism a priori measures tragedy better than does any of its rivals, by his confidence that liberalism's impositions are sufficiently small to legitimate only an opening in which the others have to "struggle" hard to receive a hearing, and by his sense that liberalism's need to learn from others about the meaning and requirements of justice is small enough that citizens need not work mightily at cultivating virtues and practices of radical receptivity that might enhance this possibility (even as they *also* cultivate a number of liberal virtues).

Instead, we are called only to "remain open" to ways in which we exclude others and to "permit" them to challenge us. It might seem nitpicky to harp upon Moon's repeated terms of choice, but they are emblematic of a weakening of the tragic sensibility that I seek to resist. To "remain open" or "maintain an openness" is to frame openness as something political liberalism largely already has, at least in ideal form, as a possession. We will have to work to maintain this virtue, but it is largely ours. Or at least it is enough so—and more so *ours* than *theirs*—that we do not expect to learn much from them about what openness might require. We will "maintain" it and "permit" them.

⚡ But tragedy significantly teaches us about *dis*possession, or often even about the utter absence of what we only thought we possessed. As such, it works to dispossess us of our secure sense of where we are and what we have, so that "remaining" and "maintaining" appear to be desperately insufficient. From this vantage point, "being open" is not primarily a quality or state; rather, it is intensely *verbal; opening; a dynamic relation that is yet to be,* greatly involving the abundance of others as a condition of possibility.

We would need to incite this sense—even as we affirm and pursue a social and political path that we judge to be best. *Perhaps justice is only possible in the midst of this tension.* Yet Moon radically undermines this possibility when he ranks a priori the impositions within the liberal framework above those at its borders. Why is the former a priori "more troubling"? Should we not also strive mightily to recall how deeply and unexpectedly troubling many of liberalism's conflicts with and impositions upon others historically has been? (Need another list be given?) Should we not also strive to project an anticipation of how unanticipatably troubling many of them are likely to remain? Would not this latter sensibility be more congruent with the recurrence of tragedy and more conducive to receptive learning, with others, about how to live less violently? Moon's manner of ranking tragedy attempts to seize possession of it more than one ought to or can, in pursuit of a sense of legitimacy that is greater than one ought to possess. He claims too much for liberal reason and thus unwittingly contributes to its unreason.

Though Moon moves admirably beyond the overly rigid closures of other political liberals, his own theory is still implicated in them. My critique is somewhat analogous with Machiavelli's critique of the rigidity of the fortress of his day. Badly needed to resist subjugation is a strategy that is more mobile, flexible, and receptive in the face of tragic dangers that repeatedly illustrate a sheer unexpectedness of character, location, and force.

If Moon is both right that every political order and identity is implicated in tragic impositions of which it has no definitive measure and right that we cannot tell ahead of time what particular features of everyone's identities will be seen to be alterable or unalterable, then *political liberalism too* ought—precisely in the name of the agency its pursues—to be drawn more vulnerably into relation to his claim that "we should not take a particular system of . . . purposes as the basis for an ideal . . . political order" (*Constructing Community*, 50–51). Tragedy, more profoundly engaged, ought to evoke a sensibility that both informs the substance and modes of acquiring and legitimating our ethical-political possessions and enlivens a certain receptive vulnerability to dispossession—which also, to be sure, is very dangerous. There is no perfect mode of disequilibrium between this "both . . . and . . . ," no perfect escape from tragedy's tragedy. Yet to strive to live in this tension, I suspect, is a basic condition of struggling against the world's tragedy and toward richer possibilities.

## The Disciplines of Unreflective Equilibrium

Yet this struggle (as well as the sense of danger and hope that informs and inspires it) is vitiated by most political liberalism. Oriented by its sense of being the single adequate response to the absolute depths of tragic conflicts of faith and by its radically diminished sense of its own impositions upon others, political liberalism for the most part pursues strategies to secure its sovereignty as the currency of public reason (or at least, its power within a small oligopoly of proximate positions).

We have seen how Rawls delegitimates political visions that exceed what public reason is "sufficient to support." But the problem is deeper. For as noted above, not only are the exclusions of public reason *defined by* principles of political liberal justice, but they are also *conditions for* its birth and ongoing existence. The "reasoning *all can share,*" in order to be and be conceived, requires that "all" bracket the differences that bring them into deep contestation. Otherwise, this reason might be drawn—by threads of connection with differences—into contestation and thus not so shared. The exclusionary bracketing, however, must be governed by this reasoning, which in turn requires it. Liberty and equality can only function as the straightforward "common currency" Rawls demands if they cease to be modulated in discrepant ways by doctrines (now excluded). Conversely, we only know what must be excluded as beyond the limits of public reason in light of clearly defined and prioritized principles like liberty and equality.

This circle has a certain viciousness to it and is theoretically untenable for reasons that I will explore in the next section, "Clarity's Concealments." Here I seek to trace *the textual-political practices of insistence and concealment* that facilitate Rawls's circling between the construction of his reason and the exclusions entwined with it. In essence, Rawls "solves" his theoretical quandary by enjoining and enacting a series of disciplinary pressures and practices. A close analysis of these moves will allow us to further articulate how the deployment of tragedy that sustains Rawls's circling undermines tragic sensibilities in their own name and generates serious political blindness and dangers.

Rawls strongly insists on the sovereignty of "public reason" for determining the borders of political discourse. Hence, even as public reason often "allows of more than one reasonable answer to any particular question," because of the play of different values or differently weighed values, Rawls "urges us not to . . . [introduce "nonpolitical" values to resolve the ambiguities at hand] in . . . matters of basic justice. Close agreement is rarely achieved and abandoning public reason whenever disagreement occurs in balancing values is in effect to abandon it altogether" (*Political Liberalism*, 240–41). If at any point we cease to offer principles and values that we sincerely believe "every reasonable person can endorse," we begin to weaken the restraining notions, habits, and dispositions that keep us from sliding down the tragic slippery slope toward the absolute depths of conflict.

The absoluteness of these limits of public reason is essentially entwined with a drive and claim to the "completeness" of its system of principles. Rawls states, "We want the substantive content and the guidelines of inquiry of a political conception . . . to be complete. This means that the values specified by that conception can be suitably balanced or combined, or otherwise united . . . so that those values alone give a reasonable public answer to all, or to nearly all questions involving the constitutional essentials and basic questions of justice" (*Political Liberalism*, 225; see also 244). Later, he writes of a public reason "suitably ordered" to achieve the same results. Lacking such ordering, the principles are indeterminate and ambiguous: They then risk being "puppets manipulated from behind the scenes by comprehensive doctrines" ("Idea of Public Reason Revisited," 145). Rawls's "original position" is offered precisely to this end. "The idea is . . . to model freedom and equality and restrictions on reasons in such a way that it becomes perfectly evident which agreement would be made by the parties as citizens' representatives" (*Political Liberalism*, 26).

At the same time, however, Rawls knows that there are and will be different understandings of which principles justice requires, as well as of how they should be interpreted and ordered. Indeed, he now offers "justice as fairness" only as one possible rendering of justice in the political liberal family. So public reason drives toward "completeness" and the "perfectly evident" not so much in order to secure once and for all a single version but, more importantly, to *impose very considerable discipline* on public discussion" (*Political Liberalism*, 227, my emphasis). The discipline imposed by the requirements of public reason—and repeatedly enacted by Rawls—consists in pressuring and being pressured to ask and respond properly to political liberal questions over all others as one's *highest responsibility* concerning fundamental political matters: Are the arguments I am offering or asked to receive from others ones that I sincerely think *all* can share? Or do they violate these limits?

Thus, even if no actual consensus on the "substance" of justice is expected, Rawls does strive to engender a consensus concerning the adoption of this "very considerable discipline." This discipline will, Rawls claims, contribute to social harmony by "greatly limiting" the range of legitimate interpretations ("Idea of Public Reason Revisited," 145). But how exactly will it do this, given our current "very deep" contestations concerning fundamental political questions? Political liberalism's response here, I think, is that a strong drive (spurred significantly by a particular rendering of tragic finitude) to completeness, unity, order, and unanimity within and concerning a framework of free and equal citizenship will create a set of pressures that help constitute citizens who are disposed to always set aside difficult differences. With our movement toward that (ever-elusive) perfectly evident situation and set of fundamental principles, we might resist the slide toward tragic conflict that inevitably befalls us when we do not set aside such differences. Political liberalism is driven by this dichotomous politics of motion: move thus or slide back.

Both haunted by a ghost it *conjures up* (with its sense of absolute tragic depth) and relieved of a ghost it *conjures away* (with its diminished sense of tragic remainders), political liberalism paradoxically insists on striving toward a certain absolute illumination—even if it knows it cannot quite attain it, driven precisely by its rendering of the ineliminable darkness of finitude. The best way to understand the mechanisms of this "very considerable discipline" is to follow its operations in Rawls's texts as he bears its weight and insists that others follow the paths imposed by its responsibilities. I suggest that what is engendered here is not only a "basic structure" of political economic principles, but a *basic structure of habitual visibilities, invisibilities, and dispositions*. Political liberalism may claim to leave these characteristics primarily to the realm of nonpolitical freedom, but in fact it does a tremendous amount of work on them and must be assessed in light of this capillary politics, as well as on the macro level.

Deeply entwined with the "original position," which aims to make

matters complete and "perfectly evident" concerning the basic framework of justice, is Rawls's understanding of "reflective equilibrium."
The original position is itself established as the "not necessarily stable"
result of a process of seeking reflective equilibrium concerning questions of justice.[12] Yet the original position also "serves as a mediating
idea by which all our considered convictions, whatever their level of
generality . . . can be brought to bear upon one another." Hence, the
original position at once represents the present outcome of a movement toward reflective equilibrium and is a "device of representation"
that "serves as a means for further clarification" in this movement
(*Political Liberalism*, 26). Crucial here is not the cessation of movement in certainty but the mode of movement and its disciplines. Rawls
(admirably) recognizes that any outcome of a process of searching for
reflective equilibrium, including any interpretation of an original position that might aid this process, is "liable to be upset by further examination of the conditions which should be imposed on the contractual
situation and by particular cases which may lead us to revise our judgments" (*Theory of Justice*, 20–21). My questioning will concern the
ways in which this liability is construed, resisted, constrained, managed, and directed *toward* zero.

   If Rawls's reflections thwart the centrifugal forces of circularity
(which disclose or even provoke irresolvable ambiguities, paradoxes,
and tensions amid various understandings of justice and levels of reflection—in ways that unravel our uncertainties and renew our vulnerability to other voices as much or more than they secure our own) and
promote centripetal forces that move toward "greater coherence,"
"deeper self-understanding," "clarification," "wider agreement," and
"reasonableness" (*Political Liberalism*, 26), it is because the process of
striving toward reflective equilibrium is constructed and operates with
a set of weights (pulling toward a center) and filters (screening out more
centrifugal forces). Rawls's reflections about this process disclose it
only in the least problematic light. Thus, it is the search for an understanding of justice that "to be acceptable, must accord with our considered convictions at all levels of generality" (8). It is a process of
"going back and forth" between universal principles and particular
judgments, scrutinizing discrepancies in a process of reciprocal critique
and revision until, "duly pruned and adjusted," they would be coherent (*Theory of Justice*, 20).

   Yet though Rawls does not announce it in his recent writings, much
more than this is necessary for him both to "assume that eventually
we shall find" a reflective equilibrium and to sustain such a singular

pursuit of *this* aspect of reflective motion (*Theory of Justice*, 20). Beyond his account of this dialectic—or a condition of its overwhelmingly *positive* character—are the weights and filters that are always at work in the movement of his texts, even if he rarely makes explicit their central role. In *A Theory of Justice*, perhaps before a certain confidence has been drawn more deeply into question, he is at his most explicit: "Considered judgments" are "those judgments in which our moral capacities are most likely to be displayed without distortion. Thus in deciding which of our judgments to take into account we may reasonably select some and exclude others. For example, we can discard those judgments made with hesitation, or in which we have little confidence. Similarly, those given when we are upset or frightened, or when we stand to gain one way or the other can be left aside. All these judgments are likely to be erroneous or to be influenced by an excessive attention to our own interests" (47). We are to give weight to the "considered" and filter out those principles or particular judgments that are accompanied by hesitation, little confidence, anxiety, or fear.

But why discipline reflection—why discipline human selves in the deepest recesses of their habitual political imaginings—only in this manner? Hesitation often discloses moral complexities and ambiguities that might, fortunately, inflect justice toward practices of more vulnerable receptive generosity toward those struggling within and beyond the established "equilibriums." Anxiety, anger, and fear often illuminate the damages and subjugations that reside in all orders, and hence these emotions engender a sense of the unending importance of also striving toward reflective *disequilibria*. All interests where people "stand to gain" are not equally and undesirably "excessive." For example, many of the "excessive" interests of the poor might be vitally informative. I am not recommending a thought process aimed simply at disruption. I am suggesting that reflections about justice ought to be forged in the tensions *between* the impulses to disrupt and those to cohere.

Ironically, Rawls's pursuit in his later work of an (un)reflective process for the overproduction of *"confidence"* is driven by a "liberalism of fear" (*Political Liberalism*, xxvi), which requires us to establish and secure a basic framework against the most tragic possibilities. Absolutizing a fear of the violent "absolute depth" of tragic doctrinal conflict, Rawls marginalizes all other judgments infused with different fears, hesitations, weak confidence, and anger—by casting them solely in a fearful light. The possibility that such conditions might also offer crucial political insight into the ambiguous, contradictory, and multifarious aspects of human existence is discarded at the outset.

Although Rawls says that the "fundamental organizing idea" behind justice as fairness is that of "society as a fair system of cooperation between free and equal persons" (*Political Liberalism*, 9), I think the fundamental organizing ideas are his rendering of tragic fear, his diminished sense of liberalism's tragic finitude, and his disciplinary/filtering response to both. These decisively shape his account of freedom, equality, fairness, and tolerance and engender a host of other "discarding" strategies to keep us moving toward the "perfectly evident." I will briefly sketch three such strategies that I think are integral to Rawls's micro-efforts to discipline people to be political liberal selves.

First, Rawls limits his analysis of fair cooperation to "normal and fully cooperating members of a society over a complete life" (*Political Liberalism*, 20). All "other questions" (such as on future generations, disabilities, international relations, animals and nature, immigration, and the like) are viewed as "problems of extension" of the principles arrived at through this greatly limited perspective. Now, Rawls is admirably nondogmatic when reflecting on this strategy. Although he thinks that the first three areas of extended questions—future generations, disabilities, international relations—can be rather easily accommodated within his framework and that political liberalism has substantial resources to address questions concerning the nonhuman, he acknowledges that there will be a "back and forth procedure" in which these questions "may require us to revise answers already reached" (245–46). Moreover, political liberalism should not be expected to answer all questions; "it needs always to be complemented by other virtues" (21). Nevertheless, the effect of his textual practice here is to build at the outset an exaggerated confidence in what is generally presented as a sovereign paradigm by shifting aside what many might consider to be among the most important questions—questions with a force that might cause hesitation, lack of confidence, anxiety, fear, and a sense of interests that would radically hamper the establishment of his framework. By framing these remainders as "problems of extension," Rawls avoids addressing, for example, the ways in which questions of human frailty and dependence might *fundamentally* alter his sense of our condition, agency, responsibilities, and the like. Similarly, Rawls guards against deeper, more problematic questioning of his framework when he suggests that where questions of the status of the natural world and our relation to it exceed public reason, they have no bearing on fundamental questions of justice and will be simply "complementary" (246). But, on the contrary, Rawls is quite mistaken: They may have enormous implications for questions concerning basics like property rights, acceptable levels of material affluence and access to "resources," and restrictions on "free choice." Similarly again, many increasingly suspect that questions concerning the identity and ethical substance of "a society" ought to be fundamentally rendered in radically more welcoming relations to "nonmembers" within and beyond various kinds of borders.

In effect, Rawls sets aside some of the most important and confusing questions in order to achieve a "clarity" and "reason" sufficient to govern them (perhaps with some revision) as mere "extensions." If one acknowledges and works with these questions at the outset, "public reason" is rendered more ambiguous, porous, and laden with contesting doctrines that greatly influence our responses to them. These characteristics might, in turn, solicit a more generous and vulnerable dialogical sensibility and politics as a *part* of what is vital to the practices of democracy. Yet if we—as Rawls does—establish the clarity, legitimacy, and sovereignty of public reason by excluding such questions, we acquire a mythically fortified mechanism with which to exclude doctrines that exceed our now "shared" public reason. This in turn operates in a significant way to minimize the possible provocations that the (now diminished) "other questions" might engender.

Second, to establish the ideal of public reason as the "common currency" of legitimacy that "we all share," Rawls tacitly exaggerates the separability of normative and empirical claims (questioned in his discussion of "burdens of judgment") and limits our appeals to "accepted general beliefs and forms of reasoning found in common sense, and the methods and conclusions of science when these are not controversial" (224). Laying claim to the "noncontroversial" in this way not only mythologizes public reason's exclusionary power against understandings of the world more obviously entwined with interpretations of "provincial" doctrines, but it also excludes things like "disputed economic theories" (what economic theories are *not* disputed?), and the plethora of central political judgments entwined with infinitely contestable assessments of how much human beings can change under different circumstances. These exclusions secure political liberalism's equilibrium insofar as they legitimate removing many important contestations from politics. The aim is, by clearing away confidence-weakening and hesitation-producing aspects of our condition, to push us along the mirage of a path to (un)reflective equilibrium that can protect us from "absolute depth." Of course, Rawls is neither the first nor the last theorist to flatten existence in the name of depth. The question is whether there might be less damaging possibilities that are concealed by Rawls's particular construal of tragedy, his related will to disciplined (un)reflective equilibrium, and his blindness to the remainders of his own theoretical and political efforts.

Third, "comprehensive doctrine" is a term Rawls works in ways that further weight and limit the process of reflection. Almost always associating "comprehensive" with "doctrine," Rawls exaggerates the comprehensiveness and immutability of many doctrines and thereby intensifies our fear of their proximity to the absolute depth of irreconcilable, thoroughgoing conflict.[13] At the same time, by calling religions "doctrines," Rawls minimizes their textured, public, and practiced character and thereby minimizes the difficulties and impositions associated with efforts to render them *nonpublic*.[14]

Perhaps even more important, by always associating "doctrine" with "comprehensive," political liberalism builds the illusion that the primary coercive forces threatening us are "doctrines." In this light, if public reason were to effectively delegitimate all doctrines beyond political liberal family limits, we would (provided a fair distribution of primary goods) have a society void of coercive forces, where we could freely choose our "life plans." This, both rhetorically and as embodied in the flow of Rawls's text, tends to deflect attention from the significance of many important forces that shape and constrain our political (un)consciousness—often quite comprehensively. Think, for example, of the effects of capitalist political economies in the development of our knowledge, perception, imagination, desire, sense of possibility and impossibility, culture industry, normalizing technologies, work, geography, wealth, poverty, education, environment, health and disease, relationships, and the limits of democracy, just to name a few.

Alternatively, if we see our world as produced and constrained by a variety of practices that are powerful but often not doctrinal, then the all-or-nothing dichotomy between a situation where comprehensive doctrines dictate the fundamentals and one where political liberalism protects a coercion-free space from doctrinal interference becomes highly problematic. If many doctrines have more capacities for dialogical transfiguration, modesty, and negotiation than Rawls acknowledges, and if our present world is awash with nondoctrinal powers that are rather comprehensive, then numerous possibilities arise in which various alternative doctrines and practices might challenge modes of unfreedom and barriers to thriving in ways that might come to be seen as broadly desirable—even if not recognized as such now. People would have to engage them and see. The point is not to argue that there are no risks here. Indeed, Rawls does a good job identifying some very

real risks. Rather, the point is to show how Rawls's drive toward clarity, spurred by his rendering of the tragic, leads him to conceal *both*
important modes of political liberal blindness and imposition *and* the
possibility that messier democratic processes of dialogical experimentation might be needed to better respond to these problems. It is good
that Rawls professes an openness to revision, but the operations of his
textual practice and the dispositions associated with it render such
revision relatively improbable.

## Clarity's Concealments:
## Bringing Political Liberalism's Borders into Question

A penetrating critique of political liberalism comes from Kent Greenawalt, who is committed to some central political liberal conclusions.
Like Rawls, Greenawalt largely concludes that ordinary citizens should
not voice their religious convictions when arguing about basic matters
in public forums. Though he departs from Rawls in affirming that
such convictions may rightly influence citizens' decisions and voting in
political matters, he is proximate to Rawls in affirming that citizens
ought to *argue* within the limits of the "common currency" of political liberalism. What most interests me are the *paths* and modes of
inquiry Greenawalt advances in his *Religious Convictions and Political Choice*. Ostensibly a political liberal, he deconstructs so many of
the pivotal mechanisms, disciplines, and borderlines of the political
liberal stance that, in my view, he is left with perhaps too little to effectively support his position. At any rate, the edifice of political liberalism in Greenawalt's hands becomes more humble, risky, and porous —
a dwelling somewhat better suited for our democratic times.

Greenawalt claims to move dialectically between principles and
judgments, "like the common reflective equilibrium way of thinking
. . . explicated by John Rawls" (*Religious Convictions and Political
Choice*, 25n1). Yet in important ways their modes of theorizing are
markedly different. Whereas Rawls discards judgments accompanied
by little confidence, much hesitation, and upsetting emotion, Greenawalt pursues such judgments relentlessly. For him, it is precisely by
exploring the essentially ambiguous borderline questions—concerning
those beings with contested moral status, reason and revelation, "public" reason and "local" claims, empirical "fact," and traditional interpretations influenced by authority, community, and commitments—that
we might best learn how to guide our political life. By lingering repeatedly with "troubling questions of value and difficult questions of fact,"
Greenawalt works toward a somewhat more capacious politics (144).

Greenawalt's path is partly animated by his sense that his own religious convictions have played a significant role in his political choices. Yet his journey is also spurred by his sense that the tragic dangers and damages of the human condition are more dispersed and multiple— not solely governed by the "absolute depth" narrative of the wars of religion.

Although Greenawalt claims that "worries [concerning wars of religion] are genuine," he thinks they have been exaggerated and writes in a different tone. "In this society religious divisiveness has occasionally been a serious problem, but not one that has overwhelmed the capacity of the society to work." Contesting Rawls's teleological claim to "complete and extend the tradition stemming from Locke," he notes that "it has never been widely assumed that religious convictions are impermissible grounds for political decision. The dangers that do exist can be largely countered by firm adherence to principles of religious liberty, nonsponsorship, and separation of religious and political authority" (*Religious Convictions and Political Choice,* 160).[15] Moreover, other dangers and damages must also be considered, such as the "psychological costs and unfairness of people conscientiously foregoing reliance" (160) on deeply held religious convictions and practices. Given the enormous complexity of many central political issues and given the ways in which even one's assessment of "the facts" is *always already* greatly influenced by personal experience, faith, communities, persons and institutions of authority, and so forth, to exclude these from deliberation would be to deprive people of the crucial frameworks through which they might learn about the world (179).

A brief sketch of Greenawalt's argument begins to open the Rawlsian paradigm to challenges based on a more profound and complicated sense of human possibilities and dangers. Greenawalt illuminates the tragic hubris and damage Rawls conceals in his drive toward "clarity," and he opens political liberalism somewhat to the possibility of other discrepant sources of insight, motivation, and discipline—as well as indirection.

Rawls's "problems of *extension*" become the troubled *heart* of Greenawalt's theorizing, from which he articulates complications concerning principles upon which political liberalism has hoped to found the sovereignty of public reason. He argues that it is at the borders— between human and nonhuman, life and nonlife, and so on—that it becomes clearest that things (and public reason among them) are not so clear. These issues are highly contestable because the distinctions and principles often used to resolve them are contestable as well. Our deliberations are inextricably inflected with visions of the good related to doctrine, in significant part because the latter influence how we construe and prioritize even liberal principles and attributions of moral status. Indeed, such doctrines—and the practices, communities, and traditions with which they are associated—often powerfully and divergently shape the very questions we ask. (For example, with respect to abortion: Is the key question when life begins?) This happens even when we accept that seeking answers in accord with public reason is our highest political duty, and it often entangles public and nonpublic reasoning in ways that make it impossible to say exactly which is (or even ought to be) which. Deeply implicated in our best efforts to seek political choices that are just are "personal bases for decision . . . that cannot be justified, in the force they are given, in terms of publicly [universally] accessible reasons. These bases would include personal perceptions, intuitions, feelings, and commitment, and deferences to the judgments of others that cannot be defended by persuasive reasons of interpersonal force [that could claim society-wide allegiance]" (*Religious Convictions and Political Choice*, 156). He argues that we often have no access to "justice" and "fairness" that is not informed by the particularities of various grand narratives to which we belong and the micro-influences of our particular social practices and experiences upon perception and emotion. For Greenawalt, these factors add dimensions of opacity, ambiguity, contestability and questionability to public reason itself, even as they do not entirely dissolve it.

Greenawalt illustrates how this contestability is significantly present not only in questions concerning "borderlines" but in our deliberations, disagreements, and decisions concerning many issues at the center of political liberalism, such as welfare and crime policy. Rawls protests that these differences do not affect the "basic questions of justice," beyond which public reason's sovereignty (not intended to be as extensive as Greenawalt takes it to be) dissipates. But, I think, issues of property law, of conceptions of proper punishment, and of just distribution are as "basic" as are any issues (on Rawls's own terms), and Greenawalt shows that doctrines, dispositions, communities of association, and the like not only inform our answers concerning these issues but also inform the very questions we take to be vital for discovering them. Greenawalt's practice of moving to and fro between universals and particulars amid the conflicts and ambiguities illuminated at the borders leads him to more-modest and skeptical conclusions. Acknowledging that there are many times when reflective equilibrium may not be reachable concerning the character, boundaries, and implications of public reason, Greenawalt concludes that (1) it is effectively impossible to exclude religious and other convictions from reflection and political choices; (2) because public reason is essentially inconclusive on many issues, the "shared clarity" argument for its hegemony is often mythical; (3) personal and associational convictions are sources of fundamental political insight and learning as well as blindness; (4) therefore, normatively, it is unwise and unfair to demand that citizens exclude such convictions when making political choices.

Greenawalt also contests many assumptions packed into Rawls's negative use of the term "comprehensive doctrine." Just as public reason is essentially inflected by "provincial" and "transcendent" influences, religious (and irreligious) convictions are modulated by multiple layers of experience and judgment that range widely in the degrees to which they are informed by sources exceeding a single tradition. Claims thus rooted vary in width and depth of accessibility, persuasiveness to other constituencies, and degrees of vulnerability to critique from nonbelievers. These messy variations mean, for Greenawalt, that when people bring aspects of religious frameworks to democratic dialogue, their arguments are often not as singularly comprehensive, dogmatic, "sectarian," and rigid as political liberals often assume.[16] For all these reasons he argues, along with Jürgen Moltmann, that theology "cannot be apolitical" (*Religious Convictions and Political Choice*, 35). Greenawalt concludes that when his calculus is compared to Rawls's, one sees that the costs of rendering religious (and other) convictions "nonpublic" increases and that the possible costs of restrained reliance upon them diminishes.

In this light, Greenawalt abandons exaggerated hopes for the power of public reason, offers only "rough guidelines for political behavior," and claims that "prudential assessment must largely supplant clear lines of principle" (216). He concludes that ordinary citizens can rely upon religious convictions in personal political decision-making processes, in voluntary associations, and when voting, *but not in directly public discussions*. He reasons that "there is a substantial consensus on the organizing principles for society, [and] a shared sense that major political discussions will be carried on primarily in secular terms" (ibid.). These are somewhat surprising and unconvincing claims, as most of his argument powerfully illustrates that beyond constitutional essentials, we lack a consensus on principles, their meaning, and relative priority. Greenawalt's account seems to warrant only a serious warning about the dangers involved in bringing relatively provincial "convictions" to public discourse—not a ban on raising them at all.

His exclusive turn to a "common currency" of nonreligious public reason in political discourse (*Religious Convictions and Political Choice*, 217) is problematic given that he has drawn its *independent* value and efficacy into question by arguing as follows:

1. The priority of its different coins is significantly indeterminate (and therefore its quantitative valuation is internally unstable).
2. The normative direction of these coins and this currency overall is significantly indeterminate (and therefore its qualitative values are unstable).
3. Because of 1 and 2, this currency's capacity to facilitate exchange-enabling agreement and cooperation can be weak at key times.
4. The currency's quantitative and qualitative value and its efficacy often seem to depend upon impurities and hybridizations with less "common" elements over which there is limited central control.
5. Given 4, the values and efficacy of this currency are entwined with discrepant specificities.
6. This "gold standard" is thus largely a myth.

Perhaps the language of "currency" and "exchange" appealed to by many political liberals does not simply refer to the myth but, even more, participates in *enacting* it.[17] In so doing, it not only "cashes in" on the prevailing imaginary of corporate capitalist exchange but, as I argue later, also constitutes a barrier to some of the more radical modes of resisting this hegemony and developing alternative practices.

My point is not that efforts to discern and invent common principles are fundamentally undesirable—far from it. Yet when they are figured as a "common currency" that would provide a *"regulating basis"* for political conversation, the effort often goes awry. Rather, the elements exchanged in dialogue must be understood to involve an essential indeterminacy that solicits hybridizing movements with terms not yet shared in order to facilitate both a reciprocal critical illumination of differences and the discovery and invention of common horizons. When "the shared" in a large heterogeneous society is interpreted as a singularly regulating "common currency," it shifts from being an important *solicitation* to illuminate commonalities and differences and becomes exclusionary in ways that weaken our judgment and capacities to cooperate in the face of problems. Simultaneously, it denies difference in ways that conceal (particularly from majorities) damages, intensify resentment (particularly on the part of various minorities), and marginalize the ever-important role of minority dissent.

One learns this from Greenawalt, even though he seems to forget it at key moments in his text. Perhaps what pulls him most strongly toward an exclusive common currency is a prudential analysis not so different from Rawls's: In a "very religious but extremely tolerant society," he writes, "public airing of particular religious views might work well, but in actuality such discourse promotes a sense of separation between the speaker and those who do not share his religious and political convictions and is likely to produce both religious and political divisiveness. . . . [Others] may feel left out and resentful" (*Religious Convictions and Political Choice*, 219).

There is no doubt that this sometimes happens, and these risks ought to chasten those who eschew efforts to translate the most local convictions into terms and practices that various people beyond a particular community might begin to understand and find compelling. And it is difficult to imagine that for most basic issues of justice in the United States, these translations would not involve concepts like liberty, equality, fairness, and democracy. Yet, again, it is a leap from these claims to claims that public discourse should rely upon these terms to the complete exclusion of religious and other local idioms that exceed them—especially as their meaning and relationship always partake of the "local" idioms that political liberals would exclude (in the name of a "public" that does not really exist apart from them). One can imagine, for example, arguments concerning nature, abortion, or property that speak to issues of liberty, equality, and fairness in ways that are significantly and explicitly inflected by religious claims and practices concerning sacredness, vulnerability, jubilee, charity, mystery, sacrifice, witness to creation, stewardship, biocentrism, and so forth, that would exceed claims of "public reason alone," yet that would resonate across a large number of diverse groups. Some would feel left out, but perhaps a significant majority would not. Alternatively, many (perhaps even many more) might feel left out of a "public" ethos that excludes all references to claims beyond those that "public reason alone" is sufficient to substantiate. If "pubic reason" is itself often highly contested, indeterminate, and not necessarily *the* decisive factor for many people concerning many important issues, then it is by no means clear that it alone always establishes a more cosmopolitan and less provincial "inside" than other idioms and networks of translation.

One can further challenge Greenawalt's claim that drawing upon particular convictions necessarily increases divisiveness by recalling Rawls's comments on the way articulations of support for a common principle or policy in and across a variety of idioms might strengthen respect across these faiths. One can analogously argue that where there are serious disagreements over shared terms across different faith traditions, *withholding* the metaphysical roots of these differences will also *provoke* resentment and divisiveness. Political liberals might take heart, believing that this withholding signifies a basic respect. Yet it seems just as probable that it will be read as duplicitous and deceitful. These complexities call for ethical stances that are more subtle, mobile, ad hoc, and receptive to particular others in their efforts to cultivate respect—as well as suppler modes of judgment concerning desirable modes of cooperation and contestation.

My point, in a nutshell, is that political understanding and disagreement, solidarity and division, cooperation and antagonistic strife, generosity and resentment are matters far too complicated to be well-judged, negotiated, and acted upon by an a priori privileging of secular public reason as either the exclusive or sole limit-defining currency. Negotiating these questions and problems more wisely will almost always greatly *involve* (different inflections of) liberalism's principles of public reason. But how much and what elements of particular doctrines and practices ought to be brought forth in public engagements of fundamental questions of justice cannot be decided once and for all. Rather, this question must be repeatedly renegotiated[18] by particular groups involved in particular problems. At least as important as a common currency of public reason, and partly in tension with it, are practices that develop commitments across different groups of people to cultivate engagements with others that are more infused with receptive generosity. Yet receptive generosity itself, as I shall argue below, is not to be a new regulative currency. Its articulations emerge from locations that are wide and deep in their differences, and the substance of these positions draws them to difficult listening as well as speaking to those who endorse visions that are neither generous nor receptive.

## Concluding Reflections

Having challenged political liberalism's narrative of tragedy and associated closures, I now suggest some alternative responses to the dangers it emphasizes. These dangers are not insignificant, even as they are distorted and exaggerated in the political liberal account of the human condition. I briefly develop ways terms of liberal discourse, when construed as a hybridizing currency and in a more minimalist manner, might help signal and solicit widespread resistance to some of the greatest dangers. I then suggest why they ought to be inscribed in practices of radical democracy that open onto richer political possibilities.

If (1) liberalism—like all orders—is likely to impose damage and subjugation in ways it does not yet recognize and (2) the emergence of such recognition is integral to developing more-just political judgment and action and (3) the likelihood of such emergence is often enhanced as affected traditions and newly forming groups seek to give voice to these damages by participating in democratic dialogue and struggle in idioms they judge most illuminating, then it would seem desirable to promote an ethos of democratic receptive generosity that might inflect—*and be inflected by*—manifold traditions and modes of being in ways that enhance possibilities for learning to live better in relations of cooperation and contestation.

Of course, vulnerable opening to others is risky, and though political liberalism's strategy of morally purging political space of deep differences should be resisted, movements toward a more receptive and generous democracy must also attend to and resist ways in which they might inadvertently lend themselves to movements *away* from desirable aspects of freedom, equality, and dialogical politics achieved thus far. We must not be deaf to this political liberal concern. Interpretations of and resistances to these dangers will differ significantly in their idioms, substance, and modes. However, it might be possible to translate overlapping aspects in order to signal limits beyond which we face most extreme dangers: dangers that might draw together a vast array of people in cooperative and concerted defense. Here, a differently rendered currency involving some political liberal terms is likely to have a role to play.

How might we differently render a notion of political signaling currency? First, it should be conceived not as "freestanding" but, rather, as reliant on a variety of traditions of moral enquiry, practice, and struggle that inflect the terms differently.

Second, this currency should not be understood as a sovereign "reasonableness" into which all other doctrines would have to be translatable to prove their legitimacy. Rather, it should be construed as a widely circulating set of principles that many parties today find to be useful for helping secure at least some of the minimal aspirations (and sometimes much more) that they embrace.

Third, this signaling language would be understood to call for a double gesture (in Derrida's words), a double movement. *On the one hand,* it would call us to question what in our own and other political directions needs to be excluded as fundamentally at odds with plausible interpretations of terms like "liberty" and "equality." *On the other hand,* it would call us to remember that such a signaling language will often need to be hybridized with and modulated by the terms and dispositions of different people's local practices in order to acquire directional specificity, wisdom, and animating power. This tensional solicitation is much less clear-cut than political liberalism claims to be, but it is, I am arguing, a condition for just judgment. What is called for, to bring specificity to this dialogical task, is an accumulation of tenacious memories of the worst events combined with tenacious memories of the many times when "defending against the worst" has been used as a false pretense to subjugate otherness—whose idioms were retrospectively integral to resisting the worst and forging richer possibilities.

Fourth, this currency should not be taken to preclude the possibility of—or efforts to create—alternative widely shared currencies that might come to function as well or better for resisting threats to democracy and other damages.

Keeping in mind the above, the effort to articulate elements of a currency signaling extreme danger can ironically benefit from a fleeting passage in Rawls. Toward the end of his discussion of public reason in *Political Liberalism,* Rawls reiterates that we ought to offer political judgments on the basis of a balance of values we think all others take as reasonable. And then he writes: "Or failing this, we think the balance can be seen as *at least not unreasonable* in this sense: that those who oppose it can nevertheless understand how reasonable persons can affirm it" (253, my emphasis). I suggest that Rawls's fail-safe, "at least . . . ," ought to simply *be* the political limit. This limit, of the "*not un*reasonable," helps secure conditions for a receptive democratic engagement while imposing fewer dangers of political myopia. How exactly does it differ from Rawls's position?

Rawls's "reasonable" constitutes a self-sufficient limit: It legitimates particular doctrines in public forums concerning basic questions of justice only if, "in due course public reasons . . . are presented *sufficient* to support whatever . . . [they] are introduced to support" (*Political Liberalism,* li–lii, my emphasis). Thus, Rawls's "reasonable" imagines a public reason that would *by itself* determine the moral limit to be obeyed by all vernacular visions. And it claims alone to know the boundaries of legitimate contestation ahead of time—prior to the encounter, not because what exceeds it violates in a determinate way something relatively determinate but *simply because the excess is more than itself,* simply because it violates public reason's (mythical) sense of its self-sufficiency. It is the aspiration to consensual democratic autonomy gone mad. Mad, as public reason itself might define madness with respect to comprehensive doctrines: "the zeal to embody the whole truth in politics" ("Idea of Public Reason Revisited," 132–33). In this way, it rules "out of bounds," a priori and without dialogical contestation, the vast regions indeterminately in excess of its own (mythical) exhaustive claims to reasonableness.

In contrast, the limit I suggest with Rawls's "at least *not un*reasonable" might be conceived as a minimal limit of necessity, and the terrain upon which it calls for dialogical engagements of receptive generosity is far more expansive and confessedly imprecise than the self-exhaustive positivity of the "reasonable." This danger-signaling minimal limit of necessity draws upon elements of the currency of liberty, equality, and fairness—among elements of other currencies, but in ways that affirm their hybridizing and reciprocally inflecting relations with particularities of tradition, doctrine, authoritative figures; histories of struggle; communities; bodily dispositions; and so on. It does not mark a desire to be the sole governor of the political limit from some freestanding "cosmopolitanism" but, rather, values the widespread and frequently deep resonances of these terms in their capacity to participate in signaling some of the worst and rallying resistance to that worst. To claim the great desirability of this participation is to gesture toward the more expansive realm of meanings that terms like "liberty," "equality," and "fairness" can have when diversely hybridized with particular traditions and struggles. Though the stance I am calling receptive generosity may not like—and may passionately resist—many of these specific hybridizations, it suspects that better articulations of justice will be indebted to many others, and it sees no way to step beyond the fray and still judge well.

Yet even if this dialogical politics is far more capacious than political liberalism, it nevertheless does gesture toward a limit—*itself always discerned in the fray*—beyond which signals of greatest alarm must sound. Those doctrines that cannot be conjoined, as "not unreasonable," with this currency without obviously destroying or abandoning the minimal conditions of its sense—those in stark contradiction to it—must from the perspective sketched here be focal points of gathered, urgent, and strenuous resistance. This minimal limit of necessity demands that this contradiction be resisted. Admittedly, such limits call for dialogical discernment and are contestable, but they do orient most people today in ways that clarify and delegitimate some of the worst practices and doctrines of subjugation and cruelty (such as totalitarianism, authoritarianism, slavery, and, in less clear and secure ways, for many, racial, gender, and nationalist hierarchies). A politics of receptive generosity belongs to efforts to maintain and enhance this efficacy. An affirmation of the "not unreasonable" articulates a commitment to providing all with the opportunities and means to full social and political democratic participation among free and equal people with different idioms. Often dialogic modes will still be the best ways (ethically and strategically) to resist those who contradict this limit, but receptivity at this point becomes focused more on learning about another's suffering and about what factors engender hostility and less on learning about the meaning of justice or flourishing.

Having affirmed a "public sense" in this manner, I am not very hopeful concerning its powers. It seems relatively ineffective for spurring widespread resistance to what I see to be among the worst dangers today, such as the de-democratization, growing inequality, and destruction of whole communities and ecosystems brought to many regions by global corporate capitalism. Indeed, the history of the terms of liberal discourse — powerfully brought to light in works like Eric Foner's *The Story of American Freedom*[19] — shows how they have been and continue to be articulated and deployed in such radically contradictory struggles that it is unclear how much they have to offer as abstract concepts. Although I think they have a modest role to play, far more effective might be coalitions among the particular traditions, ethical orientations, and struggles such as those engaged in the following chapters.

It is, I suspect, primarily *practices* of dialogue that cultivate the orientations, disorientations, virtues, and knowledges that are necessary not only for identifying and resisting the worst but also for struggling with others toward visions of what might be better. It is when associated with such practices that the public sense I have sketched above probably acquires most of its vitality. It is difficult to imagine how more-generous and receptive public sensibilities might be vivified in the absence of a widespread increase in inclusive modes of grassroots democratic participation and micro-political engagements, for these are virtues entwined with and nurtured in specific *practices*. Outside of this context they wither.

Of course, political liberalism declares all but the most instrumental movements toward radical democracy to be simply illegitimate attempts to empower "a highly contentious view of the human good."[20] But if bracketing comprehensive doctrines is no longer taken to be a necessary condition of justice, at least *this* barrier is lowered (not simply abolished). If the risks of radical democratic engagement and agonism were to be shown to be for many far less than those of a relative disengagement and adherence to public reason, and if there are overwhelming forces (within global corporate capitalism and the developing transnational and national institutions that support it) that quite *comprehensively* impose upon and subjugate our work, education, communities, environment, consumption, imagination, and desire, and if a movement such as the emerging coalition of students, labor, religious congregations, environmentalists, third world movements, human rights activists, and others (struggling for radical democracy in several idioms) shows significant signs of mounting a more powerful challenge than we have seen in decades to practices of unfreedom, disempowerment, and injustice, then the situation might be growing riper for theoretical projects and experimental movements and institutions in excess of the Rawlsian paradigm. These experiences might illustrate possibilities and shortcomings that would open several paths beyond the current impasse and involve notions of radical democracy as an intrinsic good.[21]

It should be stressed that these visions of a radical democracy strive toward dialogical receptivity with others who are by no means radical democrats (a point I will argue most extensively in chapter 8). The ends of receptive generosity require, for their ethical and political articulation, that the means be dialogical. For these ends cannot be perceived, judged, or invented—let alone exemplified, solicited, or taught—prior to and outside the difficult discernment that occurs in these encounters.

There are clearly risks that accompany the intensified engagement, increased vulnerability, expanded scope of issues and voices, and agonistic contestations associated with a politics of receptive generosity. Though such a politics seeks to cultivate greater respect, wide zones of collaboration and trust, and an anticipation of the political learning and existential abundance that often comes through difficult encounters, these do not nullify the dangers. Rather, these risks must be carefully weighed as participants consider how much and when to bring forth—or how much to insist upon—aspects of more-particular sensibilities and visions. Certainly these risks (and other considerations) often ought to move participants toward strenuous efforts to translate their positions into a variety of other perspectives and toward a reticence to impose their views on others. Yet they do not legitimate making public reason and its proscriptions into sovereign principles for the public forum. For the risks of a politics of receptive generosity are not infrequently outweighed by other risks, such as that of widespread resentment of political liberalism's (and all others') ersatz claims to "sharedness," its unsightly self-righteousness, its impotence in the face of many of today's most pressing problems, its own unacknowledged impositions, its ethos of relative quiescence and inactivity and the consequent risk that it will be drawn into complicity with injustice, and so forth. The limit of necessity suggested here rejects the limit of sufficiency's claim to have discovered an a priori calculus that settles these risks in one manner once and for all. They are the *subject* of political judgment, even as negotiating them well is also the *condition* of judgment's possibility.

In chapter 2 I elaborate further some of the political problems associated with political liberalism by examining the neocolonial consequences of the metaphor of currency (stemming from Locke) on political liberal cosmopolitanism. In later chapters, with an ear to the possibilities of more generous and receptive political practices, I engage several positions that seek to negotiate ethics and politics with a greater sense of finitude—and also abundant possibilities—than political liberalism has yet to embrace.

# 2
# Contesting Cosmopolitan Currency

CURRENCY—which John Locke called a "fantastical imaginary value"[1]—has long played a key role in modern narratives about the origin and development of the ever-more-productive selves, markets, and political organizations that have fostered globalization. Currency has been imagined as the medium of circulation that simultaneously establishes in market economies consent to (and thus legitimacy for) vast inequality and engenders a structure of valuation and devaluation that has played a key role in legitimating colonialism. That these two features of modernity, market economies and colonialism, so often work hand in hand is not unrelated to the way currency is at work in each of them. Recently, the trope has become central in political liberal theories for regulating cosmopolitan multicultural morality and politics: "Public reason" is to delineate a common currency that peoples with different "comprehensive doctrines" can use to regulate the exchange of political arguments and thus to produce deliberative agreements that define the nature of fair societal cooperation. As conjured up by this metaphor, groups oriented by different conceptions of the good resemble producers of different goods; common norms figure as agreed-upon monetary currency; and the well-being of just political agreement resembles the well-being of mutually beneficial trade. To what extent does the centrality of "currency" here suggest that the term has now been inflected toward democracy and global justice? To what extent does this centrality illuminate the way political liberalism remains complicit with capitalist political economies of vast inequality and with neocolonial relations with those in the interior or exterior margins of the new world order?

Both concepts of currency play crucial roles in framing dominant contemporary understandings of globalization: money currency in interpretations of markets, and the currency of shared understandings in political liberal discourses of cosmopolitanism. Moreover, in contemporary globalization the deployment of currency discourses and practices in one realm often engenders their deployment in the other. First, the increasingly widespread and rapid movement of capital, populations, relations of production, technologies, communications, and so forth plays an important role in bringing differently oriented groups more frequently and unexpectedly into proximity, relationship, and struggle with one another. Thus, without hope for establishing shared metaphysical frameworks, many search for a moral-political alternative that might abstract from these differences in order to govern and limit cooperative exchanges, be they economic, moral-political, or social. Just as economic currency abstracted from qualitative use values and established relations oriented toward monetary exchange value, moral currency promises to abstract from different ethical orientations in ways that will commonly guide, constrain, ease, and justify our cooperative activity.

Second, the fact that political-moral efforts strive, in this context, toward the establishment of "common currencies" is itself significantly related to the overwhelming material and ideological power of markets today in relation to our imaginations.

Third, accompanying the enormous inequalities generated by contemporary markets are foundational legitimating narratives that frame microeconomic relations in terms of fair exchange and macroeconomic relations in terms of a currency-centered consent. These accounts come under significant pressure as relationships of production tie planet-striding billionaires to billions of their fellow humans who wither on less than two dollars a day. Fixated on currency and unable to discover shared "doctrines," liberalism turns to the task of discovering a new moral currency to address this problem.

Fourth, modern currency narratives have been, from early on, deeply entwined with practices and narratives of colonization. If liberalism now eschews colonization in the name of justice for all, it nevertheless has been unable (thus far) to renounce the colonizing posture that would govern the terms of a reformed order. The rhetoric of currency combines fairness and neocolonialism in ways perfectly suited to a liberalism not really ready to renounce the colonial relation. In this way, liberalism's "gift" of a common currency of shared principles participates hand in hand (and in spite of itself) with unfettered economic markets as a part of the latest form of neocolonialism, globalization.

To be sure, these hands wrestle mightily with one another, and the stakes associated with their differences are often significant. Yet simultaneously, as two branches of neocolonialism, they both continue to discipline and marginalize the vast majority of people who are not among the privileged.

In this chapter, I situate the currency rhetoric of contemporary political liberal cosmopolitanism in the context of Locke's story of the emergence and implications of money. In Locke's writings, the legitimation of economic inequality and the devaluation of other modes of being are intimately connected through the metaphor of currency. I think that this aspect of the Lockean imaginary continues to frame the dominant contemporary neoliberal discourse of globalization in ways that justify both unfathomable levels of inequality and the quick dismissal of other cultures insofar as they participate in modes of being that are not readily compatible with capitalist markets (for example, alternative patterns of land use and ownership, relations with nature, agriculture, knowledge production, communal mutuality, and so on). In short, the most powerful themes in the discourse of globalization today have changed little since Locke's time, except insofar as they now pay lip service to a smorgasbord multiculturalism consisting of the production and consumption of folkloric, "ethnic" foods, dress, art, and so forth. Of course, neoliberalism is not an uncontested discourse of globalization, and one of the leading ideological contenders in the West in recent times is a more progressive cosmopolitanism that closely follows the contours of political liberalism. Yet Locke's currency imaginary continues to frame such cosmopolitanism in crucial ways that perpetuate the a priori devaluation of other peoples, most notably by directing, shaping, and limiting the nature of political discourse and engagement between the "cosmopolitans" and the "provincial" oth-  ers—particularly in the global "South." This devaluation continues a neocolonial operation while, at the same time, most political liberal cosmopolitans, when it comes to economic inequality, dream of a world in accord with Rawls's difference principle. Yet in spite of this more admirable aspect of their project, I think that the neocolonial mode of political engagement that generally imbues this type of cosmopolitanism engenders a certain blindness and deafness to alternative modes of practice and vision around the world, modes whose contributions would be invaluable for political struggles for greater equality. Moreover, the neocolonial stance fosters resentment on the part of many who are subjected to it, which in turn fosters resentment on the part of cosmopolitans. This poisons the waters of the political engagement through which might form the transnational political coalitions that are a precondition of greater equality. Thus this cosmopolitanism continues to be complicitous with vast global inequality. This complicity works not by directly legitimating great inequality (as is the case with neoliberalism) but, rather, by consistently eroding the possibilities of political vision, engagement, and coalition that would be necessary to respond seriously to this problem. Thus, in the second section of this chapter, "Political Liberal Currencies," I critically sketch the way the currency trope continues to frame and operate within such cosmopolitan liberalism and its vision of political discourses. I also argue that the insufficiency of the insistence upon a foundational currency for ethical-political thought further manifests itself in the seemingly interminable antinomies of political liberal cosmopolitanisms. Following this, I offer an alternative position one could call (radically democratic nepantilist generosity)(developed more fully in chapter 6), which, I argue, not only is normatively preferable but also emerges from and works with a number of global historical developments that promise certain practical possibilities.

## The Fantastical Imaginary Value of a Fantastical Imaginary Value

The invention of (money and the agreement to use it for economic exchange figure centrally in the legitimation of inequality and colonialism offered by Locke's normative political economy. In his account, before the introduction of money, "though men had a right to appropriate by their labour, each one to himself, as much of the things of nature as he could use, yet this could not be much, nor to the prejudice of others, where the same plenty was still left to those who would use the same industry." People were not yet governed by "the desire of having more than man needed." Instead, they aimed their efforts, by and large, toward "the intrinsic value of things, which depend[ed] only on their usefulness to the life of man" (*Second Treatise*, 37). Even if people were not morally motivated by the "spoilage" and "as much and as good" limitations of natural law, without currency they would have had little incentive to "heap up" goods, for most useful things are "of short duration." The finitude of human use made it so that "right and conveniency went together" (51).

James Tully[2] insightfully shows how, in Locke's account, the acceptance of currency brings about a certain "fall of man," from a "poor but virtuous age" with relatively few transgressions to a condition characterized by "heaping up," "hoarding," "covetousness[,] and ambition" (*Second Treatise*, 46, 110, 111). Yet even though money is not without its tragic effects, it also plays a crucial positive role in Locke's narrative of human purpose and development: "God and his reason commanded him to subdue the earth, i.e., improve it for the benefit of life, and therein lay out something upon it that was his own labour" (32). "Subdue," more than "benefit of life," is the operative term here, and Locke makes it clear that this command was oriented toward the production of "the greatest conveniences of life they were capable to draw from it" (34). God gave the earth to men in common, but it was "waste" until worked intensively. When land was thus worked, its value and that of things was almost entirely the product of labor and hence became the private property of whoever worked it, within Locke's familiar limits. Thus Locke concludes that God "gave [the world] to the use of the industrious and rational (and labour was to be his title to it), not to the fancy or covetousness of the quarrelsome and contentious" (34). Although money increases the psychological propensities toward and worldly occasions for conflict, it also plays a central role in making us industrious and rational.

Although Locke had a nostalgic admiration for "the innocence and sincerity of that poor but virtuous age" (*Second Treatise*, 111) of our precurrency predecessors, he did not believe that those innocents followed "God and his reason" insofar as he commanded us to produce the "greatest possible conveniences of life." Though "it cannot be supposed that [God] meant that [the earth] should always remain in common and uncultivated" (34), prior to currency, on Locke's account, the earth was precisely thus "wasted"—worked with either a light touch or no touch at all. For without money and the opportunity for "heaping up" that it affords, most people labored only enough "for a plentiful supply for [their] consumption." This led mainly to hunting and gathering economies, as men "for the most part . . . contented themselves with what unassisted nature offered to their necessities" (47). Perhaps some small and simple agricultural efforts were made. But beyond a few simple plots, *we should see [man] give up again to the wild common of nature* whatever was more than would supply the conveniences of life to be had there for him and his family" (48, my emphasis). "Thus in the beginning all the world was America" (49), where there are "still great tracts of ground to be found which, the inhabitants thereof not having joined with the rest of mankind in the consent of the use of their common money, lie waste, are more than the people who dwell on it do or can make use of, and so still lie in common; though this can scarce happen amongst that part of mankind that have consented to the use of money" (45).

Far from advocating "possessive individualism," Locke wrote that "covetousness, and the desire of having in our possession, and under our dominion, more than we have need of, . . . [is] the root of all evil."[3] Yet such covetousness is also central to the morality and practices of productivity that God commanded. Locke's aim was to incite, harness, supplement, and contain these passions, not eliminate them. Both money and the narrative of money-engendered productivity that Locke offered, partly in an effort to persuade self-interest to align with the productive purposes of "God and his reason," served this end (along with law, just government, punishment, proper education, and certain kinds of religion). With money and markets, people were drawn, by the allure of accumulating a durable and commonly desirable object, beyond laboring for their own immediate consumption and toward laboring for the "greatest conveniences" of mankind. Working long and hard, they enclosed the common, and as they heaped up their own rewards, they also contributed to improving the lot of everyone in the blessed circle of commerce: "He who cultivates ten acres of land may truly be said to give ninety acres to mankind" (*Second Treatise*, 36). Absent money, Indians lived in poverty on a fertile land (41).

As currency draws us toward the commanded productivity, it also facilitates a related distribution of property. On Locke's account, the earth given in common is to be allotted to people in proportion to the extent to which they comply with the injunction of natural law to maximize industriousness. Humans consent to and participate in this divine plan when they consent to use durable currency. "It is plain that [by agreeing to use currency] . . . men have agreed to the disproportionate and unequal possession of the earth—I mean out of bound of society and compact" (*Second Treatise*, 50). In addition to legitimating inequality within a commercial circuit, Locke's account legitimates inequality between those within the circuit and those who do not partake of it. For beyond the circulation of currency, lands "lie waste and are more than the people who dwell on [them] do or can make use of, and so still lie in common." Although the natives certainly "benefited" from the land and their labor, they fell far short of cultivating the "greatest conveniences," and thus they established "no right further than [their] use called for" in the things gathered (37). Indeed, they had "no reason to complain or think themselves injured" by settlers enclosing property in their midst (36).

Tully's reading of Locke's legitimation of colonialism is penetrating, and my account is greatly indebted to it. Yet he underplays the centrality of currency in Locke's narrative, locating the center of Locke's argument in his European bias toward agricultural labor. Yet I think currency is closer to the heart of Locke's argument, for agriculture alone does not justify possession. Following his radical limitation of the rights of hunters and gatherers, Locke states: "The same measures governed the possession of land, too. Whatsoever he tilled and reaped, laid up, and made use of before it spoiled, that was his peculiar right. . . . But if either the grass of his enclosure rotted on the ground, or the fruit of his planting perished without gathering and laying up, this part of the earth, notwithstanding the enclosure, was still to be looked on as waste, and might be the possession of any other" (*Second Treatise*, 38). The fact that some Indians practiced agriculture was not an important objection to Locke's defense of colonization. Notwithstanding his agricultural biases, it is currency, in his account, that makes all the difference by allowing and engendering productive activity beyond the producer's immediate benefit, by legitimating the producer's property rights to these products and the resulting inequalities, and by tying activities and products into the commercial circuit of exchange that ever enhances the "greatest conveniences" for mankind. Currency draws us away from the waste of "giving up [land] to the wild" and orients us toward the maximum productivity commanded by God.

Let me suggest a couple of orientations that emerge with this narrative and tend to reassert themselves importantly in more-recent liberalisms.

First, currency, as a "fantastical imaginary value" is said to be based entirely on the mutual consent of all involved—there is nothing "natural" about it. *Consent* is thus imagined to be the absolute foundation of everything essential to the commercial circuit: not only the medium of exchange, but also the micro-activities of exchange in which the self is psychologically restructured and systematic unrelenting productivity as well as inequality are engendered. It is commonly noted that Locke's reading of currency exaggerates consent. Indeed, Locke fabricates and secretes consent itself as a "fantastical imaginary value" from his narrative of money, this "fantastical imaginary value." But might it not, moreover, be the case that the very idea of social interaction *governed* by currency—this very idea of the *centrality of currency as such*—drags with it an exaggerated and fantastical aura of consent? Might it not be that whenever we use currency as the governing figure in our stories of social interaction, we inexorably tend to exaggerate consent and imagine it at the base of our intercourse, its activities, and its outcomes? Currency conceals imposition, power, and coercion and circulates consent universally, casting everything it touches in its own uncontestable image: tremendous inequality, the restructuring of the psychological structure of selves, the transfigured aims of society.[4] The movement of equivalence freezes time, as the initial moment of consent circulates identically from one moment to the next; and it unifies social space under a single consensual regime.

Second, the fantastical imaginary value of currency casts a shadow of fantastical imaginary *devaluation*. The consensual aura of currency calls forth tremendous justificatory efforts, without which the fantastic would begin to appear as "fantastic"—illusory, question begging, and contestable—rather than as obviously worthy of affirmation. Locke's story exemplifies this valuation-devaluation dynamic. The values of individual and social gain and the fulfillment of God's commandment, proclaimed by the currency narrative, press simultaneous devaluations into circulation. Individuals and peoples who live wholly outside the money-driven practices of productivity are not industrious and leave most of the earth in waste, contrary to God's command; their lives are "poor in all the comforts of life"; the lands on which they live are essentially "vacant"—vacant of indigenous rights to them; and thus they have "no reason to complain" about encroaching settlements (*Second Treatise,* 36, 41).

Might not this fantastical structure of valuation and devaluation, exemplified here, be an inexorable projection of currency narratives in which universal consent figures so prominently as the asserted factual basis for a system of interaction that those outside it must inevitably be devalued in radical fashion? Would not their presence in any other mode complicate and overburden such narratives? Would they not then open it to questioning so fundamental as to force a more tentative, uncertain, and open-ended process of negotiating social relationships— and with this, a different notion of the political? Could acknowledging this negotiated and open-ended character of relationships at the colonial edges of a system occur without spreading inward to relationships in the interior of the system itself? Might not the poor, then, find in this process support for questioning and resisting the ways they themselves had been devalued as the "indolent" mirror of the industrious?[5] To thwart such challenges, the consensual currency requires both devaluations that are entwined with colonialism at the system's borders and disciplinary operations within.

### Political Liberal Currencies

My intention is not to deny the functional value of political economic currencies but, rather, to question the political effects of making currency central in normative accounts of political economy. Similar questions appear regarding efforts to make currency the sovereign frame for political life, thus furthering the market exchange mentality and the ideological ascendancy of the logic of capital sketched by Karl Polanyi.[6] By "market exchange mentality," I mean not only the fantastical imaginary of consent and the accompanying valuation-devaluation binary but also a particular relation to efficiency and equivalency. Efficiency and equivalency have undemocratic and depoliticizing effects when they come to govern our understandings and practices of political and ethical life. They jeopardize the receptive generosity that would be necessary to undo the a priori devaluations of colonial "others," and they hamper the political engagements that would be necessary to form coalitions capable of transforming global capitalist inequality.

In "Origin and Use of Money," Adam Smith writes of how pre-money exchange relations must have been hampered: "This power of exchanging must frequently have been clogged and embarrassed in its operations" because the use values produced by different people failed to match, in a reciprocal manner, their respective needs. Qualitative differences in skills and desires in such cases became a radical barrier to social cooperation, rendering people "mutually less serviceable to one another."[7]

I am glad I do not have to try to barter copies of this chapter with the baker and the brewer to get bread and beer. Some aspects of the "conveniency" of money would be difficult to replace. But what happens when this expectation of quick, mutual serviceability becomes an insistent demand that structures more and more domains of life, when differences are increasingly viewed with embarrassment, simply as a clogging of social and political relationships?

As currency becomes a framing metaphor, the associated sense that relationships ought to follow the smooth logic of the efficient exchange of equivalents (of neocolonial design) often works together with the fantastical imaginary of foundational consent and the dichotomous structure of valuation and devaluation to reinforce certain colonizing and disciplinary effects.

Recall the prominence of currency discourse in the work of such contemporary political liberal figures as Rawls, Greenawalt, Gutmann and Thompson, and Moon: Rawls portrays the "public reason" that is to govern liberal politics as a "common currency of discussion and a deeper basis for explaining the meaning and implications of the principles and policies each group endorses" (*Political Liberalism*, 165). Kent Greenawalt writes similarly of a consensual foundation: "The common currency of political discourse is nonreligious argument about human welfare" (*Religious Convictions and Political Choice*, 217). Amy Gutmann and Dennis Thompson develop the moral meaning of common currency: "In deliberative democracy the primary job of reciprocity is to regulate public reason, the terms in which citizens justify to one another their claims regarding all other goods. The 'good received' is that you make your claims on terms that I can accept in principle. The 'proportionate return' is that I make my claims on terms that you can accept in principle. Deliberative reciprocity shares with prudence this basic concept of mutual exchange but gives it moral content" (*Democracy and Disagreement*, 165). Donald Moon affirms "a strategy that seeks to 'bracket' the difference[s] . . . in the search for common values and principles on the basis of which [the] 'interchange of giving and taking' can be regulated in a way that is fully acceptable to each" (*Constructing Community*, 8). In this way, political deliberation is thought of as an exchange that requires a regulatory currency based on common consent. The effort is to discover *in advance* the currency that will ground and limit political deliberation. With such a currency at the heart of political life, social cooperation will be—like Locke's economic cooperation—regulated in all basic aspects according to a set of consensual coins that circulate throughout the basic structure, thus shaping, nurturing, and limiting the development of the body politic.

This aim to shape societal cooperation so all involved can agree is admirable, and I think it is an irremovable *part* of the striving of any moral-political life worthy of democratic affirmation. Yet, as I have argued in chapter 1, when it becomes the sole governor of our understandings and practices of political dialogue, it tends to underestimate liberal impositions upon those who exceed its limits and to eclipse the importance of difference, radical dissent, and struggle in political life in ways that tend to be dangerous and damaging.[8] In political liberalism these dangers are manifest in exaggerated and insistent assertions about the breadth and depth of the moral-political consensus, a consensus according to which our national and global polities are said to flow. Occurring in tandem is an insistent moral-political devaluation and effort to silence that which would draw from—or reach toward—visions beyond the limits of this purported consensus.

There is no doubt that principles like equality, freedom, fairness, agency, and reciprocity have played vital parts in the historical transformations of liberal democracy as practiced in the United States and beyond. But should we think of these principles as a "currency" that *regulates* our exchanges? Or would we do better to think of them as central sites of ongoing and often radical contestation, terms to which virtually every major political struggle must appeal but whose meanings and relative prioritizations are so discrepant and often indeterminate as to stretch the term "regulate," and the notion of unitary value associated with coins of a "currency," far into the realm of the farcical? Rarely consisting of frozen coins, currency is more a relational substance that alters in each interaction as much as it regulates those interactions. Similarly, a notion of "exchange" governed by equivalence hardly captures the self-transfiguration and other-transfiguration that characterize our adoption of and appeals to principles we claim to share.

Recall again my discussion in chapter 1 of the potent critique of the notion of political liberal common currency developed by Greenawalt, a political liberal who ultimately relies on a notion of secular currency, even as his writing often moves profoundly in alternative directions. Greenawalt's detailed argument culminates in the idea that this currency's quantitative and qualitative values, as well as its efficacy for various constituencies, often seem to be entwined with impurities and hybridizations with less "common" elements the currency cannot regulate. Therefore this "gold standard" is to a significant extent a myth. The language of currency perpetuates this myth and cashes in on the prevailing imaginary of corporate capitalist exchange (by extending the logic of currency) and colonialism (by extending the posture of articulating an order that would radically precede the vibrant and often contestatory engagement of those to be ordered). It also constitutes a barrier to more-radical modes of resisting this hegemony and developing alternative practices.

The basic contours of the political liberal narrative of common currency are remarkably similar to those of the Lockean money narrative. I will briefly review these analogies in its account of domestic discursive currency and then turn to its cosmopolitan variant in more detail.

The first move of this fantastical imagination is to discern a consensus at the heart of things, and political liberalism typically anchors this consensus in fairness, reciprocity, or agency. As with Locke and money, the consent initially seems relatively unproblematic. Of course people agreed to use money; of course most people in contemporary liberal democracies agree that society ought to be a fair system of cooperation between free and equal citizens. But the devil is in the details and the deployment. Just as Locke's account exaggerates consent, so, too, the political liberal narrative exaggerates both the role of consent in the development of the notions of fairness it discerns at the heart of U.S. history and the extent and implications of this purported consensus. Thus Rawls omits the corporate, power-laden, and consent-compromising context in which working and poor people have often opted for the compromises that, for a time, consolidated into the practices and principles he affirms. His account largely omits the extent to which this notion was born in and continues to be subject to deep contestations from the Left and the Right. Thus, concerning voices to the left, Rawls's historical hermeneutic omits the struggles for far more participatory and agonistic dialogical practices of "reciprocity," "fairness," "liberty," and "equality." He omits historical and contemporary construals and contestations of nationhood that fundamentally challenge the notions of citizenship and peoples that govern his theory of justice. He omits contestations holding that really meaningful interpretations and enactments of the difference principle are intrinsically entwined with particular radical practices and doctrines of sharing and generosity. He omits current struggles by people (often marginalized, often inhabiting borderlands, literally or figuratively) to theorize and practice democracy in ways more affirmative of difference. Then, having, like Locke, exaggerated the historical breadth and role of consent, he fabricates a fantastical imaginary exaggeration of the meaning of this purported consent, so that it appears to orient "us" in a single normative direction, circulating widely to embrace and govern myriad practices. So, as it turns out, insofar as we are said to consent to the basic currency of Rawlsian liberalism, we consent to large inequalities (even if they would be far less and far more humane than current inequalities) and to theories and practices of self and relationship that are relatively disengaged and difference-denying politically; we are also to be oriented normatively in most fundamental ways by constitutional nationalism (even if far more humane and cosmopolitan than is currently the case).

Political liberalism takes contested *elements* of social practice and affirmation and misconstrues them as a *foundational currency*. It thus freezes and generalizes an aspect of the orientation and limits of complicated and dynamic processes in ways that morally proscribe or marginalize contestations. The circulation of equivalents from one moment to the next functions temporally to extend the purported consent infinitely into the future.

Rawlsian treatments of "comprehensive doctrines" exemplify this process by which the moral-political system seeks to erect a protective barrier against all challenges in excess of "public reason," as we saw in chapter 1. The legitimate moral terrain and boundaries of political contestation consist of those claims that can be converted without remainder into Rawlsian currency. Whatever is not wholly thus translatable—whatever exceeds in any way the "sufficiency" of this currency as supreme agent of convertibility—is morally illegitimate from the outset. Ultimately, this money defines the matter, this currency the constraint.

My aim here is not to resist the idea that democratic political dialogue and contestation are oriented significantly—normatively and pragmatically—toward ideas of fairness and reciprocity. Rather, my questions concern whether these ideas ought to be construed in manners that marginalize differences, in the ways Rawls suggests. Perhaps, as I will argue more below, reciprocity and fairness might better be construed to involve a far-greater element of agonistic, generous receptivity toward difference—for both ethical and political-pragmatic reasons. At any rate, conceptions of currency-based fairness make the exchange of equivalents the central paradigm for human cooperation. Long before Rawls explicitly articulated the deepening and widening of this capitalist Logos, Adorno saw it taking shape all around. As Adorno writes in *Aesthetic Theory*, "What is called 'communication' today is the adaptation of spirit to useful aims and, worse, to commodity fetishism."[9] I have interpreted this passage at length elsewhere.[10] Here my aim is only to stress that the insistent construal of communication as exchange is fueled by a mentality that—as we have seen with Smith—increasingly feels only "clogged and embarrassed" by qualitative differences that are (mis)construed exclusively as antithetical to "mutual serviceability" the instant they refuse rapid conversion without remainder into the medium of exchange. For Adorno, many modern understandings of justice result from a series of reductions: Communication is reduced to useful aims along the lines of barter (missing the radically transfigurative possibilities and virtues of dialogue), and the latter is reduced to a system fundamentally oriented and limited by the logic of equivalence and currency fetishized such that it governs— far more than it is caught up in—the dialogical practices of politics.

Paradoxically, this trinitarian fantasy of consent, devaluation, and fetishized exchangeability forms a series of mutually reinforcing pressures within the political liberal theology. These pressures constitute a closed dogmatic rigidity comparable to that which this liberalism discerns or projects in all orientations that exceed or resist it.

## Contesting the Antinomies of Currencies of Cosmopolitanism

The force of this "force" of liberal political argumentation becomes increasingly evident when it is projected beyond "domestic" politics and

⌊onto the global screen as cosmopolitan currency. Rawls projects a currency for "peoples"; other political liberals (such as Andrew Kuper explicitly and Martha Nussbaum implicitly) contest his rendering and project instead a currency for "persons." The differences are by no means trivial. Yet I am concerned here with how their discrepant dangers and difficulties stem from their shared reduction of cosmopolitanism to currency.

In the name of reciprocity and fairness, Rawls maintains aspects of a colonialist stance. His *Law of Peoples* moves along oblivious to the many contemporary postcolonial voices and movements that would call his project into question. In a concluding section, titled "Law of Peoples Not Ethnocentric," Rawls[11] summarizes his case for the currency of liberal principles with which the peoples of the globe should guide themselves:

> We must always start from where we now are, assuming that we
> have taken all reasonable precautions to review the grounds of our
> political conception and to guard against bias and error. To the
> objection that to proceed thus is ethnocentric or merely western,
> the reply is: no, not necessarily. Whether it is so turns on the *content*
> of the Law of Peoples. . . . The objectivity of that law surely
> depends not on its time, place, or culture of origin, but on whether
> it satisfies the criterion of reciprocity and belongs to the public
> reason of the Society of liberal and decent Peoples. . . . we see that
> it does satisfy the criterion of reciprocity.

This reciprocity is supposedly evident in the fact that Rawls's system is derived from a "second original position" in which "peoples" are situated behind a veil of ignorance, able to argue for principles of interaction only on the basis of their own freedom and equality. Rawls thinks this excludes all doctrines that exceed what this status alone is sufficient to support. Thus no peoples are made to submit to others unreasonably. "They cannot argue that being in a relation of equality with other peoples is a western idea!" (*Law of Peoples*, 122).

But what are "freedom" and "equality"? Many selves, traditions, and newly emergent groupings would find highly unfree a situation that excluded diverse doctrines at the outset from participating in forming basic principles (such as freedom, equality, and reciprocity) and practices of discourse and political relationship. Many would discern in this discursive constraint a continuing insistence on inequalities deeply rooted in a fantastical colonial valuation and devaluation. I am not defending those who seek to dictate comprehensive doctrines to the world; rather, I defend those many who, in various ways, would bring such doctrines selectively into play in dialogues and struggles, in a more open-ended, receptive, and agonistic manner. These people might find farcical (or worse) their utter absence as interlocutors in the text— along with Rawls's paltry attempt to "guard [his notion of reciprocity] against bias and error" by giving "an imagined example of a non-liberal Muslim people I call 'Kazanistan,'" who he then *imagines* can accept and follow his system (*Law of Peoples,* 5).

However unreceptive it may be, Rawls's effort to "assure [us] that the ideals . . . of a liberal people are also reasonable from a nonliberal point of view" (*Law of Peoples,* 10) aims to provide some space for peoples not wholly in conformity with liberal ideals. He worries that proponents of a "global original position"—in which all *persons* are symmetrically situated and which "would straightaway ground human rights in a political (moral) conception of liberal cosmopolitan justice"— beg major questions. They simply assume that "only a liberal democratic society can be acceptable" (82–83); they do not show it. To illustrate what is acceptable, Rawls says, we must "work out a reasonable liberal Law of Peoples." And when that is done, Rawls finds that behind a veil of ignorance, "peoples will want to maintain . . . equality with each other" (60) rather than submit to principles determined by (liberal) others. If such peoples are decent (nonaggressive; observant of rights to life, liberty, and personal property; and practicing a consultation hierarchy) but fall short of liberal ideals of free speech and democracy, liberals should tolerate them and forgo sanctions aimed at their transformation. Sometimes, Rawls implies this latitude is intrinsically morally acceptable. More often, he stresses that "maintaining mutual respect among peoples" is key. "Lapsing into contempt on the one side, and bitterness and resentment on the other, can only cause damage" (62).

Although the general effort to create space within liberalism to tolerate nonliberal peoples has something to recommend it, Rawls's particular efforts leave a lot to be desired, as Thomas Pogge,[12] Bruce Ackerman,[13] Andrew Kuper,[14] and others have suggested. Kuper extends a line of criticism from the vantage point of a cosmopolitanism of *persons,* illuminating numerous places where Rawls's law of peoples appears to be complicit with injustice in highly troubling ways. Recognizing the value of culture to persons, Kuper contends that "the question is not *whether* to tolerate cultures but rather *how* to do so. Only an original position that includes all the persons of the world as free and equal persons can be tolerant in the right way" ("Rawlsian Global Justice," 648). This construction—which is truer to Rawls's spirit than is Rawls's *Law of Peoples*—will lead us to endorse an ethical neutrality that is impartial to conceptions of the good and opposed to all political power thus based. In defense of a liberal pluralism of persons, Kuper compellingly illustrates ways in which Rawls's ideals make compromises with illiberal modes of power. "Peoples," as conceived by Rawls, are problematic for Kuper because they are construed as sovereign unities of sympathy along national lines closely articulated with a state. Kuper rightly points out that there are no cultures without many dissenting selves, no peoples that do not contain heterogeneous and often discordant groups, no national boundaries of sympathies that are not crossed and often contested by competing allegiances, and many articulations of nationhood and state power that are presently contested by groups who believe they were arbitrarily divided, thrown together, and marginalized. Rawls's *Law of Peoples* effectively urges liberals to look the other way when faced with many illiberal treatments of persons, and it gives contemporary nation-states an effective veto on what sympathies will have political significance.

Kuper argues that when we "get the standard right" and "specify which principles ought to be accepted by those subjects in this domain" ("Rawlsian Global Justice," 662), it becomes evident that "instead of tailoring a political morality to the concerns of those currently in power" (660), we ought to affirm unqualified rights to free speech and a democracy morally governed by the neutral currency of public reason articulated in *Political Liberalism*. Cultural affiliation and diversity are a good—and tolerable—only within these limits.

Thus oriented, the nation-state wanes as the locus of sovereignty. Kuper endorses both a vertical dispersion of sovereignty in nested territorial units that can better accommodate various allegiances and facilitate the exercise of persons' liberal rights, and a horizontal dispersion of sovereignty according to functional requirements and tasks (limited by coordination requirements that tend toward "agency clusters"). "Our practical task is to gradually pluralize the global basic structure by creating a variety of forms of democratically responsive, semiautonomous legal authority" ("Rawlsian Global Justice," 666).

I will say more later about the politics of Kuper's cosmopolitanism. Presently, I note an aporia in the disagreement between Kuper and Rawls that—though it may infect all political theory—becomes particularly acute in political liberalism. *This* aporia (in contrast to some of the paradoxes I discuss in chapters 5 and 6), unacknowledged and unaddressed as it is, is a weakness, not a strength, in the heart of political liberalism. On the one hand, Rawls—aware that it is problematic to have liberals morally legislating that all peoples should be precisely liberal or face sanctions—seeks a global moral-political currency that affirms more space for diverse peoples who, though "decent," are significantly "illiberal." He "imagines" a scheme to which decent peoples would consent (participate in as rulers as well as ruled) by showing (in however bizarre a fashion) that they could affirm the same principles as liberal societies would behind the second veil of ignorance (the first veil is that associated with Rawls's original position) without modifying their doctrine-informed basic institutions. Rawls respects diverse decent peoples by according them, in a world that contains multiple possibilities for being, the unpressured sovereignty to transform themselves only as they themselves see fit. Yet a foundational moral currency requires a foundational site of agency. Rawls locates such a site of agency in nation-states and thereby participates uncritically in some of the damages (to selves and groups) that such entities impose.

Kuper, in contrast, counters these damages by insisting on a global respect for persons that dictates which cultural affiliations and encroachments are acceptable and which are not. Although his criticism of Rawls is valuable, people(s) can, should, and will ask of Kuper the same kinds of questions they pose to Rawls: What exactly are respect, equality, and freedom? And how are their definitions to be decided? As a currency theorist, Kuper, like Rawls, decides from on high, prior to any engagement with all persons involved, not only the *content* of principles but also the *form* within which their material specificities are to be further deliberated on—that is, the logic of the original position and of an ethically neutral public reason. Yet if public reason is *always* discrepantly inflected by different traditions and doctrines, how would anyone be able monologically and neutrally to determine its content or the form of public deliberation in which it is to be elaborated? Would not respect in this case involve at the deepest levels a sense of humility in prescribing and proscribing? A sense of more-receptive, vulnerable, and open-ended dialogical engagement? A sense that democracy must somehow be as much about determining basics as about being determined by them? A sense of the ongoing value of democratic agonism in exposing both concealed damages and alternative possibilities? Would not the neutrality Kuper prescribes, by completely disengaging from the political sphere ethical differences among people(s), often tend to reinforce the doctrines, habits, perceptions, affects, and related practices of the currently established and most powerful assumptions, groups, and institutions in given times and places? Would not Kuper thus find himself subject to the charge he rightly registers against Rawls, that Rawls "ends up tailoring a political morality to the concerns of those currently in power" ("Rawlsian Global Justice," 660)? Would not Kuper overly predetermine personhood just as Rawls overly predetermines peoples? And, in so doing, would not Kuper *also* inadvertently freeze certain aspects of people(s)?

Political liberalism thus divides in ways that fundamentalize either peoples or personhood and are highly problematic, even when viewed only from the critical perspective each side casts on the other. Thus, rather than developing a stance that might more subtly, dialogically, and vulnerably negotiate between the two (as well as negotiating between these and "other" concerns), it is driven in *search of a definitive currency to regulate our differences*. The establishment of such currency requires that we imagine sovereign agents of consent. Yet it appears that such efforts short-circuit precisely the kinds of engagement in which an autonomy rooted in more-careful judgments of damage and possibility might develop.

Martha Nussbaum might be read as a political liberal who better addresses these problems. In her work the currency framework is less prominent—less the foreground and more a backdrop to efforts to cultivate a cosmopolitanism in which all are more aware that their local traditions are not natural, neutral, or exhaustive of admirable human possibilities. Does not *her* cosmopolitan "plea for difficulty" exemplify an open-ended relation to normative universality? Perhaps. Yet I suggest that Nussbaum's texts often illustrate the way the currency fetish continues to erode these more promising gestures of dialogical opening.

Nussbaum calls us beyond myopic patriotism toward a cosmopolitan concern for the equal dignity of every person on the planet.[15] She seeks to disrupt the passivity of those who unquestioningly accept the orientations into which they are born by means of a pluralistic education in which pupils are "confront[ed] . . . with difference in an area where they had previously thought their own ways neutral, necessary, and natural" (*Cultivating Humanity*, 62). We should engage other cultures in ways that teach us to "doubt the goodness of one's own way and to enter into the give-and-take of critical argument about ethical and political choices" (62). We should question how social and political power shape our understanding; how "our relationship to non-Western societies has frequently been mediated by projects of colonial domination" (116); how "real cultures," beyond the chauvinistic projections, are plural, "contain[ing] argument, resistance, and contestation of norms" (127). Nussbaum calls us to "a kind of exile . . . from the comfort of assured truths," to keep our "minds open and alive, prepared to find something interesting and valuable . . . even better than those [truths] of [our] own" (134).

I question Nussbaum's cosmopolitanism *not* because she offers us lists of core capacities and principles that would orient it. Given their level of generality, I agree with most things on the lists: life, health, and bodily integrity; equal dignity for men and women; the rights to and opportunities for free thought and imagination; serious participation in control over one's political, social, and economic environment; and the exercise of practical reason in politics and work. These are vital considerations that should inform social and political change, and they can contribute significantly to resisting many bad situations around the globe in the name of a more desirable world.

Moreover, at her most circumspect, Nussbaum tells us that the list is simply the "attempt to summarize empirical findings of a broad and ongoing cross-cultural inquiry. As such, it is both open-ended and humble—it can always be contested and remade."[16] The list is to be specified locally, in context-sensitive dialogue among those involved. Nussbaum regrets that earlier versions of her lists of Aristotelian-Rawlsian universals did "not give as central a place as Rawls does to the traditional political rights and liberties," but "now political liberties have a central importance in making well-being human" ("Women and Cultural Universals," 216). Maybe; but if so, they are *constrained* by her political liberalism and the repeated prescriptions and proscriptions of "public reason" that at once nurture such proclamations and inflect the specific power and direction they receive both explicitly and implicitly in her textual engagements with others. Forgetting to question Marcus Aurelius's claim that "it is possible to live a virtuous life in a palace" (*Cultivating Humanity,* 64), she often appears to fashion more a palace than the chuppah she would construct.

My criticism concerns the *way* she offers public reason and lists, the terms of their presence, and some of the work they do. The contestation Nussbaum morally condones is tightly constrained by Rawlsian "reasonableness" ("Women and Cultural Universals," 210n40). In the name of being "as protective of [doctrines] as it is possible to be, compatible with a just political structure," Nussbaum remarkably supposes a Rawlsian divide between the political and the nonpolitical.[17] Protection is offered "to private religious choices and to the separation of these choices from the contentious debates of the public realm. It is no sign of disrespect to any religious tradition to ask that its members use in the public realm arguments that can be understood by people from other traditions" (*Cultivating Humanity*, 37).

For normative and pragmatic reasons, participants in democracy are called on to argue politically in terms intelligible to others. But what exactly are understandable public arguments? And what is the ethical direction and weight of this request? Is the "understandable" generally a given, or is it, as I suspect, very often uncertain, contested, *yet to be*, to be brought forth precisely by something that is not now part of the "understandable" — perhaps even brought forth by bizarre forms, fragments, or premonitions of "doctrine"? Is it always "no sign of disrespect" when members of particular traditions are asked to separate those tradition-inflected "choices" from the "contentious debates of the public realm"? If, as Nussbaum suggests, her list of core values is very general, "open-ended," and "humble," "to be more concretely specified in accordance with one's origins, or religious beliefs, or tastes" ("Women and Cultural Universals," 210), then it is improbable that this specification will occur only in nonpolitical ways. Rather, the political core currency she offers itself will be — and will need to be — the site of political contestation and transfiguration.

Nussbaum's minimization of the vulnerabilities and risks of political engagement is striking in her more concrete discussions of cultural specificities and cosmopolitan education. Though "good public reasoning about the list will retain a rich sensitivity to the concrete context, to the characters of the agents and their social situation," her concern is only with how the currency can be "instantiated in a concrete situation" ("Women and Cultural Universals," 218). She never offers an instance of having learned something fundamental from encounters with others in "age-old traditions" — something that really shifted her direction, transfigured the list in a basic way, or, perhaps, somehow questioned the centrality of list-giving itself. Nor does she cultivate a yearning or expectation for such a transformative encounter in the future. Her discussion of cosmopolitan education seeks to foster a "sophisticated grasp of human variety" (*Cultivating Humanity*, 62) and a sense that one's local culture is not neutral or natural, but that is generally as far as she goes. Rarely do the many educational examples she offers or her proposals for studying non-Western culture convey the sense or expectation that such encounters may begin far-ranging, unpredictable, and difficult reorientations of one's life. There are no discussions of people's understanding of self, political economy, responsibility, sacredness, democracy, community, and the like being called radically into question or altered. She recognizes colonial violence, but she offers no voices on other sides of the colonial difference that speak powerfully in excess of her own political liberal project.

Although Nussbaum acknowledges that colonialism has influenced knowledge in the past, her texts exhibit virtually no attention to ways colonialism may still be at work in her own project. She writes to bring about one "true and great common community" but has little sense for the way liberal currency projects may be implicated *as such*—not just because of the power-laden nature of this or that principle—in exaggerating extant or "reasonable" consent, immodestly devaluing (prior to serious engagement) those others who do not share it, and creating an impatience with those who would complicate relations.[18] Given the way liberal currency is implicated in the colonial legacy, the assumption that political philosophy can continue to develop wholly within a basic currency framework is highly problematic. This is not to deny Nussbaum's claim that "we can't avoid having a notion of 'core' capabilities" ("Women and Cultural Universals," 204), which function in some sense as currency for political deliberation. "We" must pursue this project, *among others*. Yet there is more than one "we," and each leans into the "universal" in ways that contest the others, in varying manners and to different degrees. Hence practical reasoning must not be contained only *within* the currency. It must invite the contestation of the currency itself—and it must contest the hegemony of currency in our ethical-political imaginations.

One way to approach this task is repeatedly to thematize and reflect critically upon historically proximate forces that have insinuated themselves into cosmopolitan currency projects, so that, suspicious of how they might continue to operate in one's own work—and in resistance to them—one might open toward better possibilities. One might consider the deleterious effects of such projects for engaging others receptively and generously, especially in light of this history. Relatedly and equally important, one might begin to listen to the disparate struggles from which one might learn. Nussbaum falls short in these regards. As Richard Falk notes, her position "is not sufficiently distinguished from or even aware of globalist tendencies that are integrating experience across boundaries at a rapid rate. To project a visionary cosmopolitanism as an alternative to nationalist patriotism without addressing the subversive challenge of the market-driven globalism currently being promoted by transnational corporations and banks, as well as currency dealers . . . is to risk indulging a contemporary form of fuzzy innocence."[19] This innocence pertains not only to external challenges but also to the ways these powers have shaped the very *mode* of philosophizing that Nussbaum pursues. Critical considerations of the latter may be key to struggling more hopefully against the former. Within Nussbaum's writing, there are still echoes of the colonialist's immodest forgetfulness that her own view, as Robert Pinsky suggests, "is local[,] . . . the formulation of one peculiar province, the village of the liberal managerial class."[20] Reading Aurelius differently than Nussbaum does, Pinsky writes: "The weight of these quotations, for me, is to warn us how extreme an act of imagination paying attention to the other must be, in order to succeed even a little[,] . . . a caution against the arrogance that would correct *your* provinciality with the cosmopolitanism of *my* terms."[21]

But what might a radically dialogical and critical cosmopolitanism look like? How do we fashion a more receptive and vulnerable generosity without ignoring the need for orientation and a sense of the inviolable? In the next section I offer an initial response that will be articulated more thoroughly in chapters that follow, especially chapter 6.

### Toward a Cosmopolitical Nepantilist Generosity

Many who seek to move beyond an abstract common currency come to embrace rather abstract and shallow celebrations of "hybridity." The usually very insightful Jeremy Waldron, for example, orients his version of cosmopolitanism with the following image: "Though he may live in San Francisco and be of Irish ancestry, he does not take his identity to be compromised when he learns Spanish, eats Chinese, wears clothes made in Korea, listens to an aria by Verdi sung by a Maori princess on Japanese equipment, follows Ukrainian politics, and practices Buddhist meditation techniques."[22]

This is swell. But, for a number of reasons, I find this hybridity to be neither particularly meaningful nor compelling as a primary ethical and political ideal. First, in some ways this image exemplifies the insistent desire for pure fungibility engendered by the fantastical imaginary of political economy framed and driven by currency. Every component of everything can be easily detached and recombined with everything else—with no costs. As such, in the name of something new and better, this image can easily proliferate the drive for common currency and unfettered free-market exchange—the sovereignty of marketized globalization—that would proliferate the very structures of capitalism and colonial power.[23] These structures of power, in turn, erode, at the deepest levels, the democratic engagement of different people(s) in determining the basic structures of association that govern much of our lives. Although "hybridity" discourses do not always proliferate this drive, it is often unclear how much and how deeply they resist it.

Second, the shallowness of much "hybridity" discourse tends to mask the disproportionate extent to which the hybridizations are assimilated into colonizing power rather than transforming it (thus often exemplifying homogenization more than the play of differences). There is no doubt that assimilation and transformation often happen simultaneously. Nevertheless, one needs only look at the way "Buddhist spirituality" has been taken up by New Age capitalism or at the way "Native American" cultural images have been assimilated by the sport-utility-vehicle industry to see quite clearly the inequalities so frequently at work in this supposed syncretism. With Pratrap Bhanu Mehta,[24] I wonder whether a world that continued to move in this direction would really have much difference left that required negotiation, or whether such a world would offer the possibility of serious resistance to some of the most odious forms of the power that drive globalization.

Third, I question whether hybridity *as such* is compelling as an ethical-political orientation. Hybridities can be delightful, miraculous, horrifying, empowering, disempowering, democratizing, de-democratizing — any number of these and their combinations. The kernel of truth in the affirmation of hybridity is that stances against hybridity as such are almost always associated with odious modes of power, and thus it is usually ethically desirable to be *against* stances *against* hybridity as such. Beyond this, however, the more important questions concern the desirability of various kinds of hybridity, in various situations. To whom are they desirable? What modes of reflection, dialogue, and agonistic struggle ought to be practiced in these discernments and enactments?

Gloria Anzaldúa's writings on the "new mestiza" (which will be at the center of chapter 6) are helpful in approaching these questions. To be sure, she writes of the nourishing possibilities and joys, as well as the dangers and suffering, that can emerge in the crossings of different cultures. But one misses the deepest elements of her work if one interprets her primarily as a celebrant of hybridity. Most significantly, she suggests an ethical mode of thinking and democratic engagement that responds to the problems and possibilities of cosmopolitanism in the context of colonialism and global capitalism. Anzaldúa energetically enacts and solicits, in contrast to an easygoing consumerist hybridity, "mental nepantilism, an Aztec word meaning torn between ways."[25] Whereas cosmopolitan currencies strongly privilege undivided political-economic loyalty, the new mestiza cultivates "divided loyalties," not simply in terms of those to whom she offers herself but also in terms of those people(s) and traditions from whom she seeks to learn. Anzaldúa's own experience at the multiple borderlands between several developing traditions (for example, Mexican, U.S., indigenous) and emergent struggles (those of farmworkers, lesbians, feminists, Chicanas), moving with, against, and beyond each of these traditions differently, has taught her, in the most embodied of ways, about the suffering and limits of each teleology. Simultaneously, the disparate locations of rich possibilities for freedom, justice, and flourishing that appear to her in her own life drive home a belief that struggles generally benefit from a nepantilist ethos that discerns and enacts its direction in the midst of the multiple lightings of different traditions. Her wager is that the world is too full of diversely located modes of subjugation and suffering and too rich in possibilities for wisdom, justice, and thriving for any single currency or teleology to be nearly sufficient for the tasks of democratic struggling and living well.

Thus one finds in Anzaldúa's writing what might be called a "nepantilist generosity": a generosity that elaborates itself—internally and in communities with others—in dialogues torn between different sensibilities and visions of the future; a generosity torn between, on the one hand, the pursuit of what appear to be among the best political directions, principles, and practices that have been illuminated thus far by the sparks generated in the friction between these different visions, and, on the other, its sense of the radical need to listen attentively to the voices and visions that come from places it cannot or has not yet illuminated—directions it cannot or has not yet pursued. Anzaldúa's ethos would be generous in the way the new mestiza would "[make] herself vulnerable to foreign ways of seeing and thinking" (*Borderlands*, 82). It would be generous to others in its anticipation that a more worthy future is only possible *with* them, in radically receptive encounters: "Every increment of consciousness, every step forward, is a *travesía*. I am again an alien in new territory. And again, and again. . . . Every time she makes 'sense' of something, she has to 'cross over,' kicking a hole out of the old boundaries" (48–49).[26] Value here is no longer viewed in terms of the accumulation of a single currency (and the devaluations that sustain it); rather, it is seen as that which emerges in receptive engagements and tensions between different ways of being that deepen our sense of suffering, danger, and other possibilities for justice and flourishing. To be sure, principles (such as rights to free speech and association) and practices (such as radical democratic engagement) are vital elements in securing spaces for such engagements. Yet their possibility is not reducible to nor necessarily containable within the directions these principles and practices delineate in advance of the engagements themselves. For also vital to the encounter is an energetic receptivity, a willingness of the participants to listen in ways that might solicit them to radically reform their own understanding of these principles and practices: the principles' requirements, their implications, the meaning and relative importance they have in constellations of different traditions, political struggles, and emergent sensibilities and communities. These, in turn, may introduce other principles, practices, and languages of remembrance and yearning that participants in the encounter take to be just as—or more—fundamental. Critical cosmopolitanism is partly the difficult cultivation of an awareness of the limits of knowing in advance.

*Nepantilist* generosity; *torn* generosity? "This is her home / this thin edge / of barbed wire" (*Borderlands,* 82). Torn generosity of generative crossings, emerging from a life torn—a life in which tornness itself has become constitutive of cosmopolitan virtues. A bit overwrought, one might say. Perhaps. But both in the face of cosmopolitanisms that presume the primacy of a single untearable political currency and in the face of abstract celebrations of hybridity based on a problematic sense of hyperfungibility, "torn" emphasizes the difficult and wrenching work that is so often required in the encounters between deeply different traditions and visions of things. "Torn" articulates a tragic sensibility—resolutely calling us to reflect on and resist the blindness and violence that seem to accompany human practices. It calls us to anticipate these requirements; it solicits this work. The wager is that myths of cosmopolitan "ease" generally go with the flows of status quo power. I do not mean to dismiss or underestimate the tremendous possibilities for transfiguring aesthetic and ethical sensibility that are all around us or to deny that many of these may offer paths to their spirit that seem effortless (anyone who has unexpectedly slipped into the sound sphere of enrapturing music from several distant lands may know something about this). Instead, I intend to cultivate a deep suspicion concerning the adequacy of anything remotely approaching ease for the generous and receptive negotiation of either our deepest differences or serious struggles against global corporate capitalism.

Do we have any reason to be hopeful that people(s) proximate to this radically dialogical vision might actually have a chance to muster the power to significantly engage the directions of development taking place in our world? For the generous vision that Anzaldúa articulates overlaps and resonates with many others emerging around the world. In chapter 6 I will argue that many feminists of color appear to be

converging around similar themes and modes of struggle. Walter Mignolo's work insightfully elaborates the diverse, globally emerging visions
and practices of what he calls, drawing upon Abdelkebir Khatibi, an
ethics and politics of "an other thinking." Mignolo writes not of "a
new form of . . . hybridity, but an intense battlefield." The "border
thinking" struggles of many in colonial modernities against modern
colonialism(s) can be seen to have a critical cosmopolitan family re-
semblance to what I have been calling nepantilist generosity.[27] Drawing far and wide from struggles to theorize from "the other side of the
colonial difference," Mignolo sketches the sometimes independent,
sometimes interrelated developments of dialogical visions articulated
through the "double consciousness" of those situated between two or
more traditions or subgroupings within various communities. Khatibi's
"double critique" emerging from the Maghreb, W. E. B. Du Bois's
"double consciousness" and the new mestiza in the United States,
Zapatista Subcomandante Marcos's "double translation," Edouard
Glissant's "Creolization" in the Caribbean, and many others—emerging movements of thinking and acting value dwelling dialogically at
the tension-laden borders between people(s) as the most hopeful mode
of ethical and political becoming. Scholars like Homi Bhabha[28] and
Judith Butler[29] are pursuing similar directions. Beyond the territoriality of myriad nationalisms, these visions "indicate a geohistorical location that is constructed as a crossing instead of as a grounding" (*Local
Histories/Global Designs,* 69). As global flows of people, communication, capital, and technology increasingly cause people around the
world to find themselves proximate to, stretched by, suffering from,
struggling in, and dreaming from discrepant traditions, it is not impossible—*not impossible*—that our times may be increasingly ripe for the
powerful emergence of a more radically democratic, generous, and
pluralizing freedom.

Mignolo conjures a global network of local struggles that might just
generate a coalition of visions and powers to challenge capitalist colonial globalization with a diverse, democratically empowering, and more
generous globalization from below. The idea here is not to overlook
widely emerging violent nationalisms, neoliberal initiatives, and so forth
that clearly lean in very different directions. There are many contradictory developments, and writers of nepantilist generosity and its cousins
do not claim to be or to speak as representatives of "the whole."
Rather, we seek to become serious voices and ears in radical democratic dialogues and serious contenders in struggles for power.

Let me emphasize, again, "ears": a power that develops and articulates itself in and toward the activities of listening. "Postcolonialism" probably has neither more nor fewer self-aggrandizing scholars than do most other discourses. Yet one of the things that on the whole distinguishes it from many positions in academia today is its persistent injunction that "'learning from' those who are living in and thinking from colonial and postcolonial legacies"—learning from the voices and visions of those engaged in specific struggles—is crucial to "promoting new forms of cultural critique and intellectual and political emancipations" (*Local Histories/Global Designs,* 5). With Paolo Friere, postcolonialism emphasizes, in Mignolo's words, "thinking with instead of thinking *for* or thinking *about* people" (265). Why? Because there is no way to learn to resist blindness and violence, except with—and often *from*—those toward whom each currently configured "we" is constitutively blind and violent.

Although there are numerous and important points where Nussbaum's discourse and a democratic nepantilist generosity might find resonance and coalitional possibilities, I want here to underscore a difference between these two genres of world wandering. Nussbaum's cosmopolitans are "to become, to a certain extent, philosophical exiles from our own ways of life, seeing them from the vantage point of the outsider and asking the questions an outsider is likely to ask." But the "outside," for her, usually becomes the outer concentric circle of "the community of humanity" (*Cultivating Humanity,* 58). However much "lonely" questioning this may entail, when Nussbaum repeats Diogenes' claim "I am a citizen of the world," it is hard not to hear a presumptuous expectation that the comfort of patriotism will be replaced by an all-too-comforting cosmopolitanism in which her "reason and a love for humanity" will ensure that she can *be*—be a citizen of a "shared reason"—wherever she goes. Given the dangers I have raised concerning cosmopolitans who would circulate around the world like currency, let me suggest another image of world-traveling.

Anzaldúa, too, writes of exile and migration. Her more-than-territorial imagination summarizes the history of her people(s) thus: "We have a tradition of migration, a tradition of long walks" (*Borderlands,* 11). Most of those walks have been very tough journeys. But the nepantilist rose in the cross(ing) of her present is her sense that these walks have engendered tensional virtues—fragile and robust—that are likely to be crucial for ethical struggles of future journeys. She waters this cosmopolitan flower daily, and it grows. But roses have thorns, and the exiles they nurture are not so much those of the "I am a citizen of the world!" as those of the more difficult wisdom Mignolo evokes with a phrase from Bernardo Canal Feijoo concerning "not being able to be [*ser*] where one is [*estar*]." This, Mignolo continues, "*is the promise of an epistemological potential and a cosmopolitan transnationalism that could overcome the limits and violent conditions generated by being always able to be where one belongs*" (*Local Histories/ Global Designs*, 334).

I am doubtful, given the intransigent finitude of the human condition, that people(s) can "overcome" the limits and violence that shadow our identities—at least not if we mean totally, perhaps even if we mean for the most part. But, with Adorno, Anzaldúa, and Mignolo, I do think that we can resist them much more effectively—we can overcome *these* limits and *those* specific violences—as we follow the promise of not being able to be where one is. Which is to say, we can do and be much better.

Doing better hinges significantly on cultivating an enlivening tension between a tragic sensibility and a sense of rich promise and possibility. Tragedy without promise is despairing, and promising possibility quickly turns ugly when it becomes politically oblivious to the aspects of tragic finitude that are likely to accompany it. The trick is to maintain each sensibility without overwhelming one with the other. For a nepantilist generosity maintaining this balance means, in part, acknowledging the elements of affinity it shares with aspects of liberal cosmopolitanism, even as we work to articulate and practice very significant differences. Hence, for example, there are many aspects of Nussbaum's core currency that are worthy of affirmation, even if the position articulated here would affirm them in ways more solicitous of agonistic engagements among various "others," ways that would be likely to inflect, transfigure, transgress, and supplement her currency. Thus, rather than insistently proclaiming "Rights!" to other struggling people, we might offer something more like the following: "These particular rights and capacities have proved very effective in some of our past and current struggles. It appears to us that they might harbor certain desirable possibilities for your own struggles. Yet we also know they come with certain dangers, damages, and disciplines that we continue to resist and seek ways around. How might you articulate these rights in your struggles? How is their meaning transfigured, and what is their relative priority in the constellation of ethical-political traditions and visions from which you draw strength and lean into the future? What might we learn from you in this regard? To what questions and

insights are we currently deaf, and how do you understand the implications of this deafness? What alliances might be possible between us
given our resonances, connections, and difficult differences?"

To repeat, we should not—in critiquing currencies and ethical-
political stances as currency—fall into the trap of thinking we are "post-
currency"; little could propel us more quickly toward the reconstruction
of ethical-political blindness. Nepantilist generosity *needs* direction and
values—like democracy, freedom, equality, "diversality," and many others I cannot anticipate—no matter how provisionally formulated, contested, and open-ended, no matter whether they are offered more as
solicitous connectors than as universals abstracted and shielded from
the differences of others. Hence it too will—for better *and* for worse—
always partake in the formulation of currencies that it offers and sometimes insists on in the face of the worst modes of power. Beyond the
need, one must speak of the tendency. Echoing Karl Marx's words in
the *Grundrisse,* one might even speak ironically of a "law of the tendency" to convert into another currency precisely the terms with which
one would resist the reifications of currency—a "falling rate of profit,"
even, as overproduction transforms the most "torn" and tensional
terms, juxtapositions, and affirmations of lively border thinking into
hard and flat coins that begin to circulate too easily, uncritically, and
in ways that risk installing new modes of sleepy repetition and deafness, new dangers. To infuse a nepantilist generosity with a certain
sense of irony is not to erase the utmost seriousness of these alternative modes of democratic engagement; rather, it is to recognize that
there is a certain playfulness without which the seriousness will not
*become.*

To help us develop these themes in more explicitly political and institutional directions, James Tully offers our imaginations a cornucopia.
Beyond the narrow range of the mainstream hum of liberal discourses
on constitutionalism from Locke to Rawls, Tully brilliantly explores
the long minority traditions of both "treaty constitutionalism" practiced by Native Americans and "diverse federalism" made up of very
different members (as in Canada). Tully criticizes a modern constitutionalism that seeks to establish a "foundational, universal, and fixed
background to democracy," arguing that it falsely presumes an implicit
consensus and bypasses "the responsibility to listen to others" that is
the core of the democratic ethos that he finds necessary for a postim-
perial age.[30] Aboriginal treaty constitutionalism, in contrast, views each
accord between peoples as "one link in an endless chain" of open-
ended relationships, based on mutual recognition and consent, that seek

to "reach agreement on a form of association that accommodates their differences in appropriate institutions and their similarities in shared institutions" (*Strange Multiplicity,* 131). In these traditions, distinctness is presumed to continue rather than being extinguished or assimilated by the constitution between peoples. In Tully's view, the League of the Six Nations is exemplary in this respect, insofar as each member maintains its own language, customs, and government and "each negotiator participates in his or her language, mode of speaking and listening, form of reaching agreement, and way of representing the people, or peoples, for whom they speak" (129). The Iroquois League embodied the vision that "a constitution can be both the foundation of democra[tic relations] and, at the same time, subject to democratic discussion and change in practice" not based on a single communicative currency (129). Interestingly, rather than currency, in these relationships the item given and received, the lingua franca for "recording the form of agreement reached and expressing the good will the agreement embodies," was the "two row wampum belt," whose various rows of beads symbolize distinct and different peoples traveling together in dialogue, respect, peace, and friendship (127).

Tully argues that this nonassimilative spirit of relationships of mutual recognition of difference, consent, and continuity has much to recommend it for intragroup relations and for relations that cut across groups. So, for example, women within an indigenous community might negotiate their relations with men in a similar manner, in the open-ended elaboration of commonalities and differences; and women (or members of other groups, for example, environmentalists, and so on) across numerous indigenous and nonindigenous communities might form alliances that engage practices of diverse federalism, as they did in the constitutional negotiations in Canada in the early 1980s, which led to equal rights and affirmative action amendments.

Though there is much to be learned from Tully's account of these issues, I am more skeptical than he is about the possibility and desirability of generalizing even greatly modified notions of sovereignty in the way he seeks to do this. With and against his effort to generalize for democracy the idea that "relations of interdependency should be voluntarily taken on" (*Strange Multiplicity,* 194), I suspect it is descriptively and normatively more helpful to see (as Tully often does) relations of interdependence as significantly prevoluntary in terms both of their past and of emerging encroachments on each self and group. Democratic politics, then, is about endlessly renegotiating and transfiguring these relations of "historical throwness" (the way we are swept by time into the contingency of our world prior to our choosing or understanding our shifting situations), and doing so in manners more radically democratic and more receptive to differences that are tossed together in ever-new ways before people(s) have a chance to discern or agree fully to the terms of engagement. Democratic politics is the effort to constitute a discerning volition of nepantilist generosity in the midst of a world always already and endlessly taking form and generating pressures in other directions.

The vision of politics that begins to emerge from the work of Anzaldúa, Mignolo, and Tully allows us to supplement the image of dissipating sovereignty that Kuper describes in his provocative critique of Rawls. Recall that Kuper seeks to disperse and pluralize the theory and practice of democratic sovereignty along both vertical and horizontal dimensions.

The spirit of nepantilist generosity suggests a further dispersion of democratic theory and practice in a way that registers the dissonant *temporal* depths within any "now," no matter how spatially and functionally variegated. Kuper's functional dispersion remains essentially territorial insofar as it transports a relatively static spatial matrix onto the realm of "issue areas." He takes the territorial model and turns it at a right angle to imagine sovereignty dispersed along "functional lines." Hence there will be democratic "governing bodies" and "agency clusters" around "different spheres" and "nonterritorial spaces" and interaction ("Rawlsian Global Justice," 657). Although this course has much to offer, the exclusive use of spatial metaphors unwittingly risks a stinginess that nepantilist generosity would have us resist. After all, in the democratic temporality of dynamic tensions among us, we human beings move and struggle to the beat of many distinct and sometimes-dissonant drummers. These temporalities often encroach on one another, in such a way that even under the best conditions at any moment, the negotiations, agreements, institutions, and directions reached among them are likely to consider poorly and marginalize many possibilities for being and becoming. This limitation infuses the presence of all theories and practices with absence, so that "*what is proper to a culture is to be not identical to itself. . . .* There is no culture or cultural identity without this difference *with itself*" (Derrida, as quoted by Tully in *Strange Multiplicity,* 14). Movements toward radical democracies of nepantilist generosity seek to approach this temporal dispersion in each moment, culture, and institution as a solicitation, against whatever odds, to reopen the structures of present responsiveness to fresh negotiations with (and to be among) those clamoring at gates that have arisen intentionally or in spite of ourselves. As such, these movements toward tensional democracy seek not only to maximize responsiveness in institutional designs (though this they surely must do) but also to cultivate a capacious sense for and yearning to receptively engage anew those to whom our dominant modes of response have failed to respond. Concretely, this means expanding our capacity to participate in and engage groups, movements, and nascent institutions and practices that cut across and seek to reform the jurisdictional "spaces" of established institutions. It means understanding and affirming that democracy is in no small way the dynamic coexistence of practices and institutional spaces that dislocate as well as complement one another.[31]

One can see some beginning efforts to articulate a politics of nepantilist generosity in relation to institutional practices in the World Social Forum (WSF), concerning which Boaventura de Sousa Santos's manuscript "The World Social Forum: Toward a Counter-Hegemonic Globalization" is seminal.[32] The WSF is a gathering (meeting during its first three years in Porto Alegre, Brazil, then in Mumbai, India) of tens of thousands from diverse social movements, nongovernmental organizations (NGOs), and progressive local and state formations from around the world. These different groups come together at the WSF to articulate stark resistance to the central forces and damages of neoliberal globalization and to proclaim strongly that, as their fundamental principle states, "another world is possible." They share experiences, knowledges, and alternative practices, and they build relationships and networks with the aim of nurturing alternative modes of globalization that are at once equitable and respectful of difference. In their first several years of existence they have sought to create institutions that are—in diametrical opposition to the institutions of global corporations and finance—open and responsive to local knowledges and emergent democratic initiatives. By any stretch of the imagination the WSF is far more democratic in its institutional designs and aims than are the summit of economic leaders at Davos, Switzerland, the World Trade Organization (WTO), the International Monetary Fund (IMF), the General Agreement on Tariffs and Trade (GATT), and the like. One could analyze the ways dialogical democracy finds institutional articulation by paying attention not only to central institutions of the WSF but also to the way it (increasingly) *also* decenters its institutions along crosscutting lines (pregnant with tensions) that are thematic, regional, local,

group differentiated, and so on in order to deepen and diversify participation. Yet a significant portion of Santos's analysis is devoted not only
to questions of innovative design but also to the *problems* of democracy in the WSF—the way it remains insufficiently democratic, and often
along traditional lines concerning region, North-South, rich-poor, culture, scale, education, and so forth.

In the present discussion the specificities of current and proposed
institutional designs for the WSF is less important than that these designs persistently harbor tensions and the dynamic ways nepantilist
generosity infuses the relationship of many engaged take to these designs. The slogan "another world is possible" does pivotal work not
only in the WSF's relation to dominant forms of globalization but also
in its relation to its own institutional articulations at any point in time.
Santos argues that the diverse groups involved in the WSF articulate—
in ways that are both theoretical and practical—what he calls a "sociology of absences" (discerning the ways groups and practices are produced as absent) and a "sociology of emergences" (discerning insipient
alternative forms of human coexistence that challenge the claim that
the present is the "end of history"). These counter-sociologies inflect
the relation most participants at WSF take to the institutional designs
at any given point in time. Hence, given the deep attentiveness of most
participants to diverse ways power operates to silence and suppress, it
is not surprising that, thus far, one of the remarkable characteristics of the WSF is the extent to which its flourishing has been linked
to a dynamism rooted in the sustenance of tensions made possible by
a substantial generosity and responsiveness among differences. The
movement and development of the WSF—as well as some of the specific tensional designs—articulate nepantilist generosity: the *movement*
toward proliferating and accenting cross-cutting and tensional local,
regional, issue, and group forums with the aim of deepening and diver-
sifying participation; the *repeated reconsideration* of institutional design in light of a capacious and patient responsiveness to tensions that
most other political formations have sought to obliterate. The WSF
develops in a way that, thus far, seeks to sustain tensions (for example, between localism and the need for broader coordination, between
dialogue and action, between state and nonstate articulations, between
the need for proposals and the need for ongoing responsiveness, between equality and difference, between direct action and institutional
action) that, in combination with a deepening ethos of nepantilist generosity, foster a dynamic democratization that must repeatedly reor-
ganize itself. As Santos argues, "This path does not claim to solve the

issue of participatory democracy. . . . the issue of the participation
of the rank-and-file will be always there. . . . there is no machinery
of democratic engineering capable of solving the problem of internal
democracy at a single blow. To my mind, such a problem will end up
being taken care of through successive partial solution."33 Of course,
Santos is careful to caution the WSF against "throwing out the baby
with the bathwater" at each point of reformation. Ateleological impulses must wrestle with teleological orientations in the formation of
better democratic judgment and action. Possible democratizing changes
have to be considered in relation to the past successes of current institutional designs. Questions of efficacy do not just disappear in the face
of questions of radicalizing democracy; rather, such questions often
contend with one another. Yet now the contest must take place on a
more even playing field rather than on one favoring without question
the technocratic god of efficiency. Democracy moves toward developing judgment, power, and action as a "community of the question,"
as Derrida puts it (and as I will discuss at length in chapter 5). Utopia
is always "not yet."

In this push beyond politics fundamentally framed by the "fantastical
imaginary value" of currency—its presumptions of widely circulating
consent and devalued others, its readiness to feel "clogged and embarrassed" when exchange becomes tough—a heterogeneous "we" might
be able to move with enough in common to make serious radical democratic inroads into contemporary processes of global marketization.
Insofar as global capitalism is entwined with the hegemony of exchange
value, nepantilist democratic crossings are nothing if not fundamentally at odds with it.

   The meaning of this opposition cannot take the form of a few words
that seek to organize the new state of things. Rather, this opposition
would entail a strange chorus of new approaches—beyond those that
feel only "clogged and embarrassed"—to life after Babel. "Babel,"
Mignolo writes with a smile, "may not be as bad as the ideologues of
unification and purity . . . thought it was"; Tully glossing Sheldon
Wolin on Babel, agrees (*Local Histories/Global Designs*, 277; *Strange
Multiplicity*, 196). Indeed, as Mennonite theologian Yoder sees it, "Babel
in the myth of Genesis places the multiplicity of cultures under the sign
of the divine will. . . . This scattering is seen as divine benevolence."34
Babel may be significant not because it left us weak and disunited
but because recognition of this condition as gift is the condition of

any power and community worth striving for. The chapters that follow attempt to flesh out and draw into engagement diverse ethical responses to the possibilities of politics and ethics after Babel. It is my hope that the unresolved tensions embodied in the text will be as illuminating as my synthetic and constructive work.

# 3
# MacIntyre and the Confidence
# Trickster of Rivalish Tradition

URNING TO ALASDAIR MACINTYRE to explore possibilities for receptive
generosity in democratic engagements across lines of difference
will strike many as counterintuitive. Many read him as suggesting
a retreat to isolated, homogeneous, and inwardly turned local communities that cultivate their own traditions and avoid contact with difference (construed as a "pluralism which threatens to submerge us all" *Liberalism +*
into "new dark ages").[1] The political imaginary he offers is often viewed *for pluralism*
as one in which difference and conflict are so diminished as to be incapable of shedding light upon my concerns—except as an exemplifica- ↓
tion of the *bad*. In political liberal narratives, MacIntyre generally *tradition*
exemplifies a neo-Aristotelian politics unified around a single vision of
the good, against which Rawlsians define their own project. So I am
not unaware that turning to MacIntyre here will greatly strain my credibility for many.

Nevertheless, I suggest that a politics of *traditio* has much to learn
from this theorist of tradition. Even if *traditio* solicits vulnerable engagements with "other" traditions, fragments of traditions, and emergent sensibilities and practices in a manner that risks transfigurations
that may be seen as treasonous, this should not obscure the fact that *tradition*
*traditio* is also indebted to and must critically develop tradition in a +
more teleological sense. If these debts appear treasonous to those who *teleology*
would congeal ateleological sensibilities themselves into a new dogmatic
fortress, so be it. MacIntyre not only illuminates teleological development but also powerfully argues that only within a teleological horizon
can we grasp and nurture a vulnerability to the ateleological aspects
of human historicity.

To be sure, no small part of what we might learn from MacIntyre concerns what is brilliantly problematic in his thinking—that which exemplifies modes of being-together that a politics and ethics of receptive generosity might best strive to avoid. Yet while I do elaborate this aspect of what we might learn, I also focus on how his movement away from various Enlightenment and liberal projects illuminates much that political liberalism conceals. These insights are valuable in both deconstructive and constructive senses, and I seek to bring them into engagement with the movement of my own thinking.

In contrast to interpretations offered by many of his defenders and critics, I present a reading of MacIntyre's work in which contingency, conflict, difference, heterogeneous traditions, and a version of dialogical enlightenment and politics are central. Although ultimately my sense of weaknesses in MacIntyre's project leads me in alternative directions, the path I take beyond him remains significantly indebted to him, and it is haunted by certain questions and possibilities that his vision enables and that may illuminate shortcomings in the theories and practices I strive to articulate. MacIntyre's project is, for me, simultaneously and in different respects an aid toward certain thoughts and practices, an illuminating error, and an invaluable ghost.

## The Goods of Conflict

MacIntyre places questions of learning to live well amid deep historical contingency, contestability, and conflict *at the very center* of his critical explorations of liberalism and genealogy, as well as at the center of his efforts to recover and develop an understanding of selves and communities embodied in traditions teleologically oriented toward the good. His writing sometimes lends itself to interpretations that miss this, yet MacIntyre is best read as a theorist concerned with what it might mean to live well in borderlands.

For decades, MacIntyre has compellingly argued that from absolutist, dogmatic, and ahistorical assertions about morality, "we can be saved only by an adequate historical view of the varieties of moral and evaluative discourse . . . [such that] our too narrow views of what can and cannot be thought, said, and done are discarded in the face of our record of what has been thought, said, and done."[2] A profound sense that "the costs of consensus are paid by those excluded from it"[3] has oriented his work toward illustrating the "impoverished view of the range of types of moral concepts" (*Against the Self-Images of the Age,* ix) and has led him to support the "liberal values" of toleration and freedom of expression (ibid., 283).[4] In the 1970s MacIntyre argued for "the essential contestability of social concepts."[5]

So what happened? Did he so emphatically offer us a broader "historical record" only to embrace "tradition" in a way that, paradoxically, requires us to turn away from the wide-ranging messiness of history toward a relatively homogeneous social space and time? Is tradition, generally, the truth with negligible costs in no need of contestation?

Affirmative responses here overlook central themes in *After Virtue* and completely ignore the books MacIntyre wrote later in which he further develops those themes. Far from abandoning his sense of multiplicity, contingency, contestability, and conflict, MacIntyre seeks to develop a more promising mode of moral enquiry and practice precisely upon this difficult terrain.

One of the most important contentions in *After Virtue* is that liberal modernity "furnishe[s] us with a pluralist political rhetoric whose function is to conceal the depth of our conflicts" (235). One way such concealment works is through a "rhetoric of consensus" that disguises political and moral heterogeneity by claiming to discern basic agreement beneath our arguments.[6] Thus, when disagreements emerge, dominant modes of contemporary political discourse tend to sever the immediate issues from the deeply conflicting beliefs and traditions that often engender these conflicts, and then they strive to negotiate a superficial peace. The breadth and depth of contestation further disappears in numerous philosophical assumptions that "we" can, through an ahistorical individual rationality, provide moral arguments compelling to all. When such efforts repeatedly fail, emotivist theories (reducing morality to individual preferences and assertions) arise to account for the seeming interminability of moral conflict. Yet such theories further conceal moral contestability by positing at bottom a different brand of ahistorical, decontextualized selves that deflects critical interrogation. In MacIntyre's view dominant modes of modern theory and practice are invested in denying the messiness of our abode—partly in spite of and partly by means of pluralist rhetoric.

Of course, without question, MacIntyre bemoans the seemingly endless and deep incommensurability that marks modernity's numerous conceptions of goods and justice: "There seems to be no rational way of securing moral agreement in our culture" (*After Virtue*, 6). And in the absence of such rationality, our convictions remain radically arbitrary, our economics continue to be structured by rapacious laissez-faire capitalism, and our politics are still characterized by irrational impositions of bureaucratic control in the name of an illusory "reason." Yet the way beyond these problems and to *the possibility of intelligent judgment in the midst of them* is through an indefinitely long-term deepening and widening of genuine contestations—paradoxically eclipsed by "pluralism"—not through their attenuation.

MacIntyre argues that moral discourse in modern liberal societies consists of a "mélange" of heterogeneous fragmentary "survivals" from earlier narratives and practices that are no longer understood. We argue beginning from numerous (often utterly incoherent) moral premises whose larger meaning, context, and implications we poorly understand and rarely seriously investigate. Widespread acceptance of the abstraction of premises from historical narratives and practices leads us to reify moral discourse and enquiry. Under such circumstances, the proliferation of these shards leads not to an increase in difference and contestation but, rather, to the fragmentation of different rationalities until they are drained of life, substance, sense, and contestatory power. Entwined with this waning of rationalities is a waning of different modes of life, which become less and less able to organize or defend themselves in the face of disintegrative political and economic forces. We are, he claims, like the progeny of an imaginary society in which flourishing natural sciences suffered enormous persecution and historical annihilation. We rediscover fragments of sciences after a catastrophe and argue about the merits of bits of ideas found on torn, charred pages from missing books, but "almost nobody realizes that what they are doing is not natural science in any proper sense at all" (*After Virtue*, 1). When minute pieces of larger narrative practices are atomistically seized by people oblivious to their relations, function, and meaning as parts of larger constellations of living significance— when they are, with remarkable amnesia, asserted as ahistorically self-evident or arbitrary preferences—the expanse and density of their distinction dissipates. And so too does the distinction of those "individuals" who thus story themselves. Contemporary pluralism becomes a simulacrum of difference, and modern moral discourse a "simulacrum of morality." Lacking substantial narratives, practices, virtues— *traditions*—our pluralist "values" are unable to resist the dynamic forces of capitalism, individual acquisitiveness, and bureaucratic manipulation. When evoked, modernity's values often merely provide masks for arbitrary power and interests. Increasingly recognizing this, many moderns come to identify morality with power.

Hence "the notion of pluralism is too imprecise. For it may equally well apply to an ordered dialogue of intersecting viewpoints and to an unharmonious mélange of ill-assorted fragments" (*After Virtue*, 10). The greatest danger facing particular communities entering the liberal-pluralist public sphere is *not* that we are overburdened because "we have all too many disparate and rival moral concepts." It is, rather, that the requirements of this public sphere "conceal the depth of our conflicts" and impose modes and norms that incapacitate serious engagements across differences. We are pressured into unburdening ourselves of both the weight of responsibility to our own traditioned differences and the weightiness of serious listening to others. With time, these pressures extinguish the particularities of communities while corporate markets and bureaucracies constitute selves and relationships according to their logics of power. Liberal pluralism does this by requiring us (1) to (de)figure our positions in the terms of an illusory neutral reason, as if our different narratives and practices were irrelevant to ethical and political enquiry, and (2) to "participate in the cultural mélange" by employing the moral fragments immediately at hand rather than by developing our differences into more-coherent and more-reflective alternatives for engagement within and across traditions. Both impositions erode difference in an arbitrary manner that proliferates a hopelessly irrational incommensurability and erases the possibility of a more genuine contestation that *might* allow us to learn to live more intelligently.

But what exactly does MacIntyre *suggest?* Most political philosophers are familiar with his suggestion that "what matters at this point is the construction of forms of local community in which civility and the intellectual and moral life can be sustained through the new dark ages which are already upon us" (*After Virtue*, 245). Some see this as a simple reversal of the modernity he views as "not proper in any sense" and interpret him as offering a vision where ideas and practices are *proper:* where they *fit* together in a larger whole in such a way that they are entirely *appropriate* to one another, *suitable*, not disjointed, displaced or partial. We would *belong* to each other and our history, because we are *owned by* it, made *right* and coherent by it. Yet this reading misses the heterogeneity, contestation, and conflicts within and between traditions that figure prominently in MacIntyre's account. Rather, I think that his suggestion that we build local communities should be interpreted in relation to his effort to discern historical modes for engaging in disputes, engaging in contestations concerning the proper.

Certainly the idea of a proper transparent community plays an essential role in *After Virtue*, but it figures as a strange and elusive idea.

It appears both as the representation of an explicitly irretrievable heroic past that "may or may not have existed" (122) and (differently) as the ever-distant telos of a tradition's unending "quest." It is *not*, however, something that ever characterizes the present of any living tradition. MacIntyre situates tradition somewhere quite distant from either Descartes's clarity of prehistorical first principles or Hegel's harmonious clarity at the achievable end of history.[7]

In *After Virtue* the heroic age celebrated in poems and sagas represents what I called above the "proper." Each self has a determined role and status that fits together with other roles into a "highly determinate system" (115). This system and these roles determine one's values and duties and what one is owed—not just generally but in terms of the actions required. Each person has "a clear understanding" of the social order and its normative requirements. "Morality and social structure are one," and moral questions are simply "questions of social fact" (116). So tightly do the self and social order belong to one another that the heroic self lacks "the capacity to detach [it]self from any particular standpoint . . . to step back . . . and view and judge that standpoint . . . from the outside" (119). Given this identity between facts and norms, both modern ideals of free individual choice and universalism, and even the idea of a universally worthy account of the good that would teleologically orient a particular tradition are utterly absent. Life, understood as a socially located and determinate story, is the "standard of value," and "it is defeat and not victory that lies at the end" (117).

With this story of the properly storied life, MacIntyre seeks to challenge unquestioned modern assumptions about the naturalness of abstract individuality and morality. Yet it is less the Homeric world that interests him than the ideas and practices of some of those who came after, after the "proper." MacIntyre emphasizes that whether or not the heroic age actually existed as depicted in the poems and sagas is unimportant to his argument. What is important is that "the belief that they had existed was crucial to those classical and Christian societies which understood themselves as having *emerged* from the conflicts of heroic society [visible from beyond its own horizon] and which defined their own standpoint partially in terms of that *emergence*" (*After Virtue*, 123, my emphasis).

Though MacIntyre repeats "emerge" in this sentence, I emphasize it. I do so to underscore two things. First, the societies and theorists that MacIntyre finds most compelling were in fact—and understood themselves to be—significantly removed from heroic societies, even as they acknowledged significant debts to them. The Homeric kinship system lived on in ancient Athens not as a definitive context but, rather, as an unstable system within the framework of a polis that provoked questioning concerning heroic society and the meaning of social roles, justice, virtues, and the good in Athens. As displaced, heroic society becomes a condition both of orientation and of disorientation, and many discrepant philosophical, political, and dramatic initiatives emerged in response. Classical Athens understood itself as the outgrowth of this *ongoing legacy* of conflicts and questions that constituted no small part of the life of its present. The "proper," on this reading, is no longer self-evidently bestowed upon human thought and practice by the social order; rather, it takes form in this horizon of historically animated questions.

Second, I want to emphasize a certain resonance with the Enlightenment, which, as Kant put it, "is man's *Ausgangs* [emergence, escape, way out, release, exit] from his self-imposed immaturity."[8] From the outset, MacIntyre gestures not to community submerged in "the proper" but, rather, to tradition as a mode of emergence—or better, of emerging. MacIntyre should be read both as a critic of Enlightenment thinkers and as a philosopher of enlightenment understood as a commitment to the ongoing development of conceptions and practices of rationality that can gradually emerge from the blindness, untruth, and violence that are recalcitrant aspects of every historically situated community. He is critical of "Burkean" notions of tradition that affirm stasis and contrast themselves to reason.[9] The "common life" of a tradition does not consist in a satisfied attitude aimed at securing a past that has bestowed proper order; rather, it "will be partly, but in a central way, constituted by continuous argument as to what [it] is and ought to be. . . . Traditions, when vital, embody continuities of conflict" (*After Virtue*, 206). This illuminates MacIntyre's claim that "the thesis of *After Virtue* is not at all that the thinkers of the Enlightenment have nothing to teach us. It is that in order to learn from them what they genuinely have to teach us their insights have to be integrated into a quite different kind of intellectual framework and understood in terms of a quite different kind of intellectual perspective from those offered by what I called the Enlightenment project."[10]

As is well known, Aristotle significantly informs MacIntyre's understanding of the virtues and practical reasoning to be cultivated in traditions. MacIntyre claims that for Aristotle and his contemporaries, virtues are no longer transparently attached to particular social roles. Rather, they become integral to the well-being of *man as such*, in ways that make them less obvious and more questionable. Not surprisingly, most Athenian accounts of the virtues—and Aristotle is no exception—are deeply Athenian even as they make claims about what is good *as such*. At the same time however, their understandings of the virtues, indebted as they are to a specific community, make it possible for citizens to criticize particular policies of this community. Most Athenians understood well both that their virtues and capacities for judgment were made possible only through membership in the community and that this fact established neither transparent nor blind obedience but, rather, the possibility for critical enquiry into the community of their own genesis.

For MacIntyre, Aristotle, among Athenians, provides the best account of what judgment, the virtues, and the good can mean in a context where they are not transparently defined by particular social roles—and Aristotle does so by articulating "the rational voice of the best citizens of the best city-state" (*After Virtue*, 138). The telos of such selves and their community is *eudaimonia*, "blessedness, happiness, prosperity. It is the state of being well and doing well in being well" (139). The virtues are the characteristics necessary to pursue *eudaimonia* successfully as well as an intrinsically "necessary and central part of the good for man" (140). As one cultivates the virtues, one gradually shapes, orders, and limits one's dispositions in a manner conducive to flourishing. The virtues are internally related to good judgment, *phronesis*, a central virtue that both requires the other virtues and makes them possible. *Phronesis* and the other virtues, in turn, make possible movement toward one's *telos*. If people are to avoid floundering disorientation and thrive, they must take care to cultivate virtues, judgment, and practical reason, as well as friendships formed in pursuit of these.

Yet MacIntyre thinks that Aristotle oversimplifies things by imagining an emergence from the conflicts and opacities of history that is too complete in at least three ways. First, Aristotle "over-unifies" and harmonizes so that agon drops out of his accounts of the virtues, dialectics, poetics, and politics. Conflicts are no longer grasped in relation to the "sometimes irremediably tragic" human condition depicted by Sophocles' dramas but are, rather, understood as stemming merely from "flaws in character . . . or unintelligent political arrangements" (*After Virtue*, 147). The Sophoclean aspect of tragic finitude is vital to MacIntyre's reworking of Aristotle, and learning to negotiate conflicts becomes a central virtue.

Second, Aristotle has an exaggerated sense of transcendence insofar as he thinks he has entirely emerged from the errors and partiality of the past and established "*his* comprehensively true account," which could then discard the past. Yet for MacIntyre, the present never completely emerges as transparent truth but is "intelligible and justifiable—insofar as it is justifiable—only as a member of an historical series" (*After Virtue*, 137). Thus when the present claims to overcome the conflicts and errors within past alternatives, the primary means of discerning this resides precisely in its ability to narrate the conflicts between itself and past alternatives in ways that illustrate the present's apparent superiority in *this historical context*. When we fail to recognize this, we fail to achieve sufficient self-reflection regarding emerging as the condition of our own thinking.

Third, this failure, and Aristotle's related blindness to the essential finitude within which his own thought must remain open to correction, greatly diminishes his power to reflect critically on the limits of his Athenian understandings of the polis, barbarians, women, slaves, and so forth. MacIntyre argues that Aristotle thus developed an inflated sense of emergence from the finitude of history in relation to the heterogeneity of traditions within or at the borders of a society. Because Aristotle is convinced that he has established "the comprehensively true account," his work is of limited value for the project of elaborating how a rational tradition pursues relations with different traditions. MacIntyre notes that if Aristotle had realized "that it is through conflict and sometimes only through conflict that we learn what our ends and purposes are," he would have had deeper insights into the "teleological character" of ethics and community (*After Virtue*, 153).

MacIntyre argues that central features of medieval culture made these insights more difficult to avoid. Like sixth-century Athens, medieval society had to confront the problems posed by discordant "survivals" inherited from the past. But now these problems were multiplied and magnified, as medieval culture faced the challenge of "how to educate and civilize human nature in a culture in which human life was in danger of being torn apart by the conflict of too many ideals, too many ways of life" (*After Virtue*, 154). "Medieval culture, insofar as it was a unity at all, was a fragile and complex balance of a variety of disparate and conflicting elements" (155). He has in mind not just those conflicts among the three Abrahamic religions but also those within Christianity, whose discrepant regional developments incorporated highly tension-laden fragments from the heroic societies that preceded them, as well as fragments of the Athenian syntheses of its heroic tradition, fragments of pagan Roman fragments of Athenian fragments of heroic society—and so forth. It is precisely the emergence and development of traditions in *this* type of protean conflictive context that makes them interesting to MacIntyre. Of course, he also recognizes the presence of "one type of Christian teaching, influential to varying degrees throughout the Middle Ages, which dismissed all pagan teaching as the devil's work," but this consummate retreat from borderlands into a "pure" tradition left the problems of giving life an intelligent shape "insoluble" (156).

What is "proper" to those MacIntyre most admires in this period is the *way* they cultivate community traditions in a situation that is radically "improper"—incoherent, discordant, translucent. He learns from the distinct way they fashion a creative form of life that gives an intelligent and ethically ordered shape: "by generating the right kinds of tension or even conflict, creative rather than destructive, on the whole and in the long run, between secular and sacred, local and national, Latin and vernacular, rural and urban. It is in the context of such conflicts that moral education goes on and that the virtues come to be valued and redefined" (160).

On MacIntyre's reading, neo-Aristotelian Christianity is influenced by and reflexively forms this context in ways that produce a deeper affirmation of the historical, teleological character of human coexistence. The Christian virtues of forgiveness and charity constitute a vision of reconciliation that always lies in a future yet to be entirely accomplished. Yet since from within the messiness of history, that endpoint is not visible to us, the end of human life is more fundamentally a question for us than it is a determinate answer. It is *the call* to a life that is just and good—makes sense, is coherent, accords with human flourishing—but we do not know fully what such a life would be. Hence, the telos that would order our diverse practices and strivings must be understood in the general form of *the narrative quest itself*, so that "the good life for man is the life spent in seeking the good life for man, and the virtues necessary for the seeking are those which will enable us to understand what more and what else the good life for man is" (*After Virtue*, 204). Those embracing this end come to understand the structure of their practices, lives, and strivings in terms of a narrative "journey" toward redemption: the truth, justice, and the good yet to be achieved (163). This journey of people moved self-critically toward a future horizon has a distinctly Christian character, as the struggle against internal and external evil is central to it. Yet its basic structure remains, MacIntyre claims, deeply Aristotelian. Virtues and practical judgment remain as before both the primary means of achieving the good and a central aspect of it. Only now, "the virtues are those qualities which enable the evils to be overcome" (164)—those that enable us to move toward the good, and those that prefigure it: charity, faith, and hope, and also justice, courage, and honesty. This quest requires that we "subordinate ourselves to the best standard so far achieved" in myriad practices (178); cultivate our behavior, capacities, sensibilities, judgment, and passions in an effort to give these standards their due; and ultimately become beings who might further improve upon them.

Traditions "in good order" are not primarily the result of intersecting individual actions; rather, they are very significantly shaped by a community's deliberation about what they are and ought to be. Our "common life will be partly, but in a centrally important way, constituted by a continuous argument" about where we are and where we ought to go (*After Virtue*, 206). We will be asking what the good life for people is, what practices and pedagogies contribute to this end, what virtues make it possible—and we will be seeking to transform and fashion ourselves in light of what seem now to be the best responses. To live well (which is to say, to *story* well) requires having a deep sense of being a traditioned being: one whose powers of rationality and judgment can only flourish in dialogue with inherited modes of being and vision. This involves both a general sense about the human condition and a particular sense of belonging in dialogue with *these* traditions and practices, *this* community (or *these* communities) in the midst of which one lives.

Living well in these "continuities of conflict" is never easy, but two aspects of modernity pose particular challenges. First, in capitalist political economies, work has increasingly come to be organized by market imperatives and technologies aimed at maximizing profit and efficiency. This, in conjunction with the corresponding rise of the bureaucratic state, has meant that traditions and practices with internal goods and virtues have been shifted to the margins of the "official" political economy, replaced by instrumental activities aimed at goods and powers wholly external to the activities themselves. MacIntyre argues that "individuals" thus trapped and constituted, and mass societies thus (dis)organized, have very weak or even nonexistent capacities for exercising the virtues and practical judgment that thriving communities require. His political response to this situation is straightforward. For all localities, an intense and ongoing struggle will be essential between those remnants of tradition and the practices of "plain persons" that still retain some autonomy, on the one hand, and the dominant modes of political and economic organization, on the other: ("For the state and the market economy are so structured as to subvert and undermine the politics of local community. Between the one politics and the other there can only be continuing conflict."[11])

The second challenge, already discussed above, concerns modernity's dominant *modes* of responding to cultural heterogeneity. As we have seen, MacIntyre finds certain aspects of medieval culture particularly fascinating and relevant to modernity because they suggest alternative modes of cultivating communities that strive toward the good *amid cultural heterogeneity*. Vital to developing traditioned rationality is generating "the right kinds of tension or even conflict"—both within the relatively less heterogeneous terrains of a given community and in the borderlands between communities.

But more precisely: (how?) To develop MacIntyre's response to this question, I turn to *Whose Justice? Which Rationality?* and *Three Rival Versions of Moral Inquiry,* which offer the "systematic although unstated account of rationality" that *After Virtue* had mostly only presupposed (*After Virtue*, 242). Thomas Aquinas is central in these accounts.[12]

As MacIntyre (re)reads Aquinas, unity is less a transparent achievement than the teleological horizon of a tradition. Without a unifying *project of striving to bring coherence* to diverse goods, practices, and virtues in order to care for morality and the good as such, the historical dialogue in which human beings can exercise their always open and incomplete rationality is virtually impossible, and the virtues are devitalized. Absent a unifying telos, MacIntyre argues, individual claims and particular goods become so heterogeneous *in their fundamental structure* (each becomes closed off from the others, the past and the future) that they can no longer genuinely engage and contest one another. Each particular notion becomes worldless, loses the horizon that relates it to the others and to a larger whole in a way that both grants it a certain stability and opens it to meaningful interrogations. Fundamentally atomistic and closed in structure, such "goods" become purely arbitrary preferences. Intelligible and intelligent moral life becomes impossible in the midst of *this kind* of relationship to heterogeneity, MacIntyre claims, because at a most fundamental level the very question of the meaning, value, and legitimacy of a moral concept requires a relatively stable yet open horizon that can provide some discernable interrelationships and orientation. The teleological horizon of the good provides a space in which questions and genuine argument might be possible, provoked, meaningful, and powerful. Without this, the contingency and partiality of our concepts and relations are so radical as to be in essence unintelligible, unquestionable, and irresolvable. A too-radical contingency—a too-radically heterogeneous relationship to heterogeneity—can kill enquiry just as surely as can a closed structure.

Conflicts, both solicited and illuminated by the telos of a tradition, are a source of the tradition's life, because through them we question, test, and work upon the complex background of our past and present in order to advance toward a good that finite humans can never completely know or realize. In this way the particular standards and practices of a community are continually "elaborated, revised, emended, and even rejected" (*Whose Justice?* 101). Those positions that survive this process and are passed forth are the ones judged best up to this point. "If we do rest in a conclusion reached by dialectical argument it is only because no experiences have led us to revise our belief that in our *epagogai* so far, *nous* has indeed apprehended the needed universal concepts for the foundation of our *archai*, and that no alternative opinion advanced has been able better to withstand objections than that at which we had already arrived. But the possibility of further dialectical development always remains open" (*Whose Justice?* 100–101). In this way conviction and legitimacy are linked to a rationality and judgment embedded in a community's tradition of enquiry about the good life and the developing practices and virtues that make it possible. Social life thus develops a distinct order that is more than an arbitrary imposition of power and that exists with a combination of determinacy and openness that solicits and supports ongoing and fruitful moral enquiry. These insights are inscribed in both the content of Aquinas's work and its questioning/responding form.

Of course, MacIntyre recognizes the circularity here. Our virtues and capacities for judgment are always indebted to a notion of the good that guides us. Yet our understanding of the telos of the good is in turn indebted to these very virtues and capacities. On MacIntyre's reading, when a tradition is "in good order," this circularity is not vicious; rather, it is the condition of development: "We gradually learn to correct each in light of the other, moving dialectically between them" (*Whose Justice?* 118).

We cannot ascertain this development by measuring the distance between our judgments and the world in itself. Rather, as a tradition develops from its contingently given beginnings, through events that put these initial givens in question, to various ongoing reformulations or rejections of these givens, a sense of discrepancy emerges between what was previously thought to be true and the truth as it is now embraced.

We judge claims to be false when we become aware that they impede our embodied mind's ability to make anticipations that are not disappointed and recollections that "enable it to recover what it had encountered previously." We judge those claims true that allow us to rectify these failures. "The original and most elementary version of the correspondence theory of truth is one in which it is applied retrospectively in the form of a correspondence theory of falsity" (*Whose Justice?* 356). We signify this lack of correspondence—and relative improvement—between present and past judgments when we say something is false.

With Aquinas, MacIntyre suggests that reflections within a tradition upon the development of the tradition give rise to increasingly *historical* understandings of our sense of truth, justice, and the good, understandings that call us not only toward this retrospective theory of falsity but also toward a prospective theory of truth. Claims to truth thus become claims that the discrepancies and inadequacies that one now observes in relation to past judgments will never be suffered by one's present claims, "in any possible future situation, no matter how searching the enquiry, no matter how much evidence is provided, no matter what developments in rational enquiry may occur." Our sense of truth comes to be rooted in and aimed at *legitimate historical endurance*: It becomes the claim that what is held now will continue to correspond—now understood (in a different sense of this term) as the claim's ability to communicate with and win agreement from all future beings who inherit the tradition's mode of living and enquiring (*Whose Justice?* 358).

This understanding generates and inextricably unites claims to immortality *and* to the acknowledgment of uncertain "vulnerability which is the trait of all worthwhile theorizing."[13] For historical beings never know (neither by Cartesian first principles nor by Hegelian absolute knowledge at "history's end") how their encounters will turn out. Their certitude is warranted only insofar as it is rooted in their repeated and honest exposures to those encounters that pose radical challenges to themselves—indeed, they are called to engage in as many vulnerable encounters as possible and to be sensitive to their tradition's inadequacies and distortions in these encounters. "The test for truth in the present . . . is always to summon up as many questions and as many objections of the greatest strength possible; what can be justifiably claimed as true is what has sufficiently withstood such dialectical questioning and framing of objections" (*Whose Justice?* 358).

It is in this context that one must understand MacIntyre's references to "the goods of conflict." Vulnerable engagements in conflicts among those within and between traditions are integral to a tradition's well-being, as Aquinas repeatedly exemplified in the way he engaged conflicting interpretations of Christian doctrine and the conflicts with Jewish, Islamic, and Aristotelian traditions. Contra Hilary Putnam,[14] who interprets MacIntyre as affirming the suppression of dissent, MacIntyre argues that communities ought to not only tolerate dissent but also have an "active and enquiring attitude towards radically dissenting views."[15]

Hence we begin to see how MacIntyre thinks that teleological modes of living and learning call forth community and bestow it with a distinct developing shape. At the most elementary level, "if we are to achieve an understanding of the good . . . we shall have to engage with other members of the community in which our learning has to go on" (*Three Rival Versions,* 136). This primordial apprehension is implicitly community *forming,* insofar as it draws us into dialogic relations of respect and mutuality that engender an incipient sense of natural law. Yet it also *exceeds* the bounds of particular communities and specific histories, for each community is drawn by this sense into relations in which it must vulnerably expose itself to the critical perspectives of other communities. In these relations, this community-forming force works upon larger spheres of human encounter, even as it often encounters here radical issues of violence and fragmented heterogeneity that render its meaning and direction more difficult to discern for long periods of time.

For MacIntyre, all genuine claims to be developing toward the good as such "commit those making them to hold that when that scheme encounters alternative standpoints making alternative and incompatible, even incommensurable, claims, Aquinas's dialectical synthesis will be able to render those standpoints intelligible in a way that cannot be achieved by their own adherents from their own point of view and to distinguish their defects and limitations from their insights and merits in such a way as to explain the occurrence of what they themselves would have to take to be their defects and limitations at points at which their own explanatory capacities are resourceless" (*Three Rival Versions,* 125). Yet this very confidence requires that we "render ourselves maximally vulnerable" to other traditions (181), for insofar as our rivals are *not* incoherent or we can*not* render their incoherence intelligible or our rivals actually shed valuable light upon our own shortcomings, our claim to superiority falters and must open to possibilities for revision or even rejection from the perspectives of other traditions.

The outcome of these encounters, or even that there will be an outcome rather than a seemingly interminable suspense, is never guaranteed: "For very long periods of time traditions do indeed seem to coexist without any . . . resolution" (*Whose Justice?* 366). Yet many developments may heighten the possibility of resolution one way or another. A tradition may become convinced that it can no longer develop because of the proliferation of incommensurable interpretations within the community. The knowledge tacit in its practices may reveal fundamental problems in its explicit conceptual frame. A new situation may arise before which it is impotent. An encounter with another tradition may unexpectedly disclose its weaknesses and the other's strength. Under these conditions of "epistemological crisis," a tradition is brought to submit itself to revision, and in extreme cases it might undergo a radical conversion to another tradition.

These dialogues and judgments, exercised in this intercultural realm, are particularly difficult. For traditions with a sense of the distinctness and contingency of their life and sense of truth will have little faith in what MacIntyre views as the cosmopolitan liberal fiction of universal translatability—let alone ideas of ahistorical neutral standards that might resolve disputes. They come to encounters uncertain of how far their ideas can be translated into the language of another community and uncertain of how well they will be able to translate vital insights of other communities into their own language. The task of understanding here becomes one of learning the language of another life and vision as a first language. This is a demanding task, but MacIntyre argues it is our only true hope. Hence, "a tradition becomes mature just insofar as its adherents confront and find a rational way through or around those encounters with radically different and incompatible positions which pose the problems of incommensurability and untranslatability" (*Whose Justice?* 327). Confidence may grow only through these encounters, and "only those whose tradition allows for the possibility of its hegemony being put in question can have rational warrant for asserting such hegemony" (388).[16]

## Imagining Utopic Terrain

MacIntyre has yet to offer a very textured sociopolitical articulation of what cultivating tradition might look like today. Clearly it involves an affirmation of particular traditions that cultivate distinct moral narratives and practices. Closest to him are Christian traditions, yet his project extends beyond them. For all his claims to be writing about tradition in a manner richly formed by the neo-Thomist tradition to which he belongs, a significant aspect of MacIntyre's embrace of Thomism is linked to the way he thinks it *exemplifies*—in its mode and substance—the traditioned character of human beings as such. Thus he claims to offer an account of the "rationality of tradition-constituted and tradition-constitutive enquiry" (*Whose Justice?* 9) in a much more general sense.[17] MacIntyre suspects that most traditions in "good order," whether those of Jews, Muslims, pre-nineteenth-century Hawaiians, or small isolated fishing villages, embody significant aspects of this mode of rationality—certainly far more than do modern liberal cosmopolitans. Even the tacit understandings embedded in the everyday practices of "plain persons" "are in fact and to a significant degree proto-Aristotelian."[18] It would be a good if these traditions and communities of people explicitly affirmed and robustly cultivated their particular teleological practices and enquiries rather than donning the detrimental garb of liberalisms that pretend to present a neutral, universal language of truth. Hence although MacIntyre takes the Thomistic account as the best so far, he embraces with a generous agonism other communities developing traditioned rationality in ways that have significant resonance at a metalevel.

Yet most of us are not and do not understand ourselves to be members of a single tradition. Rather, we "tend to live betwixt and between": liberals of sorts in the public sphere, while drawing upon fragments of a variety of traditions in other parts of our life (*Whose Justice?* 397). The suggestion that we, as vessels of a million "half convictions," cultivate deeply traditioned communities is not compelling for most. Another strategy is needed.

Perhaps ironically, MacIntyre offers his most defined vision in a transformation of that most liberal of modern institutions: the university. His hope is that if we can initiate spaces, sensibilities, and practices through which to cultivate particular traditioned rationalities and genuine contestation here, these might (through numerous political struggles) eventually spread to the public sphere and throughout society. As Kant sought over two hundred years ago to alter the public sphere by rearticulating the "Contest of the Faculties" in the university, MacIntyre today pursues a similar task, but no longer within the limits of a neutral reason alone. A transformed university might allow us to begin an indefinitely extended journey through our "cultural mélange" in such a way that we could fashion a set of more coherent and intelligent visions. For the foreseeable future, incommensurability and incoherence are so great that we should not expect to convince others. A more realistic goal would be to "render our disagreements more constructive" (*Three Rival Versions*, 8). The task is to articulate institutional practices that help us negotiate in a more intelligent and hopeful manner the very deep differences that are not going away any time soon.

Yet MacIntyre's "realism" here is less a compromise of his vision in the face of a recalcitrant situation and more a manifestation of a utopian spirit animating his project. His call for universities that house multiple distinct rival modes of enquiry is not so much "for lack of anything better"[19] as it is an exemplification of *ideal* coexistence.

On MacIntyre's reading, liberalism colonized the space that opened with the nineteenth-century abolition of religious tests in universities. Instead of an opening of education to a variety of competing modes of enquiry (of which liberalism was but one, alongside Thomism, Nietzschean genealogy, and others), there was a liberal vaporization of difference carried out through modes of appointment, enforced liberal norms of teaching and scholarship, and curriculum formation that disallowed pedagogical commitments to distinct larger frameworks—especially those aiming to organize collective modes of such enquiry. Within this order those who systematically challenge the substance and genres of liberal scholarship are not universally banned, but when they are admitted, according to MacIntyre, they are virtually forced to distort themselves in ways that make them ineffective contenders: for example, "Thomists" who argue for decontextualized fragments of arguments in *Summa*, "genealogists" drained of aphoristic style, everyone striving to express themselves in the currency of a neutral reason. This leads to a "university in disarray," unable to make advances on moral and political questions because it thwarts more-thoroughgoing contestations. This disarray, combined with the pressures of global capitalism, increasingly leads to the delegitimation of the humanities and qualitative sectors of the social sciences.

In contrast, MacIntyre advocates a university and public sphere with more space for "antagonistic dialogue," "radical dialogue" (*Three Rival Versions*, 221). Instead of the preliberal modern university of enforced agreement and the liberal ideal of the university of unconstrained agreements based on neutral reason, MacIntyre envisions the university as a place of "constrained disagreements, of imposed participation in conflict, in which the central responsibility of higher education would be to initiate students into conflict" (231). Here professors endorsing a particular framework would engage in hiring, curriculum development, and teaching within distinct sections, in a manner explicitly designed to express, cultivate, and advance this framework of enquiry. Although they would participate in intragroup dialogues concerning what this entails and although there would be latitude for diverging views within a framework, there would also be limits imposed—beyond which one could not go and still be a member of, for example, the Thomist faculty section. Members of particular pedagogical communities would also have obligations to engage in dialogues with other groups in order to examine critically other positions and their own. Additionally, each would participate, no longer as a partisan but as one interested in maintaining the university as a forum for fundamental conflicts, in the deliberative, university-wide governance structures that would fashion the ways the particular groups engage each other, identify and eliminate illegitimate suppression, articulate commonalties, and so forth. Ultimately, in addition to the rival structures within universities, rival universities would develop, markedly distinguished by differences in organization, substance, and style. For MacIntyre, the development of more-coherent articulations of different frameworks holds more promise for shedding light on the problems facing both particular traditions and wider societies. At the very least it would better illuminate the stakes among alternative modes of being and enquiry. MacIntyre suggests that transformed universities, unlike current ones, might become places where "the wider society can learn how to conduct its own debates, practical or theoretical, in a rationally defensible way" (*Three Rival Versions*, 222). Insofar as universities became institutions that could shed light on social, moral, political, economic, and theological questions, they might reclaim their legitimacy in the face of the question, "What are universities for?" This legitimacy, along with the various modes of rationality that would develop in the various spaces of higher education, might increasingly enable universities to challenge—instead of becoming tools for—a growing capitalist unreason.

MacIntyre is well aware of the tremendous distance between the conditions that "have made the liberal university so helpless in the face of its critics" and the conditions he imagines in his postliberal university. "The charge of utopianism, so it must appear, cannot be evaded" (*Three Rival Versions*, 234). Yet, he asks, what does this charge mean? What distance does it measure?: "The gap between Utopia and current social reality may on occasion furnish a measure, not of the lack of justification of Utopia, but rather of the degree to which those who not only inhabit contemporary social reality but insist upon seeing only what it allows them to see . . . cannot identify, let alone confront the problem which will be inscribed in their epitaphs. It may be therefore that the charge of utopianism is sometimes best understood more as a symptom of the condition of those who level it than an indictment of the projects against which it is directed" (235). Often, or perhaps always, it is only in proximity to a gap—a distance—that the confines of a given present can appear.

But how are we to identify and measure such small-mindedness in a manner that might reach compellingly beyond the limits of a single tradition? With this question, we are brought to one of the most important dimensions of MacIntyre's project. For the profoundest problem with "realists" is not the distance between their particular "present-bound" vision and some perspective that would critically illuminate it in the light of a preferable alternative; for ultimately, there is probably no tradition at any given time that would not be problematic in important ways, in relation to some perspective that would cast a similarly critical light upon it. Rather, the profoundest problem with "realists" concerns their relation to temporal distance as such—their inability to open themselves to and imaginatively engage with possible futures that exceed their current calculations. Hence, "those most prone to accuse others of utopianism are generally those . . . who pride themselves upon their pragmatic realism, who look for immediate results, who want the relationship between present input and future output to be predictable and measurable, and that is to say, a matter of the shorter, indeed the shortest run. They are the enemies of the incalculable, the skeptics about all expectations which outrun what they take to be hard evidence, the deliberately shortsighted who congratulate themselves upon the limits of their vision" (*Three Rival Versions*, 234). The small-minded are precisely the "enemies of the incalculable," those who would build their invulnerability to the future with overly "hard facts." Utopia illuminates the distance between those who would live enchained in their "measures," on the one hand, and those modes of living and learning rooted in a profound sense of historical finitude and future possibility, on the other. These latter are *many more than one*. Aware of this, MacIntyre cultivates a generous pluralizing vision in tandem with his increasingly specific articulation of tradition.

MacIntyre's "utopic" university thus valorizes those modes of being that harbor a certain generosity toward a future that exceeds the grasp of every present. This futural generosity, exemplified in the historical inexhaustibility of the Thomist telos that endlessly calls Thomist communities into critical dialogic quests and work upon themselves, is inextricably entwined with a generosity toward the present, exemplified by the vulnerable relations with those whose visions stand at a distance. MacIntyre expresses this generosity in his vision of a university that would afford his own tradition and rival modes spaces in which to develop through practices of relative autonomy and dialogic engagement with the others.

This dual vision is integral to MacIntyre's "utopic" mode of becoming in time. Each calls forth and requires the other, *for there is no real generosity toward the others without a sense that one's own present community does not yet possess a transparent calculation and grasp of the truth that remains futural for us; and there is no generous opening toward the future that is not born in and borne by the enlivened sense of finitude wrought by vulnerable engagements with others whose differences bring it vividly into the foreground.* Thus, in MacIntyre's reconceptualization the university should be viewed less as a practical application than as an exemplary embodiment of the core idea.

Here the double valence of utopia—signifying both the "ideal" and "nowhere"—takes on special significance. Most profoundly, the ideal, as linked to a future that is not yet and a temporality that is becoming, is to be found fully nowhere. Or at least, it is not confined to a place but, rather, manifests itself in the mode of dwelling in the *tensions between* different places, whether these be differences within a community or between diverse communities. This ideal comes into being only through practices recognizing that it is not exhausted anywhere and that it is in perfection nowhere. It is our hope for creating places of flourishing—*eu topos*—that work to rid territories of territoriality. The *eu* that *joins* the ideal to nowhere would be the condition of the work of *separating* the *terra* (the earth as nurturing sustenance) that is one root of "territory" from the *terrare* (terror, war, exclusion) that is another. Hence MacIntyre's vision of flourishing, at its best, moves between images of specific places and modes of questing toward the good, on the one hand, and a searching eye for the more displaced, radically interrogative, and indeterminate places *between* the modes he calls his own and those other spaces of practice whose efforts at thriving he would support and critically engage, on the other.

## The Confidence Trickster

Franz Kafka tells a story of a person who is continually undermined by a voice, the "confidence trickster," that erodes the confidence necessary to face the basic challenges of life, let alone to live a flourishing one.[20] The trickster can change form—to undermine this confidence and that confidence—so it is not easy to resist.

Perhaps all modes of power manufacture this confidence trickster to thwart both the emergence of and the receptivity to those who would call them into question. All efforts toward more promising ethical and political paths must cultivate resources for responding to and resisting this trickster—especially insofar as these alternatives emerge from peoples most subjected to powers that have deployed this trickster to undermine solidarities, visions, faiths, and capacities for action.

However, like all tricksters, the confidence trickster is a shape-shifter that moves in most surprising ways toward unpredictable ends. Hence it happens (writing now a companion to Kafka's story) that the confidence trickster frequently morphs, when we least suspect it, into forms that undermine our highest aspirations and flourishing, not through the erosion but the inflation of our confidence. Kafka depicts a trickster that undermines by vitiating our capacities for form-giving force; we must also be wary of the way *this same trickster* can undermine our movement by so enhancing this force of confidence that we become rigid, unreceptive, "rigormortic." Looking back, we can see the effects of this trickster at work in political liberalism. Although MacIntyre recognizes some of these effects and articulates compelling modes of response to them, his own texts nevertheless profoundly illustrate the work of the trickster, turning MacIntyre's resistance toward the trickster's own end by drawing hubris from humility, tragedy from the movement of transcendence. MacIntyre's efforts sketched above are by no means completely defeated, yet his corpus is marked at key points by a problematic loss of suppleness and receptivity—and it appears to be the work of this trickster.

Recall that in MacIntyre's heuristic account of the development of a tradition, a stage of more contingently given beliefs and practices is followed by a stage in which confidence is challenged as it is put in question. Insofar as a tradition can successfully respond to these challenges, a stage of "reformulation" follows. As these stages alternate in ongoing developments, understandings of truth as transparent possession give way to teleological accounts of truth as that toward which a tradition moves. Correctly understood, this leads to vulnerable, risk-taking engagements with the questions and alternatives coming from both within and beyond a community. Central to intelligently negotiating such encounters is a cultivated sense of the possible inadequacies of one's tradition and an ability to listen well. Only if a tradition develops in this manner can it gain a legitimate self-confidence. But a tradition *can* gain this confidence, and if it develops in Thomistic fashion, it *does and should* gain it—and in no small quantity.

"At every stage beliefs and judgments will be justified by reference

to the beliefs and judgments of the previous stage, and insofar as a tradition has constituted itself as a successful form of enquiry, the claims
to truth made within that tradition will always be in some specifiable
way less vulnerable to dialectical questioning and objection than were
their predecessors" (*Whose Justice?* 359). At one level this is simply a
"specifiable" claim: A tradition can point to the challenges to which
it has successfully responded and is no longer vulnerable. Yet the specifiable nurtures a more general and pervading sensibility. "Their warranted confidence in their own tradition will of course increase as their
tradition shows itself in successive encounters able to furnish the necessary resources and achieve the necessary transformations" (*Whose
Justice?* 327).[21] This confidence has a generality that exceeds its sense
of its past and projects itself toward the future and the others it will
encounter as time unfolds.

Concerning the future, a tradition's growing confidence diminishes its
sense of the significance of the distance between itself and the good
toward which it aims. Hence, after noting that neo-Thomists must admit
the inadequacies of their knowledge concerning "our ultimate end" and
even more so concerning the "divine nature," MacIntyre immediately
says, "It is important, however, not to exaggerate this inadequacy." This
inadequacy only concerns our ultimate end, "*not at all* in respect of its
sufficiency in specifying how we ought to act" (my emphasis). The way
of practical enquiry is known by a rational tradition without such inadequacies, and "at every stage in this practical enquiry we have a knowledge of our good adequate to guide us further" (*Whose Justice?* 193).

Yet just how confident should any tradition be that its knowledge
of the good is adequate to guide us further? Might not the history of
human encounter and the finitude of our knowing show us that most
often current knowledge of the good is significantly inadequate to the
tasks of going further? Are we not, most of the time, significantly in
need of transfigurative learning from the others with whom we struggle,
in order to go forward at all? Does MacIntyre's affirmation of vulnerability to the *possibility* of coming up short in encounters with other
traditions sufficiently articulate the posture we ought to bring to such
engagements? Or ought we not also to cultivate a sense of the *likelihood* of coming up short in some respects, the *likelihood* that we will
learn crucial things from these others who see the world so differently?
Lacking this sense—and bolstered by "confidence"—declarations of fallibility can function more as an alloy of superiority in one's shield against
the others than as an opening. There is a likelihood that, with care,
we also will have much to offer. But might not the difficult-to-sustain

vulnerability necessary for transformative giving and receiving be radically compromised by MacIntyre's confidence that his tradition's inadequacies are as relatively insignificant as he suggests? What does such
confidence do to one's ears?

MacIntyre's sense is that it sharpens them. And the larger part of
his efforts foreground and cultivate the sources of this confidence.
Hence, related to the confidence that grows with temporal progress,
MacIntyre affirms what one might call a "confidence of systematic-
ity." He affirms that "Aquinas's procedures entitled him, on many
occasions at least, to place more rational confidence in the answers
which he gave to particular questions than is provided by the particular arguments he adduces. . . . Aquinas was engaged in an overall
work of dialectical construction in the *Summa* in which every element
. . . contributes to the order of the whole. Thus conclusions in one part
of the structure may and do confirm conclusions reached elsewhere"
(*Whose Justice?* 172).

An eye for systematizing and coherence can have beneficial effects
and is indeed indispensable for our cognitive powers, and sometimes
a confidence grows in relation to these that is not without its good reasons. Yet the will to system is also a curse, as Adorno, who at the same
time deeply appreciated the power of systematizing, so profoundly
showed. The will to system can be a mode of imposition: a will to fit
incommensurable things into an order for which they were not designed; a self-propelling engine of oblivion, as each part—confirming
and confirmed by the others—contributes to a growing framework,
confidence, and power that is increasingly deaf and difficult to resist.
Of course, MacIntyre aims to check *this* type of systematizing by
repeatedly engaging all other available arguments. Yet I suggest that
retrospectives on our systematizing efforts and confidence powerfully
suggest that the two types of practice and confidence are frequently
entangled and confused and are extremely difficult to distinguish. If
this confusion (to which we are more prone the more confident we become) is among the most characteristic features of our condition, then
we might do better to cultivate an ambivalence toward the will to system, both employing it and criticizing it. We might do well to cultivate
a studied asceticism toward the seductive confidence boosters that
accompany the growth of systems. Perhaps the ethico-epistemological
task most needed, especially the further we proceed in systematizing,
is to resist an affirmative hubristic relationship with them. Is not sys-
tematicity most suspect at the moment it gives its nod of assent to—
and thereby receives energy from—this trickster?

Often oblivious to these insights, MacIntyre forges paths of reassurance that have dangerous implications. Nurtured by and nurturing the growth in confidence is a tendency to frame the past problems of one's tradition as entirely extrinsic to what is central to it. Hence, for example, the paradoxical fact that at its height Aquinas's systematic project "largely disappears" is not taken as an occasion for critical reflection about whether there were ways in which something central to the project was implicated in this disappearance (for example, did the growing "warranted" confidence and power ultimately overwhelm even the systemizing that nurtured them?). Instead, this fact is narrated simply as a defeat due to "the power of the institutionalized curriculum" (*Three Rival Versions,* 150–51).

MacIntyre cultivates a radical "commitment" regarding all other traditions that is similarly problematic: The "Augustinian is . . . committed to [one central negative thesis:] that no substantive rationality, independent of faith, will be able to provide an adequate vindication of its claims . . . [that] each in its own historical development will exhibit its own failure . . . incoherence or resourcelessness" (*Three Rival Versions,* 101–2). Now, for MacIntyre, this commitment does not simply articulate a confidence but also makes Augustinians vulnerable, insofar as the long-term success of other traditions would tend to call the Augustinian tradition radically into question. Yet this construal of hubris as vulnerability ignores the temporal asymmetry between the confident commitment and the vulnerability. The commitment is vital, for Augustinians, *in each present moment* of encounter. The vulnerability, however, is in relation to a "prediction" of a future that "will" occur (ibid.). This vulnerability has a futural index, and as such it is endlessly deferrable. Thus the commitment energizes ungenerous readings of other traditions in the present while laying claim to a "vulnerability" that can actually feed the unreceptive confidence of we-who-are-better-than-the-others-because-we-are-vulnerable.

This process has effects far beyond epistemology, having also ethical and political effects. As the Augustinian tradition developed, MacIntyre writes, "There were elaborated large agreements [and corresponding confidences] in interpretation, so that the onus placed upon dissenting interpretation became progressively more difficult to discharge" (*Three Rival Versions,* 84). Of course, *questiones* were also identified and disputed, yet these rested upon a set of "large agreements" held confidently and protected in ways increasingly difficult to challenge. Hence, as the tradition gains increasing confidence in its agreements and recognizes that its projected direction hinges upon them, it confidently employs a variety of pedagogical and disciplinary techniques to secure its progress toward truth. Although MacIntyre recognizes that errors and injustices were committed by the guardians of practical inquiry, he nevertheless unambiguously affirms practices of "enforced exclusions . . . preferments and promotions" (224) to secure a necessarily extensive area of unquestioned agreement. Because the teleological development of reason requires "membership in a particular type of moral community, one from which fundamental dissent has to be excluded" (60), "intervening authorities" are necessary (91). Central to such intervention is the idea that our will "is initially perverse and needs a kind of redirection which will enable it to trust obediently in a teacher who will guide the mind. . . . Hence faith in authority has to precede rational understanding. . . . humility is the necessary first step in education" (84). This has significant implications not only for the prerational ordering of dispositions in the pedagogy of children but also for the operation of authority in the hierarchical institutions of the tradition as well: "It was clearly pride of will which Bernard discerned in Abelard and which Abelard acknowledged by his submission that he discerned in himself. So it is the underlying epistemology of Augustinian enquiry which requires the condemnation of heresy, since heresy is always a sign of pride in choosing to elevate one's own judgment above that of genuine authority. It was then the exercise of authority and the recognition accorded to authority which prevented the development of dialectical argument from fracturing the unity of enquiry into a multitude of disagreements" (91).

No doubt authority plays an integral role in pedagogy and enquiry, a role that is often veiled by myths of an unconstrained development of reason. Authority and constraint—always present—are not simply bad things, and it is important to listen for and recognize ways they are used and operate within modes of being and becoming we embrace, as well as within those we do not. I think one of the key—very paradoxical—challenges today is to discover modes of cultivating both practices that grant a certain authority to (and within) radicalizing and pluralizing democracy *and* dispositions that might aid us in receptively engaging those peoples and modes of becoming that yearn otherwise. This is no easy task, and it requires complex arts, many of which have yet to be invented. Yet *with and against* MacIntyre, this dual and tension-laden task illuminates the weaknesses of a too strongly teleological tradition of practical enquiry. Significant portions of MacIntyre's work articulate the way that risk, vulnerability, and more-radical contestation are necessary for any teleology laying claim to rationality and justice. (And precisely in this light, the mutually intensifying circuits of cognitive development, confidence, commitment, and associated practices of pedagogy, authority, and disciplinary intervention appear extremely problematic.) It is difficult to imagine *how* selves and communities fashioned in as thoroughly a teleological mode as MacIntyre suggests would be capable of, let alone well-prepared for, receptively engaging the conflictive terrain of human history and plurality that he himself sometimes profoundly and generously illuminates. And it is difficult to discern *why*, in light of his sharpest insights, he would affirm practices that are as disciplinary and ungenerous as his sometimes appear to be.

Perhaps, then, one must look at more than simply the theoretical arguments to discover some of the sources that drive this dimension of his account. For the theoretical aspects of his work that accent his most rigidly teleological visions do not simply engender the visceral dimension of a tremendous confidence in one's community, a deep commitment to the expectation of others' erring, particular feelings of humility in relation to authority and discipline, and so on. They are *also engendered by* this visceral-perceptual stance at work in the tradition MacIntyre affirms. This visceral-perceptual dimension is nowhere more evident than in the practices that MacIntyre points to in some recent works to illuminate and exemplify characteristics of solidarity, moral agency, virtue, and disciplined practice: the occupations of deep-sea fishing and the Marines.[22] His account of these contexts is fascinating in part because of the way they help him to deftly give flesh to themes of risk, sacrifice, recognition of common goods, justice, focused reflective desire, and the character of limited but real disagreement. Yet these examples are entangled with a perceptual-affective relation to our condition that is *also* highly problematic. And if being "thoughtful" is, as he claims, "to be unwilling to allow thought to rest content with unscrutinized metaphors or unidentified presuppositions, especially when these function as obstacles to further moral inquiry," then nothing more deserves scrutiny here.[23]

Deep-sea fishing and the Marines are occupations that viscerally shape our sense of the terms "practice" and "craft." They conjure images of deeply and positively consensual practices. If one instead employs practices like, for example, political philosophy, or guitar playing from Andrés Segovia to Jimi Hendrix, or politics, then risk, sacrifice, conflict, and goods are infused with far less concordant images, and in turn our affective responses to many kinds of strife or to robust celebrations of commonness or to the imposition of limits by authorities can shift in dramatic ways. MacIntyre's occupations profoundly work the affective level because each is constituted in radical proximity to the most visceral of the visceral: our sense of extreme danger. Marines train for the hazards of war and the goods of winning. Fishing, as MacIntyre emphasizes, is America's most dangerous industry. It is precisely in relation to these great dangers that the desirability and necessity of an agreed-upon ranking of goods, merit, system of authority, and so on are most pronounced. Danger mobilizes and valorizes this coalescence. A jealous God or a jealous reason casts the recalcitrant world in the singular image of danger, and this dangerousness, in turn, sustains the directions, limits, and disciplines of one's chosen jealousy. MacIntyre, I suspect, would not confess to having an allegiance to a jealous God or rationality, yet he not infrequently seems to remain significantly entangled in an affective response to the world in which otherness appears most fundamentally dangerous. Such entanglement is not easily escaped, because the perception of danger that sustains rigid teleological practices becomes an insistent affective response that the latter generate in turn. The *practices* of direction, exclusion, and discipline stimulate (long after the *thematized* jealousies that helped engender them become less compelling and less pronounceable) an affective propensity to continue to perceive the surrounding world as dangerous: These practices tend to generate "the dangerous" as an ongoing condition of their own desirability. Radical dissent will thus be imaged as heresy; heresy will be viewed as the most dangerous of things: pride; asystematicity will be imagined simply as self-destruction; the "others" will be viewed as bound to failure. *Integral to sustaining a sensibility in which these ideas make sense—as their condition and their effect—are analogies that intensify our sense of the dangerous (the abyss of battle, the abyss of the sea) in proximity to our discussions of moral goods.*

To critically scrutinize these analogies is not simply to dismiss them. With Foucault, I believe that "everything is dangerous." And ethical life must certainly cultivate our capacities to respond to danger. But the question, with Foucault again, is to consider what the greatest dangers are.[24] And what Foucault realized, more consistently than did MacIntyre, is that the teleologies, authorities, and disciplines that we embrace and that embrace us are likely to be every bit as dangerous (or more so) as much of the otherness they mark as the worst. This implies that we might do better to cultivate a relation to danger in the *tension* between teleological and ateleological responsiveness, as I develop more fully in the following chapters. We might seek both to mobilize perceptions, judgments, dispositions, virtues, and practices that seem most beneficial for pursuing recognized goods and justice—and resisting recognized dangers—and to mobilize paradoxically in ways that call us more vulnerably to question and let be questioned our teleologies: to cultivate radical stances of irony, humor, and patience, in which the directions we embrace can be relaxed intermittently so we might listen for damages and possibilities difficult to hear. MacIntyre might have learned more than he has about this from the likes of Foucault, Derrida, and Gilles Deleuze had he not, with an exemplary confidence and commitment, read them in a way that doomed them to the sin of hubristic willfulness and failure to which his narrative at some of its worst moments insists all others must come.

I do not mean to imply that this paradoxical task to which I think we are called is easy (it isn't) or that it could receive any final articulation (it can't) or that each side of the tension does not, in part, threaten to weaken the other (each does). Nor do I wish to embrace the indecisiveness that MacIntyre rightly criticizes for being among the all-too-familiar unhelpful modes of moral posturing today. My point is simply that efforts to reflect upon ethical life that do not take this paradox very seriously—efforts that try to turn away from negotiating the tensions between the teleological and the ateleological—magnify the dangers that we will be deaf and violent in our relations with others who resist the teleologies we embrace. My wager is that these dangers are consistently greater than those that surely accompany the ethics of *traditio* I am proposing in this book.

### Conclusion

The task then, is to try to learn from what is wisest in MacIntyre's writing (concerning, for example, the desirable aspects of specific teleological rationalities, virtues, and practices, and the vulnerability at the heart of compelling teleologies), so that these insights can be juxtaposed with more ateleological sensibilities and practices in a tensional ethical-political stance. At his best, MacIntyre articulates a teleological project that is both directed and significantly vulnerable to other traditions. I have suggested ways that this project can and does sometimes slide into a more dogmatic and disciplinary posture. But a strong argument could be made that such a slide is not inevitable and that a more compelling teleological position could be reformulated to better resist it. This is the "MacIntyre" I wish to carry forth in the chapters that follow: a MacIntyre who affirms a strong teleological position with a greater reflective awareness of and resistance to some of the dangers I have identified in his work. This MacIntyre is one from whom my learning is never finished. This MacIntyre is a ghost who haunts my project with the specter of a strongly traditional account that has significant vulnerability to other traditions as a constitutive dimension of its self-understanding and practices. My guess is that even this MacIntyre insufficiently cultivates ateleological sensibilities. Yet the vision of tradition that he offers has a decisiveness of shape, direction, and practical capacity that affords benefits as well as dangers. To be haunted by this MacIntyre is to let ourselves be made uncomfortable and solicited by the important challenge of cultivating many of these advantages and of endlessly working both to be cognizant of and to reduce the comparative losses that will surely threaten a position that, like mine, cultivates paradoxical tension at the heart of its sensibility and practices. We will perhaps, even probably, not do as well as MacIntyre in some dimensions. The task is to allow ourselves to be haunted so we do not end up doing so much worse that other possibilities we might offer are offset to the point where they become undesirable.

Before moving to philosophical and practical positions closer to my own, I wish to turn to the work of Yoder, who offers a vision of Christianity that pushes a practice of tradition closer to *traditio*—and haunts me more—than does the work of most thinkers I know.

# 4

# The Wild Patience of John Howard Yoder

ANY LIBERALS AND CHRISTIANS share a profoundly impoverished imagination of how people might live well amid others who are radically different from themselves. Many early liberals, like Locke and John Stuart Mill, resisting other odious forms of power, nevertheless proliferated a series of stories that directly or indirectly legitimated the violent exclusion of many peoples and ways of life from the charmed circle of rational beings entitled to a serious hearing in the developing "democratic" spheres of deliberation, governance, and colonization. I have argued that this basic strategy (though now less violent and more inclusive in some important respects) remains strong and finds one of its most powerful articulations in political liberalism's effort to define before the event the general principles that will guide and exclusively limit all legitimate democratic discourse and practice in pluralistic polities. "Public reason" is the mantra of those engaged in this effort, and "comprehensive doctrine" is the symbol for what is morally to be excluded from the voices and ears of all good citizens.

In recent centuries, many Christians, waking up to the violence wrought by their own a priori condemnations of nonbelievers, have sought to cultivate more-charitable relationships with those outside Christianity. Most often, these efforts are articulated through forms of liberal tolerance of all modes of faith and faithlessness so long as their particularity remains in the nonpolitical sphere and their voices in the public political sphere are strictly limited in substance to what can be affirmed by the public reason "we all share." Of course, evoking God and Scripture is fine, but only insofar as it is done according to the terms and within the limits of the purported basic consensus. Many familiar modes of Christian resistance to these (often unacknowledged) liberal exclusions take the form of resurgent fundamentalisms, which, while they certainly transgress the closures of political liberalism, appear to offer alternatives that would only return polities to worse exclusions. And so we often witness contestations to and fro between Christians who offer a bland ecumenicism and tolerance according to a liberalism that is often complicitous with—or very weak in its resistance to—odious forms of power and suffering, on the one hand, and Christians who offer fundamentalisms that are violent and eschew all dialogue, on the other. In chapter 3 I argued that MacIntyre's neo-Thomism takes significant strides toward offering an alternative to this dichotomy but that serious problems remain.

As a member of no church, I come to questions of other possibilities from the flickering shards of episodic traditions of radical democratic struggles for more-generous and more-receptive heterogeneous communities. Thus my effort to discuss outsiders and the otherness of the church will strike many as strange, and my focus on John Howard Yoder in this context, stranger yet. I must admit to sharing the first sense of strangeness, for at times in this chapter I find myself heralding a Christian body politic that is at once too close to measure and infinitely remote. I remain as puzzled as anyone by this (im)possibility, and I am astonished by anyone generous enough to listen. Perhaps I am sublimely drawn in terror and attraction to the utter lack of authority of my voice in this place at these moments. To escape the insufferable authoritative posture of academic writing is no small allure. But surely that is not all.

More importantly, I find in Yoder's writings a vision of dialogical communities that brings forth very particular and powerful practices of generous solidarity precisely *through* creative uses of conflict and a vulnerable receptivity to the "least of these" within the church and to those outside it. In fact, few today offer as compelling a vision for pursuing justice and political engagements in heterogeneous societies.

Yoder is a Mennonite. When Mennonites emerged as a minority radical reformation denomination in the sixteenth century, many other Christians agreed upon at least one thing: Mennonites should be killed. They practiced adult baptism out of a sense that the church was in important ways a voluntary community. They practiced dialogical discernment. They were aloof from coercive state power. They dressed plainly, in opposition to the semiotics of power-laden distinctions. They were pacifists. They practiced excommunication of those who violated these and other practices. These people were not good for the dominant machineries of economic, political, military, and religious power of their day.

Today there are Mennonites of many stripes, and they believe many different things, often quite different from what Yoder believes. For Yoder, being a Mennonite Christian involves belonging to a church incarnating a politics that proclaims "Jesus is Lord." This involves, among other things, complex and discerning practices of pacifism, eucharistic sharing of wealth in production and consumption, a refusal to try to "put handles on history" through coercive state power in order to mold the world to one's vision, and a commitment to the church as a community that engages otherness within and beyond its walls in a radically dialogical and vulnerable fashion. Yoder's church engages the work of reconciliation with an imagination oriented toward forgiveness, repentance, and a profound sense of the world as an abundant gift that should be received from God in the spirit of Jesus Christ. What most interests me about Yoder in the context of this book are the ways he combines bearing evangelical witness to his confessedly provincial tradition with vulnerable and receptive dialogical practices with others. Indeed, these latter practices are integral to the witness itself. Witness simply and literally makes no sense at all apart from receiving others with a radical vulnerability. As Yoder develops these themes, he articulates a theology of traditioning that addresses in a most profound manner many of the problems I identified in MacIntyre.

If one reads Yoder through the lens of an Ernst Troeltsch, a Reinhold Niebuhr, or a Rawls, one will find only a "sectarian" who offers nothing valuable for developing potent resistance to evil in the wider society or for engaging with receptive generosity those from deeply different traditions or fragments of traditions. If one reads Yoder through the lens of, say, a MacIntyre, one will do better but perhaps still miss a lot. Beyond these crafted misreadings there are other possibilities, and I try to trace a few below.

I think it is wrong to understand Yoder's affirmation of "the otherness of the church" and his call to "let the church be the church" as a turn away from engaging the world. I do not mean simply that the church as Yoder understands it is always deeply engaged with the world and (as he put it, following Jeremiah) "for the nations" in multiple ways, ranging from critical resistance, to community practices embodying and proclaiming an alternative Gospel ethics, to the flexible experimentation of a minority community in ways that often have broader implications and uses, to selective tactical alliances and forms of cooperation with other groups, and so forth. These are, of course crucial to Yoder, and they reveal the error of the "sectarian" charge. Nor do I simply mean that the church as Yoder understands it, far from pursuing a retreat into sectarian purity, homogeneity, and imposed harmony, engages the "worldliness" of the world—its inchoate aspects, complexity, heterogeneity, discordance—insofar as it is a body of endlessly unfolding manifold differences drawn into cooperation and creative uses of conflict through reconciling dialogical practices. This too is true and important, and it illustrates ways the church might be good news for the world precisely because it provides compelling modes of response to the world's murky, multifarious messiness. Yet it does not quite hit the registers I seek most to engage. Indeed, paradoxically and frightfully, theories that proclaim to be the best possible internally differentiated or differentiating communities (in Christian, liberal, and many other forms) have often been marshaled to bolster an absolute a priori privileging of their own orientations and limits and a corresponding deafness to all difference outside. The obliteration of difference in the name of difference is as familiar as aggressive war in the name of peace. I would even guess (to pronounce a horizon that this chapter strives, *with* Yoder's articulations of vulnerability and patience, to resist) that all forms of such invulnerable privileging of one's own church and community—no matter how internally dialogical and differentiated, no matter how generously "for the nations" they seek to be, no matter how much they eschew practices of warfare—will, finally and in spite of themselves, slide toward postures at war with outsideness as such.[1]

Yoder treads along other, richer paths; his vines grow in other ways. Of course, he too writes that the dialogical "church precedes the world epistemologically" and "axiologically."[2] But he understands this stance as the church's condition for engaging the world generously and with a receptive vulnerability. In other words, he interprets the binding centrality of the lordship of Christ as the opening of dialogical relations between the church and the world in which giving and receiving is possible. Thus I will argue that vulnerable relations with outsiders are integral to the otherness of the church and that when this understanding of *caritas* is forgotten and unpracticed, the church loses its otherness and is assimilated to the violence of the world. When Christians cease to engage outsiders with receptive generosity, they cease to let the church be the church; they lose sight of Jesus as Lord.

Anyone familiar with Yoder's writing will already observe the work of translation in my essay. This is, on Yoder's terms and mine, what must occur in any particular encounter, and it opens up hopeful possibilities and risks. I have tried to avoid the latter and to pursue the former through a variety of strategies. I have tried to let ring throughout the very specific language of Jesus and Scripture that provides the root from which Yoder's efforts grow and to which they always return. Simultaneously, I have entwined with these melodies contrapuntal phrasings that translate and *develop* it with terms drawn from the radical democratic struggles, theorizing, and concerns that I bring to the engagement.[3] In translating and developing, I have attempted to let Yoder's work inflect and transfigure the language closest to me with his meanings, and I know I have done the reverse as well—sometimes in ways that I do not know. By juxtaposing these two languages, neither uncontaminated by nor reducible to the other, I have tried to present some of what each might learn from the other. Each voice discovers a new yet strangely familiar sound. At the same time, the juxtaposition of their distinct terms also creates throughout some dissonance, some of which I discuss toward the end of the chapter. In this explicit lack of fit, I hope to keep alive a sense of the differences and thus alert readers to damages unwittingly imposed so that readers might creatively attend to them in the name of a more receptive generosity, the body politic of Jesus, or something yet unsung from which we all might learn. In the final section, "Reaching Back and Breaking Forth/Off/In/Out?" I sketch some of the differences that most disturb and haunt the positions with which I was more comfortable prior to my engagement with Yoder. Yoderians might well develop some ghosts for Yoderians.

My inquiry here, however, leads me to attend to Yoder *as* ghost, and, as much as possible, not to exorcise him so as to resume a slumber.

To write of ghosts, however, is not identical to being one. And this again raises the question of from where, as a member of no church, I embark upon this tensional journey with Yoder. People with self-understandings similar to my own will mightily resist affirming a stable and definitive location of authorship. We view our locations as multiple, shifting, and changing—we are uncomfortable nearly everywhere. Yet I do not write from nowhere, and it is in fact my engagements in radical democratic coalition politics that greatly shape my interests in, perspectives upon, and questioning with Yoder. As a member of an enduring progressive grassroots social movement (Peoples' Alliance) and as an active participant in a broader, multiracial, diverse coalition of religious congregations, social movements, and community and neighborhood associations in Durham, North Carolina (an Industrial Areas Foundation affiliate), I am interested in practical and theoretical modes of engagement that can contribute to enriching

democratic dialogue and action among groups with many deep differences. Within our coalition, we are diversely striving to create a
public space in which heterogeneous, community-specific narratives of
suffering and hope can be given voice and receptively engaged. Most
groups within the coalition seek to fashion their participation in a
manner that at once strengthens their particular community and tra-
dition(s) and at the same time enhances their ability to listen better
to and learn from the very different narratives of suffering and hope
brought forth by other specific communities. Together, we (and similar coalitions across the United States) are groping toward a form of
urban power that cultivates direction through a combination of heterogeneous voices and powerfully receptive ears. We are inspired, both
by our different traditions and emergent struggles and by the possibilities of our being in common, to cultivate a more generous and receptive form of democratic power—to cultivate our particular and
intersecting histories in directions that will enhance our capacities to
engage in this good work and good news. These are quintessentially
Yoderian concerns, and few people are more illuminating than Yoder
concerning these issues. I read Yoder to learn better what this project
might mean and require. I read Yoder to raise questions where I believe
his thinking might impede these tasks. And I read Yoder in an effort
to cultivate in myself an appreciation for the distinct powers for such
engagement that stem precisely from a tradition that I do not call my
own. At the limit, I read Yoder in an effort to hear good powers that
may, in some registers, exemplify admirable and even crucial capacities that people closer to me have as yet been unable to match.

## These Are a Few of My/His Favorite Things
## (To Be Sung As If John Coltrane Were a Mennonite)

Eschewing both religious and secular claims to represent with certain
superiority a universal movement and meaning in history—a meaning
that would continue to progress only if "we" impose upon the future
"the good way our recent past has taken," Yoder offers a position that
"is most openly and respectfully, repentantly and doxologically aware
of particular historical identity" (*Priestly Kingdom,* 3). Yoder's Christianity (resonating with a theme in MacIntyre on this point) understands itself as "a goal-oriented movement through time." But whereas
Constantinian Christianity and political liberalism would move into
the future by delegitimating their others at the outset and then imposing (openly or in ways less visible) upon all who would resist the linear extension of their most "progressive" present, Yoder suggests that

there is no worthy directionality that would not repeatedly have to pass through vulnerable encounters with other directions and indirections. There would be no church worth its name without both teleological (directional) and ateleological (concerning the unanticipatable) virtues and practices.[4] For beyond the tepid proclamations of a possible falli-bility, the posture of radical reformation asserts that "any existing church is not only fallible but in fact peccable. That is why there needs to be a constant potential for reformation and in the more dramatic situations a readiness for the reformation even to be 'radical'" (*Priestly Kingdom*, 5).[5] With contemporary Deleuzians, he resists the arboreal imagination. "Far from being an ongoing growth like a tree (or a fam-ily tree) the wholesome growth of a tradition is like a vine: a story of constant interruption of organic growth in favor of a pruning and a new chance for the roots" (*Priestly Kingdom*, 69).

Yoder seeks to renew a Christian "hermeneutics of peoplehood" — a radically dialogical conception of church practices of discernment — in light of a "Protestant perspective," only to note immediately that the latter has no affirmative historical center that might illuminate its discordant manifestations. "Its common marks are negative": a sense that in the history of Christianity "something had gone wrong"; "a fundamental skepticism about what everybody everywhere always thought"; a "challenge." In contrast to narratives that claim to pos-sess sovereignty by securing a continuous relation to an authorizing origin, "Jesus is Lord" is the solicitation to a "perennially unfinished process of critiquing the developed tradition from the perspective of its own roots" (*Priestly Kingdom*, 15–17). The scriptural accountabil-ity thus evoked does not signify a naive sense of transparency and a self-righteous possession of a truth that has been or can be completely restored beyond historical contingency. Rather, the wisdom of the cross that teaches *"semper reformanda"* calls communities to open to the future by way of a never completed movement of dispossession. The church does not possess the origin — Jesus Christ — like a "proposition . . . which we *hold* to be authoritative and to be exempted from the relativity of hermeneutical debate." Nor can the church escape the "need to be corrected . . . as if our link to our origins were already *in our own hands*" (*Priestly Kingdom*, 70, my emphasis). Rather, the normativeness of Jesus works primarily to "deny absolute authority to any later epoch, especially to the present." It illuminates that all is not well and calls for "midcourse correction," "reorienting our pre-sent movement forward in light of what was wrong" (*Priestly King-dom*, 87).

But how would this Gospel *root* that illuminates always-particular dissonances, discontinuities, dispossessions, and renewals within the tradition finally avoid being simply another standard (or method) beyond history, a standard that would endow with fundamentalist authority those who speak and act monologically in its name to critique the world around them? And if it was conceived simply as such an authority, might it not then more fundamentally close than open Christians' relation to history and all outsiders—thus resembling the very Constantianism (by which he means, in simple terms, all efforts to take "control" of history) that Yoder has so profoundly taught Christians to resist? If Yoder escapes this trap, it is because he understands the church's relation to Jesus as the very incarnation of practices of becoming vulnerable to encounter with the otherness of history—the exemplary possibility of dialogical liberty; or, perhaps better, the exemplary breaking forth of the ways and the desirability of such responsive freedom.

To understand Yoder here we must carefully explore his account of the relationship between "reaching back" to Scripture and practices of vulnerable welcoming. As we reach back, he writes, "what we find at the origin is already a process of reaching back again to the origins, to the earliest memories of the event itself, confident that that testimony, however intimately integrated with the belief of the witnesses . . . will serve to illuminate and sometimes adjudicate our present path" (*Priestly Kingdom*, 70). Scripture offers "the early communities' recording and interpreting [Jesus's] words in the ongoing process of defining the meaning of obedience" in their time (116). The meaning of Jesus's teaching does not stand out all by itself but can emerge only in dialogic discernment of those early communities inspired in his memory. Similarly, "the free-church alternative . . . recognizes the inadequacies of . . . Scripture standing alone uninterpreted . . . [and] locates the fulfillment of that promise [of the guidance of spirit] in the assembly of those who gather around Scripture in the face of a given real moral challenge" (117). Thus truth is always a finite historical incarnation. For Yoder what might endure is a community of vulnerable dialogic practices responsive to Jesus in their reaching back to Scripture for illumination; one that might allow truth to manifest itself ever anew in the specificities of historical encounter and discernment. Even if the early church was "fallible, divided, confused," the "structural soundness" of its major teachers lay significantly in their elaboration of such practices (129).

Yoder spent a lifetime discerning this church epistemology of disciplined vulnerability and cultivated "expectation of newness" (*Priestly*

*Kingdom*, 38). I shall only very briefly summarize a few of the most important aspects and then flesh them out in light of the concerns raised at the beginning of this chapter.

For Yoder, the good news of Christ's generosity finds expression in the literal body of the church community. But of what sort of unity does this body partake? What unity does it seek? Yoder emphatically rejects notions of church unity based upon extant agreements that would provide a lowest-common-denominator foundation for identity, direction, and tolerable pluralism. Such understandings tend to construe every serious dispute as a call for division. To avoid such division, they then often paper over difference in ways that avoid questions and contestations crucial to the vitality and faithfulness of the church. They avoid or purge precisely the differences that might make conversation worthwhile. Such efforts to maintain a "common currency" capable of circulating like lifeblood throughout the body inexorably tend to cheapen the "coins" in ways that "call for less critical perspective, less sacrifice, and less change."[6] They call for less ongoing critical reflection and reformation in relation to dominant practices. They proliferate "low expectations for dialogue"—both in terms of what each might offer and in terms of what each might receive.[7]

Far better, Yoder argues, to understand church unity as a commitment to dialogical processes of reconciliation—figured by the early churches' gathering discernment around Jesus's wisdom of the cross. This "radicalizes the particular relevance of Jesus, enabling dialogue through the content of his message: the love of the enemy, the dignity of the lowly, repentance, servanthood, the renunciation of coercion."[8] Scripture, from this radical reformation perspective, most profoundly teaches a "hermeneutics of peoplehood." Central to this teaching is the idea that meetings must be "an open process," "where the working of the spirit in the congregation is validated by the liberty with which the various gifts [of all the different members of the church] are exercised, especially by the due process with which every prophetic voice is heard and every witness evaluated" (*Priestly Kingdom*, 22). The movement of the community through time occurs as "binding and loosening," whereby it seeks to discern afresh the obligatory and the nonobligatory, the need to withhold fellowship and the need to forgive: The community literally alters its shape and direction as it binds here and unbinds there, and it thereby participates in bringing forth the temporal continuities and unanticipated discontinuities of tradition*ing*.

Essential to a dialogic process animated by *caritas*, Yoder repeatedly emphasizes, is the multiplicity of gifts within the church and the need for each to remember and witness how "*every* member of the body has a distinctive place in this process" (*Priestly Kingdom,* 29). The different gifts will contribute in diverse ways, times, and places and in ever-new ways to the shape and directions of the living body of the church. To guard against the stiffening of the corporate body into a static structure of hierarchical normalizing power, Yoder, reading Paul, emphasizes that "all the gifts are of equal dignity" and that each member should resist conformist pressures, "giving special honor to the less comely members" by offering them the utmost receptive and critical powers (*Body Politics,* 50). In the same vein, he argues that "prophecy [edifying communication] is both a charisma [gift] distinctly borne by some individuals *and* a kind of discourse in which others may sometimes participate as well" (*Priestly Kingdom,* 29, my emphasis). For this reason, "everyone who has something . . . given by the Holy Spirit to him or her to say, can have the floor" (*Body Politics,* 61), and all must listen to the "least of these."

Yoder affirms the need for diverse members of the church to participate in bringing orientation and order to this highly spirited process. Hence there are those with profound prophetic charisma who help bring forth edifying visions of the church and its place in history (*Priestly Kingdom,* 29), but they are subject to "the other members," who are instructed to dialogically "weigh what the prophet(s) [have] said" (*Body Politics,* 61). So too there will be "agents of memory" who are particularly resourceful at drawing upon the community's past to illuminate the present, but they "don't judge or decide anything" (*Priestly Kingdom,* 30); "agents of order and due process" offer their gifts to ensure that all are heard and that the spirit of conversation is conciliatory.

The conviction is that every member of the body will have a nameable gift. With each of these gifts, the expectation is that several members of a church will be particularly gifted and that episodically the gift will emerge from those among whom its manifestation is least expected. The dialogic practices of giving and receiving here are to bind and loose—to discipline and release—the expectation and ushering forth of "Spirit-given newness" in ways that illuminate previously unperceived problems and possible responses (*Priestly Kingdom,* 35). For this illumination to occur, some ordering is necessary. Yet Yoder emphasizes that for most of history, and certainly now, the need has been to renew a radically dialogic and multiplicitous "vitality." "Paul *first* said, 'Every-one has a gift'; *then* he said, 'let everything be orderly'. We too need the first truth, as Good News, before the second. In the name of the first truth we need to challenge the concentration of authority

in the hands of office-bearers accredited on institutional grounds."
Multifarious vitality needs to be "reined in only after it begins to over-
reach itself" in deaf and selfish forms of "self-validating enthusiasm"
(*Body Politics,* 51, Yoder's emphasis). Subverting the way body metaphors historically have supported hierarchy by identifying a member
as the "head," he notes that "Christ, not one of the other members,
is the head," and "Jesus" was "the last priest" (53, 56). There is a
"certain functional hierarchy . . . in that understandable prophecy is
preferable, if one must choose, to unintelligible speaking in tongues; but
Paul said he did not want his readers to have to choose. Both were valid;
he practiced both and wanted others to do so" (54). Church disciplines
must always aim to cultivate *both* the expectation of unanticipatable
and often initially inchoate newness *and* the discerning capacities to
renew the orientation, direction, and order of the Gospel tradition that
faces and works with it.

Yet if practicing and discerning the meaning of nonviolence, unco-
erced community, eucharistic sharing of wealth, and the priesthood of
all believers is to occur at the dialogical edge between order and unanticipatable emergence, between the intelligible and the visceral, is there
not still a way in which "Jesus as head" privileges the body of believers? However exemplary relations are to be *within* the church, does
not "Jesus as head" structure relations with people outside it around
a rigid hierarchical privileging of Christian vision with effects antithetical to the politics of Jesus just described? In other words, might
not "Jesus as Lord" constitute a radical deafness to nonbelievers and
a confinement of prophesy to those within the church, so that the
dialogic conditions of *agape* within give way to monological practices
toward others outside in a manner likely to proliferate blindness and
violence—certainly *not* the careful discernment that might make vital
giving and receiving possible? And would not these degraded relations
at the borders migrate inward as "members" are suspected of this or
that type of "foreignness" and treated accordingly?

To understand Yoder's resources for resisting this charge, we must
return to his understanding of the looping back to Scripture, through
which an intelligent church might move and reform in time. Just as
this looping back to the early church's looping back to Jesus has suggested the shape of traditioning practices and relations within the church
and between this community and Scripture, it is again in *looping itself*—the dispersion of the gifts that propel and inform its movements
and practices of reception—that we find the illumination and genesis of
the relations between the church and those of other faiths and reasons.

In the "perennially unfinished process" of reaching back to discern scriptural accountability, the church cultivates a "readiness for reformation": an expectation that "the Lord hath yet more light and truth to break forth from this holy Word" (*Body Politics*, 59), that the church ought to move through history as "a continuing series of new beginnings" (*Priestly Kingdom*, 133), and that Christian practical moral reason "must always expect to be at some point subversive" of the common wisdom outside the church and within it (40). Reaching back to the practices of Jesus and the early churches of Scripture provides a "considerable principled solidity" for this process (118). Yet this guidance is to spur and support—rather than spurn and suppress—vulnerable and receptive encounters with those beyond the church.

From Yoder's radical reformation perspective, Jesus and the early communities gathered around his memory teach us that *to be possible at all*, practices of *caritas* must be inflected toward vulnerable engagements with those emerging in margins within the church body *and* with those beyond it. Hence his other-inflected reading of the basic "body practices"; for example:

1. Eucharist, rather than being simply the giving and receiving of wealth within the church, "is a paradigm for every other mode of inviting the outsider and the underdog to the table."[9] (Note that Mennonites have been leading innovators in establishing emergent networks of "fair trade" around the globe.)
2. Nonviolence finds its exemplarity in vulnerable love of the enemy, and this vulnerable love is articulated not just in refusing to kill or coerce the other but in striving to extend the processes of reconciliatory dialogue beyond the church even in the most agonistic relations, where "the commitment [is] to hear not only the neighbor but even the adversary" (*Body Politics*, 69). (Note that the Mennonite Central Committee does profound work around the world to aid in reconciling long-standing violent conflicts.)
3. Efforts to discern charisma (gift) must reach beyond the church body to scrutinize incarnations of God's "providence" in manifestations of foreignness.[10]

But putting Yoder's perspective this way underestimates, really, the renewal to which he bears witness. For such a presentation might misleadingly suggest that the ethical nature of the relationship of Christians toward outsiders is known by the body of believers entirely *prior to* the encounter with the others—known, in other words, simply through the relations between those in the gathered community, Scripture, and the Holy Spirit in a way that rises above and is somehow itself exclusive and independent of vulnerable receptive engagements with others beyond the church. Yet this is decidedly not the case, for in the presence of outsiders, the looping *back* of discerning ethical practice cannot itself happen in the absence of a vulnerable and expectant looping *through* engagements with those of other dispositions, faiths, and reasons. Although the church has a certain precedence both epistemologically and axiologically as the body of focused dialogical discernment and action in light of Jesus's practices and pregnant wisdom (*Priestly Kingdom*, 11) (and thus there can be no "politics of Jesus" that could be coercive, selfish, nondialogical, or invulnerable or that could cease to loop back to Scripture), it is, as we shall see, even the case that the church has often learned about these most basic practices from "outsiders." Of course, what it learns retrospectively in the most "extreme cases" (in scare quotes to evoke the paradox of the utter normalcy of such extremity in the long history of Constantinian and neo-Constantinian Christianity, as Yoder reads things) where it has gone astray in evil is of its own unfaithfulness to Jesus and Scripture. Yet in other cases, where Christians learn more from outsiders than that Christians are being decidedly "un-Christian," they learn not primarily of their unfaithfulness but of previously unperceived meanings of faith. The outsiders participate in the very "breaking forth of more light and truth from His holy Word."

Yoder writes of "looping back" as "a rediscovery of something from the past whose pertinence was not seen before, because only a new question or challenge enable[s] us to see it speaking to us" (*Priestly Kingdom*, 69). When new questions and challenges arise from outside the church body, they often take the form of new developments and events (for example, the globalization of corporate capitalism, ecological crises, new forms of techno-genocide, consumer culture, and the like) that might solicit and thus help in foregrounding hitherto unrecognized dimensions and implications of Scripture that illuminate what it now might mean for the church to "be church." They incarnate "the need" for scriptural practices "to be selected and transformed transculturally in ever new settings" (*For the Nations*, 92).

However, more interesting in the present context are the times when it is precisely through receptive engagements with outsiders who contest

hegemonic practices (in the church, in the wider world, or in the relations between the two) that the church is enabled to "loop back" in
ways that enable new light to break forth. At these moments of receptive encounter at the discordant edge between the church and outsiders,
the latter participate in the reconfigurations of the edges, in the pruning relationships, and in the nourishing circulations between the present church and its scriptural roots.

Historically these relations have sometimes re-illuminated practices
that are absolutely elemental to the church. Hence Yoder enjoins, "[the]
hermeneutical role of the community is . . . primordial; i.e. we have
to talk about it first. It is however by no means an exclusive possession. . . . When the empirical community becomes disobedient, other
people can hear the Bible's witness too. It is after all a public document. Loners and outsiders can hear it speaking especially if the insid-
ers have ceased to listen. It was thanks to the loner Tolstoy and the
outsider Gandhi that the churchman Martin Luther King, Jr., . . . was
able to bring Jesus' word on violence back into the churches. It was
partly the outsider Marx who enabled liberation theologians to restate
what the Law and the Prophets had been saying for centuries, largely
unheard, about God's partisanship for the poor" (For the Nations, 93).
Similarly, Yoder notes that most "churches" had to learn important
lessons about religious liberty and democracy from antichurch proponents of the Enlightenment (Priestly Kingdom, 23).

When those within the church are not listening to the Bible's witness, the ears with which the church might loop back will have to receive the ears of the others—even when those ears claim to hear another
God, or gods, or no god at all. And when have those within the church
ever been listening to Scripture as fully as they might? When have they
been fully attentive? One could even say that this very possibility hinges
for Yoder significantly upon the attentiveness they bring to encounters
with outsiders. The voices, places, and times of the emergence of God's
gifts are not predictable, even as radical reformation Christians know
that the vulnerable and receptive practices of scriptural engagement are
eternally central to our ability to receive them.

Very significantly, these new and deeper senses of both the radical
unpredictability of God's gifts and the vulnerable and receptive politics of Jesus necessary to receive them might themselves most probably break forth for most Christians today if a gift, whose most potent
forces and articulations are largely outside the church, is somehow
recognized and engaged in the deeper ways intimated above. To translate this again: The fullest conditions of possibility for caritas themselves

might *emerge* historically in ways that exemplify this fullness before it fills the church in the form of disciplined practices or intentional awareness. Yoder's word for this Christian deliverance from what others might see as a question-begging or vicious circle is "grace." Let us look closer.

In "Meaning after Babble," Yoder writes: "From the Gospel perspective, modern pluralism is not a set back but a providential occasion for clarification. It may enable us to see something about the Gospel that was not visible before" (135). If you miss the uncanny element in the way "the Gospel" breaks forth in these sentences, you will miss a lot. For the Gospel perspective from which modern pluralism and pluralists might appear to be a God-given occasion for clarification is *already* the Gospel perspective that has been clarified (through Yoder's critical and receptive encounter with these outsiders of modern pluralism) and now "clarifies" something about the Gospel that was not visible before—that was *not Gospel* perspective for most (or perhaps any) moderns before and still is not for most now. The edge of this teleology-ateleology moves too quickly to be caught at rest. It can only be *offered*, by one discerning from the border of the church and affirming this vulnerable discernment, in hopes that there is or can be a body of believers who can weigh and receive it in a manner that will participate in the breaking forth of this gift. Grace: because what ought to be given has already arrived, "at once original and true-to-type, at once unpredictable and recognizable" (*Priestly Kingdom*, 133).

Yoder's looping back through the outsiders and otherness called "pluralism" is enacted in a reading of Scripture that is at once radical and strangely compelling. "Babel in the myth of Genesis," he writes, "places the multiplicity of cultures under the sign of the divine will." "Restoring his original plan," YHWH scattered them not as an act of angry retribution but in an "act of divine benevolence," "for their own good," as Paul recognized ("Meaning after Babble," 127). The renewed multiplicity of particular languages, the need for discourse dependent upon particular communities and concrete relations between particular communities, was to "save humankind from its presumptuous and premature effort at divinization," by which various particular individuals and groups tried (and continue to try) in myriad ways to enforce uniformity according to their own self-transparent Truth (132). The possibility of *veritas, caritas,* and *agape,* Yoder's reading suggests, hinges upon engagements within and between different communities that are at once evangelical and vulnerable. Or evangelical in their vulnerability and vulnerable in their evangelism. It is to this entwinement at the heart of Yoder's "politics of Jesus"—brought forth in precisely such engagements—that we now turn.

Christians cannot, Yoder argues, confine themselves to the private sphere and the secular currencies of public discourse that many liberals, from Locke to Rawls, have insisted upon. There is no Christian ecclesiology that could forego the evangelical proclamation to others that Jesus is Lord—that he calls us to peace, to voluntarily radically dialogical communities, to a witnessing of the wild heterogeneity of giftedness, to the cessation of coercive hierarchies, to generous sharing of wealth in both production and consumption, and to attention in every sense to the "least of these." The church must be a body striving to give as it has received. "The calling to witness to the Other has been a constitutive component of the self-definition of Jewry at least since Jeremiah and of Christianity since Pentecost" ("Meaning after Babble," 138)—not a "choice." "Jesus is Lord" is the Good News that the practicing church as pulpit and paradigm brings to the world. In discerning, practicing, and offering this gift to others, the church remains true to Jesus's word, oriented by his moral substance. It remains faithful to the idea that it "learns more from Scripture than other ways" about how to practice a receptive generosity, how to cultivate criticism of self-aggrandizing modes of power, how to maintain a stance of "revolutionary subordination,"[11] and how to engender a readiness for reformation.

But how is this witness to occur? For Yoder, this witness has to be discerned in each particular case. The church must always strive toward disciplined practices that incarnate and exemplify the Good News. Yet this "letting the church be the church" is never conceived simply as an inwardly turned sectarian practice; rather, it is also, at the same time, "for the nations," the outsiders.[12] As such, exemplifications of Good News must find incarnation in the church's modes of witness to the world. Christians must reject imposing their faith upon others and must also renounce foundational claims to have reached "some kind of transcultural or preparticular ground" ("Meaning after Babble," 134). Rather, they are called to validate their faith repeatedly, in one vulnerable encounter after another.

Crucial to this project is translating "our Word into their words," "one particular community at a time" ("Meaning after Babble," 132). This is not a call to trim the Gospel to whatever "public discourse" claims to be sovereign in the surrounding world. Rather, faithful to their scriptural roots, Christians should contest the discourses and powers that govern the world when those powers contradict the politics of

Jesus. But this means that, far from simply bearing witness in their "own" idioms, they must also communicate in "terms familiar to particular outsiders," as the messianic Jews did when they openly "seized [the world's] categories, hammered them into other shapes" that often radically reformed or reversed their meaning (*Priestly Kingdom*, 54). In so doing they bore witness in such a way that the others who were invited to respond could truly hear it. "Interworldly grammars" are often generated in these encounters (56), but none should "renew the vain effort to find assurance beyond the flux of unendingly meeting new worlds, or to create a metalanguage above the clash" (60). The church's assurance and the other's acceptance are the stuff of ever-renewed challenges.

To grasp the radical depth of this truth for Yoder we must return to his understanding of translation. Transcultural witness requires that "we must enter concretely into the other community . . . long enough, deeply enough, vulnerably enough, to be able to articulate our Word in their words" ("Meaning after Babble," 133). This vulnerable renunciation of violence *required for* discerning how to bring good news to the other also "*is* good news for the Other" (135, my emphasis). Hence Yoder claims, with Martin Luther King Jr. and Mohandas Gandhi, that nonviolence "is thereby an epistemology. . . . The truth of our witness needs [it] to let its credibility show" (ibid.).

But it is not simply an epistemology for the other. The vulnerability through which members of the church craft the "what" and the "how" of their witness is simultaneously the risky endeavor through which they might — beyond attesting to the church's own (re)newness — discover newness with and from the others. This is absolutely vital to the attitude and practice of engagement that the church must creatively seek to bind and loose into being. Thus Yoder writes, again with Gandhi, that even "the adversary is part of my truth-finding process. I need to act nonviolently . . . to get the adversary to hear me, but I need as well to hear the adversary" (*Body Politics*, 69).[13]

Yoder further elaborates this claim concerning nonviolence as epistemology in essays on interfaith dialogue. I quote at length a passage that captures the spirit of his arguments:

> It may be the Islamicist Kenneth Cragg who for our time has made most poignant the insight that I have only really understood another faith if I begin to feel at home in it, if its tug at me questions my own prior (Christian) allegiance anew. Likewise, I am only validly exposing my own faith if I can imagine my

interlocutor's coming to share it. Perhaps the *word* mission has
been rendered unusable in some contexts by abuse, but respect for
the genuineness of dialogue demands, *in both directions* that there
be no disavowal in principle of my witness becoming an open
option for the other. Mission and dialogue are not alternatives:
each is valid only within the other, properly understood.[14]

One cannot generously communicate one's faith without striving to
inhabit receptively the other's world in a manner that challenges one's
own faith as well as the faith of the other. Epistemological nonviolence
aims at practices in which the possibility of giving and receiving are
inextricably entwined. This is troubling to the core, for there is no
mission without dialogue and no dialogue unless one "takes the risk
of having his own ideas . . . radically changed," even as one might seek
to radically change aspects, or perhaps most, of what the other does
and believes ("Disavowal of Constantine," 255n). For this reason, Yoder
claims: "We are all 'nominal' adherents. No one's faith is final in this
life" (255). Paradoxically, to seek to radically renew one's faith in the
particularity and universal relevance of Jesus is, for Yoder, to be drawn
to him (and thus to herald others) precisely in the exemplary illumination through which Jesus makes *this* generous truth break forth and
be real. "The gatheredness of the community is the point . . . where
kerygma [heralding] and dialogue coincide, where renewed appeal to
the biblical Jesus and renewed openness to tomorrow's world are not
two things but one" (253). And *this* faith, *this* time, must proceed confessedly repentant and actively critical of the triumphalism that has for
so long vainly taken Jesus's name to justify conquest.

   To herald Jesus Christ as Lord is resolutely to cultivate this stance —
these directional practices of indirection — in opposition to the dominant subjugative powers of this world and the relentless and mobile
structures of assimilation with which they devitalize critique and resist
transformation. It is to be convinced that Jesus teaches Christians why
and how to do this better (and empowers them to do so) than the other
ways they have encountered thus far.

   Yet if the church is resolutely to resist the bad, it must also resist
an immodest tendency to conflate otherness and outsideness with bad-
ness. These conflations tend to structure encounters in a totalizing "all
or nothing" fashion. In contrast, the challenge is to "affirm a particular witness to be good news without being interested in showing that
other people are bad" (*Priestly Kingdom,* 60). Indeed, only through
the integrity of more-receptive engagement does discerning judgment

of good and bad become possible. Eschewing such conflation means that very often, and for the most part, the dialogical encounters with others in which Christian witness is brought to bear will not directly engage another's faith as a totality (gathered under a negative mark) but, rather, will selectively draw upon those church practices, habituated sensibilities, and theological perspectives that bear upon those aspects of another's faith or faithlessness that are foregrounded by a particular problem or site of contestation.

Witness to Jesus as Lord must *not* be read as a solicitation to strive for a singular and direct knockout victory over outsiders. Instead, it calls for multiple particular vulnerable encounters in which the strengths of the church body are little by little brought to light and perhaps themselves radically reformed and renewed. "Maybe [heralding] has to have several [meanings], each fragmentary, but which might severally add up asymptotically to a functional equivalent of a proclamation of lordship" (*Priestly Kingdom,* 57; the qualifiers "maybe," and "might" themselves articulate the new posture). The heralding, discernment, risk, and renewal of faithfulness occur to a great extent in contestatory and cooperative work around particular historically situated questions. What and how do those gathered around Jesus as Lord contribute to identifying—and to creatively resisting and responding with alternatives to—*this* pattern of violent conflict, *these* practices of economic subjugation and suffering, *this* set of disciplinary practices entwined with an idolatrous relation to productivity, *that* postcolonial practice of subordination, *that* authoritarian police state, *this* group of people's cynicism, *these* stingy practices of (not) caring for the unborn, the very old, or the ill, *these* selfish practices of territoriality, *these* parties' incapacity for more generous and receptive dialogue? What is the fruitfulness of Jesus relative to other alternatives here?

Yoder calls for vital and disciplined engagement *and* for a certain modesty integral to both: Given an affirmation of historical particularity and peccability, it would be "contradictory to expect that Christian commitment—even less Christians' performance—should be at the top of every scale. What we're looking for . . . is not a way to keep dry above the waves of relativity, but to stay within our bark, barely afloat and sometimes awash amidst those waves, yet neither dissolving into them nor being carried only where they want to push it" (*Priestly Kingdom,* 58). This modesty of "what we're looking for," entwined with the dialogical generosity of radical reformation Christians' mode of looking, creates the possibility of numerous tactical alliances with outsiders whose directions significantly parallel certain goals of the church (*Priestly Kingdom,* 61–62). In this sense one might even speak of a tentative, selective, partial confusing of some bodily distinctions between church bodies and outside bodies at certain points in the identity markers that constitute a border between one and another. For Yoder, these, of course, are already confused (in a good way) where the church has incorporated and reformed itself through receptive engagements with outside—and now no longer wholly outside— voices and practices. But here he broaches an additional confusion of bodies, even when reformation is not what is involved or at stake: the confusion along certain segments of borders between bodies that nevertheless remain quite distinct.

Yoder writes with *and* against these ideas of confusion of the body of the church. Although he strongly critiques Augustinian notions of the invisible true church body, neither does he reify the visible body in a manner that would wholly identify it with the practiced body of believers. The very vulnerable generosity that constitutes this body confuses its boundaries. It is, I think, no accident that Yoder draws upon outsiders and outsideness to articulate and solicit this "core" vulnerability. In the *practice* of naming and (in varying ways) receiving lessons from Gandhi, Marx, and modern pluralism, Yoder *performs* the vulnerable and ambiguous identity of the giving and receiving body of Christ. And one should remember that the outside is often not purely other in Yoder's view. Marx read the Bible, Gandhi encountered Jesus through the works of Tolstoy even as he refused to call himself Christian ("Disavowal of Constantine," 260), and modern pluralism has important debts to (and differences from) "the Hebrew and Christian intervention in cultural history . . . missionary mobility . . . love of the enemy . . . relativizing of political sovereignty . . . dialogical vision . . . charismatic vision of the many members of the body . . . disavowal of empire and of theocracy" (*Priestly Kingdom,* 60).

Yoder's point decidedly is *not* that "it all originates in Scripture"— as I hope is clear. Rather, it is that though God's providence requires visible dialogical church bodies in action, it is infinitely bigger and ambiguously more than the visible body (what it looks like, what it sees) at any point in time. God's gifts are (to borrow from Merleau-Ponty) a "perpetual pregnancy." The church body generously strives to be midwife for these gifts. Though that oversimplifies, because it is often not clear who is pregnant with what, exactly what role Christians might have played in the pregnancy, exactly what role the others might have played in the development of the midwife's own body and capacities for midwifery, or exactly whether segments of the church body's borders might not become highly indeterminate and porous as it works along-side other bodies toward the historical reception of particular gifts in response to particular problems. These bodies are confusing. One could even say that a certain vulnerability to the confusing is constitutive of the discerning and patient body of Christ.

In this vein, against the "easy rejection by Westerners of 'syncre-tism,'" Yoder is sympathetic with many Christians in the 'third world' who remind Europeans that "mixing has gone on for centuries in Europe, whereas the task of authentic communication in the forms of any non-Western culture has only recently been tackled. Until we know how faithfully to speak of Christ in some non-Western language, we can hardly know what identifies culpable syncretism" (*Priestly Kingdom*, 68).

Yet while Yoder affirms these imaginative dialogic efforts that are "newly open to far-reaching reformulations of the gospel message," he simultaneously signals what he will always *also* renew as a concern that is for him at once a condition of these efforts and at the same time a resistance to a certain direction (or indirection) they sometimes (and perhaps always must to some extent) embrace: "It has not been at work long enough for us to determine whether it will develop criteria for defining heresy" (*Priestly Kingdom*, 68). The church must renew its generous and receptive hybridizing vulnerability *and* it must renew its capacities to discern the heresy of "genuinely incompatible elements." It must not simply and undiscerningly conform to indigenous ways (145). Because Jesus is the root of the church's possibility to receive reformation through the wildly placed and timed gifts of God, Yoder will not hesitate to affirm "fidelity to the jealousy of Christ as Lord" (86)—understood as the fundamental cruciformity of the universe and the practices necessary to herald it. This fidelity indicates a certain limit to the confusion it makes possible, and it is a limit Christians are always enjoined to discern.

This jealousy, Yoder claims, calls Christians to—and is their best possibility for—cultivating receptive generosity. And it does so in no small part by resisting the deification of some antithetical value like "power, mammon, fame, efficacy" (*Priestly Kingdom*, 86). There are— within and outside Christianity—a lot of *bad* traditions, fundamental errors, and evil powers. "The need is not that *those* traditions be inte-grated. . . . They must be uprooted" (69). At a certain point (discerned by a community first and foremost pushed and pulled by the tensional entwinements of this receptivity and this jealousy), when repeated efforts toward reconciliation have failed, this will involve excommunication, or else the body of Christ as disciplined practice will cease to have any meaning.

"The linguistic line between treason and tradition is very fine. Both terms come from the same root. Yet in substance there is a chasm between the two" (*Priestly Kingdom,* 67). The differences between "faithful organic development" and "compatible extrapolation," on the one hand, and "incompatible deviation" and "sell-out," on the other, are often extremely difficult to discern. Thus Jesus calls Christians to radical dialogical gatherings vulnerable to unexpected otherness in order to discern "the chasm." The church would have to ready itself for vulnerably encountering the unwonted to have any hope of exercising good judgment. "Yet if the notion of infidelity is not to fade into a fog where nothing is verifiable, the notion of infidelity as a real possibility must continue to be operational" (68). If this church breaks forth with pregnant visibility, it also bears witness to all it sees that is abortive and antichurch. The what and how of this discernment of fidelity, Yoder calls "body politics." Vulnerable relations will, in some form or another, continue even with those who are decidedly treasonous—but not fellowship.[15]

On Yoder's list of what and how fidelity is *not:* "polytheism." For the church, the path to reformation with the unanticipatable manifoldness of God's gift must pass through the jealousy of the One. But then we must add this qualification: This paradox is too big for any *one* (individual, group, time) to handle or claim to possess entirely. Then add that "the prophetic denunciation of paganism" will always be "ad hoc," "vulnerable," and "fragmentary" ("Disavowal of Constantine," 249–50). The sum, for Yoder, is that which is beyond a "sum." It is "'Patience' as Method in Moral Reasoning," a set of reflections that Yoder patiently worked upon for fifteen years until death interrupted the unfolding of this most spectacular non-summing, list-like exposition of this practice so central to his understanding of Christian ethics. Yoder thinks of patience as, among so many other qualities, the *gift of time,* for one has been given time: time for vulnerable witnessing and discerning and participating in the unanticipatable breaking forth; patience as suspension of the socially and existentially engendered pressures upon time to summarize judgment and engage others in summary fashion. Yoder calls this gift to the self and the other the "'modest' patience of sobriety in finitude." This patience offers resistance to the insistence lodged in every teleological "now" that it *contain* within its own horizon of orientation the future to come and the others within that future. "The certainty with which we have to act one day at a time must never claim finality."[16] This radically modest stance of in-finality is the very temporality of *caritas* that members of the church must bring to reopen each particular *now*.

At its most radical, the modest patience of sobriety in finitude takes the form of a certain slackening—one might almost say suspension—of the pressures lodged in many familiar renderings of fidelity to "the jealousy of Christ as Lord." For example, suspending the finality of the idea that there is no good way that does not follow Jesus as Lord; the idea that to believe that the "rebellious but (in principle) already defeated cosmos is being brought to its knees by the Lamb" (for example, *Priestly Kingdom*, 54, 136) necessarily implies that all *must* eventually submit to Jesus (by coercion or freely—it matters not a bit to me here). These can be read as claims to finality, and they have been deployed as powerfully and as often to render Christians invulnerable as any claims ever have.

Yoder always resists these Constantinian readings of these claims. Hence, for example, the church should not a priori judge outsiders as bad, and the Lamb worthy of worship might only be discerned through vulnerable engagements (never imposition—the choice is theirs) with those who do not share this faith. Yet he appears not infrequently to suggest a singular endpoint ("His ultimate victory") brought about by a distinctly cruciform dialectic or, better, eschatology ("His hidden control"), which one might suspect would engender an overwhelming hubris in believers, a hubris that could radically vitiate the very receptivity he otherwise cultivates (*Priestly Kingdom*, 136).

I confess to having absolutely no idea what it would even mean to think and believe with Yoder here concerning victory and control. But I might have an insight into how Yoder thought these ideas must function and how they must not. They are to powerfully inspire and orient the church to resist "the *principalities* and *powers*" (my emphasis) that would subjugate creation to idolatries of "power, mammon, fame, efficacy." They call believers to resist as mythical these closures of history and to begin (again and again) to practice an alternative body politics, confident that the future belongs to *caritas*—even in the face of powers that seek to eternalize subjugation and seem to exhibit enormous capacities to assimilate or brutally crush opposition and alternative hopes. It is something like this: "We love our neighbor because God is like that. It is not because Jesus told us to that we love even beyond the limits of reason and justice, even to the point of refusing to kill and being willing to suffer—but because God is like that too."[17]

But this opening of the future *as such,* this claim that the future as such *will* open, and will open *only as caritas,* this claim about today and tomorrow based on what has *already* been reported to have happened—this opening that gives time *must not steal it.* And the unrelenting tenacity of Yoder's efforts to negotiate the complexities and risks at this point will always astound.

Hence a(n) (un)certain suspension, a(n) (un)certain patience. In an essay that reads "Jeremiah" as calling Jews and then Christians to bear witness to God's sovereignty by heralding diaspora as grace, Yoder writes again of the jealousy of God: "This enormous flexibility and creative force returns us to the question, Is there anything nonnegotiable in the dispersed minority's witness? Anything untranslatable? Of course there is; it is that there is no other God. The rejection not only of pagan cult but also of every way of putting their own YHWH/ LORD in the same frame of reference with pagan deities, even not speaking the divine NAME as others would, was tied for the Jews in Babylon with the proclamation of his sovereignty over creation and history. There is no setting into which that deconstructing, disenchanting proclamation cannot be translated, none which can encompass it. The anti-idolatry message is not bad but good news. It can free its hearers from slavery to the powers that crush their lives" (*For the Nations,* 76–77).

This liberating nonnegotiability can free the hearers, and Yoder's church *must* maintain it and invite others to it. Yet if its stance is clear toward *"the powers,"* it is radically indeterminate—radically *patient—* in relation to *"other subject peoples"* (*For the Nations,* 78, my emphasis), who find themselves named in the title of the concluding section of Yoder's essay, importantly the only one framed as a question: "Is This a Way Other Subject Peoples Might See Themselves?" With a textual maneuver of most pronounced abruptness, Yoder interrupts any and all pressures of finality that might be building in his essay, by writing, "I close by declaring my complete lack of authority to answer this . . . question." He then modulates and builds the question in a variety of ways, leaving each modulation starkly unanswered: "Is there something about this . . . that might be echoed or replicated by other migrant peoples? Might it give hope to other refugees? To other victims of imperial displacement? . . . Peoples overwhelmed by imperial immigration?" (ibid.). We will simply have to "wait and see" (a phrase from other writings); because the meaning and relevance of "His victory" breaks off into indeterminacy when faced with other subject peoples "for themselves." Those within the church simply cannot now know if their good news is the best news for other subject peoples. *Go out there. Listen vulnerably. Herald. Listen. Wait.*[18]

Yoder's most radical patience here is not simply a "pastoral patience" rooted in his sense of power dynamics and Christians' poor relations to many wounded outsiders. Nor is it simply "therapeutic patience," nor simply "'contrite' patience of repentance" that acknowledges complicity in Christian unfaithfulness and evil deeds. No, it is more radical than these forms of patience that are "for *a* time, for *a* reason."[19] In excess of these, it is for time itself, time as generous opening, time as gift, gift of time. In this sense, this patience is not where "His victory" *breaks off* into this indeterminacy (as I suggested in the previous paragraph) but where it *breaks forth* as this generous indeterminacy. Yoder's patience as *wild patience:* love for the untamed entangled growings of heralding, listening, waiting.

### Reaching Back and Breaking Forth/Off/In/Out?

Many questions spring from these soils. In a few closing words I will reach back to a position many will perhaps discern to be more "outside" than the one I have adopted thus far in this chapter. I will reach back to my locations at various intersections in radical democratic movements where Christians, Jews, Muslims, secularists, neo-Nietzscheans, populists, citizens, and those who have come from afar legally and illegally join in dialogue and action toward more generous and receptive modes of power. I reach back in the hope of an emerging question with which there might break forth not so much new light as a heightened sense of its possibility.

Reading carefully, one might discern in Yoder an intermittent sense of an element of complicity between pre-Constantinian proclamations of the jealousy of Jesus as Lord and the rise of Constantinianism. For though Yoder claims that the early churches were generally "structurally sound in their major teachings" (*Priestly Kingdom,* 129), he nevertheless indicates a flaw that, in light of the reading of Yoder developed thus far, could be called nothing less than "major." Put simply, they did not quite rightly understand traditioning as readiness for radical reformation in the sense of reaching back as the breaking forth of new light, as practiced generosity toward the unanticipatable future. They partly misconstrued the church's mode of being in time too much in the direction of identity—not enough as "excess."

The term "excess" is *not* a postmodern translation. Yoder wrote of the "original revolution" as "an ethic of excess," locating the "style of His discipleship" in the question, "What do ye more than others?"

which "is for Jesus a fitting question whereas for the common discourse of ethics one measures oneself by others in order to measure up to the average. Here it is the excess, the going beyond what could be expected, the setting aside what one would have a right to which is itself the norm. . . . It is the nature of the love of God not to let itself be limited by models or options or opportunities which are offered to it by a situation. It does more because the very event of exceeding the available models is itself a measure of its character. . . . Jesus would ask, 'How in this situation will the life-giving power of the Spirit reach beyond available models and options to do a new thing whose very newness will be a witness to divine presence?'"[20] The early church gathered around Jesus's word in Scripture was "sound in its major teachings" insofar as it creatively articulated them in church body practices. What it did not appear to grasp sufficiently, Yoder suggests in the passages that follow, is the way Jesus's question was to deconstruct the ethical indolence of even (especially?) those who would interpret Jesus himself more as a static "model" than as the pregnant incarnation of Good News, which has to be received and given *as pregnant* to remain or become good. Jesus, as the questioning solicitation of this ethic of excess, knew that to be received, he had to be received excessively. This opens church-time, or traditioning, beyond the logic of identity that otherwise prevails.

Here is a reading of Yoder's sense of a possible erring in this respect. In the face of gradual and problematic "adjustment to other loyalties" that slides into "unfaithfulness" to the body politics of Jesus, Yoder writes, "It would seem at first that the necessary corrective would be to reject all change, restoring things as they had been before. For the early centuries . . . 'renewal' was that simple; it asked for the restitution of the way things had already been" (*Priestly Kingdom*, 86). Thus there is a way the early church that was reaching back, and to whom Yoder reaches back, did not fully understand "reaching back." Only modern historical consciousness "made it impossible to think that way" (ibid.).

From this mistake emerged a false choice between "movement forward as accommodation" and reformation as "return to go" (*Priestly Kingdom*, 87), which has had disastrous effects to this day. The early churches' insufficiently generative (and excessively identitarian) conception of their restoration practices seems to have weakened their abilities to creatively translate Jesus and Scripture into forms that might have allowed them to reorient themselves toward speaking to, resisting, and offering more engaging, powerful, and seductive alternatives to the idolatry of the "principalities and powers." There was a weakening of missionary powers to engage new situations and new others. It is in this context of a devitalized church traditioning that Ambrose and Augustine drew problematically from Roman law "to speak to questions the New Testament did not help them with" (75). Those who recognized the accommodation for what it was withdrew. "It would have been good at that time to have a new prophetic voice to save the church from the no-win choice between separatism and sellout. Tragically, there was no such prophet" (ibid.). This was no accident. If the "New Testament did not help," from Yoder's stance, this is because those who read it failed to gather together in a manner sufficiently historically dynamic and receptive to the text, each other, and outsiders to enable prophetic translations through which it might have spoken. The slide toward Constantinianism might be understood in this context—at least if Yoder's suspicions have any merit. My guess is that his suspicions have a certain heuristic value for the present, regardless of their historical salience in the first centuries following Jesus.

Many factors undoubtedly contributed to the early churches' "return to go" sensibility. Here I pursue only one in the form of some questions. Could it be that the *jealousy* of Jesus as Lord—not just as a concept, but as stories, dispositions, habits, practices—is entwined with and works in spite of itself toward the closure of the church's generous and receptive participation in historical generativity? In one sense this is not a true question. History screams: Of course this has happened—Jesus has been worked over thus. Yet I aim the question in a different direction, or at least more deeply. Could it be that this jealousy in *pre*-Constantinian forms acts in part as a certain gravitational pull against the future—against newness as such—in a manner that infuses the church's *caritas* toward time and the other with a certain stinginess that erodes its generativity and generosity from within? Could it be that this non-Constantinian jealousy might pressure reformation toward identical restitution, in such a way that the church slouches toward separatism (mini-Constantinianisms) or sellout (Constantinianism)? My point here is not to valorize "newness as such" but, rather, to cast suspicion upon pressures to *de*valuate newness as such. This suspicion opens spaces and times for patient discernment of the new, in contrast to a priori tendencies toward valorization or devaluation of the new.

I know of *no* generosity that is not "peccable in fact" (*Priestly Kingdom,* 5)—none without congenital defects and damages against which it must struggle. Every extant movement of generosity has limits, and these limits both enable and disable the power of giving and receiving. Every movement of the gift must attend to these limits, working them ceaselessly and patiently in ways that address and move beyond the stinginess that remains and often emerges anew in every extant form. The call of receptive generosity is to work at these limits receptively with others—to become more capable of this working-with, especially (but not only) with those others who have been on the underside of power, especially those who claim to have been violated by powers in which we are implicated. My suspicion concerns the way Yoder's way of affirming a certain jealousy might weaken the good work at the limit, to which he is called and to which he so profoundly calls us. This jealousy, from my vantage point, is not without its power and capacity for good work, but I would suggest that it needs to be inflected differently and reshaped, not only for the radical democratic community coalitions in which I am most invested but for the work that Yoder calls Good News.

Even if these questions get at something persistently real, they are by no means devastating, nor are they intended to be devastating. But recognizing a perhaps fundamental and undesirable vulnerability within this Christian jealousy might engender different, possibly more-perceptive, capacities for discerning strengths and weaknesses of these other modes of faith and being, as well as other loci of critical and constructive practice. It might solicit and encourage more-receptive engagements with some forms of polytheism, atheism, and postsecular modes of enchantment, as well as with a lot of critical work being done by liberation theologians, critical race theorists, feminists, students of postcoloniality, and ecologists, for example. As I read Yoder, although his work often has sympathies and resonances with—as well as much to contribute to—some of what is best in these and other practices of affirmation and critique, his actual engagement with most of them was quite slim. His work would have benefited significantly, I think, from fuller dialogues with these bodies of work.

Of course, the work to which Yoder was called, the work he did, was tremendous, and it took all the time he was given. "Should have" always has a weak and pretentious ring in cases like his. If it has any merit, it is insofar as it bears upon prospective developments. Thus, perhaps those who are inspired by Yoder would do well to develop some of these points of intersection. Perhaps some Christians would then witness certain virtues of polytheisms, atheisms, or postsecularisms precisely at the points where Christians discover certain vices *within* themselves that seem hard to separate from the cross they bear.

Perhaps among these would be the virtues that might be found in certain polytheistic, atheistic, and postsecular tendencies to allow and even seek more-receptive and more-generous blurrings of the insistent inside/outside framework that has governed not only Constantinian Christianity but also, in my view, some of Yoder's reflections as well.[21] Perhaps Yoderians might then discover in others inspiring capacities for appreciating and responding to multiple sources of inspiration and orientation that aid radical democratic coalitional efforts that might be integral to and exemplary of some of the work Yoderians too seek to accomplish. Perhaps discerning these relative strengths, in juxtaposition with some weaknesses that tend to be engendered by their own jealousy (for example, reticence to work as often with outsiders, difficulty hearing and very seriously engaging their claims), might lead those inspired by Yoder to slacken, resituate, or differently consider and articulate some of their practices. Perhaps it would call them more often to elaborate, as a community, indebted affirmations—which is not to say embraces—of other communities' stories and sources; practices of recounting with a certain awe the stories and deeds of other communities in order to cultivate a more capacious joy in otherness and readiness to listen. Perhaps.

Echoing Yoder, I have absolutely no authority to say whether these reflections ought to influence how Mennonite Christians might begin to see themselves. But in the instant the question opens, before it is framed by an answer, as Derrida might say, there might be found another opening for *caritas,* another unanticipatable yet somehow recognizable breaking forth. Whether this hope is with or against Yoder, whether it is inside or outside, or whether it might help enhance powers to resist that which is evil in these distinctions without which—paradoxically—there is no resistance to evil, I am no longer sure. To Yoder, even as I lean here in another direction, I am indebted not least of all for this uncertainty, among many other things.

Yet let me not end on this note of still-too-limited discomfort—as if the discords were quite this easy, as if I could stay for the most part on top of them or stay where I was before they appeared. If I see Yoder's Jesus as a great story, it is not simply because it resonates so much with themes of dialogue and receptivity that I embraced long before my encounter with his writing. More importantly, it is great the way the sublime that is unconquered by sovereign subjectivity is great: It mightily calls into question my perception, sense-making, reach, direction, ethical and political faiths. Yoder haunts me. He is not an easy ghost, but I want to want him with me. I want him opening new doors and windows in my cave, offering new light and air, and occasionally rattling my walls until I feel in my bones "there's no place like home" and find myself engaged in a new thing.

With and in this spirit, let me close this chapter with an undigested and brief list of some interrelated challenges and questions that Yoder poses to radical democrats such as me myself, challenges and questions that I might formulate provisionally at present. Some I begin to respond to in the chapters that follow. Some remain for future works. Many are likely to remain long after me.

1. *The church as body.* To what extent and in what fashions can radical and pluralizing democrats theorize and develop enduring corporate practices of resistance and exemplary alternatives?

2. *The discipline of the church body.* How might we develop enspirited disciplines that empower without becoming "disciplinary," in the pejorative senses of this word we have identified quite well?

3. *The jealousy of the discipline.* Yoder shows compellingly how a certain jealousy might aid resistance to odious forms of power. What are the possibilities of enduring resistance in the absence of this or a similar jealousy?

4. *The generosity of the jealousy.* Is there not a jealousy infusing and partly enabling every generosity; certain refusals, certain relatively rigid limits to any "yes"? Has this been sufficiently acknowledged by neo-Nietzschean democrats? Sufficiently acknowledged to draw from this condition its highest possibilities and to respond to its dangers (as Yoder does in his rendering of patience)?

5. *The pacifism of the generosity.* In the critique of a certain "perpetual peace" and in the embrace of a certain agon, have we not avoided more sustained inquiries into war making as such, even as genealogists have contributed in important ways to critical illuminations of numerous specific war-making practices? Is any killing congruent with receptive generosity?

# 5
# Derrida and the Promise of Democracy

JACQUES DERRIDA SHARES WITH MACINTYRE the dubious fortune of having a large readership that—in celebration or dismissal—tends to register only one dimension of his thinking.[1] Yoder is read less but perhaps better. Just as many ignore difference, contestation, and vulnerability in MacIntyre and just as Yoder can be dismissed as "sectarian," Derrida's efforts to work energetically both with and beyond dialectics, phenomenological sense, reason, and democratic traditions have been most often missed as many readers register only the tropes of the messianic, of unanticipatability, and of ghostly alterity. These tropes are crucial to Derrida's project, yet the vitality of his thinking lies in his calls to cultivate ethical and political judgment *in the animating tensions between* themes of radically unanticipatable otherness and radical dialectical democratic traditioning.[2] When this paradoxical stance is missed, his project gets interpreted as either a radical (basically Habermasian) dialectic or a philosophy of sheer indeterminacy. Either way, what is most compelling about Derrida's articulation of democratic responsibility, judgment, and justice vanishes.

Derrida insightfully theorizes democracy as most promising when articulated through a responsibility and judgment that is worked at the discordant edge between substantially determinate radical democratic teleologies and an ateleological receptivity or "anticipation of the unanticipatable" that opens itself to questioning by alterity. Democracy must forever become significantly a question unto itself. If it hardens into an overly determinate teleology—even a radically democratic one—the responsibility it promises wanes. Yet if it remains only a ghostly evocation of ghosts, it is prevented from experimenting with specific modes of action, without which it would violently relegate otherness to an oblivion like that which deconstructionists would resist.

Yet what might it mean to be thus situated in relation to others? Toward what kind of ethics and politics does this gesture? And what is at stake in the difference between Derrida's position and those we have discussed thus far?

This chapter is divided into five sections. In the first section, "The Paradoxical Responsibilities of Historied Beings in the Face of Infinity," I carefully develop Derrida's early philosophical reflections on historical sense, tradition, teleology, responsibility, intersubjectivity, and our relations to others that emerged in his readings of Edmund Husserl. These reflections resonate throughout much of his later work and are crucial for an understanding of his ethical and political explorations in the decades that follow. In the second section, "Ethics and Politics of Democracy to Come," I develop his ethical and political writings with an eye to questions concerning the paradoxical teleological-ateleological character of responsibility. I argue that the most compelling aspects of his work lie in the tensions he articulates here. Miss these and you miss his project. In the third section, "Tradition of Encounter/Encountering Tradition," I pursue some of the ways MacIntyre's and Derrida's positions bring critical pressure to bear upon each other. As I read the encounter I stage here, Derrida gets the upper hand. Yet a certain *spirit* of MacIntyre (even if it is largely unnamed) reemerges in the fourth section, "Deconstructing Derrida," in the interrogative energy that leads me to read Derrida against himself to illuminate problems with the way he sometimes articulates his project. In the last section, "Rerum Discordia Concordia," I argue that contestations remain between MacIntyre and Derrida that *are themselves* vital to the life of democratic politics. Ultimately, efforts to embrace a radical democratic politics of tensiondwelling involves cultivating an affirmation of the rich possibilities between positions, not simply within the position one favors.

### The Paradoxical Responsibilities of Historied Beings in the Face of Infinity

Derrida's earliest published work, *Edmund Husserl's "Origin of Geometry": An Introduction,* profoundly reflects on responsibility, historicity, tradition, teleology, intersubjectivity, and deferral in ways that powerfully inform his later ethical and political efforts. According to Derrida, Husserl brilliantly "inscribes the advent of mathematics within the ethico-teleological prescription of the infinite task."[3]

On Husserl's analysis, modern sciences and philosophy have fallen into a crisis of "objectivist alienation" in which their "theoretical and practical activity" has become separated from its "sense for life and the possibility of being related to *our* whole world" (*Introduction*, 31). They face fragmentation, a loss of meaning, and a waning of faith in rationality (a diagnosis that has certain resonances with MacIntyre, resonances that are often overlooked). Having lost sight of their profound historicity and connection with the lifeworld, having forgotten their traditional teleological mode of being that is the ground of *all* sense, contemporary efforts "to unify [fragments of knowledge] into a whole, instead of being fulfilled, come to nothing."[4] Only by recovering these dimensions could we recover meaning, unity, and "take our position toward actualities in judging, valuing, and acting."[5] Making ourselves responsible for this recovery is an "infinite task," yet for Husserl it is entwined with the origin of sense, truth, and all that is promising.

Yet how does Husserl think that geometry can illuminate the essence of all traditional culture, or culture as *essentially traditional?* How would this seemingly most ahistorical and timeless of all the sciences illuminate the historical?

For Husserl, it is precisely because geometry is at once objective (not affected by empirical subjectivity) and only what it appears to be (there is no object in itself behind the ideal triangle) that it can transparently exemplify the meaning and original mode of being of all truth, which he understands in terms of the *unity of sense—its worthiness to be passed on across time and social space.* Without this latter continuity of sense, there would not be—nor could we comprehend the meaning of—truth, culture, or history *as such.* In this way, geometry "is the most profound and purest history. Only the pure unity of such a tradition's sense is apt to establish this continuity. Without this no authentic history would be thought or projected as such; there would be only an empirical aggregate of finite accidental units" (*Introduction*, 59). Husserl is well aware of the temporal and spatial limits and discontinuities of cultural sense-making, but it is concerning the aspect of extended sense, without which there would be no culture, that he thinks his investigation into the most transparently disclosed unity of geometrical truths has much to teach us.

Husserl knows that every de facto historical culture is marked by local contingencies of language, practice, power, and geography that fragment and limit the spatio-temporal significance of many continuities. But Husserl's point, Derrida suggests, is that these accidental limits and ruptures are themselves only *thinkable* for a being who partakes of a more profound unity and continuity of meaning that somehow endures across the limits and can thus illuminate what has been arbitrarily cut short. Contingencies are not *fundamentally* constitutive of historicity, for the latter involves a sense that surpasses the limit of each one. Of course, these broader continuities of historical meaning also have a certain provincial and provisional character. Yet insofar as they are about truth and justice, they strive toward ever-broader continuities, which themselves attain unity, Husserl claims, only insofar as they partake of the original structure of historicity exemplified and revealed by geometry. There is sense insofar as there is a unity of meaning deemed worthy of being passed on; and true unity—beyond blindness and force—is constituted in the mode of a historicity whose telos is exemplified by geometry's infinite idealities. In short, "a sense-investigation of [geometry's] conditions of possibility will reveal . . . exemplarily the conditions of the historicity of science in general, then of universal historicity—the last horizon for all sense and objectivity in general" (*Introduction*, 34).

The meaning of geometry's infinite truths originates in the finite pregeometric lived world. The "life of practical needs" depends upon the perception, retention, and gradual perfection of various shapes and processes. The demands of our finite praxis engender sense worthy of enduring, for without it, our perception and cognition would be too discontinuous for survival. Husserl thinks of these pregeometric generalities as "morphological idealities." They are not "pure" and infinite but, rather, are precipitated out of and elaborated through the movement of finite historical perceptual experience. In the first instance, shape is not experienced as such but only immediately as the contour of *something* foregrounded in the context of bodily practical need. Over time, this sensuous impulse toward sense, through which the object itself coheres and appears against a background, advances toward the recognition of shapes as such, say the roundness of a blueberry, through which a more developed sense of the lived world can appear and be considered. "Spatial shapes, temporal shapes, and shapes of motion are . . . *singled out from* the totality of the perceived body" (*Introduction*, 123). This singling out and development of a sense of generality common to diverse experiences—for example, the "roundness" of a blueberry—arises as the tacit and immediate roundness of the berry seen at a previous moment is retained in memory and made explicit in a "reactivation" of the sense of its perceptual structure that grasps something common in both the past-perception-made-present and the present perception. Through the recognition of such sensible bodily idealities, general meanings develop the perceptual field through a process of increasing explication and begin to thread through and bind the world with increasing coherence (for example, the roundness of blueberries, peas, eyeballs, the moon, and so on).

This development intensifies insofar as "the life of practical needs" involves us in a technical praxis that "always [aims at] the production of particular preferred shapes and the improvement of them according to certain directions of gradualness" ("Origin," 178). Hence concepts like "smooth," "straight," "point," and "measurement" are increasingly refined with the gradual perfection of technical praxis (which, in turn, is further enabled by these concepts). The teleological horizon of this development is "an open infinity," in which each achieved level of perfection opens indefinitely toward those still greater.

Even as the horizons of these morphological idealities *open on to* an infinite process of perfection, they are themselves not infinite but are, rather, "bounded idealities": idealities whose sense is always marked by the contingencies of their particular historical sensual origin. Development consists in inhabiting and pushing beyond—and in this sense correcting—limits and orientations handed down from the past. The developments and directions of the past are thus incorporated and overcome simultaneously. Though this process is infinitely open, the movement beyond each finite sense always is itself finite and never attains the purity we imagine for the infinite idealities of geometry.

Yet Husserl argues that the latter, though qualitatively different, are grounded in the former. "It is evident in advance that this new sort of construction [geometry] will be a product arising out of an idealizing, spiritual act, one of 'pure' thinking, which has its materials in the designated general pregivens of this factual humanity and human surrounding world and creates 'ideal objects' out of them" ("Origin," 179). This new geometrical praxis will have its "bases" in the morphological idealities "developed out of [everyday] praxis and thought of in terms of [gradual] perfection" (178–79). Derrida interprets Husserl's understanding of this new geometrical praxis as a philosophical act of "radical freedom, which authorizes a move beyond finitude and opens the horizon of knowledge as that of a prehaving, i.e., of an infinite project or task (*Vorhaben*)" (*Introduction*, 127). The "open infinity" tacitly presupposed by finite perfections of everyday concepts rooted in lived practices is never thought of transparently or aimed at as such—we do not "prehave" it as infinity per se—in our pregeometrical praxis. With the thought of geometrical infinity, in a sense we take an energy and direction acquired as we are swept up by the finite *movement* of our thinking and utilize it to throw ourselves beyond finite aims toward an ideal beyond all limits. Husserl understands this move toward such an ideal as a "passage to the limit . . . the going beyond every sensible and factual limit. It concerns the ideal limit of an infinite transgression [of finitude], not the factual limit of the transgressed finitude" (*Introduction*, 127, my emphasis).[6] The absolute infinite—which makes all other infinites possible—is that of the unity of the geometrical field and science itself. "The ground of this unity is the world itself: not as the finite totality of sentient beings, but as the infinite totality of possible experiences in space in general" (*Introduction*, 52). In other words, the ideality of concepts like "line" or "circle" ultimately requires the infinite unity of the world, without which all claims would be limited to particular locations.

Yet exactly what sort of an infinite unity of sense is this? For all his writing about absolute ideality as beyond finitude, Husserl argues that this idea never exists in fully explicated purity—even in the consciousness of the supreme geometer. Indeed, he writes of "the obvious finitude of the individual and even the social capacity to transform the logical chains of centuries [at this point themselves massive and, as a developing work in progress, still by no means exhaustive of the infinite unity of the idealized geometric field], truly in the unity of one accomplishment, into originally genuine chains of self-evidence" ("Origin," 168). In the passage of one moment of "vivid self-evidence" to the next, there is a process of retention characterized by an "unavoidable sedimentation," a fading passive acquisition through which past moments are initially retained (and these past moments themselves contain further sedimented pasts). We can actively reproduce and reactivate the vivid self-evidence implicit in this and that passively acquired past, but we are limited in our capacities for such explication of the whole. Hence there is a constant danger that we might go astray amid this massive field of unexamined past presents that are always entwined with our teleologies of progression toward and projections of infinite ideality. And hence ideality is itself construed as permanent *responsibility* to think to and fro between premises and consequences, as a law *prescribing the work* of "idealization: namely, the removal of limits from our capacity, in a certain sense its *infinitization*" ("Origin," 168, my emphasis).

It follows, paradoxically, the geometrical science that was to "pass to the limit" beyond the finite to pure infinity is shown to be none other than finitude's infinite task of historical clarification between retentions and "protentions"—origin and telos—*toward* an ideality that is never transparently given. We "leap to the limit," but the "endpoint" we produce is finitely disclosed through a history of embodied explication that is never entirely at our disposal. Thus geometry's ideality, "this eternity, is *only* a historicity" (*Introduction*, 141): not a passage beyond passage but, rather, *another passage itself*, toward an uncertain telos that was already tacitly announced in and always marked by the first primordial impulses toward sense. Thus geometry turns out both to be and to profoundly illuminate *traditionalization* itself as the unifying essence of sense and truth.

Yet as Derrida reads Husserl, the traditioning through which alone geometric ideality is gradually manifest is itself possible only insofar as it is explicitly sought and constituted under the sway of this ideality as its telos. The ideality of geometry is historically elaborated, but this history has coherence, unity, and sense—it is *history,* as opposed to unintelligible disconnected fragments—only as and through the teleological pursuit of geometric ideality. Only thus might subjectivity gather itself and its objects from one moment to the next, making sense by honing ideas of commonality from finite experiences toward gradual perfection *under the sway of the idea of infinite unity.*[7]

Thus, of this Idea of an infinitely coherent unity, Derrida writes, "It is not by chance that there is no phenomenology of the Idea. The latter cannot be given in person, nor determined in an evidence, for it is only the possibility of evidence and the openness of 'seeing' itself; it is only *determinability* as the horizon for every intuition in general. . . . If there is nothing to say about the Idea *itself,* it is because the Idea is that starting point from which something in general can be said" (*Introduction,* 138–39). Paradoxically, the ultimate meaning of this Idea would be the very processes of sense-making that it makes possible forever prior to its full determination. There is no sense, finally, in absence of a teleological explication and elaboration of experience under the sway of an Idea (tacit or explicit) that, irreducible to any determinate finite content, is ultimately the "ethico-teleological prescription of the infinite task" of progressing beyond each finitude (*Introduction,* 136). Hence geometry's "leap" beyond the lifeworld does not achieve the manifestation of infinite ideality but, rather, vividly manifests the crucial role such never-attainable ideality tacitly plays in establishment of all sense—all *history* as such.

This is further illustrated, Husserl thinks, if we consider the most basic sense of any object, which rests upon an idea of its identity and continuity across diverse points in time and social space (even as aspects *of* this identical object might change or be manifold). Without this ideal both the world and the self would disintegrate into nothing but a shear aggregate of instantaneous empirical contingencies. Our sense of an object is gradually improved through the elaboration of concrete experience as aspects previously unseen are added, those mistakenly thought to be a part of it are removed, and so on. The unattainable telos of this effort is that of the infinite ideal object purified of distorting subjective contingencies. Hence, "to *constitute* an ideal object is to put it at the permanent disposition of a pure gaze. . . . Here the act of primordial *depositing* [the gradual sedimentation of the ideal] is not the recording of a private thing, but the production of a *common* object, i.e. of an *object* whose original owner is thus dispossessed" (*Introduction*, 78).

For Husserl, the idea of common enduring objectivity is entwined with the ideal of transcendental *intersubjectivity*. The telos that temporally binds the self through the elaboration of sense simultaneously opens the self to the vantage point of others. Intrasubjective communication (between the diverse moments within the self) is entwined with the ideal of intersubjective communication across time and space: "Of course, [ultimately] the world and fellow mankind . . . designate the all-inclusive, but infinitely open, unity of possible experiences and not this world right here, these fellow men right here, whose factuality for Husserl is never anything but a variable example" (*Introduction*, 79).

Even as ideals *exceed* any concrete social instantiation, they exert a call that draws us into particular relations and traditions of teleologically engendered sense and inquiry on our infinite journey toward truth. "Every science is related to an open chain of the generations of those who work for and with one another . . . who are the productive subjectivity of the total living science" (*Introduction*, 60). As a participant in an "open chain" of others, one bears responsibility *with* them, and moreover one (and one's particular community or communities) comes to be *as* this responsibility: "The investigator's own subjectivity [and also that of particular traditions] is constituted by the idea or horizon of total subjectivity which is made responsible in and through him for each of his acts" (*Introduction*, 61).

Derrida's account accentuates Husserl's discussion of responsibility to draw out the ethical dimension at the heart of all sense-making (*Introduction*, 141). Philosophy as phenomenology is the elucidation of this Idea, which we inherit and to which we are always already responding in "lived anticipation." Yet this elucidation (described above) not only "responds *to*" but is also "responsible *for*" the Idea.

If "the Absolute is Passage," then to be responsible for this passage is to make it explicit in order to protect it from the ever-present danger of forgetfulness and straying. "Responsibility here means shouldering a word one hears spoken, as well as taking on oneself the transfer of sense, in order to look after its advance" (*Introduction*, 149). Even more: "[Philosophers] must *prescribe [commander]* [reactivation and teleological reason]; . . . assume responsibility for a *mandate*. Only in this sense does Husserl describe [the philosopher] as a functionary of mankind" (*Introduction*, 146). By making explicit and prescribing these entwined ideas of teleological sense, ideal objectivity, and intersubjectivity, we, as selves and communities, become responsible *for* the horizons that are responsible for our sense and coherence as we respond *to* them.

Insofar as these responsibilities lie at the heart of sense, Husserl uncovers an ethical condition of the world. *Only by caring for the traditionalizing structures of intersubjectivity that illuminate and are illuminated by our particular traditions—only through arts of respectful, responsible, and open communication—have we any hope of making sense of our world and our ethical being.* There is, thus, a teleological horizon of democratic—profoundly open and responsive—intersubjectivity that is constitutive of traditioning and for which we must be responsible, even if this too is an infinite idea that always exceeds our finite efforts to theorize and embody it.[8]

Derrida further develops the sense of ethical relations and responsibility in another early essay entitled "Violence and Metaphysics." Again thinking in relation to Husserl's later phenomenology, Derrida writes, "Without the *phenomenon* [read "sense"] of the other as other no respect would be possible": "The phenomenon of respect supposes the respect of phenomenality. And ethics, phenomenology."[9]

We have seen how Husserl enjoins respect for alterity by dispossessing subjectivity of its exhaustive grasp of things and other subjects. For Husserl, things offer the "possibility of an originary and original presentation [that] is always open, in principle and a priori," even as this is historically unachievable for finite beings. Yet others have, in addition to the alterity of incompleteness belonging to things, the alterity of being others perceiving the world and me, and they pose "the radical impossibility of going around to see things from the other side"—the principled impossibility of an original presentation. These two alterities combine so that I cannot be given "the subjective face of his experience *from his perspective,* such as he lived it." Instead, Husserl discovers, the other and the other's experience are always given to me "only through analogical appresentation" ("Violence and Meta-physics," 124). With this latter term, Husserl means that the other appears to me only through analogies of the other as one who *like me* opens onto the world. The other is in principle not in my "site," or place where my sense opens; rather, the other is the subject of another site of opening that I can recognize only through a fundamentally ana-logical structure. There is a certain "metaphoricity" in which I "deport" the other perceptually and linguistically onto my own site. I interpret the other through a vision that, try as I might and as I must to see from another vantage point, remains finally my own and not the other's. I can travel to an other's opening to the world only by an analogical movement in which I am stuck imagining (aided by the other's appear-ance, the appearance of the other's lived world to me, the other's sto-ries, and related accounts) what it would be *like* if I were *like* the other person perceiving the world. Our most receptive and generous travels are also deportations of the other(s). Indeed, this latter element of "pre-ethical violence," essential to opening relations to the other, alone "permit[s] access to the other to be determined, in ethical freedom, as moral violence or non-violence" ("Violence and Metaphysics," 129). Moral nonviolence can only emerge through a perceptual rendering of the other that partakes of a pre-ethical violence in which the other is both deported to my site and appears *as an other irreducible to my site*. For Derrida, it is in recognizing both dimensions of our perceptual relations with others—both the primordial inevitability of preconscious erring and the primordial possibility of a relationship in which this erring can be resisted and reduced in dialogical pursuits of justice and peace—that we might become responsible *to* the other and *for* the eth-ical opening toward the other. We never reside in a state of absolute justice or peace. Yet we can, Derrida argues, deploy "violence against violence"—we can deploy this partially disclosive yet imperfect render-ing of the other against that disclosive yet imperfect rendering—to illu-minate possibilities for more just and less ethically violent relations.

To recognize the "phenomenon of nonphenomenality" (the strange way the other is given to me as not given to me) is to mark a space where ethics *as* the question of the other can emerge and be addressed. To affirm this, "far from signifying an analogical and assimilatory reduction of the other to the same, [actually] confirms and respects separation, the unsurpassable necessity of (nonobjective) mediation" ("Violence and Metaphysics," 124). The phenomenon of nonphenom-enality elicits a radical democratic ideal because it presents the other as a question to me, and "it is profoundly foreign to all hierarchies"

(121). Democracy *as an infinite ideality*—a world where our perceptual and practical relations with others would be absolutely dialogically just and nonviolent—must remain an inexhaustible and never fully achieved horizon of our work. As such, it draws all finite practices dialectically beyond the limits of each historical incarnation, and it solicits the passage of democratic practices in a manner analogous to the way geometrical ideality solicits the passage of geometrical praxis. Under the sway of this sense of others, we are drawn into radical dialectical democratic traditions striving to articulate the ethical-political sense—the institutions, practices, principles, languages, rights, habits, affects, and so on—of our responsibility to and for each other.

Thus far, Derrida's discussion of Husserl illuminates two irreducibly related ways in which phenomenology grasps the roots of our idea of two infinite alterities entwined with the elaboration of two teleological historicities: First, regarding objects, the process of gradual perfection rooted in sensuous need coexists in a relation of reciprocal solicitation with the idea of infinite objectivity. Second, regarding others, dialogical relations to the others who are given through analogical appresentation coexist in a relation of reciprocal solicitation with the idea of the infinite other. Without phenomenology's first mode of grasping, there would be no sense regarding the world of objects. Without the second, there would be "absolute violence . . . nothingness or pure non-sense" in relation to others ("Violence and Metaphysics," 130).

Yet these very relations between absolute Ideals and correlative traditioning also draw Derrida toward a type of questioning that gives rise to different, more radical articulations of responsibility that he will juxtapose to the above formulations in ways that open his radical dialectics to energetic contestation and questioning (*not* dismissal).

The task of elaborating tradition stands in relation to an Idea "which never phenomenalizes itself": The unifying movement of time and the elaboration of sense is drawn by an Idea that is always deferred even as we continually project partial visions of it out ahead of our current historical praxis (*Introduction*, 137). Yet with this thought of unpresentable Ideal Objectivity, Derrida suggests that we have arrived at "the most profound region of phenomenological reflection, where darkness risks being no longer the provision of appearing or the field which offers itself to phenomenal light, but the forever nocturnal source of the light itself" (137). Thought discovers it is born of and borne by an absolute origin that it always already retains and anticipates—but can never possess. Derrida's suggestion here (with and beyond Husserl) is different from the one discussed above, concerning a sense that endlessly develops through gradual illuminating movement toward an inexhaustible Idea that would itself be thought of as pure infinite light. Now the accent is placed on an even more radical alterity. However much distance and deferral are integral to phenomenology's sense of traditionality and Ideal, there remains an *intimacy* between them in the reciprocal conditioning that animates and infuses their relationship, an intimacy in the shared characteristic of light, even if one is radically finite and the other infinite. There may be a zillion radical dialectical changes in direction, but the relation between tradition and Ideal is always thought within a to-and-fro cycle in which they fundamentally belong together, no matter how much we may err—no matter how discrepant their relation may be at any point in time. Yet Derrida is drawn to question this intimacy between the objectivity of our Ideal and our sense making. What if this object is in some aspect radically foreign to the sense-making to-and-fro we have described? What if that which somehow instigates our traditionality is fundamentally other than our sense and than the unified Ideal we postulate as its condition and infinite elaboration? What if traditionality is engendered in relationship to something that is, somehow, in some way or in some aspect, fundamentally outside and other than the light/illuminating process that Husserl and Derrida profoundly describe?

Derrida's point is not to dogmatically insist on this outsideness as a thesis but, rather, to show that it is a question that irrepressibly haunts phenomenology because it emerges with the distant telos that phenomenology describes as the condition of our sense. It is the question of something radically outside the relative intimacy (however discrepant and discordant) of tradition-telos. The discrepancy thematized by phenomenology in relation to an infinite ideality that cannot appear as such itself solicits this question, even if phenomenology itself does not fully pursue it. The possibility that the infinite might thus be thought of as *absolute darkness* carries with it an interrogative force that magnifies our sense of the world's alterity and our modesty in the face of it. As Derrida develops this thought in later works, his point seems to be that in the relatively intimate reciprocities in the relationship between tradition and telos, there is a strong tendency toward the overproduction of confidence and closure regarding the world and others. For even where a profound distance is recognized, we tend to think that we stand in greater proximity to the Ideal, that we have more possession of it, than do all the others. Derrida's inquiries into questions concerning a more radical alterity mean to disrupt this conviction and intensify our responsiveness to the "infinite multiplicity" of the world and other "intersubjectivities" (*Introduction*, 152).

Derrida is convinced by Husserl's argument that without an at least tacit telos of Ideality, sense is impossible. Hence we must respond to and for this Idea, which is the condition of our subjectivity, our experience of the world, and our opening toward others. Yet we do not *have* it; we *are and become* without grasping it—which is to say, without *it*. And it is nothing for us outside this history within which it cannot appear as such—for there is nothing *for us* outside of this unfolding history of sense:

> *If there is any history,* then historicity can be only the passage of Speech [*Parole*], the pure tradition of a primordial Logos toward a polar Telos. But since there can be nothing outside the pure historicity of that passage, since there is no Being which has sense outside of this historicity or escapes its infinite horizon, since the Logos and the Telos *are* nothing outside the *interplay (Wechselspiel)* of their reciprocal inspiration, this signifies then that the *Absolute is Passage.* Traditionality is what circulates from one to the other, illuminating one by the other in a movement wherein consciousness discovers its path in an indefinite reduction, always already begun, and wherein every adventure is a change of direction [*conversion*] and every return to the origin an audacious move toward the horizon. This movement is also *Danger(ous) as the Absolute [l'absolu d'un Danger].* For if the light of sense is only through Passage, that is because the light can also be lost on the way. Like speech, light can be lost only in the inauthenticity of a *language* and by the abdication of a speaking being. . . . Phenomenology . . . is . . . the free resolution to "take up one's own sense" (or regain consciousness *[reprendre son sens]*), in order to make oneself accountable, through speech, for an imperiled pathway. This speech is historical, because it is always already a *response.* Responsibility here means shouldering a word one hears spoken . . . as well as taking on oneself the transfer of sense, in order to look after its advance. (*Introduction*, 149)

In the unbridgeable interval between passage and deferred infinity, questions emerge about the Idea: Light? Or Darkness? The projection and condition of *our* sense-making? Or a question coming from elsewhere and opening our sense-making to the experience of its radical questionability and limitation in otherness? Both? For Derrida, we *must also* be responsible to and for these radical questions infusing phenomenology's good sense—and the openings toward otherness that they engender. Acknowledging the *"threatened* unity of sense and being" (*Introduction,* 151, my emphasis) is integral to resisting the closures of overconfidence that insinuate themselves in traditioning. Far from making a gesture toward nihilism, Derrida seeks to pursue questions through which we might resist nihilism—which is born in and borne by our closure to the question of others and otherness—in favor of radical responsibility, through which we might open and offer ourselves to the world and others. The aporia of the Absolute, paradoxically, calls us more genuinely to bear responsibility for "shouldering the word" and for transferring sense by opening our sense-making to energetic interrogations concerning the possessive nonsense that is always infused in and often accumulates with our traditions of sense.

Derrida's discussion of others in "Violence and Metaphysics" raises similar questions. We have seen how closely Derrida follows Husserl's account of the analogical genesis of the other who is paradoxically perceptually given to us as not given to us. This sense calls us critically and dialogically to turn pre-ethical violence of finitude against itself through critique, toward peace and offering. Yet Derrida also suspects that phenomenology itself risks a certain overconfidence (conjuring up the confidence trickster we visited in chapter 4) as it leans toward the idea that the subject *gives itself* the sense of both finitude and infinite alterity. He again discerns a question that haunts phenomenology from within its own account of analogical appresentation. Though Derrida agrees that the other can never appear to me—is not given *for me*—beyond phenomenological mediation, nevertheless this other-who-appears-in-my-site-as-beyond-my-site poses a radical question to my phenomenological sense: Can we speak so confidently of the meaning of this alterity primarily as *something we give ourselves?* Or, does not the other thus disclosed provoke the opening of my world in a way that exceeds this phenomenological accounting and calls it into question? Perhaps the opening of the question of the other originates not from my analogical sense-giving disclosed by phenomenology but from the other in excess of this? As soon as we try to articulate an affirmation that would make sense of this possibility, we would tacitly confirm phenomenology's claim that meaning (even that concerning the other who exceeds our sense) is properly *ours*—for sense is always *our* sense. "But the naked opening of the question, its silent opening, escapes phenomenology, as the origin and end of phenomenology's logos" ("Violence and Metaphysics," 133). We reside in a world where the *question* of the other has already made itself felt prior to our efforts to make sense of how this is possible and what it means. Thus, Derrida argues, Emmanuel Levinas's *questioning* of phenomenology, though always presupposing phenomenology as soon as he articulates a more determined *affirmative sense* of alterity, would have an ineliminable legitimacy.

In a nutshell: The infinite alterities that call forth teleological traditioning also always call it into question. Infinity solicits a responsibility for teleological elaboration, but it also solicits a responsibility to recall the darkness at the source of light, the alterity in excess of our sense of the other. We are called to be responsible to the ateleological aspect of inheritance and anticipation that haunts every teleology. With and beyond phenomenology, at the moment when we recognize teleology's inability to wholly account for itself, there emerges a responsibility to consider alterity as the radical "opening of the horizon, and not *in* the horizon" ("Violence and Metaphysics," 149). On Derrida's reading, though Husserl's insights are epistemologically and ethically powerful and compelling, insofar as they fail to pursue more-radical questions of alterity, they risk exaggerating our powers for making sense, approaching truth, and pursuing ethical and political justice. To become more responsive to the others and otherness of the world requires that we teleologically strive to create discourses and practices that make ethical and political sense, while at the same time rendering these discourses and practices more vulnerable to what they do not anticipate. This paradoxical responsibility requires an energy and posture that is as difficult as it is important. Derrida's aporetic philosophical journeys aim to cultivate an enchantment with the world and others as a *question* in ways that help enliven this tensional responsibility.

### Ethics and Politics of Democracy to Come

In numerous ethical and political writings, Derrida powerfully articulates this idea of a double responsibility as it pertains to democracy, justice, European traditions, capital, cosmopolitanism, and culture. As Derrida's *Other Heading: Reflections of Today's Europe*[10] provides a penetrating account of many themes that directly address questions we began to explore through the work of MacIntyre, I focus my discussion upon this book, drawing upon other texts where they deepen and broaden the enquiry at hand.

In 1990 amid increasing immigration to Western Europe from the East and South, German reunification, the emergence of the European Union, nationalisms and subnationalisms, democratization, changes

brought on by corporate globalization, and numerous other developments drawing European identity into question, Derrida wrote with a
sense of danger and pregnancy: "Something unique is afoot in Europe,
in what is still called Europe, even if we no longer know very well *what*
or *who* goes by this name" (*Other Heading*, 5). In *Other Heading* he
takes the proliferation of ethical-political questions of the past, present, and future of Europe, as well as of peoples from other shores, as
an opportunity to rethink democratic responsibility. Rejecting both
unreflective Eurocentrism and wholesale rejections of Europe, Derrida
asks, "For what cultural identity must we be responsible? And responsible before whom? Before what memory? For what promise? And is
'cultural identity' a good word 'today'?" (13). His response is significantly fashioned in relation to his philosophical reflections already discussed above.[11]

Those who are "European *among other things*"—those whose sensibilities have been significantly shaped by European traditions (*Other
Heading*, 83)—"must . . . be responsible for this discourse of the modern [European] tradition. We bear the responsibility for this heritage"
(28), Derrida writes. To be responsible for a heritage—which lives on
willy-nilly in and through us—it is essential *among other things* to
work dialectically with the traditions that significantly constitute our
perceptions, affects, understandings, powers, and interactions with the
world. We must critically juxtapose and utilize the partial insights they
afford to critically discern legacies of damage and alternative promises
in order to rework (often radically) broader future horizons.[12] Moreover, we must be responsible for these traditions because they offer
some important conceptual and practical resources for more receptively
engaging with those *beyond* "Europe." Drawing upon the philosophical reflections explored above, Derrida thinks that there are aspects
of European thinking and practice that aid our efforts to learn from
and to live well with other traditions and emergent groups within and
beyond "Europe"; that there are powerful insights that can contribute
to decentering our thinking and practice in ways that are crucial for ethical engagements with others and for democracy as a pluralizing art.[13]

Hence, Derrida's call to a responsibility for European tradition is
inherently related to vulnerable engagements with those beyond Europe.
Proliferating questions evocative of a memory and future possibility
of receptivity, he asks, "What if Europe were this: the opening onto a
history for which the changing of the heading, the relation to the other
heading or the other of the heading, is experienced as always possible? . . . For which Europe *would be,* in a constitutive way, this very

responsibility?" (*Other Heading*, 17). What if Europe sought its future through elements of its past promising receptivity to others? Derrida develops his stance by pursuing the difference at the heart of any tradition of identification and sense-making. Thus, following his work with and beyond Husserl and already distant from Eurocentrism, he writes, "*What is proper to a culture is to not be identical to itself. Not to not have an identity, but to not be able to identify itself, to be able to say 'me' or 'we'; to be able to take the form of a subject only in the non-identity to itself or, if you prefer, only in the difference with itself [avec soi]* . . . A difference at once internal and irreducible to the at home (with itself *[chez soi]*" (9–10). Cultures are not exhaustive identities but ensembles of discourses and practices gathering themselves in movements between memories of distant origins and anticipations of distant ends of their (currently incomplete) identity. Cultures develop identity by gathering themselves in anticipation of one they do not yet have. Infused with nonidentity, "the history of a culture . . . presupposes an identifiable heading, a *telos* toward which the movement, the memory, the promise, and the identity, even if it be as difference to itself, dreams of gathering itself *taking the initiative, being out ahead, in anticipation*" (18).

Yet this teleological structure of culture, Derrida emphasizes, opens it from "within" to unpredictable difference irreducible to that between the culture as it is and the culture as it longs to be. European (and every) culture opens beyond this difference of an "interior border," for the teleological structure of identity gathering "also presupposes that the heading not be *given*, that it not be identified once and for all" (*Other Heading*, 18) but rather be *questionable* to itself. The telos remains, like a shadow we chase, ahead of us, beyond our grasp: This difference is *not strictly ours*, not even as an anticipation that we would make better than all the others. As questionability, it opens us to others and otherness in ways that exceed our efforts to contain the difference within "our" culture, as "they" are drawn into contestations with "us" over which "we" have no sovereign control. The teleological difference would thus "gather this center, relating it to itself, only to the extent that it would open it up to this divergence"—and to the plethora of divergences that come from elsewhere (10). Every culture is in this sense "a culture *of* the other": a culture that both repeatedly negotiates its relations to other cultures that coexist with it and *comes into being* very much through this wild process of encountering and being encountered by alterity. And it is uncertain where the questionability of our telos comes from: An interior distance opening us to the question of the others? Or the others who throw our identifications and telos into question in the first place and to whom we must respond?

Hence we are called to a responsibility for an "opening and non-exclusion" toward that which is other than our telos, our "heading." This entails radical efforts to receive and learn with the "others of our heading" and the "other headings" (the visions coming from beyond "Europe"—and especially those that have been subjugated by various European headings for over five hundred years). "Dialectic has always been in the service of th[e] autobiography of Europe" (*Other Heading*, 26). Hence Derrida emphasizes "*the heading of the other*, before which we must respond and which we must *remember, of which* we must *remind ourselves*, the heading of the other being perhaps the first condition of an identity or identification that is not an ego-centricism destructive of oneself and the other" (15).

Pushing still further, Derrida emphasizes that we must recognize that the event of responsibility and opening exceeds teleological structure. The encounter as an *event* is "*the other of the heading*, that is to say . . . [it] no longer obeys the form, the sign, or the logic of the heading, nor even of the *anti-heading*" (*Other Heading*, 15). Our encounters with each other are infused with difference and generativity in ways that exceed the intentionality and control of those engaged, imbuing our encounters with an element of wildness. Hence Derrida writes that every culture and tradition "has begun to open itself, or rather to let itself open, or, better yet, to be affected with opening without opening *itself* . . . onto an other that the heading can no longer relate to itself as *its* other, *the other with itself* (76). To be responsive to others and this otherness we must learn to attend more receptively to this character of our becoming as the locus of unwonted possibilities that may open relations that are less violent, less unjust, and more generously democratic. Thus we are called not only to attend to the teleologies of others but *also* to attend to possibilities that are unanticipated by any of our divergent teleologies: possibilities not yet dreamed by any of us prior to the encounter. "The irruption of the new, the unicity of the other 'today' should be awaited *as such* (but is the *as such,* the phenomenon, the being *as such* of the unique and of the other, ever possible?); it should be anticipated *as* the unforeseeable, the *unanticipatable,* the nonmasterable, nonidentifiable, in short, as that of which one does not yet have a memory" (18).

Yet this call to anticipate the unanticipatable must never become a comfortable deconstructionist mantra lulling us to abandon the work of determinate democratic theory and practice in favor of messianic gestures toward "the new" and "possibility." Just as the teleological structure of culture calls us from within to a responsibility to other teleologies and the ateleological, so too responsibility to the ateleological aspects of becoming also calls us from within to the importance of teleological ethical and political work. For as soon as we evoke the new, "our old memory" of our history "tells us that it is . . . necessary to anticipate and to keep the heading"; necessary to cultivate our politics in light of a telos (*Other Heading*, 18). As corporate globalization and many of its dismal alternatives parade under the demagogic rhetoric of "the new world order," "the new man," "the new race," and so forth, we must "keep the heading *[garder le cap]*: for under the banner . . . of the unanticipatable or the absolutely new, we can fear seeing return the phantom of the worst, the one we have already identified. We know the 'new' only too well" (ibid.). It is often a return of the worst. Our power of judgment will not be enhanced if we abandon teleological projects that solicit, guide, and protect it, as painstaking memories inform and are informed by visions of the future. Ateleological anticipations and responsibilities must repeatedly be called to account in light of our more teleological sensibilities.

*And yet.*[14] We must also repeatedly mobilize our yearning for and receptivity toward unpredictable encounters with others beyond our heading in ways that draw this latter accounting into deep questioning. For we humans too often tend to respond to the uncertainties of our condition with strategies of preemptive closure toward newness as such. Our teleologies often harden into structures of insistence that deny the differences and distances that might open our cultures and history to otherness. Hence, as we must critically examine the "new" in light of our memory of "the worst," so too we must critically examine our memories and anticipations of the worst in order to deconstruct our arbitrary—but often highly organized—tendencies to mobilize and generalize these "protections" in ways that close off challenges to power and encounters with the new as such. Little is more common or more dangerous than the tendency to (mis)identify every new and unanticipated event, person, or emergent group as an instance of "the worst" that must be defeated. Indeed, much of what is actually worst originates and perpetuates itself in precisely this manner. And yet. The worst *has already come* to us and does threaten us in many ways. Hence we cannot quit our efforts to better anticipate the bad and the worst, but neither can we quit our responsibility to discern the worst *in many of these very efforts.* Thus responsibility requires a double suspicion: "We must be suspicious of *both* repetitive memory *and* the completely other of the absolutely new" (*Other Heading,* 9).

Derrida calls us repeatedly to multiple and often contradictory responsibilities. Double contradictory laws, double suspicions, and double gestures weave through his texts and interrupt each other, performatively enacting his substantive insights. With these unendingly difficult convolutions, he aims to energetically resist widespread tendencies (many in the name of universality and diversity) that would "keep at home (with [them]sel[ves]) *[chez soi]* the turbulence of the *with,* of calming it down in order to make it into a simple, interior border— well guarded by the vigilant sentinels of being" (*Other Heading,* 26). His worry is that "good sense"—lacking irony, paradox, contradiction, unexpected interruptions—will inexorably tend toward unresponsiveness to others.[15] He fears, rightly I think, that accompanying the preconscious "deportation" of the other onto my site there is an inexorable tendency toward oblivion (often reinforced and mobilized), in the face of which we must cultivate radicalized *tensional* solicitations and practices of responsibility.

This oblivion expresses itself in a "paradox of universality" that *delimits* every articulation of the universal (*Other Heading,* 71). Derrida traces how Paul Valéry describes the crisis facing Europe as a crisis of spirit that threatens not just Europe but a broader "universality for which Europe is responsible" (69). Valéry thinks this universality hinges upon the responsible memory of Europeans who know how to read, appropriate, and *extend* the "cultural capital" that Europe has accumulated over the centuries. The essence of this capital lies in how it prepares and calls us to this project of building more cultural capital toward universality: "to open onto the infinite and give rise to the universal. The maxim of maximization, which . . . is nothing other than spirit itself, assigns to European man his essence" (*Other Heading,* 69–70). For Valéry, the development of freedom—including for non-Europeans—is central to this universalizing project.

Yet where Valéry witnesses and celebrates a European—and especially French—distinction, Derrida witnesses a "paradox of the paradox." The first paradox is that Valéry defines the *unique distinction* of Europe precisely in its exemplary inscription of the *universal.* "Whether it takes a national form or not, a refined, hospitable or aggressively xenophobic form or not, the self-affirmation of an identity always claims to be responding to the call or assignation of the universal. There are no exceptions to the law." Every culture takes itself to be the "*inscription* of the universal in the singular, the *unique testimony* to the human essence" (*Other Heading,* 72–73).[16] This paradox, through which the uniqueness of a culture must be articulated as the exemplary incarnation of the nonunique, engenders another paradox: Whereas Valéry notes that his "paradoxical" "personal impression" is that France's "special quality . . . is to believe and feel that we are universal," Derrida rejoins that this feeling "is not reserved for the French. Not even . . . for Europeans" (75). It seems that every culture feels this distinction belongs to itself alone—whereas in fact such a feeling appears to be a characteristic of *every* culture. This "paradox of the paradox," Derrida argues, enjoins a sort of "fission reaction": The heading of each culture that recognizes this doubly strange situation is called to divide, to recall the division that has already occurred in the multiplicitous articulations of contested universality. Henceforth it must recognize that it inhabits a pluralizing opening toward the universal and that its distinct identity and direction is always already formed in relationships with others who co-inhabit this opening. Recognizing this, we must assume a responsibility to respond not only to our heading but also to the other headings striving to articulate universality. Illuminating this deeply paradoxical situation at the heart of what we hold dearest, Derrida hopes to open us to and beyond our oblivion.

Derrida articulates democratic theory and practice through these paradoxes and double gestures, writing of an injunction to "assume the European, and *uniquely* European, heritage of an idea of democracy, while also recognizing that this idea, like that of international law, is never simply given, that its status is not even that of a regulative idea in the Kantian sense, but rather something that remains to be thought and *to come [a venir]:* . . . a democracy that must have the structure of a promise—*and thus the memory of that which carries the future, the to-come, here and now*" (*Other Heading,* 78). In *Specters of Marx,* Derrida theorizes a democratic double promise in ways that are richly suggestive.[17]

*On the one hand,* democracy's promise, or democracy *as* promise, calls for a *dialectical* development of the progressive thrusts of democratic traditions. Here democracy develops through the to-and-fro of critical initiatives and dialectical adjustments between theory and practice. Thus, writing on how theoretical critique can bring critical transformative pressure to bear upon the world of practice, Derrida affirms a certain radical democratic spirit of Marx, that "would still remain within the *idealist* logic of Fukuyama . . . [by critiquing the world in terms of] the gap between an empirical reality and a regulating ideal, whether the latter is defined as Fukuyama does or whether one refines and transforms the concept" (*Specters of Marx*, 86). Yet although this rendering is important, it risks reifying and rigidifying ideals when it removes them from the context of historical struggles and human finitude where they are forged.

Hence Derrida conceives of radical democratic practice in relation to a dialectically evolving regulative ideal that simultaneously *both* solicits and nurtures new struggles, practices, and political applications *and* is redefined by them. For example, "the concept of human rights has slowly been determined over the course of centuries through many socio-political upheavals," as will be the future of international law as it is hewn at the murky intersection of theory and practice (*Specters of Marx*, 84). Notions of rights (combined with conceptions of empirical truth) have historically played important roles in spurring and empowering various struggles by blacks, Native Americans, women, and others for rights-bearing status and democratic empowerment. Similarly, many have struggled to extend rights to a broader field of political, social, and economic life by arguing that the realization of the freedoms and powers acknowledged in one (already recognized) area required extensions to other areas if they were to be realized at all. Yet in most instances, promised regulative ideals have not only spurred struggles to reduce the gap between "ideals" and "reality" but have themselves undergone changes as struggles and new applications transformed their meaning (for example, as freedom is no longer entwined with mastery over a spouse and the possession of slaves, as various social and economic freedoms shift the relations and proportions between negative and positive freedom, or as freedom comes to be understood more in terms of the public activity and relationships of political life). In struggling toward regulative ideals, people do not proceed according to a seamless dialectical logic but take a risky sense-transforming "leap" that seizes some aspects of a complex notion to extend and transform them in ways that alter or diminish other aspects. This occurs amid a historical situation of finitude that exceeds and infuses our ideals with contingency and significant unpredictability. The practice of democracy ceaselessly "denounces divergences between the principle of those rights (whose reaffirmation must be and can only be unconditional) and the concrete conditions of their implementations, the determined limits of their representation, the abuses of or inequalities in their application as a result of certain interests, monopolies or existing hegemonies" (*Other Heading*, 52)—and ceaselessly rearticulates rights and democracy in light of new senses born in struggles animated by such critique.

Derrida affirms the democratic promise to "reduce the gap *as much as possible*" between "reality" and "ideals" (*Specters of Marx*, 86) in order to struggle to remake the world so that it makes more democratic sense; so that it is more *sensible*. It is a commitment to democracy as sense-making in which, through transformative criticisms between theory and practice, we make ourselves responsible—drawn by the vulnerable hope of participating in a movement of democracy worthy of affirmation across generations.

Frequently, readers are puzzled by this commitment on the part of a leading deconstructionist. Yet it is drawn from Derrida's analysis of the teleological elaboration of truth and justice, an analysis that reaches back over forty years. As we have seen, long before Habermas developed a theory of communicative rationality, intersubjective reason figured prominently in Derrida's reading of Husserl. Hence his adamant support for a politics that protects and enhances "free and open discussion with a view to consensus" should not be surprising (*Other Heading*, 43). Sense *as* democratization and the sense *of* democracy impose a duty to nurture "the universality of formal law, the desire for translation, agreement and univocity, the law of the majority" (78) and to resist the "dispersion" of European cultural identity "into a myriad of provinces, into a multiplicity of self-enclosed idioms, or petty little nationalisms, each one jealous" (39). What democratic sensibility or justice could develop in oblivion to these demands?

And yet. For Derrida, exceeding dialectical promises, critique, and good sense, there is *"the other hand"* of democracy, another dimension to the democratic memory and promise. Here Derrida gestures toward a responsibility to being radically open to and opened by the other(s) beyond the determined places, times, and modes one makes for them based on dialectical common sense. Surely by creating democratic rights, laws, institutions, and habitual modes of engagement, a culture may secure openings for others to appear beyond and in opposition to the limits of the predominant order. This is, in fact, a vital aspect of the teleological ideals of radical democracy, and our interminable responsibility to these ideals is rooted significantly in their call for an order of the "the same" that nurtures practices of welcoming "the other." Hence this "one hand" of democracy is a condition for the "other hand" of the democratic promise. Yet these very openings are also often construed in ways that function as arbitrary closures toward new modes (or long-suppressed old modes) of ethical-political challenge. Similarly, our democratic openings are frequently deployed to engender oblivion when they are paraded as a sufficient evidence for the presence of democracy in order to silence all "unappreciative" critics. In more banal fashion, they can also function to de-energize our receptivity to ethical and political configurations that emerge unwontedly, as we organize ourselves toward political engagements with an exaggerated confidence in our democratic openness and good sense. Our "openings"—maybe even the best of them—have this uncanny way of putting us to sleep and acquiring fortress-like characteristics in spite of ourselves. Thus Derrida claims that democracy and justice call us also to promise a hospitality beyond every established practice and teleological ideal, to cultivate a heightened anticipation of unexpected people and struggles and a requisite readiness for radical reformations of our receptive capacities, democratic modes, and horizons, if we are to learn to engage others well:

> The idea, if that is still what it is, of democracy to come, its "idea" as event of a pledged injunction that orders one to summon the very thing that will never present itself in the form of full presence, is the opening of this gap between an infinite promise (always untenable at least for the reason that it calls for the infinite respect of the singularity *and* infinite alterity of the other as much as the respect of the countable, calculable, subjectal equality between anonymous singularities) and the determined, necessary, but also necessarily inadequate forms of what is measured against this promise. . . . [T]he actuality of the democratic promise . . . will always keep within it, and it must do so, this absolutely undetermined messianic hope at its heart . . . awaiting without horizon of wait . . . hospitality without reserve, welcoming salutation accorded in advance to the absolute surprise of the *arrivant* from whom or from which one will not ask anything in return and who or which will not be asked to commit to the domestic contracts of any welcoming power. (*Specters of Marx*, 65)

For Derrida democracy must remain a promise in excess of every regulative idea, precisely because regulative ideas are inherently tensional, torn between infinite respect for singularities and an obligation to an anonymous egalitarian fairness, to calculability, and to intersubjectively acceptable reasons. Derrida writes that we must simultaneously respond *to (répondre à)* the other and respond *for (répondre de)* the others *before (répondre devant)* a community of others.[18] Because democracy is committed to these various obligations—often mutually supportive, but often also in deep conflict—there is a certain inconceivability inherent in its concept that renders democracy always as a working journey that is significantly yet-to-be. It must be a responsiveness that does not yet know itself, or, better, that knows not to know itself too well.

Of course, we must continue calculating, reasoning, formulating ideals, constituting practices, and taking action, precisely in order to respond to, for, and before the others democratically. We must enjoin others to do so as well, even though our efforts and theirs will be imperfect. There will be absolutely no responsibility where determinate efforts are shunned or endlessly delayed in the name of an "abstract and dogmatic eschatology in the face of the world's evil," against which Derrida cautions his readers (*Specters of Marx*, 87). He is insistent and clear about this: "A promise must promise to be kept, that is, not to remain 'spiritual' or 'abstract', but to produce events, new effective forms of action, practice, organization, and so forth. To break with the "party form" or with some form of the State or the International does not mean to give up every form of practical or effective organization. It is exactly the contrary that matters to us here" (89). Yet we must at the same time insist upon cultivating a more radical sense of responsibility, welcoming, a "hospitality without reserve" that can never "phenomenalize" itself, and is "impossible."

Derrida enjoins this paradoxical responsibility not only in spite of the impossibility of anticipating the unanticipatable but also *precisely because of* this impossibility. Recall that in his early work on Husserl, the actuality of praxis and the possibility of the ideal horizon reciprocally inspire and condition each other, as theorizing and practices rooted in specific sites of enunciation frame our imagination of ideals on a distant horizon, which in turn draw forth and direct these historically specific works. Derrida discerns a certain intimacy of "actuality" and "possibility" in these coconstitutive relations, an intimacy that continually threatens to close or attenuate (theoretical, ethical, political) possibility precisely *in the name of proceeding toward better possibility.* The highest ideals delineating the directions and horizons of possibility toward which we strive are projected—oriented, inflected, limited— from historically specific conditions that these ideals also inform and make possible. These projections can be generative and contribute profoundly to opening possibilities of democratic vision and engagement. Yet they are always also infused with closure, a *horizon of impossibility* that is born in and borne by the radical intimacy and relative proximity between historically finite specificity and the horizon of possibility. This intimacy, rather, relentlessly engenders a forgetting of specificities that constitute and limit the ideality of the horizon of the possible. It persistently tends to infuse "possibility" with cramped "impossibilities" (associated with power, historical blindness, and the like) that go unrecognized because they are so close, so familiar, so obvious. And the more "we" insist upon this relatively intimate horizon of ideality as the exclusive horizon of (desirable) possibility, the more "possibility" is attenuated as *its* possession and becomes the rigid *impossibility* of the others, their horizons, and encounters that would exceed the logic of horizons.

Derrida seeks to open beyond this closing by recognizing and welcoming intimate relations with the "impossible" (the others, idealities, and events that exceed the sense of our tradition and so on) that is everywhere within and around "us" and to which we have always already begun to respond, for better or worse. By calling ourselves to an aporetical responsibility to the "impossible," we might resist arbitrary teleological closures and be opened by a world teeming with others and otherness.

Yet as we have seen, the "impossible" for Derrida is *not*, ultimately, the unanticipatable alone. Though we must strive toward a hospitality without reserve, the strange body of democratic becoming has (at least) two hands. Indeed, the unanticipatable probably comes with its own blindness and violence. Hence, the impossible, understood as democratic encounter and justice beyond the horizon of current ideals, has its best chance when the two hands wrestle with one another and stretch people to participate in an event of judgment exercised *with* the others (where "with" does not obey the logic of identity or predetermined reciprocity). The two aspects of the democratic promise "must not be added together but intertwined. They must be implicated with each other in the course of a complex and constantly re-evaluated strategy. There will be no re-politicization, there will be no politics otherwise. Without this strategy, each of the two [orientations] could lead back to the worst" (*Specters of Marx*, 87). Again: "One must therefore try to *invent* gestures, discourses, politico-institutional practices that inscribe the alliance of these two imperatives, of these two promises or contracts. . . . That is not easy. It is even impossible to conceive of a responsibility that consists in being responsible *for* two laws, or that consists in responding *to* two contradictory injunctions. . . . But there is no responsibility that is not the experience and experiment of the impossible" (*Other Heading*, 44–45).[19]

In another essay, Derrida further develops this notion of a thinking and judgment of the double gesture in relation to some of Aristotle's reflections on sight, knowing, and bees.[20] Though "resolutely in favor of a new university Enlightenment" ("Principle of Reason," 5), Derrida questions whether the sense of sight (vital to Aristotle's *Metaphysics*), when taken alone, adequately figures our capacity and desire for knowledge. Drawing upon Aristotle's discussion in *De anima*, Derrida notes that bees lack eyelids and thus *always* see. They know a lot but cannot learn. They lack the ability not only to hear but also to close off sight—that shutting of the eye at regular intervals—that Derrida links to being able to listen better, whereas "man can lower the sheath, adjust the diaphragm, narrow his sight, the better to listen, remember, and learn" ("Principle of Reason," 5). Playfully deflecting an imaginary suggestion that he seeks "to cultivate an art of blinking," he nevertheless proclaims that the university "must not be a sclerophthalmic [dry eyed and unblinking] animal." Derrida argues that we must relax our teleological energies periodically, rhythmically, like blinking our eyes, so we might practice an enlightenment (of double responsibilities and double suspicions) more infused with "listening." He evocatively seeks this possibility "'in the twilight of an eye', for it is in the most crepuscular, the most westerly situations of the Western university that the chances for this 'twinkling' of thought are multiplied" (20).

Now, what if we deploy this imagery to further consider a democratic politics that cultivates something like an art of blinking, attuned to the possibilities for receptive generosity in "the twilight of an eye"? As a blinking eye is often open, it means speaking and struggling toward a *vision* of radical democracy as a regulative ideal. Yet to work the latter so that we might better discern "how to give rise and to give place [*donner lieu*], still, to render it, this place, to render it habitable, but without killing the future in the name of old frontiers" (*Specters of Marx*, 169), Derrida also enjoins us to remember the "twilight of the eye" in which we "put . . . into question again, in certain of its essential predicates, the very concept of the said ideal" (ibid.). We should question—*and let be challenged by the others*—received ideals of the human, the animal, the sacred, rights, parliamentary democracy, representation, public opinion, technology, capital, and so forth, so that we might respond more receptively to unwonted others and otherness.[21]

If we shift from metaphors of eyes and light to focus upon modes of engaging our voices and ears, the double gesture of the democratic promise has important implications for practices of public discourse and dissent. Hence, even as Derrida affirms a notion of democratic intersubjectivity that resonates with Habermasian communicative rationality, Derrida also is suspicious that herein lie "new forms of cultural takeover" that must themselves be submitted to contestation rather than simply dictating the manner and terms of public debate. Clearly thinking of Rawlsians and Habermasians, he argues that the "best intentioned of European projects, those that are quite apparently and explicitly pluralistic, democratic, and tolerant, may . . . impose the homogeneity of a medium, of discursive norms and models. . . . Under the pretext of pleading for transparency [and consensus], for the univocity of democratic discussion, for communication in public space, for 'communicative action,' such discourse tends to impose a model of language that is supposedly favorable to this communication. Claiming to speak in the name of intelligibility, good sense, common sense, or the democratic ethic, this discourse tends by means of these very things, and as if naturally, to discredit anything that complicates the model. It tends to suspect or repress anything that bends, overdetermines, or even questions, in theory or in practice, this idea of language" (*Other Heading*, 54–55).[22] At particular risk are those influenced by genealogy or deconstruction (Habermas's "relativistic nihilists"), as well as more "local" cultural forms (those "unreasonable," "irrationally bound to traditional lifeworlds," and so on), which, as MacIntyre illuminates, often speak in terms whose intelligibility is rooted in "provincial" contexts that are more resistant to easy translation than are more supposedly "cosmopolitan" idioms. Local cultures on the undersides of colonial legacies face the greatest risks here. The danger is that contemporary liberal efforts to render a place and make it habitable "kill the future" by rendering absent the speech, appearance, and being of those people and cultures who come with "other" kinds of commitments and questions.[23] What is needed, Derrida argues, are modes of political judgment and engagement that would be both attuned to and suspicious of the responsibilities of consensual intersubjectivity, as they experiment with other modes of learning, expression, listening, and aporetical practices of dissent.

What begins to emerge in this discussion are thoughts of another mode of being in community. As early as "Violence and Metaphysics," Derrida affirms "a community of the question," evoking the tradition of those who have sought to live in ways more responsive and generous to the essential questionability of selves, the world, and others. In this "community of the question about the possibility of the question," Derrida reads both an "unbreachable dignity and duty of decision. An unbreachable responsibility. Why unbreachable? Because the impossible thus *already* occurred. The impossible according to the totality . . . there is a history of the question." If we perceive the world with philosophical integrity, he claims, we find before us—*everywhere* we look and listen, and always *already* haunting our grasp of the world— a questionability that opens the world and solicits our responsibility to this world and these people who are *not ours*. Our responsibility to others is unbreachable because the determinations with which we would irresponsibly reduce them to parts of our system have always already been breached. Hence the "unbreachable dignity" of the other, who always remains beyond our ends, a profound question before us, autho- rizing ethics and justice as an infinite question and task ("Violence and Metaphysics," 80). Intertwined with this dignity is the dignity of those who have learned from one another and who have taught—across gen- erations and in myriad ways—how to live better with a community of the question. If we live more honestly, we discover, Derrida argues, that we are indebted inheritors of traditions of those who have struggled to respond more faithfully and generously to the mysterious abundance we are to each other. Ethics and politics hinge upon an unbreachable responsibility to them and to this tradition of maintaining the ques- tion. The promise of democracy is to care for such a tradition:

> . . . a founded dwelling, a realized tradition of the question
> remaining a question. If this commandment has an ethical meaning,
> it is not in that it belongs to the *domain* of the ethical, but in that
> it ultimately authorizes every ethical law in general. ("Violence
> and Metaphysics," 80)[24]

### Tradition of Encounter/Encountering Tradition

Derrida and MacIntyre discordantly co-inhabit a set of terms and con- cerns (for tradition, community, vulnerability, risk, teleology, the oth- ers of teleology, and so on) in ways that simultaneously draw them together and drive them apart. By exploring this strange field of ten- sions we can gain a sharper sense of each theorist and the political stakes in their differences. Moreover, we can open angles of question- ing that breach the paths of each theorist even as we draw sustenance from both.

In this section I critically discuss MacIntyre's account of genealogy. Next I develop Derrida's reflections on tradition in order to challenge central themes in MacIntyre's work, including MacIntyre's vision of the genealogist's place within the neo-Thomist university. Following this I revisit some of MacIntyre's reflections to pursue a more critical en- gagement with Derrida. Finally I try to develop a more compelling posi- tion, including a vision of ethics and politics that solicits the important

overlapping and contesting work of both "traditionalists" and genealogists. I offer this position not as the sole framework within which traditionalists and genealogists must coexist but, rather, as a contestable
account that cultivates more agonistic respect and generosity on the part
of genealogists toward traditionalists—and perhaps something analogous from traditionalists.

As we have seen, MacIntyre is very aware of the often discordant
heterogeneity within and between traditions. His work explores how
we might negotiate our historical, multiplicitous, and often conflict-
ridden condition to cultivate a more generative rationality and judgment entwined with textured virtues and practices. His articulation of
neo-Thomistic traditioning strives toward justice and the good largely
through internal disputes and contestations with other traditions.
MacIntyre's formulation of teleological rationality as self-consciously
situated reason neither eschews truth claims nor clings unreflectively to
a narrow orthodoxy of "self-evident" beliefs and practices. Rather, such
rationality crafts the life of tradition through truth claims that gain
comparative warrantability insofar as they have withstood critical examination in light of contesting voices. Thus, teleological rationality
must invite other traditions to contest its claims not simply according
to its own rules and not in a piecemeal manner that would isolate fragments of a different tradition but, rather, through more-hospitable engagements that examine specific disagreements (and connecting them
to deeper issues "all the way down") in light of the larger visions in
which each discrepant claim is said to make sense. For these reasons,
MacIntyre argues that the difference and contestation engaged by traditionalists in the neo-Thomist vein is vaster and deeper than that
allowed by liberal theorists of "diversity."

At the same time, MacIntyre argues that the unifying practical-
theoretical horizon with which the Thomistic tradition negotiates conflicts helps it develop a coherence that is more rational, desirable, and
capable of cultivating widespread allegiance and authority than are
the others. As we have seen, practices aiming at the telos of the good—
with their systematic interlocking coherence of habits, sensibilities,
desires, pleasures, ideas, and unifying impulses—engender a striking
confidence among those formed by them that their tradition is closer
to truth than are the other cultures around them. They tend to engender a tremendous visceral faith that the tradition to which one belongs
will be able to render an account of the defects of other traditions in
a manner that teaches the others about errors they could not grasp
from within the confines of their own tradition—and not vice versa.

Yet within this remarkable mobilization of energy, drives, and confidence toward coherence there is, he insists, an obligation to "render ourselves maximally vulnerable." There is an obligation to listen, to learn the other's language and way of life deeply, and to risk seeing things we do not desire and are not prepared to see about ourselves. No happy dining at the liberal smorgasbord—this is difficult work indeed. We might have to change our heading: not just that of an eddy but perhaps that of the main stream. We go into these encounters with great confidence that we will meet no such difficulty, and yet we know that our past, present, and future confidence is ultimately only as good as our ability to intelligently survive our vulnerability to the others.

Thus, instead of seeking order by flattening, fragmenting, and narrowing the range of differences, MacIntyre seeks rationality by striving to bestow a certain order upon our *modes* of engagement with a very wide and deep set of differences. In the context of higher education today, this implies a double strategy. He seeks to revitalize and shape in an increasingly textured way a neo-Thomist tradition of virtues, practices, and modes of inquiry; and he seeks to engage a larger audience consisting of other specific traditions, Nietzschean genealogists, and selves of liberal societies who are awash with fragments of heterogeneous beliefs and half commitments. For moderns who are not neo-Thomists, he offers a kind of minimal-Thomism-for-non-Thomists: a mode of more seriously engaging the formerly more coherent traditions out of whose fragments we have taken what he views as our rather pathetic and dysfunctional forms. This mode of inquiry is highly indebted to MacIntyre's reading of Aquinas, but one need not be a Thomist to partake in the advantages it offers. Liberals, genealogists, and Jews might all live more intelligently, MacIntyre suggests, if we transformed our institutions and practices of inquiry in directions deeply inspired by the University of Paris of the thirteenth century.

In the context of this chapter engaging Derrida, I am interested in how "genealogists" appear in MacIntyre's scheme: both his perception of genealogical theory and its role in the universities he recommends. MacIntyre credits genealogists with having launched a devastating attack on the liberal and encyclopedic positions. Although he counts genealogists among his most serious nontraditionalist contenders, ultimately he finds their project to be self-contradictory in ways that are self-defeating and immoral.

MacIntyre thinks Nietzsche rejected all truth claims as illusions whose unreality has been forgotten by their adherents. Beneath every truth claim is a will to power striving to subjugate the world by stabilizing significations that enhance the proponent's power and suppress that of its rivals. The grand illusion about truth is that there is a real, true world existing beyond the multiplicity of perspectives. Yet there is none; only a wild tossing sea of waves of "will to power."

Some of Nietzsche's critics and adherents view this as an ontological claim, but such a view misses the heart of genealogy, according to MacIntyre. Perspectivism is not a claim teleologically oriented toward the truth of the world (for example, perhaps accomplished by understanding the power-truth of truth better than all previous truth-seekers). Instead, Nietzsche *rejects theory as an end* and orients himself toward the telos of shear "utterance on the move": He seeks to incite and communicate *movement as an unending-end in itself*. If one reads Nietzsche's claims as anything but moments wholly subservient to this task, one misses his project. And criticisms based on this mistaken interpretation will always leave genealogy unscathed, for genealogy laughs ironically at those slavish enough to take seriously what were only temporary masks intended solely as ways to disrupt and mock all rabblish truth or to celebrate one's distancing from it.

Thus the genealogical trickster joyously evades the traps of those who thought they pursued a truthful truth-seeker. Yet MacIntyre promises a trickier trap. Though Nietzsche unravels the net that would ensnare him in the contradiction between claiming there is no truth and claiming that that itself is true (escaping this net entirely), MacIntyre thinks *Nietzsche himself unravels* in contradictions between the necessary suppositions of writing and the mobility celebrated in his antimetaphysical movements.

MacIntyre argues that some minimal continuity of self is presupposed in order to maintain the continuity necessary for the genealogical *project*.[25] The genealogist must have a sufficiently stable coherence to decide what mask will be worn next, and how and why it will still be genealogical. Even the aim of endlessly subverting all continuity is itself—*at bottom and most profoundly*—a continuity and thus repeatedly presupposes securing the very substantiality and aspect of stasis that it rejects. "Make of the genealogist's self nothing but what genealogy makes of it, and that self is dissolved to the point at which there is no longer a continuous genealogical project" (*Three Rival Versions*, 54). The genealogist similarly contradicts himself insofar as the very act of writing involves addressing someone and opening oneself to a response. "Yet this cannot be done without adopting a fixity of stance" (ibid.). In the shared "now" when the reader and genealogist encounter one another, there must be an *appeal* at some level "to impersonal,

timeless standards" and textual identity to engage the reader. Nietzsche thus remains in and even generates—in his very movement—the
metaphysical traps he would escape. In his effort to break with confession there lurks a confession; and confession (Nietzsche taught) always
carries a lot more Christian baggage than post-Christian selves ever
care to acknowledge. The tricky Thomist sets a Christian trap for the
trickiest trickster and says, "Look inward! *Truth* dwells within you
and confesses itself in your every word, even as you deny it. Confess!
Only by confessing the truth can you turn away from the error and
evil that you will."

Indeed, the Thomistic genealogy of genealogy claims that genealogists err not just logically and metaphysically but morally: "The roots
of intellectual blindness [stem from] moral error, with the misdirection
of the intellect by the will and with the corruption of the will by the
sin of pride, both that pride which is an inordinate desire to be superior and that pride which is an inclination to contempt for God. . . .
The Thomist can elaborate . . . an account of the will to power as an
intellectual fiction disguising the corruption of the will. The activity of
unmasking is itself to be understood . . . as a mark for pride" (*Three
Rival Versions*, 147).

Though MacIntyre thinks Nietzscheans have yet to muster a decent
response to his critique, he readily acknowledges that the case is not
yet closed. Genealogists have their work cut out for them, but their
defeat is not guaranteed. Everything hinges upon how the genealogist might intertwine "fixity" and "mobility." How might they utilize
masks without succumbing to their metaphysical fiction? How might
they do this and still maintain enough continuity so that "genealogy"
is a discernable movement even as its telos is beyond "theory"? In
MacIntyre's view, we cannot yet say definitively that this is an impossible program that must self-destruct from parasitism and lethal intes-
tinal wars.

MacIntyre claims no genealogist has tried more impressively to negotiate these questions than Foucault, yet the *path* of Foucault's thinking
is not promising. Foucault starts as a radical genealogist but increasingly moves toward "the plain academic style." MacIntyre suspects that
Foucault drew "less and less covertly upon nongenealogical sources
and methods," to avoid what must have become increasingly clear to
him was the inevitable "progressive impoverishment" of pure genealogy (*Three Rival Versions*, 55).

Yet, MacIntyre suggests more generously, if Nietzsche fled the academy to wander in pursuit of a genealogy that could find no air there

and if Foucault began as a wanderer only to end up on a pedestal at the Collège de France, perhaps these paths are metonyms for something more than genealogy's inherent erring. It is possible that the failure inscribed here is due as much to the insidious constraints that structure the discursive space of the liberal academy (and liberalism more generally). In other words, genealogy might have become weaker—as have many rival modes of inquiry—from the liberal pressure to adopt modes of enunciation that undermine its capacities to articulate and develop itself. Thus Foucault's retreat from pure genealogy would be due in part to liberal-Enlightenment demands for articulations that privilege "neutral reason" over mobile perspectivism, seriousness over irony, and academic treatise over aphorism. How many nonliberals of any stripe hold the fort under these pressures of the liberal academy?

Ultimately, MacIntyre thinks that the only way to discerningly separate the inherent failures of genealogy from those due to constraints of Enlightenment liberalism is to give genealogists a real space to muster up mobile modes of discursive practice as they see fit. "For what forced fundamentally dissident thinkers, such as Foucault, into the conformism of the university was in fact the absence of any independent forums for debate, of any organized institutions for enquiry, of any nonacademic genres for communication outside it. The impoverishment of the wider culture presented them with a harder choice than any that Nietzsche had had to make, that between some considerable measure of academic conformity and almost complete ineffectiveness" (*Three Rival Versions*, 221).

Although MacIntyre leaves to genealogists the task of crafting strategies for opening nonacademic genealogical spaces, he does offer them less-constraining academic spaces in his "post-encyclopedic university," where they would both work as partisans and nurture the university as a place of constrained conflict in nonpartisan ways. Genealogists, MacIntyre imagines, would be free to cultivate aphoristic styles, to replace the lecture with a "theater of intelligence" that deploys endlessly shifting masks that call themselves ironically into question, and to solicit such questioning practices from other genealogists and their critics. No longer would liberal pressures infuse genealogy with impurity.[26] In this genealogical theater we would finally learn whether genealogy's "derivative" "and even parasitic" tacit reliance upon themes it explicitly rejects is due to the constraints and pressures of liberal society or to genealogy's own failures. We would finally learn whether the "schisms" between the Nietzschean and the non-Nietzschean that appear *within* genealogical projects like those of Paul de Man or Foucault "only confirm the difficulties arising . . . in [genealogy's] admitting into itself any conception of the person which involves accountability" (*Three Rival Versions*, 213), or whether "genealogy can discover within itself, or at least from sources not alien to it, the resources to provide a solution" (215).

But would genealogists like it in this "theater of intelligence," where they would be expected to discover what they need "within" and to thrive on "nonalien" resources alone? Indeed, in this space of purification offered by the charitable Thomist, might they not perish? What if MacIntyre's image of pure genealogy misses the impurity explicitly articulated by most genealogists? What if this "miss" engenders a trap genealogists might perceive in the institutional space MacIntyre offers as a refuge from liberal traps? And what if his reading of genealogy obscures a reading that would put more difficult pressures upon "tradition" itself? What if the contaminations, inconsistencies, and tensions that MacIntyre notes in Nietzsche and Foucault can be read as *vital* to the quest for truth and justice, even as they are difficult and risky for both genealogical and deconstructive projects themselves? In my response to these questions, genealogy appears more compelling than in MacIntyre's account—and more troubling for his Thomism.[27]

As we have seen, Derrida's analysis of traditionalizing rationality has significant resonance with MacIntyre's neo-Thomism. Yet at the same time as Derrida works themes like distance and the invisibility of teleological ideality, dialectical tradition opens beyond itself to thoughts of exteriority, radical contingency, darkness, and ateleology inextricably entwined with Logos. Although teleological reason remains crucial to striving toward democratic justice, with Derrida's investigations our exaggerated and deleterious confidence in the priority of our own sense and teleological directions is profoundly shaken and radically opened to alterity. In light of Derrida's analysis of contingency and otherness, the opening of justice (calling us to be mobile/moved/moving but not, contra MacIntyre's, an abstract affirmation of movement as exclusively the end in itself) requires a double contradictory obligation toward two kinds of responsibility—one for dialectical teleological sense and one to the other to come. We are called to the difficult task of intertwining a teleological faith with practices of more radical opening to questions that come from beyond our teleologies. Juxtaposed with and implicated in the development of teleological prophetic vision and critique is the paradoxical effort to slacken our teleological energies so that we might pursue the democratic promise in a manner analogous to the "blinking of the eye"—so that we might become more receptive to others and more appreciative of the incalculability of democratic encounters. We must *energetically* cultivate—in excess of teleology—the strange arts of and tastes for radical listening, welcoming, waiting, patience, ambiguity, and paradox. Of course, we can no more achieve perfection in these arts than we can reach the revelation of our telos. Yet work called by both impossibilities is vital to mobilizing the kinds of energy, reflective intelligence, learning, and virtues essential to democratic responsibility.

Although MacIntyre also seeks to render each tradition "maximally vulnerable" to contesting traditions, as an Augustinian he is "committed to one central negative thesis about all actually or potentially rival positions: that no substantive rationality, independently of [Augustinian] faith, will be able to provide an adequate vindication of its claims" (*Three Rival Versions*, 101). From a Derridean perspective this commitment is entwined with the overcultivation of teleological confidence, authority, discipline, pedagogy, and habits in ways that greatly engender cognitive, visceral, and relational invulnerability. Although MacIntyre's account affirms a certain vulnerability,[28] it is rooted in and animates an intense confidence—shall we say *"pride"?*—that shapes encounters with other people and traditions in ways that are theoretically and ethically unwarranted and undesirable. What, *given MacIntyre's own reading* of the radical finitude of our sense and faith in relation to the immensity of being, could justify such a strong commitment to the thesis that the others must fail absent our faith? Are we really big enough—are we certain the world is sufficiently small and homogeneous—to justify this commitment to the impossibility of other legitimate narrative practices? Are we sufficiently big to be committed to a good so small as to be a priori this jealous? I doubt it.

Nevertheless, a tradition committed thus is likely to educate sensibilities in ways that engender a blindness and deafness toward others, a lack of receptivity that is prone to remarkable invulnerability and erring for a long period. For this commitment makes the other *a priori* a "rival" first and foremost. And as the energies, passions, and investments of rivalry predominate, our teleological efforts so intensify that our ears fill solely with the bustle of our own motion and become nearly incapable of hearing other voices within and beyond the limits of "our" community. Nearly everything in human history suggests that it takes very difficult and rarely cultivated capacities—along with a lot of luck—to hear well beyond the horizons of our teleological anticipations. For Derrida, we must *always* work hard to cultivate this receptivity. We must seek to learn from the others beyond our tradition, strive to be open to possibilities of radical transfiguration, anticipate the events of those encounters as that which exceeds teleology, ripen to the possibilities of acknowledging coexistence in excess of agreement or rivalry. It is not that Derrida seeks to flee agon; indeed, he seeks to intensify it. Yet he seeks to do so in ways that do not bestow upon our encounters the singular pressures and flattening structures of (im)possibility that accompany MacIntyre's notion of rivalry.

MacIntyre's exaggerated confidence circulates through his understanding of the education and incorporation of a people. Because "membership in a particular type of moral community, one from which fundamental dissent has to be excluded, is a condition for genuinely rational inquiry" (*Three Rival Versions*, 60), pedagogy must fashion souls to pursue the community's teleological ends as singularly authoritative. Masters or philosopher-educators within this tradition enjoy and bear responsibility for a great deal of authority. Though in the final analysis this authority rests on rational assessments that they embody the "best so far," for a significant period "humility," "obedient trust," and "faith" in the tradition and its representatives are central to pedagogy. Rational assessment is always only possible retrospectively, because "only a self transformed" by the teachers and texts of the tradition is "capable of reading aright" the texts, teachers, and tradition (82). Hence, teachers aim to cultivate attitudes, dispositions, and virtues—"pre-rational reordering"—that enable students to recognize as rational and pursue a community's telos.

This pursuit of rational enquiry is ultimately to open beyond the limits of a particular tradition to vulnerably encounter other rival traditions. Yet it is doubtful whether selves prerationally reordered into such a singular structure of authority and commitment to the wrongness of other traditions would acquire capacities and virtues to experience others beyond the harsh unending light of a teleological interrogation chamber.

MacIntyre does not wish it. Thus, for example, he pursues a university that is in some important respects more generous than that provided by numerous liberals. Yet by construing his university as a set of spaces for rival modes of enquiry, *each one primarily in pursuit of its own telos*,[29] MacIntyre's Thomist generosity unwittingly fabricates a trap. To clarify this we must consider the unruly and unwanted displacements and receptivity that many Derrideans and Mestizas would probably bring to their newly assigned place.

Genealogists are unruly because they do not reject teleology, metaphysics, accountability, and traditionalizing rationality. Derrida urges us to pursue these tasks and embraces the responsibility to cultivate selves capable of practicing and further developing the traditions of radical democratic generosity they inherit. But, and in addition, genealogists also seek to orient themselves and others toward a receptivity to otherness beyond their horizons of expectation. This otherness may come from another tradition "outside," or it may come from "inside" in a way that confuses the opposition "inside and outside." To be open to and opened by this otherness is vital to learning to live well, and we must care for this extremely paradoxical caring.

Derrida's stance—in contrast to professed commitments to one tradition being better than all the rest—finds expression in his tendency to affirm tradition with more modest tropes, such as "it helps us recognize and avoid the worst." Similarly, he persistently illuminates conflictive heterogeneity within each tradition: "We should not forget that we are first speaking of the tradition of a certain concept of friendship. . . . Now if this tradition is certainly not homogeneous . . . Our main concern will indeed be to recognizing the major marks of a tension, perhaps ruptures and in any case scansions . . . to make ourselves once again more sensitive to this heterogeneity and its internal potentialities, to make it and them a springboard for a leap further out" ("Politics of Friendship," 234). Derrida listens to tensions and heterogeneity in an effort to resist "covering over and destroying the archive" (ibid.) of other abundant possibilities that teleologies tend to conceal even when they make other advances. Will the "leap further out" be toward a distant heading that we already anticipate but do not yet possess? Or toward an other heading? Or the other of the heading? Derrida cultivates a sensibility attuned to the ineliminable uncertainties here. With these questions he points to a difficult terrain where the responsibilities of caring for "one's own traditions" and caring for "the other traditions" are not as clear or separable as we thought; where *purity itself* may be one of our greatest dangers.

Hence responsibility is bound to two contradictory tasks—divided between tradition and treason (*traditio* is the root of both). It is bound to a democratic tradition of finding a way to avoid the worst and coexist well, but it is also "tied to heresy"—even "a decided predisposition towards a certain principle of heresy."[30]

Vital to this task are intricate efforts to diffuse the "yes or no" pressures that tend to heighten as purity and rivalry become the central motifs. Thus Derrida offers narratives of traditions by which he is inspired (for example, certain streams of Christianity) in ways that stress the tradition's *debts to other traditions* that remain vital on their own terms (for example, Judaism, by which he is also inspired), or narratives that emphasize how the very manner in which a "superior" tradition "supercedes" and suppresses an "erring" tradition intensifies the identified erring in what is taken as an advance. Or he will provide an account of "us" in a way that locates the strengths of our history precisely in the aporias and tensions that provoke endless interrogations, developments on different sides, partial hybrids, but, thankfully, never a pure synthesis.[31]

The genealogists whom I imagine will also orient us ethically through a growing collection of stories about surprisingly helpful heterogeneity within what were thought to be relatively homogeneous spaces, stories of unexpected and retrospectively affirmed transfigurations through engagements with feared and loathed peoples, stories of encounters with others that evoke alluring indeterminacy and wondrous open-endedness, and stories of the vibrant renewals and rich possibilities that appeared unexpectedly through strange processes of hybridization.

Hence, juxtaposed with a tradition of relatively determinate aspirations and practices, genealogists would cultivate a memory and anticipation of heresy—one that would nurture even a spirit of the "heretical with respect to that very heresy" (*Gift of Death,* 27). The success of genealogy would rest upon its ability to maintain the tensions among multiple responsibilities in ways that mobilize modes of receptive generosity and learning that are retrospectively recognized and deemed worthy of being renewed for future ethical and political engagements.

These people would fit poorly in MacIntyre's university. Relentlessly impure, they would be "all over the place": grafting and hybridizing, proudly parasitical, traveling to other sections with unpredictable agendas and receptivity, drawing in to their wing myriad nongenealogists, forever failing to evaluate themselves in the "right" terms. They would work toward modes of engagement that resisted both "rivalry" and "conciliation"—even as they frequently participated in the latter as well. They would probably challenge the structure in order to open spaces of encounter more conducive to such things.

## Deconstructing Derrida

I have argued that a great deal hinges upon cultivating lively tensions between teleological and ateleological responsibilities, and I have shown that MacIntyre insufficiently acknowledges these tensions in ways that damage possibilities for engagement. Perhaps this is due to how persistently he has leaned in one direction to develop a notion of historical rationality in contexts that deny it. Analogously, I suggest that

Derrida's own articulations of these tensions have been wrought in struggles where he too has leaned in one direction to raise questions of ateleology that have been repeatedly concealed. One consequence is that he sometimes overemphasizes the ateleological so that dialectical teleology gets more lip service than actual development. This overemphasis may have certain strategic uses, but it courts the very danger he seeks to resist, namely, that deconstruction might become an "abstract and dogmatic eschatology in the face of the world's evil"—weak on textured judgment and practice. Below I rework some of Derrida's formulations to dislodge a sleepiness that sometimes reemerges in Derridean discourse. When the teleological side of the tension slackens, the atelic side becomes too "adjusted," too "in joint." Deconstructive trembling and indeterminacy become too comfortable to spur the work of democracy and justice (as I will argue further in chapter 6 in relation to Jean-Luc Nancy).

At issue here is whether Derrida sufficiently *cultivates* a dialectical relation to the traditions by which he finds himself animated. If he does not respond often or powerfully to this responsibility he has formulated so well, his genealogical practice risks becoming too pure, too singularly bent on atelic disruption and abyss as such. It would cease to disrupt itself or to let itself be disrupted. Thus fetishized, "abyss" becomes blind to questions of democracy and justice and unresponsive to others. Ateleology and teleology can engender the work of responsibility when each is juxtaposed in ways that critique and supplement the other so that our dialectical advances and radically vulnerable openings with others challenge, animate, and transfigure each other. However, each alone, we have seen, risks the worst. A juxtaposition vibrant enough to throw us out of comfortable and oblivious adjustment requires powerful work on both sides of responsibility.

Yet there is a certain one-sidedness in many of Derrida's discussions. For example, "Violence and Metaphysics" develops compelling and extensive arguments concerning the "violence," "deportation," "dissimulation," "inaccessibility," "war," "wound," and "absence" entwined with the birth of perception and language while problematically marginalizing the expressive, generative, and powerfully illuminating potentials of language and perception—precisely reversing the strong accents of MacIntyre's marginalization.[32] Derrida's bent is so strong that the hope of language is almost always put in negative terms, so that nonviolence and respect appear *only* as language's violence against its own violence and the illumination of the deportation inherent in it. Yet do we not *also surpass* violence and practice respect in the profoundly expressive and revelatory aspects of our seeing, speaking, hearing, thinking, and feeling relationships with others and otherness? Everyday perception and language offer abundant evidence of both aspects, even though they are rarely given in clear separation from each other.

To poorly articulate this tensional double character—to become too adjusted to the transgressive dimension alone—is to engender a lack of confidence in perception and language that is potentially as problematic as the overconfidence that is far more common. To better negotiate our relation to language and otherness we would do better to articulate positions that remain conflicted by both a "perceptual faith" and a "perceptual skepticism"—each rubbing the other against the grain. Lose this, and we lose our weak but highly significant ability to "learn (teach) how to live."

Derrida's strong accent on the transgressive aspect of language is entwined with formulations of respect and responsibility that quite often accent efforts to release others from our interpretive grasp toward a radically indeterminate sense of difference and futurity. This mobilizes us toward a problematic version of the asymmetry between self and other. Derrida performs a very textured deconstruction of the *self,* a deconstruction in which difference, contingency, mediation, deportation, violence, blindness, and finite responses to infinite otherness figure most prominently. This reading of the self tends to inhibit generalizations that would extend these themes in relation to other selves, for fear of once again concealing the other under the categories of the same.

Yet I think this concern for concealment conceals far more than it illuminates and risks a complicity with violence as great as the one it resists. Are not the others *also* sites of deportation, finite openings entwined with blindness and violence? Are not the others *also* born in and borne by networks of mediated sociality that always carry, in varying degrees, historically specific modes of suppression that exceed the power of any single person's ability to resist completely? Does not the other *also* have responsibilities to the "double contradictory law"? My reading of Derrida above indicates that his response—often implicit in his work and sometimes explicitly elaborated—would be *"of course."* But too often these insights are lacking or comparatively undeveloped.

Hence Derrida occasionally writes of the other to arrive, the *"arrivant,"* as being as "disarmed as a newly born child,"[33] seeking to evoke a radical responsibility for hospitality to an indeterminate singularity in excess of our calculations of the other's acceptability or guilt. Yet at times such metaphors and analogies seem to hold sway in ways

that "disarm" the tensions, contradictions, and suspicions that he compellingly enjoins in other places. When this happens, the metaphors of
innocence and indeterminacy *overdetermine* the other in ways that
radically conceal and curtail questions for and *from* the other. When
Derrida writes of an "other who looks at me, but who looks without
the-subject-who-says-I being able to reach that other, see her, hold her
in the reach of my gaze" (*Gift of Death*, 25), do not these eyes that
see me from where I can never see simultaneously present the paradox
of the other seeing *me at a distance,* without really seeing *me*—without reaching me-seeing-her (even as they deeply haunt me with this
possibility)? Yet Derrida suppresses this paradox (and the rich questions that come with it) when he writes, "It is dissymmetrical: this gaze
that sees me without my seeing it looking at me. It knows my very
secret even when I myself don't see it" (*Gift of Death*, 91).

This is a pregnant thought. By hesitating and dwelling on my side
of this dissymmetry, Derrida strives to avoid a type of "common sense"
that would avoid the profundity of this aspect of our condition. This
common sense quickly acknowledges Derrida's observation and then
immediately adds that the reverse is true and erases/folds the double
dissymmetry entirely into a logic of symmetrical reciprocity according
to a system of rules governing all participants. Although Derrida
acknowledges a responsibility here, he clearly thinks it becomes irre-
sponsibility when deployed to avoid responding to the question of the
other in excess of all systems. By dwelling on my side of the dissymmetry, he thwarts our tendency to refuse the weight of this question.
Yet though symmetrical reciprocity is a crucial part of ethical striving,
it must be supplemented and resisted in part, with difficult considerations about the other's side of this dissymmetry, *not just to think about
symmetrical reciprocity but to explore seriously the paradoxical intri-
cacies of this double dissymmetry* itself: the excessive responsibility of
the other toward all her "others," and my responsibility to this other's
responsibility. "I would like to learn/to teach to live finally," Derrida
emphasizes at the outset of *Specters of Marx.* Yet much that we might
learn from others alternatively comes from and must negotiate what
is not "disarmed" and like a "newly born child"; and much that I
might teach others must address the condition they share with me of
responding to others who exceed their perception.

By resisting reflections on double dissymmetry, Derrida often marginalizes such questions in ways that position the other at the height of
unquestionability. Thus, throughout *The Gift of Death,* Derrida writes
of the other's secret gaze that "commands me" (27). He is concerned

here with more than an excessive responsibility to the other, responsibility that opens the law to suspicions, reformulations, and questions of exception while also being *opened by* the law to difficult questioning in order to avoid an idolatry of the other that might lead to "the worst." Rather than a double contradictory law involving a duty to singularity that must engage in a contest of questions with an other duty to a dialectically accountable responsibility, Derrida writes of being "bound by an absolute, unconditioned obligation, by an incomparable, nonnegotiable duty" to singularity that entirely sacrifices teleological responsibility—and does so in secret. Because every other is totally other ("Tout autre est tout autre") and figured as "infinite love" (55) and "goodness itself" (41), like Abraham we find ourselves wholly unable to resist the tragic sacrificial acts that the other commands from on high. Hence, "what the knights of good conscience don't realize, is that the sacrifice of Isaac illustrates—if that is the word in the case of such a nocturnal mystery—the most common and everyday experience of responsibility" (67). Every time we respond to an other we sacrifice and betray the other others, each of whom would also command us infinitely—"every one being sacrificed to every one else in this land of Moriah that is our habitat every second of every day" (69). Judgment appears useless: We simply cannot know to whom to give.

Who could deny the profundity of these thoughts on our condition? Yet—to move too quickly now—singularly accented as they are, they seem to suppress responsibility in any meaningful sense. The problem is not that they call into question our determinations of responsibility but that they suppress them entirely. If Moriah is always everywhere, our guilty feelings will be absolutely impotent, for no historical-dialectical development of our sense, no better and worse, would be possible— we would always be simply in "the worst." If this is our situation we should not blame Derrida for telling us. But is it?

I do not think so. Our responsive sense, deconstruction, and judgment cannot conquer the echoes of Moriah in the topos of our lives, but we have ample evidence that they can, together, help us reside here in better or worse ways. They can make some sense of and modify this landscape in ways that reduce these echoes, even if this sense will always be subject to tragedy, trembling, and transfiguration. There are better and worse ways to respond to the "*other* others." Indeed responding ethically to each other *in her singularity* immanently requires responding to and for the other others, as each other is in her singularity born in and borne by this nexus of responding and being responded to. For starters: To refuse to receive or give an utterly arbitrary command to murder is to respond ethically to the other—to respond to her and for her responsibility to the others. To raise the ontological presence of sacrifice to the status of an irresistible command that we must obey in secret is to be raised and razed by injustice.

What gives in *The Gift of Death* (for example)? I suggest that in Derrida's most vertiginous renderings of sense as violence, responsiveness to singularity completely overwhelms its otherwise tensional relationship with our responsibility for dialectical judgment. Yet with this twist we see reemerging a strange form of the metaphysics of presence. No longer a characteristic of the self, it now resides in the other who is absent to me yet construed as the pure presence of love unstained by transgressive finitude—a presence that simply commands me and thus reintroduces hierarchy in a project that was to be "profoundly foreign to all hierarchies" ("Violence and Metaphysics," 121).

I do not want to make too much of this intermittent trope, which so much of Derrida's own work critically illuminates and interrogates. And indeed, in works like *Specters of Marx,* in his provocative discussion of *Hamlet,* ghosts, unwonted political possibilities, and the juxtapositions of teleological and ateleological responsibilities, Derrida deploys proximate figures such as the "visor effect" ("we do not see who looks at us") along with the "helmet effect" ("supreme insignia of power") (*Specters of Marx,* 7–8) to elaborate some of his most powerful insights and injunctions concerning the power of unanticipatable others. Yet as these become fetishized as absolutely unquestionable commands, visors and helmets become less and less distinguishable from the panoptic gaze that sees without being seen; is in this way the absolute insignia of power; commands in a manner that is irresistible, for it knows us better than we know ourselves; isolates us from the others; and sacrifices our relations to them as well as all otherness within that would resist its command.

### Rerum Discordia Concordia

I have argued that the receptive generosity of ethical and political engagement hinges significantly upon working with the tensions between teleological and ateleological responsibilities of the democratic promise. But could one ever find the "right" tension? I doubt it. In the above discussions, we have discerned how responsiveness might wane as one pole of responsibility is diminished in the face of another. Yet the task of responsibility is more like perpetual reanimation of our dis-adjustment than maintenance of properly adjusted tensions.

Why? Because we must respond to two *infinite* duties that, while they also participate in relations of overlap and supplementation, greatly *contest* each other, suspect each other, call each other to silence. There is, among other things, a *polemos* here that disrupts and resists all efforts to clearly articulate a proper tension. Moderation may be an important part of responsibility, but the task as such is not moderate. Each pole of our responsibility is greatly endangered at the mean (if such a thing were imaginable between infinities): at the zero point where our responsibility to others often loses the vitality of both its illuminating orientation and its capacity for savoring disorientation to a monotonous, immobilized, weakened, and complacent sensibility. At best, we might partly inform each through the other, and we might partly learn to articulate each pole in juxtapositions that help us resist being fixated by the spell of each in order to keep more alive to the demands of democratic engagement and the promise of justice.

But to be called away from fixation is not to seek to avoid it entirely. And practices of tensional juxtaposition and alternation are messy if necessary arts. People are rarely "good" at them—even if we are worse when we cease to try. Moreover, these arts of responsibility are always articulated in the murkiness of complex historical judgments: How much and what kinds of human organization most engender responsiveness to others? What levels of disorientation and disorganization open us to otherness? How might we entwine these? What levels and types of disorientation might provoke individual and collective forms of closure? What levels and which types of ambiguity disrupt egoisms? Which allow it to run wild? Always required, as Derrida put it, is "a complex and constantly re-evaluated strategy" (*Specters of Marx*, 87).

Insofar as a careful reading of our teleological and ateleological responsibilities leads us to sense that we never achieve a perfect articulation of this tension, we would do well to cultivate greater receptivity and esteem for other traditions and emergent efforts to articulate democracy in manners cognizant of the tensions between teleological and ateleological responsiveness. Hence, even as genealogists struggle to open "tradition" more radically to otherness, they might seek a greater appreciation of enviable strengths that more teleologically accented projects offer, strengths that genealogists have as yet not achieved. Thomists and other traditionalists might strive to acknowledge admirable possibilities of responsibility in genealogical projects, even if those projects push traditionalists beyond where they seek to go. We ought to learn better to appreciate *the tensions among myriad peoples articulating historical responsibility with different accents as the very condition*

*of responsibility.* We ought to cultivate a deep thirst for the illuminations, provocations, and mysterious suspensions that discordant efforts
provide one another.

Thus, although the genealogist strives for a university that provides
greater space for discrepant projects beyond the limits of liberal reason, she does not view such a university as an unfortunate transitional
phase to be surpassed in a distant future when one group might finally
"get it right" and defeat the others. The space of discrepancy with its
patient generosity toward unanticipatable developments—encounters
and mixings for which we as yet have no names—themselves prefigure
utopia and constitute vital conditions of the democratic promise. With
Thomists and peoples inheriting different traditions across the globe,
genealogists seek to release the future from the "enemies of incalculability . . . who congratulate themselves upon the limits of their [short-
sighted] vision" (*Three Rival Versions,* 234). In tension with Thomists,
genealogists seek to render incalculability *essentially* plural—reliant
upon discordant efforts to both open to it and resist its dangers.

*Some* others ought to be converted to something other than they are.
Yet the genealogist, as I imagine her, does not seek to convert MacIntyre's Thomist; rather, she seeks to coexist with Thomists in states of
mutual transformative provocation while developing political coalitions around common elements and aspirations of a somewhat "reck-
less generosity."[34] In chapter 6 I turn to works by feminists of color
(especially Chicanas), in order to explore a "nepantilist" rendering of
*traditio* that avoids some of the pitfalls of Derrida's most ateleological accounts while working in modes that are more reflective in some
ways about the uses and abuses of specific loci of enunciation. Almost
always, the writings of feminists of color construe the relation between
teleological and ateleological responsibilities as a tension rather a contradiction. Moreover, they tend to articulate visions that are more
attuned to the *generative* possibilities of these tensions—less shrouded
in darker tropes such as democracy and justice *"if there is any."* There
is some.

# 6

# Feminists of Color and the Torn Virtues of Democratic Engagement

F EW QUESTIONS OF DEMOCRATIC THEORY provoke as much disagreement as
those concerning the legitimate scope and modes of disagreement
and difference. This paradoxical situation produces uncontrollable
effects within and around all efforts to theorize democratic responses
to it. The paradox usually grows as we strengthen our efforts to discover a single paradigm within which we might resolve it. Typically,
as advocates insist they possess an uncontestable framework for regulating disagreement, they simultaneously reinforce their deafness and
provoke alternative positions that sharply reveal contingencies, blindness, and exclusions that they would deny, or disclose only in softer
light. This often engenders *ressentiment* in those who insist they possess the best political path and loathe those who deny their claim. No
democratic theory can entirely escape this predicament, but responding to it is part of what it means to live well, or at least less poorly.

"Political liberalism" seeks to maximize space for diversity by offering universal principles and virtues to guide our political interactions
while leaving unresolved a broad range of moral, metaphysical, and
philosophical questions—to be respectfully tolerated in nonpolitical
spheres. Oriented by this common moral currency, we could rationally
limit the scope of diversity in public life and more constructively negotiate our disagreements. Within the limits and according to the contours
of this moral-political geography, our diversity would be at liberty in
our private lives and would often edify us in our public deliberations.
Understood thus, the task of political theory would be to identify the

bedrock necessary for a mobile pluralism restricted to layers closer to the surface.

Of course, political liberalism is not entirely homogeneous. Important differences remain concerning both how far "comprehensive doctrines" must be excluded from public discourse and how much theorists acknowledge the contestability of their own positions. Hence, one might sketch a spectrum ranging from Bruce Ackerman's more exclusive theory; through John Rawls, Amy Gutmann and Dennis Thompson, and Ronald Dworkin in the middle; to Kent Greenawalt and J. Donald Moon, on the less exclusive side. Similarly, there is a significant difference between Rawls's claim that "no sensible view can possibly get by without the reasonable and rational as I use them," Moon's effort to affirm much in Rawls and yet simultaneously "seek to maintain an openness to the possibilities [he] implicitly denies," and the ineradicable contestability and "tragic conflict" in political life.[1] These differences aside, however, political liberals devote most of their efforts to elaborating the general project I sketched above. Even when contestability, contingency, and tragedy are acknowledged, they are typically folded into arguments that secure and mobilize our allegiance to a liberal bedrock far more than they are allowed to challenge and transfigure it.

In this chapter, reflecting upon writings of feminists of color, I sketch an alternative to this effort. Although this position has important kinships with several themes in political liberalism, it does not understand the ethical task simply in terms of seeking to construct a framework, "whole cloth," or bedrock of ethical principles and virtues to guide our political lives. Rather, political generosity toward others also requires that we cultivate a vibrant recognition of the limits and shortcomings of all such projects. It requires torn cloths, torn virtues: the cultivation of virtues torn (or at least stretched) between the often (though not always) discordant tasks of constructing an ethical-political *framework* for engaging others and cultivating an awareness that such constructions are only one part of striving to live ethically. Political relations also require virtues that call us to the difficult tasks of heightened receptivity and listening well to those beyond our moral-political frameworks and of engaging others in ways that significantly exceed the orientations—or "rules of engagement"—of our vision. Cultivating ethics is always both a teleological *and* an ateleological project. This paradox at the heart of a more desirable democratic ethic is a response to the paradox of difference seemingly at the heart of our condition. *Traditio*—the Latin root (meaning "to hand over") of both "tradition" and "treason"—names the overlapping and tensional intermingling of these two aspects of the movement toward a more generous democracy. Many feminists of color sketch provocative democratic visions of living, learning, and teaching amid our differences, visions that evoke and sustain the vitality of this tension.[2] Striking deep philosophical and political registers, they call us beyond the sterile oppositions between the more reified versions of both liberalism and identity politics that often shape our debates. Integral to a democratic ethos of *traditio* are practices of engagement with others whose differences and unwonted proximities challenge us to repeated refigurations of this constitutive paradox of ethical life. This injunction toward a deepening, broadening, and transfiguring political engagement is entwined with visions of the good that many feminists of color articulate in response to the problems and possibilities of their particular histories. Simultaneously, they argue that the insurgency of those with particular visions of the good into arenas that political liberalism would limit according to "public reason" might sometimes serve more to enhance than to impede receptive generosity among different people and might empower political mobilizations of (and with) the "least well off."

This chapter begins by juxtaposing Arthur Schlesinger Jr. and Gloria Anzaldúa in order to clarify both the similarities and the differences between one kind of U.S. liberalism (akin *in principle* with much political liberalism) and the challenge that many feminists of color pose to that liberalism. After exploring some of the central differences and the political stakes involved, I deepen and sharpen the understanding of *traditio* by juxtaposing Chicana feminist understandings of the new Mestiza with those of postmodernist Jean-Luc Nancy. Combined, the juxtapositions with Schlesinger and Nancy allow us to situate a politics of torn virtues between a teleological understanding of these tasks in the former case and an ateleological understanding in the latter. I further elaborate this perspective by juxtaposing the political histories of feminists of color with those of political liberalism. Finally, I return to a theme and expression in writings by many feminists of color that I do *not* work with in this text (anger), in order to open the directions I sketch to future, more-ateleological engagements.

### Juxtaposition I: The New Mixed Race and the New New Mixed Race— Schlesinger and Anzaldúa

For all political liberalism's shortcomings, I suspect that efforts to do better will remain in important ways indebted to it. Indeed, these debts may be so large as to lead us to wonder what difference these efforts to create a "politics of difference" really make. Do such efforts really improve upon what is most admirable in liberalism or better address its most the serious problems?

Highly influential among feminists of color is Gloria Anzaldúa's *Borderlands/La Frontera: The New Mestiza,* which articulates a vibrant ethos for learning to live in the midst of and from our differences. As her subtitle indicates, she does so in the name of a new "mestiza": of *mixed* race and of a *transfiguring mixing* of races, cultures, dreams, and identities. What is to be "new" about this mestiza is the way in which she would overcome precisely the politics of race or nationhood understood as an exclusive essence delineated by a rigid boundary within which would lie purity, homogeneity, and truth and beyond which would lie the "others," to be variously excluded, dominated, assimilated, converted, condemned, or annihilated. This vision would be "opposite . . . to the policy of racial purity that white America practices" (*Borderlands,* 78). Yet the stakes are greater here than a critique of "white American practices." If this were all, she might simply endorse and struggle for the liberal ideals belonging to "the best part" of America in order to help create a more "inclusive" and "tolerant" democratic society more worthy of the claim to offer "liberty, equality, and justice for *all.*" In excess of and partly in tension with such a project, however, the mestiza points "toward a new consciousness," from which deeper political transformations are thought to follow.

There is an instructive irony here that we should not overlook. For the ideals in the name of which the United States was constituted, and toward which many have since struggled, were also born of a "new consciousness" entwined with the idea of a "mixed race." And the irony only intensifies as we recall that Schlesinger—author of *The Disuniting of America: Reflections on a Multicultural Society,*[3] which is surely near the top of most multiculturalists' list of "books from hell"— passionately denounces the politics of difference precisely in the name of an ethics and politics of the "mixed race." Schlesinger narrates the development of this ideal from the period of the U.S. founding to the present and marshals it as the most desirable promise for a future where we will find unity and richness in our diversity instead of intolerant nationalisms, big or small.

By exploring this unwonted mixing and contamination of metaphor and vision that seems to occur between Schlesinger and Anzaldúa, we can flesh out some of the distinctiveness of the visions presented by many feminists of color: The contamination of metaphor helps us grasp the paradoxical proximity they have to certain liberal aspirations. Yet this proximity engenders a paradox at the heart of their ethos and politics, a paradox that, in turn, provides much of the very distinctive energy, political movement, and ethical texture of the new mestiza.

Schlesinger's United States[4] was born with the idea of a "new mixed race," a "mongrel race," a "promiscuous breed," as Hector St. John de Crevecoeur put it in 1759, made up of nationalities previously attached to exclusive histories, essences, and identities that lived in hostility and often warred with one another. The new mixed race was to be a new beginning—a new relation to the new. Shedding the myopic inhospitable pasts of its constituents, the United States was to forge itself according to new principles of political equality, liberty, and democratic citizenship. In the United States, anything—even this grand dream of democratic mixing—was possible, because its essence was *possibility itself*, a new race and nation formed in the warm light of a future yet to be made by each and by all, rather than chained to a past like the others. Americans had, in Thomas Paine's famous words, "the power to begin the world all over again." Drawn together in undreamed-of mixtures to build the future, they welcomed newcomers; inclusivity was the name of the game for this nation of immigrants.

Of course, this demanding morality and politics of openness to others and the future was not formless. It required allegiance to a set of fundamental political principles and a democratic vision; it required forming a new political identity around the American dream of freedom and opportunity and shedding everything in one's past that weakened or contested this allegiance. The United States is "open to all oppressed nations and religions," as Schlesinger quotes George Washington; "let them settle not as groups, but as individuals, prepared for intermixture with our people, assimilation to our customs, measures, and laws." The U.S. identity was exclusive, permitting no coexisting national allegiances. John Quincy Adams wrote that the American "must cast off European skin, never to resume it." Such were the requirements of U.S. liberty: The mixed race was not itself to mix, except with those willing to assimilate to its own terms, the terms of freedom.

Schlesinger knows how limited these inclusive ideals originally were and often have been. Even if Ralph Waldo Emerson's vision of the new race included "Africans and Polynesians," for most adherents the vision was limited to northern Europeans. Though the vision has slowly expanded in the minds of many to include blacks, Native Americans, Hispanics, Asians, and so forth, the history of the United States as Schlesinger reads it contains vast periods of harsh injustice in which practice falls far short of ideals. These ideals were fraught, he says,

with a notion of assimilation that was often far thicker and more restrictive than was necessary or desirable to ensure the future of U.S.
unity and freedom in the context of mixedness. "Americanization"
screened out immigrants' differences in many ways that impoverished
the American dream best sketched by political liberalism.

Schlesinger's narrative of the United States is one of slow, halting,
difficult, but nevertheless palpable and awe-inspiring progress toward
justice. At the heart of this progress lie the core values of universalist
liberty, equality, and representative democracy uniquely rooted in
America's Anglo-Saxon heritage. Yet their origin does not preclude a
telos of general inclusivity. Progress toward this telos is made possible
and spurred by the way American ideals make space for and affirm
heterodoxy, leading us to criticize those of our practices and interpretations of our ideals that do not live up to their highest and most genuine impulse. Future progress will hinge upon our powerful allegiance
to this Anglo-Saxon core, which makes it possible. This in turn means
that while our different (that is, "non-Western") traditions can contribute greatly to our music, food, architecture, our literature, to the
district rhythms and textures of our daily life, and so forth, they must
not be allowed to question or interfere with our core political values.
Cultural differences must be depoliticized, Schlesinger insists; we must
assimilate morally and politically to the "American Creed."

Ironically, in Schlesinger's view, it is members of those minorities
that are just beginning to benefit from the progress made possible by
this creed and their previous struggles to realize it who may most
threaten the very existence of this creed, let alone its progress. For we
increasingly hear calls from their ranks for what Schlesinger regards
as the "virus of tribalism," the "cult of ethnicity," which if realized
would mortally wound the democratic life, ideals, and practices of the
new mixed race.

There are few gray areas in Schlesinger's narrative. Generally, he
reduces the diverse contestations concerning our moral and political
values to "multiculturalism," which in turn he reduces to its most rigid
and nationalistic forms, to the most hateful and myopic authors, or to
those ungenerous readings he gives of authors far more interesting
than he acknowledges. Much in the form, content, and textures of his
efforts bears the stamp of paradigmatic modes of marginalization that
work to suppress precisely the heterodoxy he praises.

I return to Anzaldúa now, not primarily to argue that Schlesinger
gets America wrong, that America is more incoherent than he suggests, or that he gets the politics of difference wrong (all-important but

well-worn paths) but, rather, to examine carefully her relation to Schlesinger's American liberal ideals. I seek to explore her criticisms and
understand the character of her differences as well as her proximities
to the more admirable moments in his account.

In a manner resonant with the earlier Americans in Schlesinger's
narrative, Anzaldúa too writes of a new mixed race, a hybrid inclusive
of all races. And her spirit is animated by freedom, democracy, equality, fairness, and tolerance. Even when she does not extensively thematize these principles, they are important in her new mythos and
would be significant concepts in further elaborations. But from the first
pages of Borderlands, one senses something very different from the
political liberal accent on building the definitive principles of an architecture to secure the just abode within which diversity is both limited
and free to do the interior decorating.

For Anzaldúa, that version of liberalism tends excessively to reify
the generative crossing of races, nationalities, cultures, and ideologies.
It turns this pregnant movement into a fundamentally static—albeit
hybrid—thing united and structured by new principles that give it
permanent form and direction. Certainly Schlesinger's new mixed race
leans toward the future and develops. But if things go best, the development will rest on principles that are relatively timeless and unchang-
ing (Anglo-Saxon ideals) in their deepest core of meaning—at least
from the inception of the new race in the founding of the United
States.[5] A crossed breed, less than an ethos of crossing.

This difference between the new mestiza and the bedrock liberal
marks the structure of their respective narratives in an unmistakable
and illuminating fashion. Schlesinger's narrative begins with a grand
founding in which the truth of a nation with territorial sovereignty is
created by a relatively homogeneous people and then undergoes a rather
linear development toward realizing in practice the inclusivity of its
original dream. In contrast, Anzaldúa's story is one of perpetual wan-
derings into alien territory. My favorite line in Borderlands is the ter-
rifically understated "We have a tradition of migration, a tradition of
long walks" (11). From the migrations across the Bering Straits, to
those toward Aztlan in what is now the U.S. Southwest, to Mexico and
Central America, back to Aztlan as porters and guides for conquista-
dors and missionaries, back south in the face of Anglo terror during
and after the U.S.-Mexican War, back north, again, to avoid political
persecution or in search of economic opportunity, and deported back
across the border—a tradition of long walks. Anzaldúa's narratives—
of history, myth, ethics—wander in their journeys through the violence,

subjugation, and risks of this wandering, but they also wander in their discussion of "certain joys," wisdoms, faculties, solidarities, and visions that can emerge in such crossings. They are stories of surprise, unwonted proximities, impossible mixings of contradictory things, wisdom from unexpected people, places, cultures—trickster stories of ambiguity, ever aspiring to the difficult Navaho saying: "Out of poverty, poetry; out of suffering, song" (*Borderlands*, 65).

Indeed, the characteristic of the new mestiza that Anzaldúa finds most inspiring and seeks to cultivate is her repeated "crossing over," the movements back and forth across the borders of culture, nation, race, gender, ideology, values, and language that surround and run through her. This crossing has been forced upon the Chicana and other feminists of color through multiple forms of hybridity and subjugation that make it impossible to be harmoniously "at home" in any single group. Yet it turns out to be her most vital ethical resource for leaning into the future and "making herself vulnerable to foreign ways of seeing and thinking" in manners conducive to human wisdom, freedom, and justice (*Borderlands*, 82). Whereas a dominant liberalism develops by privileging undivided political loyalty—if not to a nation, at least to bedrock principles—the new mestiza cultivates "divided loyalties," in terms of the cultures from which she seeks to learn politically and in terms of those to whom she offers herself. The mestiza provokes "mental nepantilism, an Aztec word meaning torn between ways" (78), because the world is both too full of myriad modes of subjugation and suffering and too rich in possibilities of wisdom and thriving, for any single set of principles or teleology to be nearly sufficient for democratic struggles. From her history on borderlands, she urges us to cultivate a certain "psychic restlessness," and "malleability," an awareness that learning and teaching to live well involve us "in a state of perpetual transition" (78). Her quest is not one for freedom grasped fundamentally as the realization of fixed ideals; rather, in contrast, "every increment of consciousness, every step forward, is a *travesía*. I am again an alien in new territory. And again, and again. . . . Every time she makes 'sense' of 'something', she has to 'cross over', kicking a hole out of the old boundaries" (48–49) Though painful, the mestiza's "energy comes from continual creative motion that keeps breaking down the unitary aspect of each paradigm" (80).[6]

Yet—the paradoxical character of Anzaldúa's project deepens—with all her affirmation of crossings, she is also involved in "creating a new mythos," re-creating perception, thought, values, and behavior. She writes in a language that employs, among other things, principles and virtues. She "participates in the creation of yet another culture, a new story to explain the world and our participation in it, a new value system with images and symbols that connect us to each other and to the planet." Playing one culture off another to illuminate violence, dangers, and richer possibilities of experience and relationship, the mestiza seeks to "reinterpret history" in a new vision. This new story and value system calls us to a "crossing over," to a "strengthened tolerance of ambiguity," to a "willingness to share, to make herself vulnerable," all of which make this *travesía* possible (*Borderlands,* 80–82). In short, Anzaldúa is cultivating a new *identity,* a new way of perception, thought, and relationship, a new way of *passing on* (in the senses of "carrying forth," "letting pass," "living," "dying") tradition. We might call this new mythos *traditio,* for both traditional and treasonous yearnings and possibilities are entangled with one another on her reading, as are loyalty and heresy, faith and blasphemy.[7] She is engaged in creating a culture that better understands the virtue of this migrant way of being and cultivates the values and virtues it would seem to require.

There is much movement here; there is crossing and being crossed. But like Marx's violin playing, it is "damned hard work." It is dangerous and easy to botch things. The crossing Anzaldúa offers does not usually just happen; it must be brought forth and cared for—people in the plural must be *drawn together* and *oriented* toward it. Habits must be formed. Even if Anzaldúa lives for a telos that is significantly ateleological—crossing toward and welcoming the others, the other traditions, the unpredictability of the future—it is still a telos, a way, "the mestiza way." However much more fluidly generous and receptive it strives to be in comparison to bedrock liberalism, its fluidity too is paradoxically entwined with efforts to build something with stability, orientation in the midst of flux, a system of values, a culture, a new mythos. The indirection Anzaldúa offers itself *requires a direction,* the creation of educative practices, an ethical, economic, and democratic topography and temporality that better prepares us for the *travesía* to and from the beyond.[8]

Like any pursuit, this requires privileging some perceptions, sensibilities, values, and practices and marginalizing others, and this always takes place in relation to our finite inscription in past modes of doing so. What distinguishes Anzaldúa is her profound awareness of the constitutive paradox (between the teleological and the ateleological) at the heart of her project, her awareness that this paradox is not simply tragic but is also *generative* of the highest possibilities and transfigurations of democratic engagement. Her negotiation of this paradox is key to her efforts to form a culture that is more hospitable toward crossing and being crossed than is political liberalism. Yet it also distinguishes her from an influential postmodern rendering of *mestizaje*.

## Juxtaposition II: The New Mestiza and the "New New"— Anzaldúa and Nancy

There is nothing easy about this effort to dwell on the edge, crossing back and forth between "deconstruct, construct." But then, Anzaldúa's history perhaps facilitates the development of certain sensibilities and faculties for this endeavor, sensibilities and faculties that are more difficult to acquire from many other places: "This is her home / this thin edge of / barbwire" (*Borderlands*, 13). Lacking such a sensibility, one is likely to succumb to the temptation to create a bedrock for freedom that is ultimately quite rigid and deaf to learning from and being transfigured by others. But it is easy to slide in the opposite direction too, easy to construe freedom as a pure movement of deconstructing all identity and form. This construal would seek its becoming and truth solely in the sublime instant of crossing's unpredictability, or in crossing *as* (nothing but) unpredictability. From this perspective, Anzaldúa's efforts to cultivate orientations, identities, and cultures that might be more conducive to this crossing would get it wrong. They would reify her deepest insights. Guidance as such would be only misguidance. The true event of the mestiza, and a familiar theme in one strand of "postmodernism," would henceforth be understood and sought in the complete letting go of all substantiation, the disorienting release from all orientation.

Such is the dominant theme in Jean-Luc Nancy's essay on the mestiza, "Cut Throat Sun."[9] Nancy, addressing Chicanos as a people of cut and cutting identities, writes of the way Chicanos "open on the undefined, multiple, radiating, reticulated, and broken track of *mestizaje*, of metissage, of the cutting, of the uncountable cuttings" ("Cut Throat Sun," 115). Although this has a certain resonance with themes one finds in Anzaldúa, for Nancy, the "opening on to the undefined" is singularly important here. It is an abyss of overwhelming gravity in his text that, like a black hole (or "dark radiance," in his words), devours everything. Aware that though the Chicano gains identity in cuttings, "it is no less an identity for it" (117), he calls us to the pure event beyond (or the beyond within) this: "Chicano does not appropriate any meaning: it exposes an event" (121). Relentlessly he calls us to recognize that all identities "never cease not totalizing themselves," and he resists any efforts like Anzaldúa's to cultivate new identities or cultures as part of an ethical-political project: "Isn't it already going too far to talk about *mestizaje?* As if *mestizaje* were 'some thing', a substance, an object, an identity (an identity!) that could be grasped and processed" (122). (As if Anzaldúa would reduce it to this!) Rather, he calls us to a radically indeterminate opening to otherness. "So in the end, what we call 'mestizaje' is the advent of the other . . . always arriving, always arriving from elsewhere. There is no point in waiting for, predicting, nor programming the other. . . . mixing . . . should not be turned into a new substance, a new identity" (123). There is no way to prepare, cultivate, or strive to practice an ethos, a learning and teaching of crossing and being crossed, because "everything has yet to be done: everything has yet to be learned, the ways, the art, and the strength needed" (120). Everything. Not just now, but always. All preparation is preclusion. To seek the advent of the other we must stop seeking and witness the raw opening of possibility. Otherwise we would slip back into an assimilationist dream of "a 'transculture' with its multiple and enriching facets." We would find ourselves creating the very situation we sought to escape: "a world that pretends to be reclaiming differences in general (is there difference 'in general'?), but that can always trap those differences into its own indifference" (119).

Anzaldúa, as we have seen, surely agrees that ontologically and historically "the other is always arriving" ("Cut Throat Sun," 123), and that all identities and preparations harbor preclusions. Yet from her vantage point, Nancy's understanding of the ethical-political significance of this comes up short. For no matter how cut open and exposed to the cutting and crossing of all identities we may be, we are, she might cut from Nancy's text, "no less an identity for it." We are never simply raw opening. Paradoxically, *opening involves preparation.* Furthermore, though identities are always and everywhere exposed to the arrival of others, as we know—and as Anzaldúa knows particularly well—most others with which we are familiar historically have mobilized intensively to variously deny, degrade, enslave, assimilate, and obliterate the otherness of this event. We would quit preparing for the arrival of *these* others—the "new" we know only too well—only at the cost of our own subjugation. There is no identity—or other, or otherness—that would itself be entirely beyond blind and problematic forms of encroachment, and there is no place or mode of witness or listening, no matter how displaced, that is entirely beyond identity. One denies this, Nancy denies this, only at the cost of proliferating an unnecessary degree of blindness to one's finitude and to the way it, too, partakes of and engages identity, position, and damage. With this denial, the "advent of the other" toward which Nancy would summon us becomes all the less available, all the less desirable, and, in the face of an overly rigid and self-blind identity, all the less possible. To learn and to teach to live well will always involve preparations and disciplines that engage questions of direction and limitation. We tend toward stinginess and poverty when we forsake these tasks.

Just as one can see the preclusionary effects of bedrock liberalism in Schlesinger's quick and dirty treatment of his others, we can discern similar effects in Nancy's text, as Alarcón notes.[10] Hence, Nancy tells us, or warns us, with one of his generalizing moves, "we are all mestiza, and everything, everyone . . . who alters me, subjects me to *mestizaje*. This has nothing to do with mixed blood or mixed cultures" ("Cut Throat Sun," 123). Thus one must not think of the mestiza in relation to one's own specific and multiple historical locations, practices, cultural aspirations, or ethical sensibilities. Nor can one think of her in terms of specific others coming from different traditions and cultures that importantly contribute to who and how they are. Yet these are precisely among the important questions that feminists of color are struggling with among themselves and struggling to bring before others in their participation in ethical-political contestations and coalitions. Might not Nancy, with Schlesinger, have Chicanas leave all this at the door—now not as a precondition for entering a secure abode of freedom but rather so we might step beyond "abode-ness" to abide with the "advent" of the other? In either case—coming or going—the new mestiza with her very specific narratives of suffering and desire, disillusion and enchantment, is stopped at the door. And her absence is evident in the way Nancy's text drifts along a certain postmodern current unperturbed, never allowing the mestiza to call his text into question. The mestiza is banned in her own name: a politics of marginalization in the form of a call to transgress borderlands.

Yet Anzaldúa's participation in creating a new culture and in engaging specificity is due not to a lingering essentialism but to her understanding that this is integral to a more generous and receptive relation to the practice and event of crossing over/being crossed.[11] It is integral to resisting the thick and multifarious legacies of subjugation within and around one in the present.

Few stories illuminate these tensions between teleology and ateleology as poignantly as those surrounding Malinche (given in slavery to Hernán Cortés, she was his translator, adviser, and mistress for a time), the hybridizing mother of Chicano/as; and Chicano/as have wrestled mightily with her legacy. Whereas Our Lady of Guadalupe, "the Mexican people's native version of Virgin Mary," has been considered the "national patroness of Mexico" for centuries, Malinche has been the "monstrous double," representative of the Fall and of treason, a traitor.[12] Mexican nationalists, Octavio Paz notes, have successfully deployed the term *malinchista* "to denounce all those who have been corrupted by foreign influences."[13] As Cherríe Moraga writes, in *Loving in the War Years,* beginning in the mid-1960s Chicano movements used the term *malinchista* to denounce Chicanas who questioned their subordinate roles in their culture and in *el movimiento*.[14] In resistance, many feminists appropriated Malinche to re-imagine and invent alternative—even "treasonous"—visions of Chicana/o community. Chicana feminists offer discrepant reinterpretations of Malinche, yet their various approaches to her form a constellation that illuminates the ethical-political tensions of a more receptive movement toward democratic engagement.

One cluster of reinterpretations admire Malinche as one who suggests the importance of an ateleological sensibility in which opening to otherness, the unexpected, and crossing is integral to negotiating spaces of resistance, understanding, and empowerment amid practices of subjugation linked to notions of purity.[15] These interpretations evoke integral aspects of the new mestiza, yet they have also been subject to criticisms that illuminate ways the constitutive tensions of democratic *traditio* exceed this ateleological moment. Criticizing Donna Haraway's appropriation, Paula Moya argues that "neither marginality nor survival are sufficient goals for a feminist project." Moreover, "Haraway conceals the painful legacy of the Malinche myth."[16] Indeed, those against whom *"Malinchista!"* has been deployed may know something about the dangers of margins that other theorists might do well to consider. As Alarcón notes, "Malinche demonstrates that crossing ethnic and racial boundaries does not necessarily change the status of Indian women or women of color, for example."[17] There are too many traps in the world for a Malinche narrative reduced to an unproblematic celebration of crossing over and hybridity to suffice. Also needed are stories of the dangers and the subjugations, of the hopeless confusions that can result, of the potential lack of justice and possibility in the "new territory," even newly *generated* territory. A fuller constellation of Malinche interpretations calls us to negotiate both the higher possibilities and the deep dangers of the new mestiza.

Another danger: *"La Malinche!"* is the story of the story of Malinche, a five-hundred-year *history* of her story.[18] And this is a history in which she (and other "traitors") have been isolated, marginalized, insistently forgotten, excommunicated. Could she have acted and spoken in ways more susceptible of being remembered and admired? More resistant to being forgotten? Could her daughters today? Any ethic wishing to take risks beyond established and accepted communicative "currencies"—as the new mestiza must—needs an ear tuned to the Malinche who *also* pronounces the dangers *here*. Worried about possible isolation that could result from an overly "individualized vision" in Moraga's affirmation of *Vendida*, "traitor," "sellout," for example, Alarcón asks, "the new insight arrived at in writing needs to be communicated to millions of women who still live under such metaphoric controls. How are they to be persuaded to accept the insights if they still exist under the ideology 'Guadalupe-Malintzin'"?[19] Do we who would break from undesirable teleologies of tradition—and tradition understood mainly *as* teleology—also consider sufficiently questions of the transfigurative reach and power of our language, art, and politics?

These particularities of Chicana history exemplified by Malinche illuminate paradoxical inspirations and warnings that constitute the new mestiza way of torn allegiances. The new mestiza seeks life *through* negotiations of the agonism and overlaps between the striving to create a way that forms and prepares us to live with others well, and the difficult task of remembering and expecting that the ethical relation with others will involve much more than this. It will often involve an uncanny welcoming of the other, a jack rabbit–like listening, trickster malleability, a critical engagement that is both radically receptive and agonistic, and a transfiguration that will—*at the disjointed moment of encounter*—demand far more than any preparation could ever satisfy.

This in turn demands torn virtues. So justice, for example, will always require the cultivation of principles, virtues, and dispositions that we believe will best help us give what is due (optimal ways of questioning, understanding, and practicing it, resisting injustice). But it will also involve us in striving to cultivate thoughts, virtues, and dispositions of a more radical receptivity toward those who do not share our "way," our telos—toward those beings and events that call for its radical distension, for changed subjects, for possible engagements at and beyond our limits. Ateleological justice seeks to open to the future by cultivating memories and expectations of the innumerable times when teleological orientations to resist the bad overshoot themselves and erect a priori barriers against otherness as such. Justice, charity, love, courage, reciprocity, and so forth call us to orient ourselves and to open ourselves through them to a certain disorientation. Torn virtues call and help us to stay in the middle, in the profoundest moments, playing teleological and ateleological accents and insights against each other. The remembrance that Malinche keeps coming back in new and unexpected ways helps cultivate this *traditio* insofar as Malinche exemplifies ateleological encounters with the radically other who keeps changing the subjects of justice. She returns to nationalist teleologies with solicitations toward a hybridizing mode of justice. She returns to hybridizing modes of justice with questions of marginalization, excommunication, dangers, and sufferings of such efforts. Each appearance calls for the careful work of reinvention in her light. (From) where will her next apparition call us?

Yet the teleological and ateleological dimensions are not *simply* in tension with each other: Each *also* facilitates the other. It may even be that most often they do operate in relations of significant overlap and collaboration, as is indicated, for example, in the ways preparation and otherness inform each other in the above discussion. From this angle, "torn" is perhaps an overwrought term. Perhaps "stretched" more adequately evokes the relation. My use of "torn," then, is not simply a philosophical choice but is equally an existential-political one. Even if "torn" exaggerates, it nevertheless foregrounds that aspect of ineliminable tearing that is an integral *part* of the paradoxical teleological-ateleological relation; and as the existential and political pressures to deny or minimize this tearing are always great, I use the word to resist them.

Yet "torn" and "stretched" evoke something very different from Nancy's terms. His discussion of *mestizaje* dismisses all projects that partake of identification, direction, and preparation as "totalizing" "traps." Although I have argued in this section that Nancy's project harbors numerous dangers, from another vantage point, one that many Chicana feminists explore, it also misses generative possibilities that accompany many projects that mobilize political direction, preparation, and identification (even as they do so in ways that are also keenly sensitive to the dangers involved). For writers like Anzaldúa, these generative political *possibilities* are entwined with cultivating generative *sensibilities*. The latter weave throughout their texts and tend to animate a more constructive political stance than one finds in Nancy or even in significant portions of Derrida's writing. I find this sensibility compelling, and it animates my writing in this book, including, no doubt, the way I read Derrida.

### Juxtaposition III: Political Liberal Tradition and *Traditio*: Rawls and Feminists of Color

But the question posed earlier returns: What ethical-political implications and practices might come into view from the vantage point of *traditio* that are precluded by the liberalism it would contest? One way to initiate a response is to carefully juxtapose the politics of feminists of color with that of political liberalism. This juxtaposition also provides an example of an encounter with the radically other—liberalism's encounter with feminists of color—that both solicits and further cultivates ateleological virtues if it is to be wisely negotiated. I resume this encounter through the lenses of their dueling political-philosophical historical narratives. In this light we can see the position(s) of feminists of color both as a radicalization of the Rawlsian dialectic and as an ateleological challenge to it. This enables us to more carefully clarify some of the stakes.

Rawls offers the following dialectical history of political liberalism to situate and make more compelling the overlapping consensus he aims to secure (*Political Liberalism,* lecture 4). Some liberal principles were perhaps first affirmed pragmatically, not on shared moral grounds but as part of a modus vivendi that allowed diverse groups to negotiate contingent conflicts and power relations in ways that moderated conflicts and facilitated the reduction of violence from which they were all exhausted (such as wars of religion). However, this minimal strategic framework of electoral democracy and a few basic rights generates internal contradictions that threaten its own survival. *As purely strategic,* its ability to generate trust is minimal. Each group suspects that others' allegiance will last only as long as they are insufficiently powerful to dominate. Hence groups scheme in ways that can proliferate instabilities that erupt in violence. At the same time, many experience certain benefits of democratic peace for themselves, their groups, and the wider society. If their doctrines are not *entirely* comprehensive and have a "certain looseness," many might adjust them in ways that facilitate wider affirmations of liberal principles as *"inherently good."* Hence the modus vivendi is *"deepened"* and moralized in ways that make it clearer and more reliable, trustworthy, and public, and that remove it from deep contestation—it becomes a more stable *constitutional consensus.* But this generates problems as well, problems that propel the liberal dialectic forward. To begin with, this consensus—affirming democratic procedures and some political rights—is still shallow and narrow, and hence the constitution will be a very unstable document. It must be interpreted to be meaningful, yet because it lacks deep and broad roots, interpretative processes and amendment struggles threaten to draw forth incommensurable positions that might erupt in violent conflict. The same lurking incommensurability threatens governmental deliberations occurring upon a now-more-heterogeneous political table. These threats, in combination with the need to convince others with broadly accessible viewpoints, create pressures upon political actors to *"deepen"* their consensus in ways that make available a "common currency" of principles of justice (liberty, equality, citizenship, and so on) that aid in interpretation, amendment, and deliberation. Increasing cooperative relationships across different groups, as well as certain loose and *non*comprehensive aspects of particular doctrines, aid this process. At the same time, newly enfranchised groups bring forth serious conflicts that create pressures toward a *"broadening"* of the consensus to include social rights and economic needs, so that over the long term democratic traditions develop an overlapping consensus concerning justice for the basic structure of society.

Political liberalism seeks to further deepen this process by means of a "self-clarification" of the tradition that reaches beneath the "very deep" conflicts in liberal culture to make perfectly evident the principles of justice that best express our deepest sense of society as a system of fair (reciprocal) cooperation between free and equal citizens (*Political Liberalism,* 26). Yet if Rawls understands previous deepenings to be transfigurative and generative in their responses to destabilization, he claims to "complete and extend" the tradition now in a way that *secures* the ideals already underlying our most basic democratic practices from those who, like the new mestiza, would threaten it.

As we have seen, central to Rawls's theory is a "common currency" of principles that would (1) regulate distributive inequality to the maximal advantage of the "least well off" (difference principle); and (2) protect and regulate individuals and groups with different moral, philosophical, and religious views. He seeks the latter by securing a "tolerant" nonpublic realm in which these differences can freely flourish and by strictly limiting their expression, in public deliberations concerning fundamental issues, to that which accords with public reason.

Differences concerning the good that emerge from particular traditions and modes of life and that cannot find sufficient support on the grounds of public reason must be excluded from playing a role in such deliberations, or else reciprocity will be violated as some find themselves governed by particular doctrines with which they, as reasonable people, disagree. Hence, for example, the following different positions would be morally illegitimate as contenders in directly political forums concerning fundamentals: views on abortion policy framed partly in terms of religious arguments concerning sacredness of life at conception; arguments about wilderness and environmental politics that move beyond enlightened anthropocentricism and are partly framed in terms of reverence for the nonhuman; arguments concerning punishment informed by a comprehensive doctrine's particular understanding of forgiveness as a sacred virtue; arguments for pacifistic policies based on interpretations of "Thou shalt not kill"; radically welcoming immigration practices informed by very particular borderland histories and visions; radical democratic political-economic policies advocated in terms of an ethos of crossing.

These limits are not legal but normative, taking the form of a model of citizenship. As such they are to prescribe and proscribe the patterns of our utterances and receptivity. Good citizens make their public claims concerning basic matters accord with the directions and limits of public reason. Moreover, not only are good citizens in a liberal democracy never called in public deliberations *to* listen receptively to others' claims that exceed in substance what could be sufficiently maintained by public reason alone, they are called *not* to listen, insofar as such claims are denied legitimacy from the outset. Justice, as political liberal tolerance, would thus call us to a nonpublic flourishing and a public disengagement of our deeply contestable differences.

Although a politics of disengagement is not prescribed in such strong terms for issues of distributive justice, it nevertheless resonates here and has effects that are at work in the vision Rawls articulates. Hence, although citizens voting and speaking in public forums should always argue issues of distributive justice with their eyes on the advantage of the least well off, the primary aim here is *not* toward movements that empower the mobilized voices of the latter and call more-fortunate people to the difficult work of receptive engagements with them.[20] Rather, it is to frame a basic structure that relieves us of any necessity for such considerations and encounters in the everyday, assured that the system is addressing their just needs. Hence Rawls writes that the difference principle should be inscribed in public law and should not apply "to particular transactions or distributions, nor to decisions of individuals and associations, but rather to the institutional background against which these transactions and decisions take place" (*Political Liberalism*, 283). "Secure in the knowledge that elsewhere in the social system the necessary corrections to preserve background justice are being made," "individuals and associations are then left free to advance their ends more effectively within the framework of the basic structure" (269).

Yet the work of many feminists of color suggests that political liberalism's dialectic of contemporary conflicts and responses comes up radically short *on its own terms* and must be reinterpreted and enacted in ways that move beyond Rawls. These shortcomings can be illuminated in relation to the way Rawls frames political (dis)agreement concerning both the least well off and different visions of the good. I shall focus on each in turn, though it quickly becomes clear that they are deeply entwined.

From the vantage point of feminists of color, better perception and knowledge of things like the conditions of the least well off, the relationship between these conditions and dominant practices, modes of effective response, and the political will and emotion necessary to mobilize action all hinge upon more-frequent engagements with those suffering from various modes of exploitation. The point is not that redistributive structures are undesirable, nor is it that distributive justice should be accomplished by random state interventions into the everyday life of citizens.[21] Rather, they question Rawls's confidence in the "division of labor" between background structures and individuals' everyday actions. They suggest that the cultivation of everyday practices for more-receptive encounters with the least well off are inextricably entwined with any real hope of building and sustaining more-just background institutions. This would involve radical transformations of currently class-segregated schools, housing developments, shopping centers, work locations, transportation systems, public parks, and so forth to facilitate frequent intermingling. And too, it would involve a different structuring of relations within such altered spaces. For example, what if corporations were required to meet regularly with members of surrounding poor communities in public forums significantly designed by the latter? What if many were required to have elected representatives of poor communities on their governing boards?

As frequently articulated by Anzaldúa, Audre Lorde, and many oters, distributive injustice is enacted and sustained by structures of cultural perception, affect, knowledge, and geographies of spatial, temporal, and (dys)functional distributions of the bodies of different peoples. *Re*distribution and *re*cognition are inseparable, and little progress will be made on these entwined fronts without a proliferation of spaces and practices of political encounter and participation. The encounters are dialogical, and they often involve *bodily* contestations and engagements. Emerging repeatedly in writings by feminists of color is a "theory and politics of the flesh"—analyses of power and possibility at the level of bodily perception, abjection, and emotion—and a call for a more contestatory politics involving both the mobilization of subjugated peoples and discomforting work by those more powerfully positioned to see and hear them differently (to see their desires, pleasures, sweat, and embodied visions of the good).[22] Citizen concern for those who are least well off is empty if they are variously objects of disgust, marginalization, and everyday indifference.

Sufficiently pressed, a progressive Rawlsian might acknowledge the need for a much more engaged politics, maybe even for some modes engaging the bodily. In principle nothing prevents this dialectical-teleological extension. Indeed, such a Rawlsian might move thus because she has been convinced (for example, in a variety of empirical, pragmatic, and psychological ways) that the values of political liberalism (themselves sovereign and unscathed) require it. Even as he rejects the "political sociology" behind such a move, Rawls himself goes some distance to note its principled possibility in relation to a "classical republicanism" that claims "that without a widespread participation in a democratic politics by a vigorous and informed citizen body . . . even the most well-designed political institutions will fall into the hands of those who seek to dominate" (*Political Liberalism*, 205). Hence, political liberal values might require for their own possibility more-robust forms of political participation.

Although this move would be welcomed, from the vantage point of *traditio* it would fall short of acknowledging the depth of the challenge posed by many feminists of color. For the visions they offer (the radicalness of their political dreams and the energy of their activism), though greatly indebted to liberal notions of liberty, equality, fairness, tolerance, reciprocity, and efforts to realize them, *exceed* these in significantly ateleological ways and refigure them in light of broader constellations of subjugation and human flourishing that emerge in complicated relation to the dense specificities of their histories. And precisely at this point political liberalism must oppose them, not only because they seek to bring specific visions of the good into political engagements but also because they tend to affirm political engagement across differences as *itself a central one of these goods.*

Thus Rawls states his "fundamental opposition" to "civic humanism," where "participation is not encouraged as necessary for the protection of the basic liberties of democratic citizenship, and as in itself one form of good among others, however important for many persons. Rather, taking part in democratic politics is seen as the privileged locus of the good life. . . . From the standpoint of political liberalism, the objection to this comprehensive doctrine is the same as to all other such doctrines, so I need not elaborate" (*Political Liberalism*, 206). Arendtian celebrations of politics as *the* privileged locus of the good life are not dominant in the writings of most feminists of color. But notions of political engagement and affirmations of encountering differences are nevertheless more than "one form of good among others" for many, and these visions play a key role in the basic transformations that they seek and argue for in public forums.[23]

Anzaldúa's mestiza suggests a *traditio* of spirit, consciousness, and politics addressing fundamental issues of justice and flourishing. The new mestiza is about political struggles around maquiladoras, farmworkers, immigrants, health care, race, gender, sexuality, history, property, language, education, environment, deserts. There are important debts to liberalism here, but only a very cramped optic would reduce liberalism to this teleological form. For out of the hybrid(izing) particularities of her history and struggles comes a yearning—a vision— toward a new politics of encounter and culture of crossing and being crossed as a very high *good in itself,* irreducible to—and sometimes transgressive of—the liberal principles it also facilitates. Throughout *Borderlands,* Anzaldúa writes not only of the hatred, anger, and suffering of borderlands but also of the "joys," "exhilaration," and "faculties" involved in the *way* of border being; of the emergence of relationships previously tabooed; of lesbian relations among Chicanas; of surprisingly powerful relations across national boundaries; of new entwinements of diverse struggles; of transfigured senses of the land. She strives toward a politics that might facilitate this sense of possibility at "confluent streams." Anzaldúa slips across borders patrolled by political liberalism, and she does not recognize its sovereign proprietary claims to the terrain of political discourse and practice.

The way this vision transcends political liberalism receives fuller illumination when we focus more directly on the limits of Rawls's dialectical narrative as it circumscribes the political (dis)engagements of "comprehensive doctrines." The radicalizing counternarrative of the "new mestiza" or "sister outsider" goes something like this: At present, liberal ideals of tolerance help animate and open some new spaces for groups with diverse histories and yearnings. Simultaneously, the yearnings and expectations for freedom and equality for diverse modes of being that are nurtured by these ideals far exceed the reality in which multiple sexualities, genders, ethnicities, "races," religions, and visions remain subject to a priori ideological condemnation, unjust constraint, abjection, or malignant indifference in their struggles to move beyond disempowering markings and marginality. These discrepancies between liberal expectations and liberal reality, combined with the limited but not insignificant nonpublic spaces and public resistances protected by liberal rights, lead to multiple conflicts in which differences become politicized (articulating affirmative aspects of their specificity and aspirations and challenging "unmarked" hegemonic identities). Increasingly, struggles fueled in part by liberal ideals generate political practices that exceed these ideals, as different constituencies repeatedly fail to attain the nonpublic freedom and equality accorded to members of the acknowledged "diversity" without hyperintensive *politicizations* of difference. This dynamic is entwined with and reinforced by the discrepancy discussed above, that between liberal ideals of economic fairness and a reality in which many are subject to forms of economic suffering that correlate disproportionately along lines of marginalized difference. Add to this the following: Most subaltern groups politicizing difference replicate *internally* conflicts and resistances analogous to their struggles with the dominant society.[24] Hence Lorde, Bernice Johnson Reagon,[25] Moraga, and Anzaldúa experience normalizing pressures from, say, movements for racial *or* gender *or* sexual freedom because they refuse to prioritize one dimension. Each sub-subaltern group formed in response to these pressures again brings up new conflicts—the presence of one's "manchild" for lesbians; a wandering sexuality, attitudes toward anger, or a poetic spirit that resists the confines of liberal deliberation.

After a series of these struggles (for example, with white women or misogynist Chicanos), many people begin "*deepening*" and "*broadening*" in a dialectic that draws some energy and direction from but moves beyond the limits of political liberalism.[26] Tolerance, in this context, comes to be seen as "gross reformism" because its *nonpublic vision of benign mutually indifferent diversity* tends to deflect political attention away from the endlessly reoccurring ways identities and differences (often very seriously) impinge upon each other. Its shallow vision of diversity conceals (and sometimes plays important disciplinary roles in) the deeper and thicker textures of perceptual, emotional, cognitive, and structural power that continue—and seem always in some degree—to operate. Simultaneously, those engaged in a politics where differences are given more agonistic play begin experiencing possibilities for dialogical freedom and flourishing in these relations that illuminate an "*inherent goodness*" of these new differential engagements. Such recognition provoked transformative directions in response to earlier conflicts of liberalism, and so it does again. *Traditio* is born, as the democratic imagination moves forward *with and beyond* relatively set teleological governance: "Revolution is not a one-time event. It is becoming always vigilant for the smallest opportunity to make a genuine change in established, outgrown responses; for instance, it is learning to address each other's difference with respect" (*Sister Outsider*, 141). Increasingly voiced among many in such movements is an affirmation of practices more generous and receptive in relations across the tensions of difference—a sense that ongoing critical explorations and contestations of all modes of being is a good thing.[27] *Borderlands* goes some distance—in content and in structure—to *enact* this surprising and significantly ateleological sensibility. After many deeply critical and angry discussions of dominant white culture, near the end of the prose section Anzaldúa opens a path of mediation, expresses vulnerabilities, suggests both that Chicana/os are the denied "doppelganger" of the white psyche and that Chicana/os should strive beyond rage and blame and stop disowning "the white parts," calls for agonistic coalition, and writes, "And finally, tell us what you need from us" (*Borderlands*, 86).

This ethos, indebted to liberalism but also animated, solicited, and haunted by other spirits, is precisely what Lorde has in mind when she writes, "Advocating the mere tolerance of difference between women is the grossest reformism. It is a total denial of the creative function of difference in our lives. Difference must be not merely tolerated, but seen as a fund of necessary polarities between which our creativity can spark like a dialectic" (*Sister Outsider*, 111). Lorde's strivings for tolerance in an intolerant world gave birth to a vision of engaged differences that go beyond tolerance. The "sparks" from the friction between differences illuminated, for her, a mode of flourishing and wisdom with its own seductive force. And with Anzaldúa, Lorde is not content to develop this ethic for herself or for her most proximate groups alone. Her vision of "interdependencies of difference" yearns for others moved by more-generous and more-receptive dialogical spirits, others with courage to "descend into the chaos" (ibid.). Mobilizing and soliciting, she wants this vision to *move* us and to participate in transforming the practices of this world. "I am who I am, doing what I came to do, acting upon you like a drug or a chisel to remind you of your me-ness, as I discover you in myself" (147). There are traces of the evangelical here, mixing with and tempered by radical receptivity, to form strange overtones and oscillating dissonance.

This "deepening" and "broadening" opens the future to more ateleological possibilities precisely through relations of exposure and indebtedness to multiplicitous pasts that exceed teleological bounds. For the new mestiza, these include Native American beliefs and practices, folk Catholicism, and sensibilities drawn from more nomadic and hybridizing modes of being. For Lorde it includes some practices of female bonding in African cultures and black communities in the United States.

For bell hooks it includes a history of thick practices of mutuality and resistance in the marginalized black communities and strong churches actively involved in black subaltern public life.[28] The politics of *traditio* emerges, then, from ateleological developments indebted to more-chaotic encounters among diverse groups, histories, and selves. It has debts to liberalism, but these should not be exaggerated in ways that diminish its multiplicitous origins and generativity, that generate understandings that divert efforts to listen, or that reinforce the self-congratulatory moments of liberalism and conceal the many ways voices historically central to liberalism have resisted (in ideals and practices) what liberalism now recognizes to be justice. The movement toward justice and flourishing *has been* and *will be*—if it will be—teleological and ateleological.

From the perspective of *traditio* one can imagine transformations going beyond the directions and confines of liberalism in relation to "fundamental issues of justice": Land use and property law might be radically altered as human-nonhuman relations come to be seen more as a rich borderland for crossings of receptive enrichment and generous letting be and less as a resource to be instrumentally exploited through private and public territorial sovereignties; immigration law might be dramatically rewritten qualitatively and quantitatively as our sense of debts to and possibilities for mutual enrichment with those beyond "our" borders increases; work might be structured far more dialogically; selves and communities might seek to reduce material inequality to levels unimaginable in political liberal societies, by means of a capacious commonwealth politics engaging different communities toward collective purposes;[29] multilingualism might become public policy in light of more-heterogeneous senses of "we"; social movements might cut across and challenge the prerogatives of territorial states as more of "us" began to interpret ourselves less territorially and more as peoples with "histories of long walks." These changes might alter "fundamental structures" through alliances built significantly around visions of justice sharing much with Anzaldúa, Alarcón, Lorde, and Reagon. As such, they would in origin and in aim transgress political liberal limits relegating such differences—including differences enchanted with difference—to the nonpublic realm. Less directly, but no less fundamentally, a politics of *traditio* would be engaged in experimental transfigurations of sensibility that might, in ways currently unimagined, feed into institutional transformations affecting families, punishment, welfare, public spaces, technologies, land use, and relationships with other-than-human beings.

*Traditio* thus evoked marks differences that make political differences. In Rawls's terms they are politicized "doctrines." They are thick and transfiguring—but are they comprehensive or totalizing? No. First, they are born *of* struggles and alliances across multiple modes of life, groups, and selves in which much ongoing tension-filled difference of history and aspiration remains and is encouraged. Relatedly, they draw from multiple sources—for example, liberal tolerance or tolerance of intense trickster ambiguity and contradiction—to cultivate modes of being more affirmative of difference *as such*, and this feeds their generosity in relation to particular differences that arouse their anger. Finally, even as this affirmation politicizes difference and transgresses some of liberalism's absolutist delimitations, it hinges on a sensibility that highlights the importance of receptivity to the unwonted, to the fecundity of the ateleological. It does not, then, aspire to be "the whole." Taming this drive, it counterposes the increased volume of its public voices with an increased receptivity to the others who do and unexpectedly will contest it—especially those who do not seek totalizing establishments deaf to their others.

Clearly there are risks with a democratic politics of *traditio*. Its commitment to more-receptive openings might make limits to encroachment more porous in ways that afford opportunities for undesirable transgressions. Its commitment to participatory engagements might put inordinate pressure upon those who would rather pursue more apolitical lives or might facilitate the power of the active over the inactive. Its greater embrace of emotion in politics might inadvertently feed undesirable forms of demagoguery and intolerance. The wager, however, is that no system and teleology will alone provide the most desirable way to assess risk and generate ethical-political responses *and* that a vision of democratic *traditio* can draw together and mobilize diverse people seeking to respond both to specific subjugations and to the possibilities of building dialogical political and economic practices capable of soliciting voices and listening across much greater ranges of human modes of being. In view of its own risks, this range must include and even solicit many who would challenge, resist, and chasten it—certainly political liberals. For it is precisely the contestable probability and relative weight of these real risks that is part of what opens wide the door to the paradox of openness and closure with which I began. *Traditio* claims to negotiate these risks better than the alternatives under discussion here. Yet if there might be a claim to possess a certain authority in this, its legitimacy would significantly hinge upon the vitality both of its ongoing practice of vulnerability to others (dispossession) and of the practice of sharing power with others who contest it (uncoupling possession and authority from sovereignty).

## Juxtaposition IV: Other of the End

If I have gathered from and worked with several voices to articulate the disposition I am calling *traditio,* perhaps *traditio* itself makes it fitting now to signal—ever so briefly—a certain lack of fit. With this, the chapter might end not so much by underscoring its aim—its end—but by opening its end to ateleological voices beyond and within it; a listening that is just beginning. This, after all, is precisely the move Schlesinger and Nancy guard against.

I have developed *traditio* in ways alive to the ethical complexities of borderlands. But the "angrier parts" of the work of many feminists of color are markedly diminished in my work. Lorde writes repeatedly of her anger at white feminists' inability to wrestle with her anger. Black women's "anger has meant pain" for them, "but it has also meant survival, and before I give it up I'm going to be sure that there is something at least as powerful to replace it on the road to clarity" (*Sister Outsider,* 132). Similarly, Anzaldúa writes,

> Some of the writing is glossed over as, particularly, white critics . . .
> often pick just some part of *Borderlands.* For example . . . *mestizaje*
> and *borderlands* . . . The angrier parts . . . are often ignored as
> they seem to be too threatening and too confrontational. In some
> way, I think you could call this selective critical interpretation a
> kind of racism."[30]

Maybe the more comfortable one is, the easier it is to be critically dismissive of anger, to show how it can impede more "sensible" deliberation or how it can fuel a politics of *ressentiment* that is "reactive" and becomes invested in "wounded attachments."[31] Each of these critiques identifies very important dangers, and they do not fail to strike me. But they miss much that is of value in the positions they seemingly dismiss.

I do not mean only that feminists like Lorde have carefully distinguished between hatred ("fury" toward difference, "and its object is death and destruction") and anger ("a grief of distortions between peers" that is "a powerful source of energy serving progress and change" and that seeks not annihilation but a "meeting on a common basis [of respect] to examine differences").[32] Nor do I mean only that usually the very writers who thematize the importance of anger also underscore its limits and the need for more-creative vision and receptivity than anger can provide.[33]

More importantly, writers like Lorde and Anzaldúa are profoundly aware of the crucial—even irreplaceable—role anger so often plays in ethical-political-epistemological struggles against subjugation. Anger is not simply a passion that sometimes helps a person listen to someone or something—to an opinion or to some information deliberatively gained without anger—that they are predisposed not to consider (though this is important). Lorde has something more profound in mind when she writes that "anger is loaded with information." It does not simply *provoke* a shared deliberative rationality that would, at least in terms of "shared values," ideally be free of anger. She thinks of an anger that participates, through resistant and alternative perception, in the very genesis of knowledge and value through "a basic and radical alteration in those assumptions underlining our lives" (*Sister Outsider,* 127). If anger is "loaded with information," this is in no small part because information is so often born with anger; anger is partly generative of value and thus has itself a value.[34] "It is not the anger . . . that will destroy us but our refusals to stand still, to listen to its rhythms, to learn within it" (*Sister Outsider,* 130).[35] In contrast, unexpressed anger can turn into and nourish a hateful *ressentiment* that incapacitates our ability to learn. Hence many feminists of color distance themselves markedly from political liberalism by affirming a larger role for anger in political relations.

For these briefly sketched reasons, I am drawn to affirm anger as an incredibly important part of ethical life—even drawn to say, in a context where it may seem inappropriate, that I am deeply angered at most of the things that anger Anzaldúa and Lorde. But.

But to say it now is not the same as to voice it and work it frequently throughout one's texts and politics. I could recite how my sense of dangers and other possibilities may diminish this voicing and working of anger. I could state my uneasiness with the charge that "this selective critical interpretation" could be called "a kind of racism." (But what *is* being said by the unsaid anger of the scholarly essay?) I could perhaps construct an argument that people more "privileged," like myself, might best contribute precisely their less angry voices to coalitions with feminists of color.

But my sense of these things, my confidence in their direction, is less certain now than ever. In the face of these voices that do not quite fit— voices from elsewhere—I am beginning to wonder whether one of *traditio*'s most important challenges might not be to listen to, learn from, be transfigured by, and engage the "uses of anger." I have in mind neither incorporating nor being incorporated by these other, more angry voices. I am often no more compelled by their *work* in angrier keys than I am by my diminished capacities there. Rather, what seems needful now might be to invent or to be invented by "uses of anger" in the face of these questions opening in this space of encounter. Might it be that an emotion so potentially laden with closure would nevertheless not infrequently be integral to a more generous and receptive opening toward otherness? But how are we to negotiate this difficult manifestation of the paradox with which we began?

Democratic *traditio* calls for and is called by tasks like these. It is, admittedly, a lot to ask. Yet my sense is that the "easier" alternatives ultimately ask more and give less. In chapter 7 I explore a form of receptive democratic politics that self-consciously deploys "cold anger."

# 7

# Moving Democracy:
# The Political Arts of Listening,
# Traveling, and Tabling

N THIS CHAPTER I explore a politics of nepantilist generosity through the
lens of efforts to organize radical democracy in urban areas across
the United States. In part I am interested in discerning possible textured ethical and political practices related to the stance I am exploring
in this book. Yet far more importantly, I seek to learn *from* this radical democratic work about what democracy might mean today. In other
words, I engage Industrial Areas Foundation politics not primarily as
an example of a politics of *traditio* that would leave the general framework untouched but, rather, as a nexus of theory and practice from
which theorists (myself included) might receive profound insights into
the most fundamental kinds of political questions—and even some
new questions. I am interested here in developing a receptive practice
of theory in relation to insurgent political life, as much as I seek to
elaborate a more receptive politics. *Traditio* must find articulation first
and foremost as a textual practice if it is not to become a mockery of
itself. What matters most is not a particular thesis but *what happens*
in theory.

Following a period in the 1980s and 1990s during which students of
politics too often uncritically celebrated a cure-all notion of civil society, many are beginning to articulate more-nuanced perspectives. On
the one hand, civil society harbors emergent democratic associations,
fosters broader grassroots participation, spawns movements that offer

resistance to corporate markets and state bureaucracies, and is a site of various forms of "micro-politics" that tend to transform our sensibilities and practices in more-pluralizing and more-egalitarian directions. On the other hand, when one examines associational life in terms of things like resources, membership, access, norms of identity/difference, circuits of power, and capacities, one sees it is often colonized by corporations and bureaucracies, is the abode of myriad fundamentalist movements, and tends to manifest racial, class, gender, and other biases.[1] Given this messy complexity, there is a growing sense that our analyses of civil society must be more subtle and variegated.

I suggest that this more careful attention should be pushed further in ways that might transform our very modes of engaging democratic practices. Consider how we often engage the associational terrain. Generally, theorists formulate questions that assume a given definition of democracy and then show its presence with reference to civil society, or show how strengthening elements of civil society might reinvigorate devitalized democratic powers and practices, or rearticulate and relocate those powers and practices in the conditions under which we live.[2] At most, our analytical and theoretical investigations of this terrain lead us to understand new sites and configurations of democratic practice, yet our core normative or ethical ideas of democracy remain unchallenged, undisturbed, and relatively unreformed in these undertakings. I suspect that this relative lack of disturbance is hampering our ability to perceive and engage new directions, inspirations, and movements of democracy emerging in certain struggles. I argue that the normative bases of various democratic theories—and the associated analytical lenses that many typically employ—significantly impede our capacities to witness and interpret democratic practices in ways that not only remove much that is most salient from our view but also shield us from engagements with democratic ventures that might solicit radical reformations of democratic theory itself.

Thus a crucial step toward addressing these weaknesses, insofar as they are connected to the ways democratic theorists typically engage the world of democratic practices, is to alter the mode of engagement. Hence part of my purpose in this chapter is to experiment with an alternative relationship to practices of democracy. I suggest that democratic theory ought to develop significantly (but by no means exhaustively) in dialogical and more receptive encounters with democratic struggles in ways that might allow the emerging practices and purposes of democratic associational life to call into question and possibly alter our core assumptions.[3] By this I emphatically do not mean to gesture toward some new unity of theory and practice, which, as many have powerfully argued, would impair both.[4] Democratic theory and democratic practice must both cultivate their capacities to sharply criticize one another, for these distances and tensions constitute a crucial part of the field in which each, indebted to the other, might thrive. Yet when the movement of distancing hardens into a posture of deaf invulnerability, when it is not juxtaposed with movements that draw theory and practice into risky proximity with each other, dogmatisms of distance arise that easily match the dogmatisms of unity. What follows might be thought of as an effort to practice democratic theorizing in a way that is more vulnerable to the knowledges tacit in democratic practices: I seek to theorize in the tension-filled zone between a theoretically distanced critical and utopic vision and a radically proximate receptivity in which the world might "start talking under the lingering eye."[5] The idea is, periodically, to let ourselves get swept up in the messy world of democratic practices and see how theory might look from there.

In this chapter I engage one of the more promising modes of democratic organizing in cities and states across the United States, namely, those associated with the Industrial Areas Foundation,[6] founded in 1940 by Saul Alinsky. The IAF is a rapidly growing grassroots organizing network involving tens of thousands of people in over sixty cities in the United States. It draws together strong and enduring coalitions of poor and middle-class people across lines of race, ethnicity, religion, and neighborhood to address poverty, housing, education, public infrastructure, environmental justice, and many other issues. Yet rather than being primarily an "issue group," its deepest aim is to build an intergenerational counterculture of vibrant participatory and pluralizing democratic practices that would dramatically—if gradually—transform political and economic power. The IAF's success (compared to many other efforts) at empowering enduring coalitions of historically marginalized groups stems significantly from its focus on "relationship building" among diverse constituencies. Issues tend to be chosen and negotiated with an eye to how they might strengthen and broaden grassroots democratic relationships. The IAF has been very successful at drawing thousands of people who did not understand themselves as insurgent democrats into enduring radical democratic practices. It is an "organization of organizations," typically drawing upon religious congregations, neighborhood associations, some social movements, community centers, unions, PTAs, and so forth. One obfuscates much that is most important and original about these efforts if one readily assimilates them to a kind of civic republicanism—as is commonly done.[7] Whereas these organizing practices draw many traditional types of associations into political activity that in part involves pressuring and working with traditional governmental institutions (such as city councils, school boards, state legislatures), the IAF draws its members into bridging relationships that cross lines of difficult difference, proliferate new democratic practices, and forge new political configurations that greatly exceed the traditional elements of their work. Indeed, it is the IAF's negotiation of the edge between the traditional and the emergent that is, I think, the most promising aspect of its practice. To appreciate and understand its vision and strategic success[8] requires, I think, that we both rework the lenses through which many theorists often interpret politics and, perhaps, transfigure the ethos that governs many visions of democratic engagement.

Interestingly, as we initiate more-receptive engagements with certain modes of insurgent urban democracy, among the important themes that come somewhat unexpectedly to the fore are those concerning practices of receptivity itself. Hence I organize the following discussion of democratic theoretical and practical possibilities around three aspects of empowerment through political receptivity. First, I discuss the importance of moving beyond the accent on voice that orients a lot of democratic theory (the work of Albert Hirschman and Mark E. Warren and much of the social movements literature) to focus more on the centrality of practices of listening. Second, I discuss the limits of listening and theorize the need for practices of receptive corporeal traveling beyond the power-saturated material-symbolic borders and carefully scripted flows of human bodies that characterize most cities. Third, I articulate how dwelling upon the first two insights might significantly change a basic metaphor that underpins many democratic theories. Hence one might ask: If listening and receptivity are given more-prominent places as we theorize democracy, how might we be pushed to re-envision the space-time of democratic engagement? It turns out that a thick description of some IAF spaces of democratic engagement points in some fruitful directions: These directions gesture critically toward the limits of the imaginary of the solid democratic table that guides a lot of democratic theory (that of Arendt and many others), and they suggest that democratic theorists ought to work more with an imaginary of democracy as "tabling." Democracy should be rearticulated more as an activity in which the tables of engagement for governing must be repeatedly altered through practices in which they are *moved and multiplied*.[9] Last, I reflect upon some of the difficulties and challenges facing this type of democratic politics. My hope is that this discussion of listening, traveling, and tabling might move some democratic theorists to travel attentively beyond the solid tables upon which we so often imagine the world, write, and teach.

### Beyond the Limits of Voice: Receptivity of Listening and Traveling

It is commonplace among proponents of democratization to look for and propose political transformations in which politically marginalized people would gain voice in relation to the processes in civil society and political economy shaping their lives. And what democrat could not be in favor of that—especially when so many people have so little voice; when the power-saturated and overused operations of "exit" (leave any situation that is dissatisfying) erode democratic practices that might address problems and, at the same time, often increase these very problems for those who cannot leave and have few resources for voice; when freedom-as-exit often functions as an ideology that obscures how hard, even impossible, it is for so many people to exit the subjugative aspects of markets, work, the cities in which we live, deteriorating environments, and so forth? Empowering marginalized *voices* is a crucial democratic project. But what if this current emphasis also conceals key elements of democratic vision and practice?

To begin to gain a sense of this possibility, let us critically examine the limits of the emphasis on voice in analyses of civil society. Consider, for example, how Albert Hirschman's often illuminating classic *Exit, Voice, and Loyalty: Responses to Decline in Firms, Organizations, and States*[10] gives paradigmatic expression to a focus on voice to the preclusion of listening, in a way that makes explicit widely shared background assumptions and that has occasionally had a direct influence upon some of the most interesting radical democratic theorists.[11] Thus, for example, Mark E. Warren's discussion of communication in *Democracy and Association* is often framed by his use of Hirschman's theoretical-analytical lens that emphasizes the centrality of the voluntary-nonvoluntary axis. With Hirschman, Warren tends to assume that exit and voice are the two most important modes of addressing problems in an association—be they difficult conflicts, decline, inefficiency, unresponsiveness to certain constituencies, and so on. Hence, "When conflict develops within associations, individuals have the choice of (1) speaking up, (2) maintaining the association at the cost of suppressing the conflict, or (3) leaving the association."[12] With Hirschman, he very insightfully develops the interrelations between these important modes of response, noting that associations can combat exit by cultivating loyalty and that they can "cultivate loyalty through the device of internal democracy"—or, primarily, through enabling the possibilities for exercising voice.

But should these alternatives so heavily orient the field of analysis? Do they do justice to the range of extant practices and possible democratic alternatives? I suggest that this lens often distorts and diminishes important practices of horizontal receptivity that some of the most interesting democratic associations are beginning to cultivate as a third dimension—a third option at work alongside and in relation to voice and exit. In a sense, just as Hirschman—echoing Thorstein Veblen—argued that economists had "a blind spot, 'a trained incapacity'" for perceiving the importance of voice and that students of politics similarly missed the importance of exit,[13] I think the "exit, voice, and loyalty" frame issues in a "trained incapacity" to discern the importance of receptivity. Thus, for example, as Warren's analysis unfolds, he offers sharp insights into the dynamics between voice and exit in democratic associations, but he has little to say about practices of receptivity.[14]

One finds a similar focus on voice in the various literatures on democratic social movements. "Resource-mobilization" theorists, such as Charles Tilly, develop a paradigm that focuses on how groups come to mobilize in order to be recognized and included as players in the political process and, in turn, to gain material benefits—in other words, to gain and empower their voice and the interests it articulates.[15] As Jean Cohen and Andrew Arato argue, although this position offers important insights, it also tends to marginalize the way movements often seek to "defend spaces for the creation of new identities and solidarities and seek to make social relations within the institutions of civil society more egalitarian and democratic."[16] "New social movements" theorists, like Alain Touraine, draw these latter dimensions to the fore, even as they underplay the strategic elements focused on states and markets that are elaborated by the resource-mobilization position. Yet for all the dialogue and receptivity between theorists and social movement actors in Touraine's pivotal book—significantly titled *The Voice and the Eye*—the focus is on the way social movements develop an articulated, theoretically reflective, and empowered democratic *voice* (no longer construed simply in terms of recognition and resources but now aimed ultimately toward broader political vision, or "the social history of tomorrow"). Hence, as Richard Sennett insightfully notes in his foreword to Touraine's text, the focus of the book is on how a social movement comes "to say what it is, to see its contours in order to speak in its name."[17] Cohen and Arato draw upon some of the most compelling insights of theorists like Touraine and Habermas to emphasize further that social movements often reach beyond an exclusive focus on giving voice to their own needs for recognition, resources, and reflective practices of democratic voicing to move toward broader and more-reflexive goals concerning the protection and enhancement of democratic spaces more generally. Yet for all their attention to "communicative infrastructure," their neo-Habermasian account tends tacitly to construe communication primarily in terms of voice and to marginalize receptivity across lines of difference in both their analytical discussion and their historical analyses.[18] This is apparent in their discussion of the U.S. feminist movement, where they try to exemplify and historically substantiate their approach. Their voice-accented narrative focuses on how the movement, "aimed at spreading feminist consciousness and achieving institutional changes,"[19] increasingly united its grassroots and institutional wings as it came to see the mutually supportive entwinement of these goals. In other words, the movement was about proliferating feminist voice in civil society and empowering this voice politically. Remarkably, the difficult history in which "feminists" (read, "white, middle-class feminists") have been gradually brought to recognize the importance of receptivity in the face of challenges from feminists of color, lesbians, working-class women, and so forth is entirely absent from their account. Yet the intensely agonistic processes (involving to-and-fro criticisms from a variety of positions) through which there has developed both a deepening recognition of receptivity and practices of more receptive engagement are among the most innovative and potentially empowering aspects of feminist movements.[20] Remarkably oblivious to this, Cohen and Arato write, "One may speak of the contemporary feminist movement in the singular, composed of various associations and organizations engaged in a wide range of strategies yet sharing a feminist consciousness."[21]

I suggest that both democratic theory and historical analyses of many insurgent democratic practices would benefit substantially by attending carefully to the development of practices of difficult receptivity. Consider some of the best elements in IAF organizing in this regard.[22] In response to problems in cities (political marginalization, inequalities, conflicts, unaccountable and odious structures of power, and so on) the IAF organizations focus heavily on cultivating practices of receptivity as *central* for generating orientation, solidarity, voice, loyalty, a sense of justice—central, moreover, to their sense of the desirable democratic communicative modes and identities. This latter point is particularly important, for while receptivity surely functions as a means to other ends, it is also becoming a deeply valued practice in itself, an "internal good," as MacIntyre discusses in *After Virtue*.

I emphasize the term "receptivity," rather than using the term "listening," because I think that the former term evokes a broader notion of responsiveness and helps attune us to a broader range of practices. Thus practices of receptivity supplement and challenge both exit and elements of the paradigm of voice, juxtaposing listening to voice and literal corporeal world-traveling to exit.

Along the first axis, the IAF challenges the dominance of voice with listening by repeatedly accenting the cultivation of listening practices. Of course, IAF organizing is very much about cultivating hitherto disempowered democratic voices. The IAF is famous for this. But its organizing approach strongly accents and front-loads the arts of listening—especially (but not only, for this is an ongoing emphasis) during its first few years of organizing in a community.[23] Long before the IAF makes any attempt to articulate a new coalition's substantive vision and voice, it patiently cultivates horizontal relationships by emphasizing practices of listening between individuals and among the religious institutions, political associations, and neighborhood groups that it tries to weave into a deep alliance that will bridge differences. Our capacities to listen to others develop very differently in different contexts; hence the IAF seeks to create relationships in which people might cultivate the arts of listening in a variety of different settings for reasons that are epistemological as well as ethical and political. Listening is less a single capacity than a complex art that must be developed in a variety of different kinds of relationships.

Thus one of the foundations of IAF organizing is "one-on-ones." In these meetings (of which there are hundreds), those active in organizing efforts attempt to seek out other current or potential participants and develop political relationships. Yet far from being a staging ground for trying to voice and sell an IAF message, these meetings are generally two-thirds listening on the part of the initiators. As Ernesto Cortes, Texas IAF organizer, says, "'When you sell, you tend to be arrogant . . . know it all. . . . you build yourself up and you quit listening. You're not attentive.' . . . Cortes believes you have to have flexibility, curiosity, patience, and a little vulnerability." Again, "For you to grow and develop, you have to get out of yourself and into the skin of others. . . . It is the most radical thing we teach."[24] Typically, IAF leaders and activists will begin such meetings with questions designed to encourage the other to begin probing the visceral depths of public perceptions and involvements: What is it about your basic sense of things that really propelled you to become a [social worker, pastor, imam, teacher, union member, or ———]? What contribution in your work as county commissioner, or your involvement in this community, do you most dream of being remembered for? There is a lot of suffering in this neighborhood; what are the things that most anger you about how this city is run? Being a pastor, what do you think Jesus and the Beloved Community mean for Durham, North Carolina? Or perhaps a leader will ask a provocative question about the other's response to a recent event they both experienced. These questions often catch people off guard. They often open lines of dialogue, paths of relationship, and political possibility that might otherwise be shut tight. When public officials experience this style of engagement, they not infrequently begin to listen a bit better themselves—and sometimes unexpected, substantive directions open up.

The never perfectly achievable effort to "get under the skin" of others involves a radical receptivity—even an *aspect* of listening that is in some senses relatively passive insofar as we try to hear and perceive the world as others do. Yet the matter is far more complicated. To begin with, in a world where deafness and oblivion are pervasive, these characteristics take up residence within the self as well as between selves. In other words, we are often deaf to ourselves, and especially to the public dimension of ourselves. Hence listening well involves an *active and powerfully provocative* aspect in which the one listening solicits others to listen to themselves more attentively and hopefully better than they might have done before. Listening, therefore, is an art cultivated through the active negotiation of discrepant points in a constellation of agonistic concerns that together might make it possible: a receptivity that paradoxically aims at a moment of passivity; a provocative, immanent engagement with the words of the others so that they might hear themselves better; an imaginative activity in which one tries to picture *oneself* in the position of others in the Arendtian sense of wondering what one would think if one resided in this other life; critical interventions that aim to bring one's own perspectives into play with the others while attentively listening to their responses, in a way that generates friction from which new understandings might emerge from both participants—if we are listening carefully.

We are not used to others being radically curious about us, drawing out the political passions and perceptions that we so often hide from strangers. In one-on-ones, current leaders and activists also reveal their own passions and vulnerabilities in an effort to draw the others to begin to articulate their political anger, passions, thoughts, interests, and hopes. The aim is "to elicit from each other their personal story."[25] People who become adept at one-on-ones become artists of crafting and sharing their own stories and of provoking and soliciting the stories of others. Through hundreds of dialogues in pairs, stories circulate that would be difficult or impossible to bring to the surface in larger settings, and they begin to weave together into a complex, variegated fabric of democratic knowledges about an urban area and its people. In this more responsive and receptive context, relationships are formed and deepened in which a rich complex critical vision of a community develops along with the gradual articulation of alternative possibilities. Yet what emerges is not simply an aggregation of different self-interests; what also materializes is a growing articulation of interest as "*interesse*—which means to be among or between."[26] As different positions, problems, passions, interests, traditions, and yearnings are shared, through careful practices of listening, participants begin to develop increasingly relational senses of their interests and orientations in ways that often transfigure the senses with which they began. And as relationships deepen, bonds are formed that are more capable of enduring the rough and tumble of more-agonistic politics. These transformative effects are recorded in narratives that populate many accounts of IAF politics.[27]

The IAF pursues listening-accented relationships in a variety of other contexts, each of which enables particular receptive capacities and has qualities of resonance that render voices audible in distinct ways. Each congregation and association conducts numerous house meetings of about ten persons each, in which members more likely to share traditions and outlooks can talk with and listen to each other in order to deepen relationships and to discern the tradition's or association's sense of key problems in need of analysis and action, sources of inspiration and direction, and group visions of alternatives. After each group formulates the vision of its city, town, or neighborhood that emerges in these meetings, the groups meet together in an effort to discern both the different and the overlapping concerns of the many groups. Here the art of listening (and voice) moves beyond the smaller more homogeneous house meetings and is now exercised in a larger and much more heterogeneous context. Although the aim of these processes is to find common ground for political action, outcomes vary. Sometimes straightforward common ground emerges (for example, a citywide living-wage campaign in Baltimore or a plan to construct affordable homes in Brooklyn).[28] Sometimes an internally variegated common effort emerges, such as "safety," which might include measures to curb drug dealers, fix up abandoned houses, prevent violence against gays and lesbians (as was the case in Nashville, Tennessee), and eliminate domestic violence in the Hispanic community (as in Durham). Sometimes diverse issues are heard but are not yet collectively "actionable" because of the organization's limited current capacities, lack of consensus, and so forth.

Listening is not accented just as a means to voice, just judgment, and power—though it certainly is these too. At least as important, however, is that it is an important democratic sensibility in and of itself. The accent on listening is an approach to the world that makes the presumption that if things are not going well, if democratic relationships are poor or lacking, if people are politically dissatisfied, if power is odious and unresponsive, if work with others seems impossible, if one's city is in decline—only part of the problem concerns lack of voice. A big part of the problem is also likely to be that most of us do not listen to one another well, if and when we listen at all. We have not only marginalized the arts of voice, we have, relatedly and perhaps even more so, marginalized the arts of listening. Certainly the democratic arts of voice and listening are deeply related, but all too often we interpret and seek to nurture democracy through a lens that greatly accents the former and addresses the latter almost as an afterthought. The alternative idea here is that if democratic voices are weak in a community, it is probably significantly because efforts to develop political voice have neither dwelled in nor sufficiently passed through the arts of listening. At its best, the democratic counterculture emerging in the IAF aims at *cultivating a power for democracy and justice that grows precisely in and through its capacity to listen.*

Yet in IAF politics the practice of receptivity exceeds listening in important ways. In a world as structured and segmented as is ours by gated geographies and social practices of oblivion (the various physical, symbolic, visceral, and psychological walls between neighborhoods, people of different races and classes, citizens and foreigners, and so on), listening is crucial, but it is usually not enough.[29] For it is often nearly impossible to hear another person or group of people well if one has not spent time in their very different spaces and been proximate to their discrepant conditions and modes of being. The abysses between people located very differently just minutes apart in urban areas today are often so deep that the idea that we are likely to hear one another well simply by communicating in a relatively neutral place— across whatever table located wherever between us—greatly obscures and possibly undermines the task at hand. It is very easy, when the other is speaking from a place—or places—one has neither inhabited nor experienced them inhabiting, to shed inadvertently all too many of their words, expressions, and gestures; to fail to absorb their depth, register their weight, and taste them; or to dismiss them altogether. This is, I think, the common course of things far more than we usually acknowledge.

Hence, rather than speaking so easily of a common world that we already share—a space we cohabit that separates and relates us in a way that provides a uniform sound chamber that works equally well for the myriad voices and ears of a polity, we might do better to say (or to say *too*) that we do not share the same world today. Or that in a literally and figuratively gated world—a world where we are so often oblivious even in the face of the plenitude of others and otherness that do pass through the gates—the trope "common world" distorts our condition at least as much as it illuminates. Of course, the world is "common" in the sense that the different segments are, in fact, related to one another through practices of exploitation, encroachment, violence, the moving of bodies, goods, crime, pollution, and so forth. But the gated oblivion of so much of our lives makes appeals to the "common world" significantly ideological unless those appeals pass through difficult and patient practices of listening *and literal bodily world-traveling* that might begin to bring together our segmented experiences so they become more truly a fabric of spaces and times that is worldly in the sense of being a volume of intersecting and communicating different experiences.

Hence, if our voices are poor, perhaps we have not listened to one another; if our listening is poor, perhaps we have not traveled receptively around our city. Listening across difficult divides must be supplemented with broader receptive practices that develop through literal, corporeal, geographical traveling.[30] These practices are not sufficient, as our blindness and deafness easily accompany us on our travels—but they are necessary. Giving a paradoxical spin to the word "traveling," one might almost say that an element of exit—a way out—is affirmed as a necessary part of a more hopeful response to urban decline. However, now the effort becomes not to exit one's place or set of associational relations altogether but, rather, to escape from the oblivion and gated structures within which one's self, capacity to receive the others, place, and associations have been largely confined and constructed. The movements out to other places—and back—foster a deeper and more complicated relationship of difficult hope within a broader urban area. Far from being a leaving, finally, world-traveling is a to-and-fro, a way of beginning to *dwell* in an urban space as a "frontier" where relationships are new, uncertain, challenging, disruptive of the reigning order of things, and democratically renegotiated across often-trying divides.[31] This movement beyond the limits of one's familiar spaces, faces, and primary associations is not an end to one's relationship with an organization or area (as in Hirschman) but, rather, the means by which one's self and associations are transfigured and new relationships are cultivated. We must literally travel away from our spaces, associations, and familiar bodies if we are to return and remain with them in a transfiguring and richer way.[32]

For these reasons, central to IAF practice is the continual movement of meetings and members around the various neighborhoods and institutions of an urban area. So, for example, IAF work has put me in numerous meetings in very poor black neighborhoods in Durham—places I had never been before. It has put me in the basements of religious buildings in these neighborhoods, listening to people speak and pray and sing and tell stories and work hard and patiently toward justice, democracy, and power *from those places*. It has put me in El Centro Hispano practicing nascent democracy with dozens of people who speak little if any English, who lack citizenship and perhaps, for some, even legal-resident status. We periodically engage in "neighborhood audits," practices of walking more receptively in strange neighborhoods with strangers, taking inventory of the conditions of houses and streets and gaining an initial sense of the shape of lives we have never experienced. This actual world-traveling bends, broadens, and nurtures one's hearing and vision, and it transfigures the imagination as our bodies experience the reverberations of music in strangely worn buildings, the textures of worn doors, a patched broken window, buildings sloping and shedding paint. I would suggest that such traveling is a basic condition of democracy's possibility at the dawn of the twenty-first century. If voice must pass through listening to find and invent itself, listening must pass through world-traveling to begin to experience other worlds or aspects of world that intersect and bear upon each other but are not simply common objects experienced from different angles. World-traveling can help engender the volumes and assemblages of experience capable of resonating in ways that can carry the words and lives of others into our depths.

Many political theorists, in the course of this chapter, have probably heard resonances with some of Hannah Arendt's notions. And this should not be surprising, as IAF organizers like Gerald Taylor and

Ernesto Cortes refer to her ideas—of action, of putting ourselves in the places of others, of "enlarged thought," "inter-esse," and public freedom—not infrequently in conversation. A striking characteristic of IAF organizing is the high level of reflexivity and democratic theorizing lodged not only in its members' direct actions but in other settings as well. The Southwest regional network of the IAF, for example, conducts two-to-three-day meetings once every couple of months in which organizers and activists meet with academics to read and vibrantly debate democratic theory, theology, race, civil society, political economy, and so forth, in relation to issues that arise in organizing. The dialogue between theorists and activists that I suggested above has been hotly pursued from the other side for quite some time.[33]

Yet at the intersections between democratic theory and practice, I am suggesting, there are ways in which dimensions of the practices significantly outstrip some of the theory that informs and inspires them. One can see this in Arendt's work. Drawing on Kant, Arendt understands the development of political judgment in terms of a "representative thinking" in which "one trains one's imagination to go visiting," or, in Kant's own words, exercises one's imagination by "comparing our judgment with the possible rather than the actual judgments of others, and by putting our selves in the place of any other man"—thereby generating an "enlarged thought."[34] This is a vital element of political judgment. Yet like Kant, Arendt is somewhat murky and inconsistent about both the relation between actual others and possible others and the relation between the work of imagination and the receptive element of listening. Though it is clear that critical and representative thinking both hinges upon experiences of and opens itself to "a community of men who can be addressed and who are listening and can be listened to," too often in Arendt's work it appears that her construal of imagination and judgment truncates listening more than listening is allowed to weave a more radically open sensibility into judgment.[35] Hence she warns us that "the trick of critical thinking does not consist in enormously enlarged empathy through which one can know what actually goes on in the mind of all others. . . . To think . . . means . . . to think for one's self, which is the maxim of a never-passive reason. To be given to such passivity is called prejudice. . . . To accept what goes on in the minds of those whose 'standpoint' . . . is not my own would mean no more than passively to accept their thought, that is, to exchange their prejudices for the prejudices proper to my own station."[36] Again, "This process does not blindly adopt the actual views of others, and hence look upon the world from a different perspective . . . as though I tried to be or feel like somebody else . . . [this is a question] *of being and thinking in my own identity where actually I am not.*[37] Thus in a lecture on representative thinking in which she imagines that she "look[s] at a specific slum dwelling," she emphasizes "representing to myself how I would feel if I had to live there" far more than she emphasizes the judgments of the "inhabitants, for whom time and hopelessness may have dulled to the outrage of their condition."[38]

IAF practice suggests that an element of more radical receptivity, in which we *do* try to get a sense of "what actually goes on" in the minds of others, is crucial. It calls us in part to more passively listen and be receptive to others and their lived spaces, accepting for a time what and how others tell us they experience and judge—their angers, loves, prejudices, and stories of hope and hopelessness—as an essential element of less myopic political experience and judgment. Echoing Cortes again, you have to attentively "get out of yourself and into the skin of others. . . . It is the most radical thing we teach." The point is not that judgment should culminate in the blind acceptance of the other's perspective (Arendt's fear), but that without being "curious, patient, and a little vulnerable," without efforts at passing through the other's opening onto the parts of the world they inhabit in deep ways, we are likely to miss much of what is ethically and politically most decisive for politics in a world of gates and oblivion. Surely judgment happens through agonistic interactions among my judgments from here, my judgments as I might make them from other positions, and other people's actual expressions of their experiences and judgments from very discrepant standpoints. Yet without a receptive and generous countenancing of the last, we risk a politics that is deaf to others. Moreover, the effort to get attentively "into the skin" of others calls us to travel receptively to the places where their skin most often lives, breathes, struggles, feels, judges, articulates, and expresses itself. In a world as antagonistically segmented as is ours, that effort calls us to be radically suspicious—epistemologically, ethically, politically—of Kant's claim that "he had no time to travel precisely because he wanted to know so much about so many countries."[39]

Pondering this nascent movement with and beyond Arendt, it is possible to discern the emergence of a sense of democratic engagement that solicits significant reformulations of some of the core ideas of many contemporary democratic theories. Here I am thinking not only of the theorists who study associations and social movements mentioned at the outset of this section but also of many other major voices in contemporary theory as well. Whether one considers political liberal "reciprocity" (where listening, voice, and affect are confined at the outset to the secular lingua franca of political liberal voices), Habermasian critical theory (which, though generally more openly communicative, often tends to marginalize affect and to reduce heterogeneous lifeworlds and traditions to the status of "ethical life" that must a priori be subordinated to a morality of communicative action whose own voice is made to appear "above the fray"), or visions in which significantly homogenized nationhood, or community, would prescribe and proscribe our political encounters according to visions relatively fixed in advance—what consistently receives little attention are practices of radical democratic listening and receptivity.[40] "Radical" here means a sense of democracy that is less rooted in an a priori framework and more aimed at *going to the vulnerable roots of inclusive receptive engagement*—at being more open to the challenges of receiving others and of engaging the substance of the differences and commonalities that unwontedly arise. Thus religion, affect, and putting oneself in uncomfortable spaces are important elements of many IAF encounters. It is crucial that such encounters are negotiated with a will to inclusiveness, mutual responsiveness, and an effort to discern paths of collective action toward common goods. But they are given less circumscribed, less scripted, and more generative political roles to play in recognition of the fact that no single constituency controls the field of democratic relations and vision in advance.

There is no simple list of principles to be gleaned from these practices—but there is much to be learned. Though listening and traveling are principles in a sense, I think it is more helpful to think of them as practices that both *embody* principles like equality, justice, freedom, and democratic engagement and, at the same time, enable us repeatedly to *rearticulate* the meaning of these in different contexts with different people. They point toward the salience of practices of a difficult democratic judgment that might be more capable of discerning worthy political vision and animating political action. In the next section I suggest that a politics more attuned to the limits of voice and the need for arts of receptivity is likely to transfigure the spatial metaphors that guide and constrain our political imaginations. Some of the lessons here might be offered in images we could use to (re)orient ourselves toward the heights and depths of democratic politics. One of the key reigning images in this regard is that of a democratic *table,* which often figures the political space around which members of a polity are to deliberate and exercise judgment. In the next section I argue that one way to focus the insights of the previous discussion is to shift the democratic imaginary away from the solid table and toward visions of democratic tabling. Once again, certain IAF practices are richly suggestive in this regard.

### Beyond Fixed Political Tables: Democratic Tabling

At the heart of the democratic promise one finds a series of dramatic tensions—they may even be what makes this heart pump the lifeblood that enables democratic action.[41] Here I am interested in how one of these tensions—between the need for tables of democratic engagement and the element of marginalization that always seems to accompany each democratic table—is imagined and negotiated in IAF organizing toward more receptive empowerment.

A vital promise of democracy is that of "collective self-rule" by the "demos," consisting of selves who are free and equal and engaged in ongoing practices of ruling and being subjected to rules and modes of engagement discerned to be vital to their sustenance. Such self-rule must strive to fashion a world of equality and freedom and must simultaneously disavow political inequalities based on inherited and arbitrary distinctions. Yet as Greek tragedians sensed and as centuries of modern struggles have repeatedly demonstrated, the demos of democracy has never been free of arbitrary inequalities—neither in its interiors nor in relation to the borders that distinguish it from the others beyond.[42] This means that the democratic promise of equality and freedom has an intrinsic tension: Not only does it circulate *in* the orders and spaces that are established by a democracy, but it is also inextricably connected to the politics of unrecognized different groups (and selves) who struggle from the margins *against* the arbitrary inequalities and closures of the demos and grope toward new possibilities of freedom and equality.

Mark E. Warren sharply articulates this tension, arguing that democracy requires a mix of democratic associations, some aimed at participating in deliberations and formal representative institutions with an eye toward collective action, and others aimed at resisting hegemonic forms of power or at representing excluded differences. Though a politics aimed at deliberative commonality and the politics of difference can frequently be complementary in important ways, their relation is agonistic as well.[43] All democratic deliberation hinges upon the recognition of others as free and equal speakers, yet it is also infused with unacknowledged nondeliberative modes of governance and myriad practices of power that render many people inaudible. Thus representation in public spheres and in democratic institutions must not be limited to representations of commonality and deliberative means but must also, importantly, include agonistic representations of difference and resistance. "Without [groups committed to disturbances and representations of difference] deliberation will be limited to the agendas of *those who already have a seat at the table*, and whatever consensus emerges will be exclusive."[44]

*How might we strive to better represent and practice democracy as this tensional promise of the relation between representations of commonality and representations of difference? How might we solicit and nurture more-promising calls of democratic politics to attend more directly to this tensional relation?* As noted above, many construals (offered by many political liberal and Habermasian theorists) of deliberative commonness are insufficiently helpful here because they do not go far enough to address problems of exclusion and disempowerment. They articulate an overly circumscribed receptivity that tends to be only weakly attentive to the way democratic tables of deliberation harbor exclusions in terms of *who* is present, *what* types of issues can be raised, *how* they can be raised and negotiated, and so forth. Imagining a deliberative table that would be free of these exclusions, deliberative democrats rarely articulate ideals that would have us permanently and strenuously address questions of how to illuminate and respond to the significant exclusions that will probably reemerge in spite of—or because of—the configuration of the participants, norms, and modes of the deliberative table itself. Representations of difference, on the other hand, resist these exclusions by raising the volume, pressure, and level of disturbances of marginalized people and voices. Their aims are often either intransigent resistance itself (important, but limited, as an ideal that might inspirit a horizon beyond interest-group politics) in the face of little hope for fundamental change or, ultimately, "expand[ing] the boundaries of the public deliberation by reminding us of issues, injustices, and needs that are not addressed within the mainstream."[45] Yet what vision might illuminate this expanded sense of democratic politics?

The image of a common inclusive "table" is not only at work in many visions of democratic theory but also arises frequently in the everyday language of IAF politics as well. The table conjures up dialogue and politics as taking place in an inclusive public space: at a table around which political actors are seated, a table that, as Arendt famously tells us, separates us and relates us to a common world.[46] "Table" has associated with it two contradictory meanings, meanings that evoke its illuminating and problematic nature as a symbol of the democratic commons. "To table" means, on the one hand, "to put on the table or agenda for discussion," and on the other, "to remove from the table and from consideration indefinitely." I think the polysemy of this word, as with so many polysemous words, evokes an ambivalence that we ought to restore to the heart of democratic theory and cultivate in practice—if we are to strive to be true to democracy's promise. Mark E. Warren registers this ambivalence in his discussion of the table as both an inclusive and exclusive space. Yet this continual fluctuation of attraction and repulsion does not leave the table in place: It calls us both to move the table around and to let the table be moved around us, and it sets in motion an endless multiplication of its being. Democracy will not be or become solely or primarily at a central table of fixed being and location, but only from tables that let themselves be moved and that move us to very different spaces and modes of relation.

The table of radically reformed democratic theory and practice is neither the solid relatively stable "table" of Arendt's common public realm of separation and relation, nor is it the "spiritualistic séance table" that might "vanish from our midst" with which she represented the space of mass society in which we are simultaneously neither related nor separated.[47] Rather, this table moves and transforms but does not vanish. And it summons us to this moving and changing: It summons us *into relation through* this moving and transforming in which the space and lines of separation and relation undergo repeated and unwonted change. It is this table, I suggest, that better represents and enacts a democratic politics of receptive generosity.[48]

The IAF practices a politics of representing commonalities and differences at the "common table" of city politics in the United States. Hence it is famous for regularly turning out hundreds of people to the common public spaces of city councils and school board meetings. In this way people generally marginalized from public spaces and processes—poor people, working people, people of color, women, and so forth—show up before the table and gain some voice and response that they would otherwise not have. This practice of mobilization helps people "gain a seat at the table" and "extends the margins of public deliberation and judgment," in Mark E. Warren's words.[49] But this is, I think, the tip of the iceberg in terms of the democratic practices that are developing through IAF organizing and through the reinventing of the democratic table—and the *democratic imagination*—along two dimensions I wish to discuss briefly.

First: Within the IAF coalitions, the table of democratic engagement is continually moving, from this neighborhood to that, from this religious or secular institution to that. And as it travels, it morphs in the changed light and shadows of the neighborhood, in the varying feel of the room, in the different cadence of the opening prayer. Each institution that participates in the coalition takes a turn hosting the meetings of the broader group. This practice aims not only to engender a sense of ownership among the diverse groups but also, I have argued, to broaden and deepen each group's sense of an urban area, of its neighborhoods, traditions, and historical and emergent struggles, and of its peoples. The aim and effect is to work subtly on the limits that might accompany each incarnation of the table by relocating it repeatedly to different places where previous limits are variously made more apparent, perhaps transcended, perhaps rendered less operative, less rigid. In small but important ways—ways both visceral and more explicit—the coalition's modes, limits, possibilities, and sense of itself are slightly reconfigured with each move of the table. As groups gather around a differently located table, there is a palpable sense that "we are here again, at our table, but this time it is the table that your specific community gives us, with your color, your history and traditions etched in these walls and floors, your stories still subtly reverberating in the corners of the room—one or two of which you might share with us today, the enchantment and constraint of your spaces, your very specific power and style of hosting, your specific vulnerability as you open your doors to the rest of us, your prism differently refracting the light of this 'we' in an ongoing and open-ended process of shaping ourselves."

The table becomes something that, in the words of Merleau-Ponty, "initiates me into the world . . . by encroachment. . . . Perception is not first a perception of things, but a perception of elements, of rays of the world, of things which are dimensions, which are worlds[;] I slip on these 'elements' and here I am in the world."[50] The moving, changing democratic table of IAF practice is now less like Arendt's "world of things between those who have it in common"[51] (though it is not *not* this) and more like particular communities' "elements," "dimensions," "rays of the world" that we slip on in a way that subtly distends our meeting toward their ground, even though we are, all of us, there, and as such the ground belongs to each and none. At his most radical in the above passage, Merleau-Ponty writes that these dimensions, elements, and rays "are worlds"—worlds that simultaneously open onto and are constitutive of the common world of their intersections. The changing IAF table of democratic practice moves beyond being primarily like an object between us that, with the others around it, would be a "figure on our ground." It begins at a very visceral level "to initiate me into the world," to solicit and facilitate a difficult receptivity in which a heterogeneous "we" begin to allow ourselves to be figured by the table and those who most often frequent it—figured by their dimension of the world on their ground; their ground, and *they gain some sense that we are undergoing this.* The hosts experience us figuring in their space, rendering ourselves vulnerable there. At this very corporeal level an enactment of reciprocity among different people is initiated that can begin to alter the fields of experience of both the guest and the host, fields that have been hitherto saturated by dominant powers. The next time the ground of our table will change. And as the coalition broadens, new institutions and groups will act as host, and our table will be moved beyond its extant limits. "We" are becoming peoples, differently and together, through the practices associated with this moving democratic table of the "interesse." With this mode of tabling—more responsive to the problems of inequality at work in democratic tables as well as to the possibilities for addressing them that reside in and among different spaces—we might begin to create a volume of democratic experience and practice that is richer, more just, and more susceptible to moving and to being moved receptively beyond its limits.

Second: Beyond the porous edges of the IAF coalition itself, the organization stages dramatic actions that encroach upon and refigure officially sanctioned representations of "the public," as well as the experiences of the official representatives of the public. Hence, the IAF not only mobilizes for traditional public meetings but also organizes *its own public accountability meetings,* where elected officials (and the media) are called to participate in, say, a large meeting in the low-ceilinged basement of a church in a very poor black section of town, with an agenda, process, and temporality that is not of the official's design or custom and with a group of Mexicano/as who respond after official pronouncements with cicada-sounding instruments. Suddenly, those who typically preside—and who are seen to preside—over the "common" public space find themselves situated in a common space where they are decidedly not in control, a common space where the topics under discussion, the framing of these topics, the duration allotted to various speakers, the mood in the room, and so forth are disproportionately organized by the peoples of neighborhoods mostly ignored by the hegemonic halls of public deliberation. At their best, these meetings, often called "accountability sessions," are artfully and reflectively crafted "public dramas."[52] These meetings are symbolic spaces that resituate public officials in such a way that they are no longer those presiding over public space from the heights of their elevated chairs, no longer the ones deciding who among these others will be "included" as serious voices in the discussion and how, no longer the ones deciding who and what will not. Rather, they now find *themselves* as the "others and otherness to be included," initiated into the world *by others,* figuring on their ground. These representative dramas of public space decenter the official representations (inscribed in the architecture and practices of official meetings) that engender an exaggerated sense that the order and limits of democratic publicness are in official hands.[53] They transfigure the official representations all the more powerfully because they include official representatives within a drama that is not of their own making. A central question frequently posed to officials in these dramas is this: Will you promise to participate with us in future works and dramas?

One hope of such meetings is that some officials might experience some of the power lodged in public spaces from the underside, so they might become more aware of and less comfortable with its limits. Perhaps they might even become more generous and receptive in their management of the council chamber. What is more likely is that people so often marginalized, who are now organizing the public meeting, will experience some of the transfigurative power of their own spaces, tables, and voices. They might gain a sense that the geography of this neighborhood and church, these new relationships, the clothes and flesh of these bodies, are not just things to be framed within and governed or ignored by a public space and power that comes from elsewhere. Rather, they are "elements" in Merleau-Ponty's sense: rays and dimensions of the world that are capable and worthy of framing the figure-ground articulations of public space and thus of participating in the myriad framings through which the public might be represented and common power might be brought ever anew into being. They and we participate in making the common table of the city move, transform, and multiply. In this, we participate in re-representing the democratic relationships between commonalities and differences, between "margins" and "center."

When we take these images of democratic tabling and combine them with the image of the solid table of official public spaces, we get a vision of democracy as a movement of many interacting changing tables. The idea here is not to entirely supplant the solid table of official public space but, through practices of more receptive tabling, to decenter its hold on our imagination of what democracy ought to look like. The hope is that these alternative tables might develop sufficient power to transfigure our tension-laden democratic ideals and perhaps even alter the official tables toward greater receptivity. At any rate, these insurgent democratic practices offer an image that is more evocative of the difficult work of democratic responsiveness at the intersections between our commonalities and our differences. We democratic theorists might do well to squint and look closer.

## Conclusion

"Learning what 'representation' means and learning how to represent are intimately connected," wrote Hanna Pitkin.[54] From IAF practices, theorists might learn that to represent democracy as a practice of those gathered around an inclusive, stable table is perhaps to "table" democracy in the bad sense, namely, that of taking democracy (or an essential aspect of it) off our agenda, removing it from consideration. To represent democratic practices of representation and thus to learn how better to represent and act responsively in concert with others, we would need a more *interesting* table, a table of the *interesse*. Pitkin reminds us of three meanings of the IAF's favorite Latin verb, meanings that speak most powerfully to the issue at hand: the democratic table, as this practice of moving the spatiality of our "being between," would have "to differ," in order "to make a difference" — in order not to repeat a flaccid politics of indifference.[55]

Yet we risk seriously misrepresenting these democratic practices if we focus only upon their verbal nature, neglecting all that endangers such listening, traveling, and tabling. It is crucial to bring these dangers into view, in order to focus on additional tensions that insurgent democratic movements must repeatedly negotiate, precisely because the dangers reside in some of the very elements that are integral to what is hopeful. To ignore the dangers, I think, is to increase the risk that they will partly undermine the promise of democratic receptivity. I end by discussing briefly three dangers.

The first is related to the politics focused on achieving common goods. As should be clear by now, there are many mutually supportive relations between this politics and a politics that cultivates a growing receptivity with and among those in the margins. The struggle for and achievement of important public goods — and a record of concrete successes — is a key part of what allows the IAF to build an enduring, diverse, and growing membership engaged in receptive democratic practices. Democratic engagement is hard work drawn from people who are overworked and undercompensated before they ever enter these political arenas. Without specific, winnable issues, the IAF's long-term project of building a more generous "inter-generational" democratic counterculture[56] seems unlikely to go far. Moreover, as Mark R. Warren and Mark E. Warren have both recently argued, political work around specific public goods can paradoxically "underwrite and even enable differences to be segmented and bracketed sufficiently for them to be democratically negotiated" in ways that make confrontations less totalizing and warlike.[57] By generally focusing the dialogues on problems that arise around difficult differences on specific issues, by shying away from frequent investments in more-general and more-searching confrontations among incendiary differences, and by creating a cooperation-based solidarity and trust that lowers some of the risks when the issues do get intense, the IAF often makes more-receptive relationships across differences less risky and more probable for most people.[58]

Yet there are also dangers that a politics focused on common goods poses for radical democratic promises of a more mobile and receptive table of engagement. Shying away from engaging volatile differences can have its costs. For example, although issues related to gay and lesbian sexuality may occasionally surface in relation to "safety," the deeper engagements associated with queer politics have not found a place in IAF politics. Nor is it likely that issues like abortion, animal rights, or several similar others will appear at these tables in the foreseeable future. More direct, probing, and systematic questioning concerning race, class, and gender is often dissuaded in the organizing process.[59] Hence, although a large amount of transfigurative work on these issues is done at the practical and visceral level, the moving table of IAF democracy still struggles when it comes to moving far enough to address some of these limits directly and thematically. The danger is that these general tendencies to shy away from certain types of conflictive issues might harden into ideologies of closure that damage our ability to successfully understand and respond to the problems at hand.

A second related danger concerns pragmatic politics. The IAF is remarkably successful when it comes to cultivating relationships and receptivity in its pragmatic work. At the same time, pragmatic demands can risk overwhelming some of the deepest and farthest-ranging elements of this action. Hence, as organizers and activists get swept up in struggles around immediate issues, time and focus constraints make it easy for the deeper relation-building work to be set aside—especially when a coalition is already sufficiently powerful to win on issues concerning relatively small infrastructural improvements in poor neighborhoods, small job training programs, and the like. Forming working relationships with powerful political and economic actors enhances efficacy, but it can dampen efforts to discern paths toward more radical change with respect to these very powers. Meeting people "where they are at" can blunt efforts to imagine and work toward more transformative visions of what and how we might become.

A third and related danger is that because IAF groups often seek to articulate themselves in moderate terms (even when aims are quite radical) in an effort to broaden their appeal and enhance their persuasiveness to those with whom they struggle and negotiate, under the sway of their own rhetoric they might not sufficiently recognize important and radical aspects of their own practices. This, in turn, might diminish the extent to which they attentively cultivate such practices and draw out their implications for other aspects of political life. Part of what I have in mind here are ways in which Tocquevillean interpretations of this politics might conceal more innovative aspects such as those discussed in this chapter. In this sense, they might (in Sennett's words) weaken efforts of this insurgent political organizing, "to say what it is, to see its contours in order to speak in its name." Yet there is an even greater danger here, which is that in becoming enamored with a moderate lens, they could come to know *too well* what democracy means—in a way that could weaken their receptivity to profoundly new aspects of their work more generally.

These tensions are with us to stay, because what is dangerous is also very important and valuable to what it endangers. By turning our eyes and our ears toward these tensions, by being attentive to the overlapping but also agonistic values and practices of democratic politics, and by resisting the temptation to reduce democratic politics in the name of one set of concerns, we might cultivate a judgment more capable of democratic empowerment. This chapter is one contestable voice— and a yearning to hear—in this task of democratic theory and practice.

# 8

# Reconsidering the Politics of Education

BEGAN THIS BOOK by noting several pressing dangers to democracy that have been gaining strength in recent decades. I have argued, in relation to a variety of idioms, that protecting democracy and helping it flourish depends on cultivating an ethos that is at once far more politically engaged, more generous, and more receptive to differences than the political liberal paradigm urges. Liberalism seeks to protect freedom in a way that often accents an ethos of tolerance according to which people should leave one another alone to pursue their own goods within the limits of the "harm principle" (tightly or loosely construed). This involves removing contested differences from the public realm (the condition for arguing that they do not encroach upon each other) and teaching tolerance of these apolitical differences (without which differences become repoliticized). Yet I have argued that though there is much that is appealing in this dream of peaceful coexistence among such differences—especially in relation to many extant alternatives—it comes up short in several important ways.

First, many of people's supposedly private differences inexorably come into play in significant ways around a whole slew of political issues. This means that they are not, in fact, as private and apolitical as liberals would claim. Second, as these differences manifest themselves politically, they fuel liberal resentments that, not infrequently, manifest themselves in a policing posture—sometimes moral, sometimes legal—above the fray, which in turn fuels resentments on the part of those who would be thus policed and excluded. Third, in the midst of a political economy of vast inequality, the fear and loathing of differences is continually mobilized by the powerful in order to further foment a politics of resentment that divides would-be coalitions for change, distracts people from issues of greed and inequality, and mobilizes support for the extension of police, surveillance, prison, military, homeland security, gated communities, disciplinary pedagogical institutions and technologies, cuts in public programs and taxes, growing inequality, and so forth. One needs only look at the politics around race, "welfare queens," black criminals, immigrants, gays and lesbians, Islamic people, and so on for examples. As long as we reside in a political economic system that produces tremendous economic inequality, it is unrealistic to think that similar forms of other-loathing will not be repeatedly fueled. Finally, a greater generosity toward differences and a more vigorous sense of political engagement than political liberalism offers are both conditions for political coalitions that might begin to alter this deteriorating state of things.

Hence, in response to political liberal claims to be the most "realistic" solution to the problem of coexistence in heterogeneous societies, I think there is a great deal to suggest that a politics of disengagement above the fray of differences unwittingly helps engender—and at any rate is incapable of defending against—the inequality and intolerance they would resist. A political movement toward equality requires a broad, strong, and enduring coalition across difficult differences. Developing a broad coalition hinges upon the cultivation of widespread engagements across divides, an engagement that will require a great deal of receptivity and generosity on the part of many people. I have argued that such engagements are part of the good life, part of human flourishing, part of what enables the deepening of justice and democracy— part of what allows us to witness and redress currently unacknowledged modes of suffering and to better respond to new expressions of human existence. Yet these engagements are also, I think, a vital condition for defending and extending that which is most admirable in the liberal tradition—including the diminishment of generalized difference-loathing. Absent a politics of receptive generosity and moving democracy, I suspect that the best of liberalism will increasingly become an empty dream—an increasingly "distant constellation fading in the corner of the sky." The question becomes, then, how to begin to work toward such engagements across the divides that are among the most challenging. In this chapter, I turn to political questions emerging around Christian fundamentalist parents in Hawkins County, Tennessee, who were angry about what they saw as a hegemonic secular liberalism in their schools. I look at some important liberal efforts to formulate a response and then develop the general contours of what a radical democratic alternative might look like. Thus this chapter extends the ethos I have been developing to engage some of those whose differences pose the most difficult challenges for my position, and it offers a direction for a grassroots politics—articulated in some detail in relation to the issue of education—that might begin to cultivate the coalitional power to resist the dangers to democracy I sketched in the introduction.

In chapter 7 I sketched a "moving democracy" that sometimes brackets particularly divisive issues and generates action around an agenda of common goods in order to form enduring relationships that bridge difficult differences. Part of the idea here is that as relationships develop, a deepening and broadening set of intersecting experiences (albeit differently perceived by different constituencies)—crossing different geographies, stories, bodily modes of being, modalities of preaching, expressions of suffering, anger, and vision, and so on—might support ongoing transformative negotiations over segmented portions of more-difficult divergences and might increase the general propensity to be more generous toward differences. This is perhaps beginning to occur in places like Charlotte, North Carolina, where PTA members in Jesse Helms strongholds have joined progressive black pastors and church members around issues concerning schools, with an eye toward a long-term coalition. The event of "being together" in these divergent groups, as they begin regularly to engage one another by sharing stories, spaces, and engaging in collective political action, is perhaps more significant than what is or is not said about the most conflictive divisions between them—at least for a while. Thus I explore this alternative and theorize a more "rhizomic" account of taking political responsibility for avoiding war and disengagement among vastly different constituencies (in contrast to the political liberal strategy focused solely on declaring and defending a hegemonic, trunk-like center).

The prominence of many heated political disputes concerning various aspects of civic education amid radical societal differences has given rise to numerous theoretical responses to questions regarding the proper aims of civic education, as well as to questions of how and to what extent the claims of dissenters to various civic pedagogies should be addressed. One prevalent approach to this challenge is that of political liberalism, which, as we have seen, formulates a norm of the "reasonable" in order to determine the proper modes and limits of public discourse and an education that would adequately prepare students for the responsibilities of citizenship. On the other hand, with many others, William Galston criticizes political liberalism for its constraining impact on public discourse and its potentially invidious effects on various subcommunities. Accordingly, Galston defends an alternative conception of "liberal pluralism," one that strives toward greater accommodation for particular communities—often deemed "unreasonable" by political liberals—to allow them to pursue their ethical-pedagogical vision, constrained only by certain minimal civic norms.

We will consider these approaches by examining the divergent responses of these two approaches to the much-discussed *Mozert v. Hawkins County* court case, which involved a group of Christian fundamentalist parents who objected to a reading curriculum intended to foster students' tolerance and respect for other cultures and worldviews on the grounds that it threatened their efforts to raise their children in accordance with their religious faith. Although they evaluate the outcome of the case differently, both approaches remain in important respects bound by similar presuppositions about how to theorize diversity and its political implications. Namely, both approaches assume a hegemonic theoretical stance for addressing the issues involved. This leads each to avoid bringing—or allowing others to bring—the contestability of their own presuppositions to the fore and leads each to offer somewhat caricatured depictions of the central issues in dispute. Both approaches thus avoid fully *engaging* the challenges posed by the *Mozert* families, and this raises questions about the adequacy of their attempts to come to terms with the way radical plurality affects social and political life.

After presenting our appraisal of each of these approaches, we draw out the general similarities between two rather disparate sources, namely, the theology of Yoder and the politics of receptive generosity, to defend a response to these challenges that, in its greater desire to welcome particularity and *engage* otherness, is not only better able to respond to the challenges of the *Mozert* case and others like it but also furnishes us with a more compelling approach to the numerous challenges of plurality and public life we currently confront. Yoder and a politics of receptive generosity both contest the hegemonic stance of most theorizing by cultivating a more vital dimension of vulnerability and engagement at the heart of their ethical stance. This, in turn, opens onto more promising political engagements.

## Political Liberal Responses to Mozert
Many political theorists view the *Mozert v. Hawkins County* case as an exemplification of the tension between the defensible norms of

civility and tolerance, on the one hand, and the unreasonable demands of religious fundamentalists, on the other. For political liberals, the case serves as a cautionary tale that reveals rather sharply the limit beyond which a properly constituted liberal polity should cease to make room for those who take issue with its core political ideals.

The dispute arose in 1983, when seven families in Hawkins County, Tennessee, filed a complaint contending that the public schools' use of a Holt, Rinehart, and Winston basal reading series violated their religious freedom. The parents claimed that the series, intended in part to inculcate tolerance and respect for diversity, in presenting other worldviews took an approach that directly jeopardized their own attempts to teach their children to rely exclusively on the Bible for guidance in their lives. The eventual suit was filed after the school board rejected an "opt-out" arrangement that some schools had worked out with the parents whereby their students were excused from class during reading periods in order to study from a different textbook. After a district court judge ruled in favor of the plaintiffs and the opt-out accommodation, the school board appealed, and the U.S. Court of Appeals for the Sixth Circuit reversed the decision. Despite the parents' assertions that the reading series denigrated their religious faith and weakened their children's convictions by exposing them to other worldviews, the appeals court ruled that the "mere exposure" to objectionable ideas provided by the readers did not constitute a constitutional burden on the families' free exercise of religion. Because the court's opinion anticipated key aspects of the political liberal position, we will review it in some detail.

Chief Judge Pierce Lively, who wrote for the court, argued that although the plaintiffs might indeed have been offended by material in the readers, their children were required only to read the stories; they were not compelled to accept as true or signal agreement with anything they read. Lively found persuasive the superintendent's affidavit maintaining that though the textbooks expose students to diverse values and religions, "exposure to something does not constitute teaching, indoctrination, opposition or promotion of the things exposed" (*Mozert v. Hawkins County*, 827 F.2d [1987], 1063). The readers were taking a "neutral" approach to the whole question of religion and truth, choosing simply to present students with a range of viewpoints that they could evaluate for themselves. Far from constituting a coercive pedagogy, the readers never encouraged students to abandon or even question their own convictions (1065).

Lively defended the readers' basic aim of teaching "civil" tolerance, which, as he interpreted it, "does not require a person to accept any other religion as the equal of the one to which that person adheres. It merely requires a recognition that in a pluralistic society we must 'live and let live.' If the Hawkins County schools had required the plaintiff students either to believe or say they believe that 'all religions are merely different roads to God,' this would be a different case" (1069). The plaintiffs were wrong, therefore, in attributing a sinister animus to the school board's selection of the readers; the board members were not intending to sway the children's convictions away from their parents' but were merely pursuing a legitimate civic goal. The readers' objective was simply to ensure that students became aware of and could learn to respect the fact that other people interpret the world in different ways. Judge Cornelia G. Kennedy concurred and argued that even if the plaintiffs could demonstrate that their religion had been burdened by the readers, the civic aim of teaching tolerance would constitute a compelling state interest, since it is crucial to democratic citizenship. "Teaching students about complex and controversial social and moral issues is just as essential for preparing public school students for citizenship and self-government as inculcating in the students the habits and manners of civility" (*Mozert v. Hawkins County*, 1071).

Both justices implied that the *Mozert* parents were obstructionist troublemakers, intent on subverting the legitimate purposes of public education. By insisting that the readers "*appear to us* to contain no religious or anti-religious messages," Lively left little room for the notion that the *Mozert* parents might have had valid reasons to be concerned about the readers' detrimental impact on their children's faith (1069, emphasis added). Kennedy further argued against the opt-out accommodation, citing the school board's interest in avoiding "religious divisiveness" and speculating that to grant the parents' request would result in "a public school system impossible to administer" because of the landslide of requests for exemptions that would be likely to ensue (1072–73). In sum, the *Mozert* families were unreasonably insisting upon their own private religious views as a basis for altering a curriculum narrowly and properly tailored to accomplish valid public aims.

Recent analyses of the case by Stephen Macedo and Amy Gutmann and Dennis Thompson largely follow the reasoning offered by these justices.[1] Macedo explains that in a manner consistent with political liberalism's commitment to avoid grappling with "comprehensive ideals of life" when determining legitimate civic aims, the justices sought to avoid delving into the specific features of the *Mozert* families' worldview; instead, they attempted to identify whether the reading series could reasonably be understood as furthering reasonable public purposes ("Liberal Civic Education," 473). The virtues of tolerance and respect for diversity and the "critical reading" methodology the readers used to try to instill them are consistent with public aims that can be defended on political terms alone. The plaintiffs, by denying the legitimacy of these aims and by preventing their children from developing their capacities as citizens who can contribute to the perpetuation of a just society, have thus excluded themselves from participation in the project of liberal citizenship. Macedo stresses that "leaving religious questions to one side is the best that our educational establishment can do with respect to religion. Indeed, maintaining an educational establishment that teaches children that important public issues can be deliberated upon without considering religious questions is itself part of the education for liberal democratic citizenship properly understood" (*Diversity and Distrust*, 121–22). Macedo argues that within this framework, "public schools may, in effect, teach that all religions are the same in the eyes of the state, not that they are all the same in the eyes of God" ("Liberal Civic Education," 473–74). Furthermore, by working within public values that can serve as mutually acceptable grounds, "and by leaving aside the religious question as such, Lively rightly leaves the school door open to reasonable fundamentalists— that is, to those willing to acknowledge *for civic purposes* the authority of public reasonableness" (*Diversity and Distrust*, 175, emphasis in original). Macedo argues that because the *Mozert* parents vigorously reject the importance of moderating their claims in accordance with the constraints of public reason and are instead intent on introducing their nonpublic convictions as grounds for an exemption from legitimate public purposes, we are under no compulsion to honor their wishes (*Diversity and Distrust*, 203).

Similarly, Gutmann and Thompson fault the *Mozert* families for violating what Gutmann and Thompson call their "reciprocity" principle, which requires that citizens "press their public claims in terms accessible to their fellow citizens" (*Democracy and Disagreement*, 55). By relying on their *particular* religious convictions as a basis for dissenting from a curriculum that was a "reasonable, even if not uniquely correct, way for a public school system to teach democratic values," the *Mozert* families are offering an unreasonable claim, one that cannot justifiably be presented for the fair and reciprocal consideration of their fellow citizens (68). Political liberals agree that groups or communities like the *Mozert* families stand outside the legitimate bounds of liberal citizenship and that hence their fellow citizens are under no obligation to consider their appeals with solicitude or to respond generously to their claims.

Perhaps, however, the situation is messier than this. For, as we have seen, the notion of "public reason" and its corresponding virtues are mightily contested in both theory and practice. As Greenawalt, Connolly, MacIntyre, Anzaldúa, Mignolo, Lorde, Tully, and others have contended, our visions and arguments concerning the "reasonable" and "the public" are infused with and are significantly and discrepantly shaped by particular histories, doctrines, perceptions, and sensibilities with which we identify—in ways that seem powerfully to elude transparency.[2] This implies that the lines between the reasonable and the unreasonable, as well as those between nonpublic doctrines and public terms of reciprocity, are themselves often significantly opaque and elusive. In this uncertain situation it is probable that what lies on one side of these contestable lines is essentially contaminated by the other and that our provinciality—rather than being something we can leap beyond—will be integral to our efforts to discern our political situation. Consequently, our interpretations of the nature and legitimacy of the damages imposed by nonpublic doctrines upon reasonable public aims and vice versa are themselves inherently contestable.

Recognizing this complexity should not lead us to conclude that reciprocity, aspects of tolerance, legitimate public purposes, and prerequisites for political dialogue are politically unimportant—far from it. But it does suggest that such norms more often appear as politically contested questions than as clear, pure, and commonly possessed meanings that direct and limit citizen action. Given what we take to be the *fact of a pluralism that descends into the depths of the question of the reasonable itself,* and given the limits of any one person's or group's capacity to negotiate and rise beyond these depths, we suggest that an essential requirement of political and ethical life is the cultivation of more-generous and more-vulnerable modes of engagement with those who contest the terms of our particular political visions—a reticence, in other words, to seize the throne of "the reasonable." Relatedly— and especially because *we generally teach more by how we act than by what we say*—pedagogies appropriate for cultivating capacities for engagement among people with deep differences will have to search for practices that embody a radical and vulnerable generosity that expands the range of those differences we are willing to engage, extends the spaces and modes for accommodating those with alternative visions, and widens and deepens the critical receptivity of our engagements. In pursuit of these possibilities, we turn to alternative renderings of politics and pedagogy.

## Liberal Pluralism

In his book *Liberal Pluralism: The Implications of Value Pluralism for Political Theory and Practice*, Galston offers "liberal pluralism" as a capacious and generous stance toward diverse minorities, and he criticizes political liberal "public reason" for being "highly restrictive," overly exclusive, and likely to provoke antagonism among those who feel excluded by it.[3] Galston's alternative is an "inclusive" conception in which elements of radically diverse doctrines are deemed legitimate in the public sphere, provided that they are offered to defend spaces for their own dissenting particularity rather than to deploy coercive power toward sectarian ends (*Liberal Pluralism*, 115–17). Galston recommends a politics of "maximum feasible accommodation" (20) animated by "a robust though rebuttable presumption in favor of individuals and groups leading their lives as they see fit, within a broad range of legitimate variation" (3). Only individual security and compelling state interests in basic civic unity, effected in such a way that encroachments on minorities are minimized, warrant limits to the accommodationist posture of the "diversity state."[4]

Despite these evident differences from political liberalism, an important similarity is also apparent. Like political liberals, Galston too defines a core of principles, purposes, and practices to be shared by and binding upon all citizens; he argues that these are the conditions most inclusive of a broad range of diversity and stresses that "a liberal pluralist order must have the capacity to articulate and defend its core principles, with coercive force if needed" (*Liberal Pluralism*, 121). In more emphatic terms: "It manifests the unyielding defense—and (where necessary) enforcement—of principles, institutions and practices that constitute the core requirements of shared citizenship. The more seriously we take diversity, the more seriously we must take the unitary public structure that both protects and circumscribes the enactments of diversity" ("Two Concepts," 529). Yet for Galston, to a greater extent than we find in political liberalism, these core civic concerns are often in tension with parents' diverse expressive interests in raising their children, and he maintains that neither should trump the other absolutely; in addition, following Berlin, his vision is infused with a greater sense of essential contestability in politics. How are we to parse out the significance of this overlap and tension? To approach this question, we focus first on how liberal pluralism works, as this will better illuminate Galston's mode of engaging deep differences and afford us a better sense of what his principled path entails—where it leads us.

Whereas Macedo's position is constructed and fortified in antagonistic relation to "unreasonable" people on the verge of holy war, Galston's diversity state takes form in relation to "defensive" others who may have much to contribute to a liberal polity. The fundamentalist parents he discovers/invents in Hawkins County have no intention of coercing the rest of us according to their vision of God; nor do they harbor an endless set of unmanageable defensive demands; nor are they without important virtues. Rather, they are portrayed as narrowly defensive, seeking neither to change the curriculum nor to opt out of the "curriculum as a whole" but simply to object "to one specific line of English readers" they thought were "at odds with the faith they sought to transmit to their children" (*Liberal Pluralism,* 120, 114). They readily accepted a principal's offer to let their children go to the library during reading period to read an alternative textbook, and "if this accommodation had been accepted . . . that would have been the end of the matter." "The parents were willing to play by the rules, enter into a civil dialogue with the school officials, and accept proposals that fell short of their original desires. . . . There was no slippery slope" of endless demands (120–21). Moreover, although fundamentalist education may be weak on deliberation and tolerance, it may cultivate "better citizens in other respects," such as "law-abidingness, personal responsibility, and the willingness to do one's share" (118). Arguably, students of a committed tradition might in at least one sense be *better* deliberators than thoroughly skeptical liberals who never settle deeply into a particular set of strong commitments: The former may have a profounder grasp of the stakes between real differences.

As noted, Galston agrees with political liberals on the need for a strong defense of a civic core that is shared by all. Although his concern for expressive liberty creates space for defensive differences, he, like political liberals, is nonaccommodationist toward offensive threats. Thus his disagreement with political liberals' assessment of *Mozert* is perhaps less theoretical and more a matter of different descriptions of the parents and their demands. But the two are interestingly related. Galston's ideal diversity state, founded on an uncontestable core of civic unity, requires the presence of others who radically diverge from that core, but who do so in ways that are only defensive, and defensive only in modes that are manageable and do not gradually draw the core into contestation or risk its power. These others constitute precisely

the type of deeper diversity that is central to his case for the prefer-
ability of his alternative to political liberalism: Their presence nicely
illustrates the capaciousness of the diversity state while posing no basic
challenges to it. Yet Galston repeatedly affirms that education must
cultivate an allegiance to and capacities for the norms and practices
that fortify the basic "unitary public structure that protects and circumscribes diversity" ("Two Concepts," 529) and that foster "a sense
of membership in the political community strong enough (in most
circumstances, anyway) to override ethnic and religious differences"
(*Liberal Pluralism,* 65–66). Although Galston calls us to negotiate the
tensions between this aim and parental expressive interests, this nego-
tiability and the accommodating spaces it might engender hinge upon
the discovery of differences that do not offensively seek to contest his
core. To the extent that parental challenges resemble the kinds of concerns Macedo ascribes to the parents in Hawkins County, it is doubtful Galston would accommodate them.

It is thus evident that Galston's "pluralist generosity" is rooted very
much in a vision of sociopolitical conditions and of "others" who pose
little challenge to him. Carefully examined, it is perhaps less a political generosity than a *depoliticized* and *depoliticizing* generosity. It is
depoliticized in that it strongly resists the possibility of engaging in a
politics that involves the vulnerable contestability of *its own* positions.
Like political liberalism, it imagines itself as the foundation for legitimate contestability. Yet many elements of Galston's core are, in our
view, highly contestable, such as his embrace of state sponsorship of
"functionally traditional two parent families"[5] or many possible renderings of his claim, which he does not explain in detail, that civic
education should be oriented and limited by the requirements of "liberal social unity," such as fostering the "social rationality" required
"to participate in the society, economy, and polity" ("Two Concepts,"
524, 525). It is depoliticizing in that it redescriptively converts political challenges into a diversity that would be at home *within* it. Its politics of redescription tends quietly to erase the apparently indigestible
aspects of different groups' otherness in ways that maintain the illusion of its being a generous and therefore unproblematic foundation
in relation to their differences. Thus Galston erases the more aggressive
political manifestations of the *Mozert* parents, such as those described
in Stephen Bates's perceptive account of the case: the elements of their
critique that were likely to involve challenges to other parts of the curriculum, the fact that their position was from the outset partly informed
by a perspective forged in heated national antagonisms concerning

theology and the politics of education, and so on.[6] As the possible encroachments and damages of Galston's position surface, questions about its desirability might threaten the centrality of Galston's voice as *the* speaker for the "core," the state, those practices and principles to be shared by all.

Whereas established traditions are redescribed, newly emergent others within or at a polity's borders hardly appear in Galston's text. We suspect the absence of any discussion of movements of pluralization—so important in contemporary contestations concerning group differences and power—is less a simple oversight than a consequence of a perceptual weakness engendered by elements of his politics of description at work in his account of the past and present for which he stands. Concerned about "centrifugal forces" that may lurk in moral pluralism, Galston advocates an "ethical presumption" that is to exercise a counteracting centripetal force to secure political community (*Liberal Pluralism*, 65). This presumption consists of a strong favorable bias toward "ordinary universal morality" and "the arena of public culture . . . the ensemble of practical principles that gives each political community its distinct identity" (77). This strong "presumption in favor of past decisions" is "rebuttable"—not absolute—because no general principle fully anticipates the future particularities of history (69–78). Yet the burden of proof falls heavily on those advocating changes. Hence Galston accents the strength rather than the vulnerability of this presumptive orientation when he writes of it as "a well-defended fortress that would require a powerful assault to conquer" (73). Galston's defense of this fortress orientation itself hinges on a confidence in a polity's present assessment of itself: "The reasoning underlying this stance is straightforward. The merits and defects of the status quo are well known" (71). The burden on those proposing changes is to show that their proposal will not make things worse.

Now, at a certain level, who could argue with the claim that those proposing changes must show their proposal won't worsen a situation? Yet virtually everything hinges upon the kind of political accounting that a polity engenders through the descriptions and presumptions we are encouraged to bring to our assessments of such proposals. We think Galston's sketch of the "core" of our polity and civic culture—a sketch constructed with lines of ethical rectitude, lines that are strong, clear, and "well known" in their positive and negative implications, colored seductively to orient us like a "well-defended fortress" against seriously transformative visions—makes it unlikely that we will be able to listen vulnerably and receptively to newly emergent challenges. His picture risks fabricating a hubris that is erosive of the more capacious elements in his theoretical efforts. And just how "straightforward" and obvious is this picture? If one thinks of the struggles and new directions concerning race, gender, sexuality, colonialism, capitalism, democracy, nationality, and the environment that have deepened or emerged in the twentieth century, to what extent could one legitimately have said, at the point of their emergence, that "the merits and defects of the status quo are well known"—much less that the principles and civic culture of the status quo were worthy of our "ethical presumption"? And at exactly what recent moment did they become so? If emergent others and many of the important questions they raise are largely absent from Galston's theoretical engagements, might this perhaps be related to the way an exaggerated sense of the worthiness and clarity of the present tends to erect a fortress-like barrier that too readily dismisses new challenges as unworthy of serious consideration? And might this sensibility have resisted and imposed great costs upon past struggles, struggles that Galston now embraces? If this is so, perhaps we would do better to resist this "ethical presumption" and cultivate at the core of democratic traditions a stream of memory and anticipation of the value of democratic insurgency and radical reformations.

In the process of redescribing or ignoring a variety of contenders, the impositions of Galston's order are rendered invisible, an exaggerated sense of its generosity and capaciousness is engendered, alternatives disappear, and upon this illusory foundation he writes as the spokesman for the norms that are to guide the state and citizens' political activity. He then further reinforces the walls of his liberal pluralism by contending that, notwithstanding those "issues on which the political community as a whole cannot but take a stand," citizens should remove "as many contested issues as possible from the sphere of national legislation or regulation"; they should engage in "issue differentiation" in order to reduce "gross oppositions" and "geographical differentiation" in an effort to encourage "local community option[s] on issues such as pornography" ("Two Concepts," 529, 530).

These strategies are intended to prevent citizens from encroaching upon each other. But they also prevent citizens from calling into question the "basic structure" of the order Galston provides for them (and its encroachments, for example, concerning levels of inequality or the nature of political identification and orientation). And how wise are these general counsels? Have not political struggles often (and rightly) involved placing previously uncontested issues into zones of heated— often national—agonism and legislative action? Have they not often also involved "issue connection" in ways that are now affirmed as illuminating and beneficial? Galston's counsel here seems designed more to secure his own conception of political order than to facilitate the ongoing pursuit of democracy, liberty, justice, or pluralization, insofar as any of these might involve ongoing receptive engagements across difficult differences and the possibility of radical, large-scale reformations in the face of newly articulated wrongs.

Within their carefully crafted defenses, political liberals and liberal pluralists rarely theorize in a manner that sufficiently acknowledges their own finitude, their own blindness and currently unseen damages, their own contestability, or their need to cultivate a degree of receptivity and vulnerability concerning the depths of their own political vision. If these positions are built and sustained through a politics of erasure, it is perhaps time to explore alternatives that might take finitude more seriously and seek to theorize within, rather than above, the fray.

## Toward a Generous and Vulnerable Provinciality

The political stance sketched below draws together common themes from Yoder's theology (discussed in chapter 4) and what I am calling a "politics of receptive generosity" in the broadest sense. I am using "Yoderian" in a very broad sense *in this section* to refer to a vast range of Christians who follow Jesus and believe that he calls them to vulnerable dialogical discernment and practices with others. My experience in and knowledge of growing interfaith coalitions suggest that there are many churches from different denominations that seek to practice their faith in ways that understand cruciformity and vulnerable receptivity to be inextricably intertwined. "Yoderian" evokes this crucial shared sense of witness, even though I am very aware that significant theological differences remain. "Politics of receptive generosity" refers to the general pattern of more-responsive orientations to difference (discussed throughout this book and elsewhere)[7] that are increasingly emerging with a variety of disparate but partially overlapping political and theoretical developments, including those at the difficult *intersections* between democratizing struggles around gender, race, class, sexuality, and nationality; theories of democracy indebted to deconstruction, genealogy, existential phenomenology, and first-generation critical theory; the border ethos emerging in relation to numerous postcolonial struggles; and grassroots democratic coalitional efforts for public goods in urban areas across the United States. This is confessedly a motley crew—and that is part of the point: A politics of receptive generosity draws on numerous cosmologies, theologies, practices, and sites of struggle that have been intermingling in unexpected and often promising ways. To draw together these differences in a brief articulation of a general orientation is to overlook many significant ethical and political distinctions and tensions. Yet it also allows us to sketch a position that powerfully contests both political liberalism and liberal pluralism in a more capacious direction and to suggest some hopeful possibilities for alliance with theological positions proximate to Yoder's.[8]

Both of the alternative orientations (or all the different positions mentioned above) to plurality and democratic engagement, while diverging markedly in important and obvious ways, nevertheless share certain core proclivities that engender strong elements of political affinity and the possibility of tactical alliances. Each accepts as basic and irreducible the fallibility, finitude, and partiality that significantly limit any particular community's ability to transcend unwitting elements of blindness and imposition. These similarly weaken any community's claim to speak for all communities or to establish a noncontestable "public" standpoint for the adjudication of disagreements or conflicts between communities. This acceptance of provinciality, along with the partial resonances between the sense of the abundant richness of being and the faithful expectation that the gifts of God are often surprising, manifold, and discrepant in their unfolding, mobilize a profound receptivity toward the claims of other communities and traditions and a commitment to the practice of patient intercommunity encounter and engagement whenever possible. Moreover, each orientation is suspicious of theoretical approaches that would tend to threaten, as opposed to treating capaciously, the plurality that is manifest among diverse communities. Accordingly, both stances are similarly disposed toward seeking provisional and localized solutions to negotiating difference and plurality rather than all-encompassing frameworks that would deny flexibility and creativity in response to particular conflicts by too exhaustively legislating in advance the directions and limits of our voices and ears.[9]

With both political liberalism and liberal pluralism, we share a strong resistance to efforts to establish a single doctrinal truth by means of state power. Yet rather than seeking to establish a definitive civic core that would purport to be neutral among differences, we instead embrace a politics in which myriad constituencies draw elements of their particular doctrines, sensibilities, and practices into engagement in ways that establish lines of contestation and affinity with others around issues that have unavoidable and significant macro-collective dimensions, such as those concerning borders, economy, political institutions, punishment, ecological practices, education, and so forth. As I have suggested, there are important dimensions within both a politics of receptive generosity and Yoder's radical Protestantism in which an "evangelical" impulse is an essential animating force. Our particularity does not and need not preclude us from pressing our particular truth claims on the wider world; indeed, a politics of vulnerable *engagement* demands that we do so. We take the basic ideas and practices of these modes of becoming to be good news that we hope will play a significant role in transforming a world that is frequently stingy, violent, and dogmatically Constantinian. This politics—like all politics—will not eliminate peccable encroachment, but it does promise to broaden and deepen the agonistic spectrum of visions, sensibilities, and receptive capacities through which we perceive and judge the damages and more hopeful possibilities of our political activities.

Clearly the directions and limits of such a politics at any point will be determined in no small part by the changing sensibilities and judgments of different groups and alliances and by the relative political power they can mobilize. Does this then mean that the spaces created for difference and collective direction will be no more than a modus vivendi, or balance of power, as Rawlsians would probably charge? We think not. The combination of tolerance, receptive engagement, patience, generosity, and restraint that is central to our overlapping ethos is not simply a consequence of balances of power; rather, it stems from the deep sensibilities and faiths discussed in earlier chapters. As such it holds a powerful sway. Yet the very faiths and sensibilities that engender these fundamental practices call us *not* to reify them but, rather, to solicit repeated discernments concerning where they might lead and how they might limit our action. These discernments will frequently draw the different constituencies that significantly converge on the above ethos into relations that also agonistically engage their differences of faith, understanding, and sensibility. Moreover, they require from us vulnerable engagements with those who dissent fundamentally from the ethos itself, such as political liberals, liberal pluralists, and religious fundamentalists. Thus the particular shape of the "basics" of such a politics is submitted to the political fray in which we must listen and persuade in order to engender collective power or, alternatively, to resist it when it runs amuck.

This said, we do affirm strong alliances with others to defend basic constitutional principles without which even the most minimal spaces and practices of democratic engagement are repeatedly crushed. If there is a "constitutional (near) consensus" among diverse constituencies concerning some basic principles of liberty and equality inscribed in rights of conscience, speech, assembly, processes of democratic representation, and so forth, we take this to be a *largely* good thing.[10] We join a large majority of people in democratic societies in denouncing antidemocratic efforts to erode this core; we would even call such efforts "unreasonable," and in so doing we would mark them in political contexts as *positions* in relation to which we think it important to *strongly emphasize resistance over receptivity*—even if the latter comportment remains vital and crucial in our mode of relationship to the *persons* behind these efforts (and especially those who are not among the very powerful). It is this emphasis in these most extreme cases that distinguishes our alliances around these issues from many others into which we enter.

Yet—as the above italicized *"largely"* suggests—our strong commitment to such a core of principles as a condition of democracy's possibility is itself not devoid of paradox. We generally prefer the directions of "diverse constitutionalism" sketched by Tully over the constitutionalism of uniformity that he compellingly criticizes.[11] Hence, *even in our alliance around a certain core* of widely shared democratic basics, we wish to acknowledge very significant elements of agonistic discrepancy that we take to be vital to the (as yet uncertain) advancements of justice. The core is porous and not without an element of multiformity; it oscillates this way and that depending upon the position from which it is affirmed, and we anticipate that democratization will engender its transformation in ways we cannot predict. Our sense that the constitutional core is and should be thus thereby conditions the *way* we affirm it. It calls us to scrutinize carefully differences among those who contest it, in order that we may resist the tendency of "reason" to become a bludgeon against contestation as such. Even when we do deploy a "democratic reason" that is largely shared in our society, a modesty borne by our sense of finitude and paradox leads us to prefer an injunction that contestation be *"not un*reasonable" (as Rawls occasionally says), rather than saying it must be *reasonable* (as Rawls does most often). The latter formulation tends to slide into a sense of reason that knows too well what it is and makes exaggerated claims about its own sufficiency.

The double negative marks a limit that is known more through a history of resisting the worst violations than from a positive grasp of definitive "truth itself." The injunction to be "not unreasonable" regarding basic constitutional rights and principles that apply to all thus makes a broad appeal to defend spaces of indeterminate democratic practice; at the same time, it emphasizes two things. First, this mini-mal form of "democratic reason" is not something self-sufficient; rather, it is more like a beacon of warning against the worst. Nevertheless, this warning somewhat paradoxically requires difficult *phronesis,* en-gaging particular places, times, and specific vulnerable contestations in an endless effort to rediscover and reinvent democratic reason itself. The double negative indicates that this reason will frequently *require* unexpected supplements that will be perceived as exceeding the limits we currently recognize but as not ultimately *against* what the indeter-minate horizons of democracy, mutual recognition, equality, and free-dom come to appear to demand.

Second, the double negative urges a modesty regarding "reason" as a limit marker accenting resistance over receptivity: a great reticence— even refusal—to deploy it freely to silence political voices and plug our ears in any but the most extreme cases. We at once both affirm the specificity and excess of *our own* political voices with respect to this reason—affirming and struggling mightily for far more robust practices of agonistic dialogue, receptive engagements with difference, egalitar-ian economics, care for the earth, and nonviolent modes of engaging conflict than political liberals and liberal pluralists employ—*and* seek to cultivate a receptivity in our engagements with *others* who are greatly at odds with our political sense of things. We do not endorse a far-ranging "public reason" that would draw into equilibrium our political order, our voices, and our ears. Rather, we think democratic reason can be rendered to defend against the worst while leaving far greater room for the *reflective disequilibriums* that we take to be an essential con-dition for more desirable modes of democratic practice and judgment.

Our position shares a certain affinity with Galston's accommoda-tionist effort to protect groups' and communities' ability to pursue their distinctive visions of what makes life meaningful. Yet it differs impor-tantly from his approach in two key respects. First, whereas Galston limits his protection of diversity to those groups that seek defensively to preserve a threatened way of life, we argue that a vulnerable poli-tics of engagement must also make more room for groups that are "messily" defensive, and even aggressively "offensive," in bringing their particular claims forward to shape public space. And second, we view the imperative of providing accommodations not as stemming princi-pally from a desire to legitimate and circumscribe particular kinds of diversity in advance, as Galston does, but rather as reflecting the fini-tude of our own ethical-political stance. The partiality of our own position demands a receptive and generous response toward even those communities we find deeply at odds with our own orientation, and thus it prompts us to seek a variety of ways to engage and approach such communities. In this light, Galston's tendency to limit the protections of his accommodationist framework to those groups that leave his core civic principles intact appears to be merely a way of preserving a political monologue. He refuses to open up the possibility of having his own position challenged by dissenting voices that would either contest his core or conceive it in radically different terms.

Many groups—some more and some less fundamentalist than Galston—are not simply desirous of preserving "private" space for their own distinctive convictions; they (and we) wish to participate in the transformation of public space as well, often on the basis of those convictions. Within educational settings, such contestation should be allowed to play a role not only in shaping acceptable opt-out kinds of accommodations but also to some extent even in influencing schools' curricular decisions. "To some extent" here means that, with political liberals and liberal pluralists, we fear and resist those who would seek coercively to impose the totality of their doctrines on the rest. Yet this fear and resistance extends to important elements of these liberal stances themselves insofar as they seek morally and politically to impose their political vision in the name of an uncontestable reason or civic core. Absent the kind of transparency that would allow us legitimately to design all-encompassing and impermeable political frameworks for delineating acceptable differences, we are left (beyond the most basic democratic constitutional principles discussed above) with the messy realities of forging tactical alliances and acceptable arrangements in particular contexts as particular conflicts emerge and are wrestled with on a case-by-case basis. This demands the flexibility, capaciousness, and patience that a politics of vulnerable generosity seeks to provide. With our political vision, we seek to affirm the role that particular traditions, doctrines, emergent identities, and so forth can and ought to play in shaping collective life when they are brought to bear selectively, in alliances with others, through modes of engagement that are patient, receptive, forbearing, and attentive to the dangers of imposing on others with different allegiances.

This stance has numerous implications for the pedagogical cultivation of political ethics and the politics of education. In terms of the common ground between our particular visions, we seek educational practices that truthfully illustrate the vitally important historical role that particular doctrines, practices, and sensibilities have played in shaping political life. Like all those who wish to see their position endure in the world, we seek to cultivate the kinds of dispositions and orientations that can foster and sustain the politics we embrace. Thus we affirm educational practices that engender the arts of patience, forbearance, vulnerable dialogical negotiation, receptive generosity toward others who are different, capacities to tolerate and even acquire a taste for restrained agonism, and so forth. Yet though this position can and should be *proclaimed,* its substance requires that it also be made manifest (perhaps by junior high school) in texts that discuss ethical-political life from a wide variety of contending positions, including many that may be antagonistic toward the ethical postures we articulate in this chapter and wish to see strongly cultivated in educational practices. Insofar as texts bear our stamp, they would exemplify the ethic we profess in the *manner* in which we engage the other voices present.

Insofar as the politics of vulnerable engagement is itself a practice, it requires exemplification in particular contexts if it is to be successful. Indeed, it is perhaps by working toward exemplary practices in the politics *surrounding* education, as much as by practices in the classroom, that our position best illuminates and enhances a broad pedagogy of receptive generosity. To the extent that we see all political visions, including our own, as being contestable and necessarily provisional, it becomes all the more vital to recognize the importance of refraining from assuming an imperial posture when fashioning and implementing an educational curriculum. This means that though we seek to participate in fashioning various curricula, our own position calls us to do so in ways that welcome dialogue with constituencies whose perspectives profoundly contest our own and to resist the impulse to dictate the terms of the opposition.

When the solicitous negotiations affirmed by such a politics fail to shape a curriculum that is acceptable to all, accommodationist remedies have the advantage of allowing for flexible and creative responses leading toward further negotiating the challenges of diversity, responses that would simply not be possible under "one-size-fits-all" approaches to public education. Thus an educational curriculum that makes wide use of opt-out policies can be seen as exemplifying the kind of careful and restrained approach to diversity that is necessary if we are to make a politics of engagement possible. Far from being simply a "strategy" for dealing with difference, then, such an approach is a vital reflection of an attempt to recognize the limited and partial perspectives that all of us bring to bear in approaching difficult public questions. In this sense it is not only a politics but also a pedagogy, a teaching by example, of the kinds of actions essential to the politics we embrace.

How then do we envision this stance being applied to the *Mozert* conflict? The first step, attentive to the importance of the politics of description in our relations with others, should involve providing a fuller characterization of the families' concerns—one that reflects the tensions that the separate accounts of Galston, Macedo, and Gutmann and Thompson fail to grasp. In this way it becomes possible to see that while the *Mozert* families indeed pose challenges to our own approach to politics, we may have resources at our disposal for engaging those challenges that these other theoretical positions lack.

We can begin by recognizing that the concerns expressed by political liberals clearly have some validity: The *Mozert* families had deep reservations about the legitimacy of any curriculum designed to foster a respect for diversity, and their criticisms often went beyond merely securing defensive space for an alternative reading curriculum, to the point that they challenged the wider curriculum fairly aggressively. Especially during the early period of the dispute, the families publicly decried what they perceived as the school board's effort to root out "Judeo-Christian values" from the schools. For many of these parents, an understanding that the mission of the public schools is to reinforce "love of God and country" was deeply ingrained, and they thus regarded the readers' emphasis on cultural diversity with suspicion.[12] Some of the parents sought to remove the readers from the schools altogether under the rationale that the readers were spreading "secular humanism."[13] Although it is true that the families did eventually narrow the scope of their complaints once their legal strategy was underway, it is plausible to conjecture that if they had successfully achieved their opt-out accommodation, other interventions might have followed, possibly with divisive effects.

Yet it is important to emphasize that this characterization represents only one dimension of the conflict. Galston reminds us that there *was* a defensive aspect to the parents' concerns. They were genuinely fearful of the coercive aspects of this curriculum, and it is certainly arguable that their foremost desire was simply to ensure that their children's faith would not be jeopardized by it. Indeed, their fears in this regard do not seem unjustified: As Nomi Stolzenberg has forcefully argued, a curriculum that purports to treat all worldviews or traditions on an evenhanded, impartial basis will leave some students with the impression that individual choice is what matters most in determining religious truth, that these issues are best left to personal opinion.[14] Nor should we overlook the significance of the mere fact of the parents' desire to be involved in influencing school policy. In trying to advance what they genuinely believed to be the best interests of their children and of the school as well, they displayed a quality of citizenship that is often absent in today's public schools, where parents often seem unwilling or unable to lend their perspectives to the process of determining how the schools should be run. It is thus only by coming to terms with both dimensions of the *Mozert* families' complaints that we can appreciate both the challenges they pose and the opportunities for engagement that are visible here.

It is also important to bear in mind that these challenges and opportunities for engagement emerge within a larger spectrum of relationships that we think are highly significant and essential to cultivate. Thus, for example, another essential way we might more fruitfully pursue and better weather agonistic engagement with groups like the *Mozert* parents is by building cooperative, grassroots coalitions where specific common goods can be discerned. Mark R. Warren calls these relations "bridging social capital," referring to strengthened connections across communities divided by race, class, religion, and political ideology.[15] As we saw in chapter 7, urban democratic organizing, such as that done in cities across the United States by the IAF, often draws divided communities together to work on shared issues such as education, housing, livable wages, and urban infrastructure. Though its membership often tends to be predominantly moderate or progressive, the IAF declares itself to be open to conservative participation as well. In some of the most impressive organizing, unwonted grassroots coalitions and relationships are formed and endure across remarkable divides. For instance, in Charlotte, North Carolina, PTAs throughout predominantly Helms-voting Union County joined with progressive urban black pastors and church members in an IAF coalition that fought successfully for a major school bond, and they have continued to work together on a variety of other issues.[16] In forming such relationships, different communities gain a more textured and durable sense of each other as human beings worthy of deep respect. To be sure, these relationships and sensibilities do not dissolve all deep differences, yet they do engender registers of connection that can help sustain less shrill and more receptive dialogue in the midst of deeply agonistic disputes, as practices of speaking, listening, frequenting other spaces, tolerance, humor, and patience that have developed around less divisive issues can be drawn upon and put to work in areas of more heated conflict.

Through the formation of numerous networks of relationships around multifarious common issues discerned by various constituencies, an image of a polity emerges in which cohesion is engendered through connections that are usually partial in two senses: First, they form in some registers and not in others. And second, they usually form between particular sets of constituencies that partly overlap with other such sets, rather than across the whole polity. To affirm political stances that are resolutely provincial in the sense that they eschew the various thrones of "public reason" and "civic core" is *not*, therefore, to abandon responsibility for engendering strong elements of peace, comity, affinity, forbearance, and generosity among the various other groups with which one is related. Yet rather than doing so upon a common foundation, these more modest political stances call us to pursue this responsibility in ways that are usually more partial, rhizomic, multiple, ad hoc, and appreciative of the way deep vulnerable agonism itself is both the ineliminable testing ground and part of the condition of possibility for these sensibilities and virtues.

But what about "extreme" differences? Without a rigid and extensive civic core, will these differences not threaten to dissolve a polity into chaos? "It depends" is probably the best answer to this question. But at any rate, appealing to a mandatory allegiance to an illusory common core is hardly a convincing alternative. More hopeful, in our view, is a political strategy that responds to this problem by pursuing political possibilities akin to those William Connolly sketches, following a line of thinking that John Stuart Mill opened but did not develop. Here the idea is to foster a deeply pluralist sense of community, not by assuming we have a civic reason that can extinguish huge differences and foster a nationalist center, but by (in Mill's terms) "softening their extreme form and filling up the intervals between them" or by (in Connolly's terms) "cultivat[ing] intersections, hybridities, and alliances among ethnic, religious, sensual, and linguistic diversities."[17] In Hawkins County one can imagine this responsibility being pursued by a variety of constituencies that engaged the spectrum closest to them, in part to fill in some of the distances in ways that might soften extremes hardened by a mythical sense of their own purity and an unbridgeable chasm between them and their "others." Most members of the fundamentalist church to which the *Mozert* parents belonged did not embrace the latter's curricular politics, radical suspicion, and so on. Had these members pursued a politics of "cultivat[ing] intersections" and "filling up [some] intervals" by more robustly engaging both the school board and the *Mozert* parents in ways imbued with elements of respect and concord as well as tension, they might have nurtured elements of a far less polarized context for more vulnerable, generous, agonistic dialogues and struggles across deep differences.

Similarly, some members of the PTA could have responded by solic-iting the *Mozert* parents' participation in a dialogue on the curriculum, along with some work toward better after-school care, student-teacher ratios, and a school bond to address common problems. In re-imagining Hawkins County in this fashion, we can envision a few possibilities for a more rhizomic ethical-political responsibility. Without question, differences would remain dramatic and heated, but as some partici-pants "filled in" the apparent chasms between "extremes," as others cultivated certain hybridities and unwonted alliances, and as still oth-ers invented new formations of difference that confused the existing spectrum, differences might have been "soften[ed]" and reworked to engender more receptive and more generous modes of engagement. The politics and pedagogy we embrace would seek to engender such respon-siveness on the part of numerous constituencies (including political lib-erals). These aims enhance the possibility of—and are enhanced by— the organizing efforts of moving democracy, efforts that cultivate polit-ical coalitions through receptive engagements and work that generates common goods and addresses problems of inequality and suffering. By decreasing gross inequalities (which are unjust in themselves), this pol-itics addresses one of the sources of the politics of difference-loathing. Thus, over time, such political engagements enhance the likelihood of cultivating a more "virtuous circle": Rhizomic relationships (within and outside grassroots political coalitions) enhance both the fund of generosity toward differences and the possibilities that coalitions will work toward common goods and lesser inequality, which in turn dimin-ishes important sources of blind hostility and thereby augers well for future engagements across differences.

Having sketched elements of affinity and alliance between a Yoder-ian politics and that of a radically democratic receptive generosity, it is important to emphasize some of the broad differences between these positions. Perhaps most obviously, whereas Yoderians work and yearn toward the Lordship of the Lamb, the postsecular radical democrats discussed above work and yearn toward a politics in which differences that exceed and resist themselves continually reemerge. On the one hand, this difference should not be exaggerated: It is possible (as argued in chapter 4) to read the Lordship of the Lamb in ways that valorize ongoing pluralization and hybridizations between Christian and non-Christian practices. And it is important to recognize the *horizons* that generally form around articulations of the politics of pluralization, horizons that generally yearn in a direction beyond particular groups that empower capitalist exploitation, tyrannical normalization, sexism, racism, homophobia, ecological destruction, and the like. This said, these meta-differences are not politically insignificant. A rooted evangelical moment is likely to receive greater accent in Yoderian politics, whereas a rhizomic sensibility that emphasizes riskier experimentation is likely to be more energized among those affirming receptive generosity. These differing sensibilities, along with others, are likely to manifest themselves in a variety of political contestations regarding questions of abortion, suicide, sexuality, the tenor of cultural-aesthetic experimentation, and so on, even as broad areas of affinity promise significant enduring alliances on a wide spectrum of questions.

Should these differences be a source of regret? It depends. It depends on what is discerned in each case in light of experiments and receptive agonistic encounters between advocates of each stance. Responses prior to the event are rarely reliable and are never guaranteed in advance. It is just possible, however, that after a series of discrepant transformations resulting from their intense struggles, each constituency here might come to see many past difficult differences—and thereby anticipate many future such differences—as gifts that enable clarification, reformation, and growth that would not be possible in a world governed by one language, or even by many saying very similar things. And it is just possible as well that they would discover that even in their areas of affinity and alliance—Eucharist sharing/economies of greater equality and generosity, difference as providential gift of God/ difference as potential site of ethical-political richness and generativity, vulnerability/receptivity—the practical differences articulated by their diverse general temperaments and experiments have been crucial to the way their coalitional efforts have been able to cultivate a supple dynamism more worthy of and successful in a messy world. Drawing on both the strength of our commonalities and a receptive generosity toward difference, a strange community might just gather and create the powers to make the world both better and more possible. We could take the perfect storm threatening democracy as an occasion—an instigation—to reinvent boat(s) more worthy of journeys of democratic promise.

# Notes

## Introduction

1. Sheldon Wolin began to offer a powerful analysis of some of these developments in the United States in the 1980s with his discussion of the "economic polity" in *The Presence of the Past* (Baltimore: The Johns Hopkins University Press, 1987).

2. Ian Dury, Chaz Jankel, and Davey Payne, "Reasons to Be Cheerful," on *The Very Best of Ian Dury and the Blockheads—Reasons to Be Cheerful* (Papillon Records, 1999).

3. They do not *always* become aware of this, of course. Many pressures can and frequently do lead insurgent democrats to refundamentalize their newly acquired judgments and modes of being in ways that undermine this second sense of moving beyond democracy as we know it.

4. Yet the general impulse to move from theory toward practical engagement also informs people as divergent as John Caputo (in *Against Ethics* [Bloomington: Indiana University Press, 1993]) and Ed Chambers with Michael A. Cowan (in *Roots for Radicals* [New York: Continuum, 2003]), who have very different agendas.

5. See those mentioned in the first paragraph for starters.

6. For an insightful discussion of this, see Harry Boyte, *Everyday Politics* (Philadelphia: University of Pennsylvania Press, 2004).

7. See Michael Warner's provocative "Styles of Intellectual Publics," in *Publics and Counterpublic* (New York: Zone Books, 2002), chapter 3, with which I am largely sympathetic.

8. Ibid., 158.

9. Again: I do not take political liberalism to be the only source of these problems, but I do think it is related to them insofar as some of its central thrusts articulate analogous operations and patterns that often reinforce the problems or offer insufficient resistance to them.

10. My most extended critical engagement with deliberative democracy along these lines (especially regarding the work of Jürgen Habermas) is in *Rethinking Generosity: Critical Theory and the Problems of Caritas* (Ithaca, N.Y.: Cornell University Press, 1997).

11. With apologies to Bob Dylan, "Not Dark Yet."

12. John Howard Yoder, *The Priestly Kingdom: Social Ethics as Gospel* (Notre Dame, Ind.: University of Notre Dame Press, 1984), 5.

13. Industrial Areas Foundation (IAF) democratizing organizing efforts are, like everything, a mixed bag of tricks, and in different places and times they range fairly widely in terms of how intensely they cultivate practices like those I discuss in this introduction. Nevertheless, I think such practices are integral to their continual vitality as a countercultural force for democratization in a polity that, like ours, is marked by many power-soaked lines of difference. At its best, the IAF cultivates a politics that discerningly strides along the edge between cultivating a distinctive vision of radical democracy and broad-based leadership and being responsive to being reworked by others just entering the coalition as well as by those who are not participants. At its best, the IAF vitally inscribes in very practiced, corporeal, and reflective modes an interpretation of some of what a struggling *traditio* of radical democracy looks like in U.S. cities at the dawn of the twenty-first century. Of course, there are also complacencies, ego trips, party lines, and ideologies that conceal and (mis)direct the radical character of democratizing practice, with which democratic efforts must always contend. Yet the shape of the work thus far is very promising.

14. This is one metaphor; democracy needs many.

## 1. Tragedy's Tragedy

1. Peter Euben, *The Tragedy of Political Theory: The Road Not Taken* (Princeton: Princeton University Press, 1990), xi. Hereafter in this paragraph cited as *Tragedy*.

2. John Rawls, *Political Liberalism* (New York: Columbia University Press, 1996), 154. Hereafter cited in text as *Political Liberalism*.

3. John Rawls, "The Idea of Public Reason Revisited," in *The Law of Peoples* (Cambridge, Mass.: Harvard University Press, 1999), 174. Hereafter cited in text as "Idea of Public Reason Revisited."

4. See Kurt Baier, "Justice and the Aims of Political Philosophy," *Ethics* 99 (July 1989): 771–90.

5. One could even argue—Rawls does—that the previous limits exaggerated the exclusiveness required by political liberalism's notion of reciprocity and that recent revisions offer an unobstructed view of this fundamental terrain for the first time. Additional evidence of Rawls's move toward greater accommodation is found in his new emphasis on the legitimate variety within the family of liberal public conceptions of justice subscribing to "reciprocity between free and equal citizens" ("Public Reason Revisited," 141, and *Political Liberalism*, lii–liii) and on the more dynamic ways in which the latter open up to new articulations ("Public Reason Revisited," 142–42, and *Political Liberalism*, liii).

6. Here is a brief sample of such positions: Kent Greenawalt argues, in *Religious Convictions and Political Choice* (Oxford: Oxford University Press, 1988) (hereafter cited in text as *Religious Convictions and Political Choice*), that where public reason is highly indeterminate on an issue, ordinary citizens can morally draw upon comprehensive doctrines in their internal mental deliberations but ought not speak of them in public political forums. Robert Audi, in "The Place of Religious Argument in a Free and Democratic Society," *San Diego Law Review* 30 (Fall 1993): 677–702, allows that although "religious arguments may properly play a variety of roles in liberal

democracies," concerning laws and policies that would "restrict human conduct," citizens should constrain their religious arguments to positions within limits of what secular arguments alone are sufficient to sustain both "rationally and motivationally" (677). Amy Gutmann and Dennis Thompson, in *Democracy and Disagreement* (Cambridge, Mass.: Harvard University Press, 1996), stake out a position (that perhaps shifts about a bit) close to Rawls's "wide view": On the one hand, they acknowledge that shared principles "can often be discovered only in the process of deliberation itself" (56). This applies to principles of deliberation too, and they admirably acknowledge that they themselves are also implicated in this always-provisional state of affairs (50). "Conceptions of the good life" can inform our deliberations about principles and policy (39), but they must remain within the ideal of "reciprocity" that "regulates pubic reason" so that "the reasons must be mutually acceptable in the sense that they can be mutually acknowledged by each citizen" (54). Reciprocity's "'goods received' is that you make your claims on terms I can accept in principle. The proportionate return is that I make my claims [the same way] . . . mutual exchange" (55). If these terms cannot be discovered, reciprocity "prescribes accommodation" (56). Yet this apparently open process contains pressures that heavily filter in advance the kinds of reasons people can bring to deliberation. Hence, one must avoid at the outset moral claims that "require other citizens to adopt one's sectarian way of life as a condition of gaining access to the moral understanding . . . essential to judging its validity." Gutmann and Thompson contrast such claims with those that can be "accepted by individuals . . . committed to any of a wide range of secular and religious ways of life" (57). But *how wide* does this range have to be? And why should arguments of radical minorities be delegitimated at the outset? And in what sense is the majority necessarily exercising reciprocity in so doing? The potential closures take a rather stark form in their criticism of Ronald Dworkin's claim, in *Life's Dominion: An Argument about Abortion, Euthanasia, and Individual Freedom* (New York: Knopf, 1993), that "our concern for future generations is . . . of sacred importance" (78). We must, on Gutmann and Thompson's reading, be wary of this, for it "comes close to legislating religion." If there are "differing interpretations" of what this means, then deliberative justification of laws on this basis would violate the principle of reciprocity. Even if there were convergence, Gutmann and Thompson reject such appeal to the sacred, as "it is more likely to lead citizens to think in religious terms . . . encourage them to affirm their moral differences rather than their agreements" (158–59). Charles Larmore's position, in *Patterns of Moral Complexity* (Cambridge: Cambridge University Press, 1987), is similar in its affirmation of "neutrality" of procedure as a response to pluralism. Neutrality screens out all political decision based on the "superiority of a particular conception of the good" (44). This means that while Larmore affirms public discourses in which one "clarif[ies] one's notion of the good life and tries to convince others of the superiority of various aspects of one's view of human flourishing . . . so long as some view about the good life remains disputed, no decision of the state can be justified on the basis of its supposed . . . superiority" (47). Rather, we should "abstract" from what we dispute and focus upon the "rest of our beliefs." Drawing what he believes is a universal norm of rational dialogue that seeks agreement, Larmore states that "in the face of disagreement, those who wish to continue the conversation should retreat to *neutral ground,* with the hope of either resolving the dispute or bypassing it" (53). J. Donald Moon, in *Constructing Community: Moral Pluralism and Tragic Conflict* (Princeton: Princeton University Press, 1993), argues for a position nearly identical to Larmore's, though in a more tragic mode, as discussed below.

7. For example, in addition to Rawls, Moon, in *Constructing Community* (hereafter cited in text as *Constructing Community*), draws on Berlin in chapter 2, as does Larmore in *Patterns of Moral Complexity.*

8. Isaiah Berlin, *The Crooked Timber of Humanity* (Princeton: Princeton University Press, 1990), 11. Hereafter cited in text as *Crooked Timber of Humanity.*

9. Isaiah Berlin, "Two Concepts of Liberty," in *Four Essays on Liberty* (Oxford: Oxford University Press, 1979), 166–67.

10. Larmore, in *Patterns of Moral Complexity,* chapter 5, presents a critique of Herder along these lines but draws different conclusions, based, in my view, upon a highly exaggerated sense of the neutrality of his own position.

11. Among the most compelling aspects of Moon's work are his extended and often very thoughtful encounters with other liberals and critics of liberalism and his pushing of the sensibility and limits of liberalism in ethically and politically desirable ways.

12. John Rawls, *A Theory of Justice* (Cambridge, Mass.: Harvard University Press, 1971), 20. Hereafter cited in text as *Theory of Justice.*

13. Except, it should be noted, in the historical emergence of political liberalism itself, where, in Rawls's account, the mutual revision of partial doctrines plays a key role. See Rawls, *Political Liberalism,* chapter 4, sections 6 and 7.

14. One of the best alternative accounts of religion is Talal Asad, *Genealogies of Religion: Discipline and Reasons of Power in Christianity and Islam* (Baltimore: The Johns Hopkins University Press, 1998).

15. For an argument concerning both Rawls's retreat from the religious-political commitments of many early tolerationists and ways in which his theory erodes the political space for religion that they sought to provide, see Andrew Murphy, "Rawls and a Shrinking Liberty of Conscience," *Review of Politics* 60, no. 2 (Spring 1998): 247–76.

16. See Jeremy Waldron, "Religious Contributions in Public Deliberation," *San Diego Law Review* 30, no. 4 (1993): 817–48; and Viet Bader, "Religious Pluralism: Secularism or Priority for Democracy?" *Political Theory* 27, no. 5 (October 1999): 597–633.

17. The language of common currency and exchange occurs in many texts by political liberals, and the concepts are frequently at work even when they are not explicitly utilized. A few references where this language is explicit: Rawls, *Political Liberalism,* 165; Greenawalt, *Religious Convictions and Political Choice,* 217; Moon, *Constructing Community,* 8, where Moon seeks common values as a "basis" for "regulating" "interchange" (though on page 220, he acknowledges that common values many have different meanings and may conflict with and be overridden by unshared values in ways

that allow of no "ultimate court of appeal"); Gutmann and Thompson, *Democracy and Disagreement*, 55.

18. This does not mean that we negotiate outside a constitutional framework; it means, rather, that the constitutional framework itself must be renegotiated in an ongoing manner. See James Tully, *Strange Multiplicity: Constitutionalism in an Age of Diversity* (Cambridge: Cambridge University Press, 1995), for a sharp discussion of this issue from a position proximate to the one I am defending here. I address this question more fully in chapter 8.

19. Eric Foner, *The Story of American Freedom* (New York: Norton, 1998).

20. See, for example, Moon, *Constructing Community*, 197, and Rawls, *Political Liberalism*, 205–6.

21. I take up the issue of theories and movements that take radical democracy to be an intrinsic as well as an instrumental good in chapters 5 and 6.

## 2. Contesting Cosmopolitan Currency

1. John Locke, *Second Treatise of Government* (Indianapolis, Ind.: Hackett Publishing, 1989), paragraph 184. Hereafter cited in text as *Second Treatise;* all citations are to paragraphs.

2. James Tully, *Discourse on Property: John Locke and His Adversaries* (Cambridge: Cambridge University Press, 1980).

3. John Locke, *The Educational Writings* (Cambridge: Cambridge University Press, 1968), 213.

4. Hence Locke omits from his account many struggles, discordant orientations, and ways in which contingent power relationships compromise the consensual elements he discerns. Areas he does not explore include (1) the struggles of the poor to maintain certain service exchanges in which a modicum of security was sometimes obtained in feudal practices (Locke's failure to examine this dynamic is in tension with the rise of universalized monetary exchange); (2) the efforts of the poor to maintain specified, circumscribed use rights to property that was less governed by sovereign property rights prior to the consolidation of mercantilist and capitalist practices in which monetary exchange relations and absolute property rights become central; (3) the miserable feudal conditions that call into question the meaning and range of "consent" in the cases where the poor opted for powers and institutions that elevated the importance and structuring force of monetary exchange in political economies; and (4) the way the extreme discipline of the "poor laws"—which Locke himself helped author and which were required to discipline the poor into the new modes of self, exchange, labor, and relationship that this system required—might compromise the notion of consent.

5. John Locke, "Draft of a Representation Containing a Scheme of Methods for the Employment of the Poor: Proposed by Mr. Locke, the 26th October 1697," in *Political Writings of John Locke*, ed. David Wootton (New York: Penguin, 1993).

6. Karl Polanyi, *The Great Transformation* (Boston: Beacon, 1957).

7. Adam Smith, *The Wealth of Nations* (Buffalo, N.Y.: Prometheus, 1991), 29.

8. See, for example, Martha Nussbaum's critique of Judith Butler in "The

Professor of Parody: The Hip Defeatism of Judith Butler," *New Republic,* February 22, 1999, 37–45, especially in light of Butler's thoughtful rejoinder to Nussbaum's "Patriotism and Cosmopolitanism" in Nussbaum et al., *For Love of Country: Debating the Limits of Patriotism,* ed. Joshua Cohen (Boston: Beacon, 1996), 157.

9. Theodor Adorno, *Aesthetic Theory,* trans. C. Lenhardt (London: Routledge and Kegan Paul, 1984), 109.

10. Romand Coles, "Identity and Difference in the Ethical Positions of Adorno and Habermas," in *The Cambridge Companion to Habermas,* ed. Stephen K. White (Cambridge: Cambridge University Press, 1995); Coles, *Rethinking Generosity.*

11. John Rawls, *The Law of Peoples* (Cambridge, Mass.: Harvard University Press, 1999), 121. Hereafter cited in text as *Law of Peoples.*

12. Thomas Pogge, "An Egalitarian Law of Peoples," *Philosophy and Public Affairs* 23, no. 3 (1994): 195–224.

13. Bruce Ackerman, "Political Liberalism," *Journal of Philosophy* 917 (1994): 364–86.

14. Andrew Kuper, "Rawlsian Global Justice: Beyond *The Law of Peoples* to a Cosmopolitan Law of Persons," *Political Theory* 28, no. 5 (2000): 640–75. Hereafter cited in text as "Rawlsian Global Justice."

15. Martha C. Nussbaum, *Cultivating Humanity* (Cambridge, Mass.: Harvard University Press, 1997). Hereafter cited in text as *Cultivating Humanity.*

16. Martha C. Nussbaum, "Women and Cultural Universals," in *Pluralism: The Philosophy and Politics of Diversity,* ed. Maria Baghramian and Attracta Ingram (London: Routledge, 2000), 209. Hereafter cited in text as "Women and Cultural Universals."

17. Martha C. Nussbaum, "A Plea for Difficulty," in *Is Multiculturalism Bad for Women? Susan Moller Okin with Respondents,* ed. Joshua Cohen, Matthew Howard, and Martha C. Nussbaum (Princeton: Princeton University Press, 1999).

18. See also chapter 6, where this position is developed much more extensively.

19. Richard Falk, "Revisioning Cosmopolitanism," in Martha Nussbaum et al., *For Love of Country,* 157.

20. Robert Pinsky, "Eros against Esperanto," in Nussbaum et al., *For Love of Country,* 87.

21. Ibid., 87–88.

22. Jeremy Waldron, "The Cosmopolitan Alternative," in *The Rights of Minority Cultures,* ed. Will Kymlicka (Oxford: Oxford University Press, 1995), 754.

23. Michael Hardt and Antonio Negri, *Empire* (Cambridge, Mass.: Harvard University Press, 2000); Arif Dirlik, "The Postcolonial Aura: Third World Criticism in the Age of Global Capitalism," in *Dangerous Liaisons: Gender, Nation, and Postcolonial Perspectives,* ed. Anne McClintock, Aamir Mufti, and Ella Shohat (Minneapolis: University of Minnesota Press, 1997).

24. Pratrap Bhanu Mehta, "Cosmopolitanism and the Circle of Reason," *Political Theory.* 28, no. 5 (2000): 619–50.

25. Gloria Anzaldúa, *Borderlands/La Frontera: The New Mestiza* (San Francisco: Spinsters/Aunt Lute Books, 1987), 78. Hereafter cited in text as *Borderlands.*

26. Also see William Connolly's helpful discussion of this point in "Speed, Concentric Circles, Cosmopolitanism," *Political Theory* 28, no. 5 (2000): 596–618.

27. Walter Mignolo, *Local Histories/Global Designs: Coloniality, Subaltern Knowledges, and Border Thinking* (Princeton: Princeton University Press, 2000). Hereafter cited in text as *Local Histories/Global Designs*.

28. Homi Bhabha, *The Location of Culture* (New York: Routledge, 1996).

29. Judith Butler, "Competing Universalities," in *Contingency, Hegemony, and Universality* (with Ernesto Laclau and Slavoj Žižek) (London: Verso, 2000).

30. Tully, *Strange Multiplicity*, 135. Hereafter cited in text.

31. I explore a few concrete suggestions regarding these themes in the last few pages of my "Pluralization and Radical Democracy: Recent Developments in Critical Theory and Postmodernism," in *American Political Science Association's 2002 State of the Discipline* (New York: Routledge, 2002).

32. Boaventura de Sousa Santos, "The World Social Forum: Toward a Counter-Hegemonic Globalization" (presented at the Twenty-fourth International Congress of the Latin American Studies Association, Dallas, March 27, 2003), originally published at http://www.ces.fe.uc.pt/bss/fsm.php.

33. Ibid., 38–39.

34. John Howard Yoder, "Meaning after Babble: With Jeffery Stout beyond Relativism," *Journal of Religious Ethics* 24, no. 1 (1996): 122–43.

### 3. MacIntyre and the Confidence Trickster of Rivalish Tradition

1. Alasdair MacIntyre, *After Virtue* (Notre Dame, Ind.: University of Notre Dame Press, 1981), 210, 245. Hereafter cited in text as *After Virtue*.

2. Alasdair MacIntyre, *A Short History of Ethics* (London: Routledge and Kegan Paul, 1967), 4.

3. Alasdair MacIntyre, *Against the Self-Images of the Age: Essays on Ideology and Philosophy* (Notre Dame, Ind.: University of Notre Dame Press, 1978), 10. Hereafter cited in text as *Against the Self-Images of the Age*.

4. As I discuss below, MacIntyre continues in his most recent work to affirm toleration and freedom of expression in relation to state power. See MacIntyre, "Toleration and the Goods of Conflict," in *The Politics of Toleration in Modern Life*, ed. Susan Mendus (Durham, N.C.: Duke University Press, 2000). His view on freedom of expression in relation to local communities, as we shall see, is far more complicated.

5. See Alasdair MacIntyre, "The Essential Contestability of Some Social Concepts," *Ethics* 84 (1973–74): 1–9.

6. Alasdair MacIntyre, *Whose Justice? Which Rationality?* (Notre Dame, Ind.: University of Notre Dame Press, 1988), 2. Hereafter cited in text as *Whose Justice?*

7. I think we should doubt this reading of Hegel, but that is not my task here.

8. Immanuel Kant, "What Is Enlightenment?" in *On History*, ed. L. W. Beck (Indianapolis, Ind.: Bobbs-Merrill, 1963). The extent to which it is fair to characterize (as MacIntyre generally does) Kant and "the" Enlightenment more generally as advocating an *abstract* rendering of *Ausgangs* (understood as a rejection of the past and particularity in the name of a presentist, formal reason) is a question I leave aside

for now. For alternative readings see James Schmitt's edited volume *What Is Enlightenment? Eighteenth Century Answers to Twentieth Century Questions* (Berkeley and Los Angeles: University of California Press, 1996).

9. For a much more interesting reading of Burke, see Stephen White, *Edmund Burke: Modernity, Politics, and Aesthetics* (New York: Sage, 1994).

10. Alasdair MacIntyre, "Bernstein's Distorting Mirrors: A Rejoinder," *Soundings* 47, no. 1 (1984): 40.

11. Alasdair MacIntyre, "Politics, Philosophy, and the Common Good," in *The MacIntyre Reader,* ed. Kelvin Knight (Notre Dame, Ind.: University of Notre Dame Press, 1998), 252. In chapter 6 I address one dimension of this problem in terms of grassroots democratic practices in urban areas.

12. In *After Virtue* Aquinas is a relatively marginal figure, and MacIntyre's account of intercultural relations is relatively undeveloped. Aquinas is treated briefly and criticized for having an exaggerated sense of the exhaustiveness, consistency, unity, and tragedy-free character of moral life. Not long after this text was completed, however, MacIntyre significantly revised his reading of Aquinas, and the latter becomes a central inspiration for MacIntyre's more focused efforts to respond to this question of how to cultivate the right kinds of tension in order to live well amid difference.

13. Alasdair MacIntyre, *Three Rival Versions of Moral Enquiry: Encyclopaedia, Genealogy, and Tradition* (Notre Dame, Ind.: University of Notre Dame Press, 1990), 125. Hereafter cited in the text as *Three Rival Versions*.

14. Hilary Putnam, *Renewing Philosophy* (Cambridge, Mass.: Harvard University Press, 1992), 185–86.

15. MacIntyre, "Politics, Philosophy, and the Common Good," 251. In this discussion MacIntyre acknowledges that this is contrary to the general inability of Christian societies, for example, "to listen and learn from . . . dissenting Jewish communities."

16. For MacIntyre, the brilliance of *Summa*'s substantive insights lies in its mode of dialogical relation with at least two traditions (most fundamentally Christian and Aristotelian, but also Jewish and Islamic). Aquinas develops his thought systematically, integrating and interrogating each part in the context of a unified, open-ended whole. With this teleological systematic structure, Aquinas develops the coherence and illuminative power of his insights and the distinct shape of his vision. At the same time this teleological structure offers a terrain for meaningful critical inquiry. MacIntyre claims that because Aquinas's system develops its insights dialectically, reforming itself immanently and through dialogues with other traditions, it gradually acquires a warranted confidence that the answers it offers are the best available. Without this dialectical systematic structure, his wide-ranging engagement would be fragmented, "eclectic," and weak. Without this wide-ranging engagement, he would have little reason to trust that his claims concerning the systematic order of morality represent more than the assertion of his particular community.

17. Though this is not a universal, because it is possible to live life—albeit in miserable and contradictory fashion—in explicit denial of this structure.

18. Alasdair MacIntyre, "Plain Persons and Moral Philosophy," in Knight, *The MacIntyre Reader,* 138.

19. Hence he does not think of it as appropriate only for a period like what J. S. Mill called our discordant "age of transition"—soon to be surpassed by a "natural age" of reestablished unanimity.

20. Franz Kafka, "The Unmasking of a Confidence Trickster," in *The Transformation (Metamorphosis) and Other Stories*, trans. and ed. M. Pasley (New York: Penguin, 1992).

21. This general confidence is not akin to the liberal cosmopolitan confidence that the truths of a particular tradition will be translatable into other traditions of enquiry or desirable to them. Many truths, according to MacIntyre, might only be understood and affirmed through the right ordering of selves and communities through a relatively specific set of practices.

22. See Alasdair MacIntyre, "Toleration and the Goods of Conflict," in *The Politics of Toleration in Modern Life*, ed. Susan Mendus (Durham, N.C.: Duke University Press, 1999), and "The Recovery of Moral Agency? The Dudleian Lecture," *Harvard Divinity Bulletin* 28, no. 4 (1999): 6–10.

23. MacIntyre, "The Recovery of Moral Agency?" 7.

24. Michel Foucault, "Afterword," in Hubert Dreyfus and Paul Rabinow, *Michel Foucault: Beyond Structuralism and Hermeneutics* (Chicago: University of Chicago Press, 1983), 231–32.

## 4. The Wild Patience of John Howard Yoder

1. In fact, this suspicion (articulated in my critical reading of John Milbank's totalizing neo-Deleuzianism in *Theology and Social Theory* in Romand Coles, "Storied Others and the Possibilities of *Caritas:* Milbank and Neo-Nietzschean Ethics," *Modern Theology* 8, no. 4 [1992]: 331–51) provided the initial horizon of questioning that I brought to my reading of Yoder.

2. John Howard Yoder, *The Priestly Kingdom: Social Ethics as Gospel* (Notre Dame, Ind.: University of Notre Dame Press, 1984), 11. Hereafter cited in the text as *Priestly Kingdom*.

3. For my earlier theoretical accounts of these positions, see especially my chapter on Merleau-Ponty in *Self/Power/Other: Political Theory and Dialogical Ethics* (Ithaca, N.Y.: Cornell University Press, 1992) and my *Rethinking Generosity.*

4. We should note that Yoder sometimes refuses to employ academic terms like "teleology" and not infrequently signals his reluctance when he does use them. See, for example, his sarcastic comments on "teleology" in "To Serve Our God and Rule the World," in *The Royal Priesthood: Essays Ecclesiological and Ecumenical,* ed. Michael G. Cartwright (Scottdale, Pa.: Herald Press, 1998), 128–29. I must postpone discussion of this issue for another time, even though it has everything to do with questions of translation that are at work in the present chapter.

5. One could say without exaggerating that Yoder's "wisdom of the Cross" is one forever stretched between a faith in a certain sense of the *adequacy* of the believing community gathered around Scripture and informed by the Holy Spirit and a faith in a sense of the peccability or epistemological *inadequacy* that will always to some degree somehow be at work. Thus Yoder writes of the discerning community's

"morally adequate knowledge," where "'morally adequate' means good enough to work with, sufficient to enable the community process of discernment. It did not mean absolutely clear, immutable, or without exceptions. It means that my brother or sister within the discerning community has a basis for counting on me, blaming or praising me, correcting or commending me as we together proceed through the discernment process in the midst of our being and doing." At the same time, the epistemological effects of sin "poisons . . . even our ability to know [the good]." See Yoder, "Theological Revision and the Burden of Particular Identity," in *James M. Gustafson's Theocentric Ethics: Interpretations and Assessments,* ed. Harlan R. Beckley and Charles M. Swezey (Macon, Ga.: Mercer University Press, 1988), 77–82. This affects selves and the church body. Although the latter is the locus of the practices of "regeneration" and "change in orientation," it can only be such, as I claim below that Yoder argues, through practices of receptive generous vulnerability with outsiders. If Yoder does not always stress such vulnerability, this lack is due to the context in which his work so often intervenes (namely, to resist dominant church practices of assimilation to the dominant "public reason"), *not* to some intermittent awareness of the centrality of vulnerable receptivity. Yoder resists a neo-Constantinian "receptivity" that would receive and govern itself according to "public reason" precisely because it would thus greatly diminish giving and receiving in dialogue. He thus resists the church's reception of hegemonic liberal "receptivity" in the name of radical vulnerability, not to avoid it, as I fear many mistakenly believe.

6. John Howard Yoder, "The Imperative of Christian Unity," in Cartwright, *The Royal Priesthood,* 294.

7. Yoder, "Theological Revision and the Burden of Particular Identity," 84–86.

8. Yoder weaves other forms of church "body politics" into this account as well, including, importantly, eucharistic bread and sharing in economic consumption and production. See Yoder, *Body Politics: Five Practices of the Christian Community before the Watching World* (Nashville, Tenn.: Discipleship Resources, 1992), chapter 2. Hereafter cited in the text as *Body Politics.*

9. John Howard Yoder, *For the Nations: Essays Public and Evangelical* (Grand Rapids, Mich.: Eerdmans, 1997), 32. Hereafter cited in the text as *For the Nations.*

10. For example, Yoder elaborates this point throughout "Meaning after Babble: With Jeffery Stout beyond Relativism," *Journal of Religious Ethics* 24, no. 1 (Spring 1996): 125–39, which I discuss in more detail below. Hereafter cited in text as "Meaning after Babble."

11. For an extended discussion of "Revolutionary Subordination," see chapter 9 in Yoder's *The Politics of Jesus,* 2nd and rev. ed. (Grand Rapids, Mich.: Eerdmans, 1994). It is beyond the scope of this chapter to engage the questions raised in that text and responses to it concerning women and revolutionary subordination. I think Yoder aims to articulate a radically postpatriarchal vision in line with his reflections on women in the church in Yoder, *Body Politics,* 60 (and also 61–62). He also seeks to resist certain forms of feminism that would seek liberation simply by opening to women patriarchal institutions, such as the role of exclusive priest, or masculine

sovereign subjectivity. That said, I am skeptical about whether Yoder's work engages feminist theology and theory as deeply as it should and as we must.

12. This does not, of course, mean for the nations as sovereign sources of meaning and state power.

13. Yoder draws here on the outsider Gandhi in part to textually exemplify his substantive position toward engagements with outsiders.

14. John Howard Yoder, "The Disavowal of Constantine: An Alternative Perspective on Interfaith Dialogue," in Cartwright, *The Royal Priesthood*, 255. Hereafter cited in the text as "Disavowal of Constantine."

15. This, of course, raises numerous important questions concerning punishment, but they exceed the bounds of what this chapter can carefully address. One place to begin to explore these issues more fully is John Howard Yoder, "You Have It Coming: Good Punishment. The Legitimate Social Function of Punitive Behavior" (unpublished, 1995).

16. John Howard Yoder, "'Patience' as Method in Moral Reasoning: Is an Ethic of Discipleship 'Absolute'?" in *The Wisdom of the Cross: Essays in Honor of John Howard Yoder*, ed. Stanley Hauerwas, Chris K. Huebner, Harry J. Huebner, and Mark Thiessen Nation (Grand Rapids, Mich.: Eerdmans, 1999), 31.

17. John Howard Yoder, *The Original Revolution: Essays on Christian Pacifism* (Scottdale, Pa.: Herald Press, 1971), 52.

18. Historically, and in a colonial context, Yoder sees an initial and imperfect but significant practical working out of this stance in William Penn's relationship to Native Americans: pacifism; friendship; nonviolent, discursive dispute-resolution processes with equal representation on both sides; repentance for past settlers' wrongdoings; "paying the Indians again for land that according to Imperial law was already his"; no insistence on conversion or condemnation of Native Americans' paganism. Yoder countenances the imperative to go further but abstains from condemning Penn, writing, in response to a student's comment that "they should have given [the land] back to the Indians": to have gone further than Penn and "ask the Indian rulers for their authorization to be guests/immigrants under their sovereignty, or to forsake immigration completely, would probably have been beyond the scope of anyone's imagination at the time." Penn's radically generous *and* radically presumptuous erasure of theological differences between the Quakers and Native Americans would also have to be radically reformed in light of the Yoder's reflections, but again, was beyond most imaginations at the time. See chapter 13 in John Howard Yoder, *Christian Attitudes to War, Peace, and Revolution* (Elkhart, Ind.: Goshen Biblical Seminary, 1983).

19. Yoder, "'Patience' as Method in Moral Reasoning," 27, 29, my emphasis.

20. Yoder, *The Original Revolution*, 49–50.

21. As when, for example, in "Meaning after Babble," 132, Yoder assumes too persistently that Babel is primarily about distinct traditions and communities, when in fact almost all known communities are mixtures of different traditions. Yoder acknowledges and works with this latter point very perceptively at times, as I have tried to show. Yet if he were to think it through in his essay, I think he would have

to struggle with "babble" in somewhat different, more difficult, and, I think, more fruitful ways. The inside/outside framework also works to elide some important questions in Yoder, "On Not Being Ashamed of the Gospel: Particularity, Pluralism, and Validation," *Faith and Philosophy* 9, no. 3 (July 1992): 285–300, where his exaggeration of the distinction between newbearers and host culture perhaps weakens his ability to open certain questions and responses to problems of heralding in late modernity. I realize that his essay strains against liberal assimilation, but would this straining be weakened or strengthened by a greater acknowledgment of the discursive hybridities with which most late moderns always already must begin?

## 5. Derrida and the Promise of Democracy

1. Until the past decade, most commentators largely ignored the ethical and political themes Derrida has repeatedly explored since his earliest work on Edmund Husserl. Recently, ethical and political issues have become more prominent in the commentary of both his admirers and his critics.

2. These themes are related but nonidentical.

3. Jacques Derrida, *Edmund Husserl's "Origin of Geometry": An Introduction* (Lincoln: University of Nebraska Press, 1989), 136. Hereafter cited in the text as *Introduction*.

4. Edmund Husserl, "Origin of Geometry," in Derrida, *Introduction*, 165. Hereafter cited in the text as "Origin."

5. Edmund Husserl, *Formal and Transcendental Logic*, trans. Dorion Cairns (The Hague: Martinus Nijhoff, 1969), 5–6, cited in Derrida, *Introduction*, 31.

6. As noted, there is a sense in which this geometrical idealization is based upon and partially legitimated, inspired, and animated by the movement and direction of experiential idealizing. But it draws upon such idealizing in order to leap beyond its limitations to the idea of infinite ideal objectivities themselves: for example, the absolutely ideal concept of a "line" beyond all finite approximations.

7. If it were not thus governed, contingency, fragmentation, and nonsense (aspects of which are sedimented in every cognition) would proliferate. Thus governed however, contingency is weeded out, ideas gain a deepening coherence and perfection, and they thereby become more capable and worthy of being reproduced and retained across time.

8. Thus on Derrida's reading, Habermas's frequent characterization of the later Husserl as a "philosopher of subjectivity" who was oblivious to the fundamental status of intersubjectivity does not ring true.

9. Jacques Derrida, "Violence and Metaphysics," in *Writing and Difference*, trans. Alan Bass (Chicago: University of Chicago Press, 1978), 121. Hereafter cited in the text as "Violence and Metaphysics." Here Derrida affirms a central dimension of Husserl's work, a dimension that is profoundly at odds with those aspects that Derrida elsewhere interprets as a "metaphysics of presence." See Derrida, *Speech and Phenomena and Other Essays on Husserl's Theory of Signs* (Evanston, Ill.: Northwestern University Press, 1973).

10. Jacques Derrida, *The Other Heading: Reflections of Today's Europe* (Bloomington: Indiana University Press, 1992). Hereafter cited in the text as *Other Heading*.

11. Katherine Zuckert, in *Postmodern Plato's: Nietzsche, Heidegger, Gadamer, Strauss, Derrida* (Chicago: University of Chicago Press, 1996), misses most of these philosophical underpinnings of Derrida's argument and hence misses much of its coherence.

12. Efforts to leap beyond this difficult labor often unwittingly carry with them the traditional structures and substances they wish to escape, and they often do so in ways that accent the damaging legacies (which thrive behind our backs in conditions where unreflective oblivion is widespread) and diminish what is more promising (which is often deeply entwined with practices of responsibility linked to careful reflection upon the possibilities lodged in our particular history).

13. Derrida's claim is decidedly *not* that Europe has some privileged relation to this project. It is that those who inherit Europe's particular gifts have a duty to receive them carefully—a duty not to squander them that is as great as (and is related to) the duty to work beyond damages of European legacies and to learn from others.

14. And yet the movement of Derridean thinking here must interrupt itself repeatedly and abruptly with tropes such as "and yet," for smoothly flowing rhetorical forms are insufficient to articulate the textures of a democratic responsibility that must be cultivated through contradictory doubling. Responsibility requires the cultivation of discourses that repeatedly fold back on themselves and rub their discrepant articulations against the grain to animate receptive engagements with others and otherness.

15. Derrida argues that even the best articulations of "sense" (for example, Husserl's), have a tendency to eclipse alterity. For a discussion of Husserl's erasure of the non-European, see Immanuel Eze, *Achieving Our Humanity: The Idea of the Post-Racial Future* (New York: Routledge, 2001).

16. Whether or not there may exist cultures that do not understand themselves in this way, I am not prepared to say—though some cultures seem to be much less insistent on their own exceptionality than are others. Yet Derrida's claim seems to be true of the vast majority of cultures today, and certainly true of those that are dominant.

17 Jacques Derrida, *Specters of Marx* (London: Routledge, 1994). Hereafter cited in the text as *Specters of Marx*.

18. Jacques Derrida, "The Politics of Friendship," *Journal of Philosophy*, 85 (November 1988): 632–48, at 638; hereafter cited in text as "Politics of Friendship." See also Derrida, *The Politics of Friendship* (London: Verso, 1997).

19. Encore: "The condition of possibility of this thing called responsibility is a certain experience and experiment of the possibility of the impossible: the testing of the aporia from which one may invent the only possible invention, the impossible invention" (*Other Heading*, 41).

20. See Jacques Derrida, "The Principle of Reason: The University in the Eyes of Its Pupil," *Diacritics*, Fall 1983, 3–20. Hereafter cited in the text as "Principle of Reason."

21. Derrida's mention of "the most crepuscular, the most westerly situations of the Western university," in conjunction with his discussions elsewhere of North-South issues, colonialism, economic imperialism, religious imperialism, and the like, suggests that it is precisely when "the West" blinks, or when the sun of "the West" has

dropped below the horizon, that the chances for a "'twinkling' of thought are multiplied." Genealogical and deconstructive questioning can play a valuable role in cultivating modes of blinking, listening, remembering, and learning from the others beyond
the West. Yet these "non-Western" others arrive as the twinkling of *other light(s)and
thoughts* with and from which we might learn something about how to live well.
"Twinkling" suggests that among the most important arts we might learn in these
crepuscular encounters are precisely modes of understanding and enlightenment that
develop not via an insistent tractor beam but through modes of flickering, intermittent, fluctuating, and fluttering patterns of lighting. Perhaps the West might learn
with and from the others (and perhaps at dusk these others are discovered within as
well as beyond the geographies of "the West") that we learn to live less violently and
better as we learn how to learn through more crepuscular and twinkling types of
light. This, it seems to me, resonates strongly with the sensibility cultivated by Chicana feminists and numerous other postcolonial voices from around the globe, which
we shall explore in chapter 6.

22. I explore proximate themes extensively in *Rethinking Generosity*.

23. The idea of constructed absences comes from Santos, "World Social Forum."

24. Of course, this questionability never appears purely or immediately. To be indicated and protected, it must always be partially enclosed in a horizon of narratives,
arguments, and practices that conceal as well as reveal the questionability we are to
each other. The "community of the question" is thus the tradition of those engaged
in a double responsibility—both teleological and ateleological—to keep alive our sense
of the breach that authorizes the unbreachable: democracy to come.

25. MacIntyre explicitly distances his critique from the mantra-like weapon of
choice these days—charges of "performative contradiction" concerning the normative presuppositions of all communication.

26. MacIntyre argues that given the vast differences between genealogy, Thomism,
liberalism, and other traditions on questions concerning not only theses but genre
and authority as well, alongside his post-encyclopedic university, "surely a set of rival
universities would result . . . each advancing its own inquiries in its own terms and
each securing the type of agreement necessary to ensure the progress and flourishing
of its enquiries by its own set of exclusions and prohibitions"—as well as participating in debates with its rivals (*Three Rival Versions*, 234).

27. It is beyond the scope of this chapter to explore the proximity and distances
between Derrida and other genealogists. Suffice it to say that I see a kinship between
Derrida, Foucault, and Nietzsche that would place profound pressure on MacIntyre's
reading of the latter two.

28. That is, in MacIntyre's scheme, Christianity's failure would be indicated not
only by its own internal incoherence but also by the success of its rivals as defined
by its rivals.

29. Even if, for MacIntyre's genealogists, this is a telos beyond all teleology.

30. Jacques Derrida, *The Gift of Death*, trans. David Wills (Chicago: University
of Chicago Press, 1995), 26, 48. Hereafter cited in text as *Gift of Death*.

31. Derrida's effort to locate the strengths of our history in aporias and tensions
is exemplified by his account of the tension in Western philosophy between "the Jew"

and "the Greek" in "Violence and Metaphysics." The former strategies are worked repeatedly in the *Gift of Death*.

32. Although Derrida occasionally writes with Heidegger here—of the "epiphany of Being," of "unveiling," of language as the possibility of giving to the other, of the possibility of defeating nihilistic violence—these passages are as sparse as MacIntyre's acknowledgments of the Derridean themes I address in this chapter.

33. Jacques Derrida, *Aporias*, trans. Thomas Dutoit (Stanford: Stanford University Press, 1993).

34. Borrowing here a trope MacIntyre uses to acknowledge an agonistic debt to the liberal encyclopedist Adam Gifford (*Three Rival Versions*, 30).

## 6. Feminists of Color and the Torn Virtues of Democratic Engagement

1. Rawls, *Political Liberalism*, 219; Moon, *Constructing Community*, 10. Key texts by others mentioned in this paragraph include Bruce Ackerman, *Social Justice in the Liberal State* (New Haven: Yale University Press, 1980); Gutmann and Thompson, *Democracy and Disagreement;* Ronald Dworkin, *Taking Rights Seriously* (Cambridge, Mass.: Harvard University Press, 1977); Greenawalt, *Religious Convictions and Political Choice.*

2. My approach in this chapter should be distinguished from those who would continue to follow Allison Jagger's (much more understandable in 1983, when she wrote it) claim that feminists of color work "mainly at the level of description" and have no "distinctive" theory of freedom. See Jagger, *Feminist Politics and Human Nature* (Totowa, N.J.: Rowman and Littlefield, 1983), 11. I write more in the spirit of her later observation, with Paula S. Rothenberg, in *Feminist Frameworks*, 3rd ed. (New York: McGraw-Hill, 1993), xii, that feminists of color have been elaborating what amounts to a "radical overhaul of feminist theory." I argue here that they make an important contribution to democratic theory and educational theory.

3. Arthur Schlesinger Jr., *The Disuniting of America: Reflections on a Multicultural Society* (New York: Norton, 1993).

4. All quotations in this and the next two paragraphs are from Schlesinger, "'A New Race'?" chapter 1 in *The Disuniting of America.*

5. Gutmann and Thomson, in the final chapter of *Democracy and Disagreement,* provide a more supple reading of liberal principles, arguing that they will develop somewhat in the ongoing process of deliberation. Yet the development they describe is simply an internally dialectical development that occurs as each liberal principle is read and interpreted through the concerns of the other liberal principles. The possibility—let alone the importance—of an openness to transformations that come from engagements with values and visions beyond their liberal bedrock is not considered. The pressures of their construal of the liberal project leaves little or no space for such considerations.

6. In a resonant vein, Maria Lugones writes that "world-travelling is part and parcel of our experience and our situation." Lugones, "Playfulness, 'World'-Travelling, and Loving Perception," in *Making Face, Making Soul/Haciendo Caras: Creative and Critical Perspectives by Feminists of Color,* ed. Gloria Anzaldúa (San Francisco: Aunt Lute Books, 1990), 39. Cultivating a sense of the virtue of (as well as virtues for) this

situation, Lugones writes of the "richness," wisdom, freedom, and solidarity in difference that world-traveling makes possible. Integral to this ethic is "welcoming" the other and "witnessing" the other within her own world. This involves an "attitude of playfulness," an "openness to surprise," openness to "being a fool," the virtues of a trickster's ambiguous malleability. World-traveling is animated by a generous "love" that largely exceeds any determined principles: "We may not have rules, and when we do have rules, *there are no rules that are to us sacred*" (400, her emphasis). Compared to Anzaldúa, in this particular essay Lugones exaggerates both the dimension of "play" and possibilities for smooth traveling and proximate witness of others. This sometimes leads to a relationship to principles that is more cavalier and less agonal than one finds in Anzaldúa.

7. Derrida explores these relations in many texts. The most pertinent here might be *The Other Heading*, but *Specters of Marx* and *The Gift of Death*, where he writes of a "predisposition towards a certain principle of heresy," are also important in this context. See also Donna Haraway, "A Manifesto for Cyborgs: Science, Technology, and Socialist Feminism in the 1980s," in *Feminism and Postmodernism*, ed. Linda Nicholson (New York: Routledge, 1990), 190.

8. Hence Nancy Fraser is right to argue, in *Justice Interruptus: Critical Reflections on the Postsocialist Age* (New York: Routledge, 1997), that we must try to "distinguish just from unjust differences" (182). Iris Young, in *Justice and the Politics of Difference* (Princeton: Princeton University Press, 1990), sometimes comes up short in this regard. On the other hand, Young has a much more profound awareness of the limits of our efforts and hence of the need to make "listening" central to our relations with others. See, for example, Young, *Intersecting Voices: Dilemmas of Gender, Political Philosophy, and Policy* (Princeton: Princeton University Press, 1997), especially chapters 2 and 3. I am arguing for simultaneously and robustly pursuing dimensions of both projects—with all the tensions this involves.

9. Jean-Luc Nancy, "Cut Throat Sun," in *An Other Tongue: Nation and Ethnicity in the Linguistic Borderland*, ed. Alfred Arteaga (Durham, N.C.: Duke University Press, 1994). Hereafter cited in the text as "Cut Throat Sun."

10. My discussion of Nancy is indebted to Norma Alarcón's very provocative critique of Nancy's appropriation of the mestiza in "Conjugating Subjects in the Age of Multiculturalism," in *Mapping Multiculturalism*, ed. Avery F. Gordon and Christopher Newfield (Minneapolis: University of Minnesota Press, 1996), 132. For a provocative reading of Nancy that elaborates some of the contributions his work can offer to a politics explicitly informed by Anzaldúa, see Shane Phelan, *Getting Specific: Postmodern Lesbian Politics* (Minneapolis: University of Minnesota Press, 1994), chapter 5. Phelan also offers a compelling critique of Nancy that has affinities with my critique here. However, her criticism of him and her alternative suggestions focus primarily upon Spivak's "strategic essentialism" (86) and the "political necessity of common construction and (limited) identity" (88). Although sympathetic to Phelan's position, my criticism here aims more at Nancy's ethical-political rendering of the opening of "being-in-common" as such. Whereas Phelan's work develops more specifically some of the political implications of Anzaldúa's work, my chapter develops explicitly ethical themes that Phelan raises in the last few pages of her book.

11. On this point, see Yvonne Yarbo-Berjarano's incisive essay, "Gloria Anzaldúa's *Borderlands/La Frontera*: Cultural Studies, 'Difference,' and the Non-Unitary Subject," *Culture Critique*, no. 28 (Fall 1994): 5–28. Yarbo-Berjarano argues that "perhaps more productive (and more interesting) than firing off the label 'essentialist' as a 'term of infallible critique' [she draws upon Diana Fuss's analysis here] is to ask what *motivates* the deployment of essentialism" (12), or how it functions in a text. She offers a compelling case that Anzaldúa deploys identity to "give voice and substance to subjects rendered mute and invisible" (12–13). Anzaldúa maintains a vital "tension . . . between . . . activity . . . and crystallized production" and writes with great awareness that naming "both extends the possibilities of 'crossings and mixings' and 'inevitably sets up boundaries'" (*Borderlands*, 17).

12. See Norma Alarcón's provocative analyses of Chicana reinterpretations of Malinche in "Traddutora, Traditora: A Paradigmatic Figure of Chicana Feminism," *Culture Critique*, no. 13 (Fall 1989): 57–87, at 58, and her "Chicana's Feminist Literature: A Re-vision through Malintzin/or Malintzin: Putting Flesh Back on the Object," in *This Bridge Called My Back: Writings by Radical Women of Color*, ed. Cherríe Moraga and Gloria Anzaldúa (New York: Kitchen Table Press, 1986).

13. Octavio Paz, *Labyrinth of Solitude*, 86.

14. Cherríe Moraga, *Loving in the War Years* (Boston: South End Press, 1983).

15. See, e.g., Octavio Paz, *Labyrinth of Solitude* (New York: Grove Press, 1985), 86–87; Tzvetan Todorov, *The Conquest of America* (New York: Harper, 1985), 101; Moraga, *Loving in the War Years*; Adelaida R. del Castillo, "Malintzin Tenepal: A Preliminary Look into a New Perspective," in *Essays on La Mujer*, ed. Rosaura Sanchez and Rosa Martinez Cruz (Los Angeles: Chicano Studies Center Publications, University of California, Los Angeles, 1977); Haraway, "A Manifesto for Cyborgs," 217–19.

16. Paula Moya, "Postmodernism, 'Realism,' and the Politics of Identity: Cherríe Moraga and Chicana Feminism," in *Feminist Genealogies, Colonial Legacies, Democratic Futures* (New York: Routledge, 1997), 131.

17. Alarcón, "Traddutora, Traditora," 86.

18. See Paz, *Labyrinth of Solitude*.

19. Alarcón, "Traddutora, Traditora," 82.

20. Rawls *does* seek this in a modest way by means of some structural adjustments such as public campaign-finance reforms. See, for example, *Political Liberalism*, "Introduction to the Paperback Edition."

21. Rawls is surely right to argue against libertarians that the difference principle does not necessarily imply random state interventions that slide inexorably toward totalitarianism.

22. The phrase and idea "theory in the flesh" is elaborated by numerous authors in Moraga and Anzaldúa, *This Bridge Called My Back*. It is also extensively articulated by Anzaldúa in *Borderlands*; Audre Lorde in *Sister Outsider* (Freedom, Calif.: Crossing Press, 1984) (hereafter cited in the text as *Sister Outsider*); Moraga in *Loving in the War Years*; and numerous other works. Connections between "abjection" and justice are explored in Young's *Justice and the Politics of Difference*, and William Connolly's *Why I Am Not a Secularist* (Minneapolis: University of Minnesota Press,

1999) contains extensive discussions of "affect" in relation to the issues at hand. On "flesh" and "intercorporeality," see also my *Self/Power/Other.*

23. The right not to participate in such politics should not be confused as a principled banning of this vision.

24. But as Chela Sandoval shows in "U.S. Third World Feminism: The Theory and Method of Oppositional Consciousness in the Postmodern World," in *Feminism and Race,* ed. Kum-Kum Bhavnani (Oxford: Oxford University Press, 2000), the periods of conflict around essentialist reductions tend to be significantly shorter in movements among women of color.

25. Bernice Johnson Reagon, "Coalition Politics: Turning the Century," in *Homegirls: A Black Feminist Anthology,* ed. Barbara Smith (New York: Kitchen Table/Woman of Color Press, 1983).

26. See Sandoval, "U.S. Third World Feminism."

27. On receptive generosity, see my *Rethinking Generosity.*

28. bell hooks and Cornell West, *Breaking Bread: Insurgent Black Intellectual Life* (Boston: South End Press, 1991).

29. For an interesting discussion of neopopulist coalition politics in the U.S. Southwest that cuts across and transfigures lines of class, religion, race, and gender, see Mary Beth Rogers, *Cold Anger: A Story of Faith and Power Politics* (Denton, Tex.: UNT Press, 1990).

30. "Interview with Gloria Anzaldúa," 232. The interview was conducted twelve years after *Borderlands* was first published, and it appears in the second edition: Gloria Anzaldúa, *Borderlands/La Frontera: The New Mestiza,* 2nd ed. (San Francisco: Spinsters/Aunt Lute, 1999).

31. For example, Wendy Brown, "Injury, Identity, Politics," in Gordon and Newfield, *Mapping Multiculturalism.* See Susan Bickford's thoughtful critical responses to Brown in "Anti-anti Identity Politics: Feminism, Democracy and the Complexities of Citizenship," *Hypatia* 12, no. 4 (Fall 1997): 111–31.

32. Lorde, "The Uses of Anger," in *Sister Outsider,* 127–29. See also Rogers, *Cold Anger.*

33. Thus, Anzaldúa writes that "all reaction is limited by, and dependent upon what it is reacting against" (*Borderlands,* 78). Similarly, Lorde writes, "Anger is useful to clarify our differences, but in the long run, strength that is bred by anger alone is a blind force which cannot create the future. It can only demolish the past" (*Sister Outsider,* 152).

34. At this point Gutmann and Thompson get off the boat. See *Democracy and Deliberation,* 135–37.

35. A similar point is made in Rogers, *Cold Anger.*

## 7. Moving Democracy

1. See, for example, Sidney Verba, Kay Lehman Schlozman, and Henry E. Brady, *Voice and Equality: Civic Voluntarism in American Politics* (Cambridge, Mass.: Harvard University Press, 1995).

2. I think this is true of a wide variety of work in democratic theory today. (My

work here is critical of but nevertheless remains significantly indebted to some of these theories.) I think that across a broad array of theoretical positions there is a problem of "formalism": Normative, ontological, or political logics are first elaborated in contexts quite removed from textured and responsive interpretative engagements with everyday political practices, and theorists hastily point to the world for particular instances that support the theory or show how its aspirations might be further realized. Frequently elided are modes of engagement with associational life that seek to learn about democracy in fundamental ways from the peoples, practices, and associations being studied. Habermas's analyses of social movements (and those of many following in his steps) have changed over the years, but in every instance, he constructs a normative framework in conjunction with a political sociology developed in conversation with "the greats" and then points to civil society to show that the norms have some reality and efficacy in real-world democracy and modernity. Ernesto Laclau and Chantal Mouffe, *Hegemony and Socialist Theory: Toward a Radical and Plural Democracy* (London: Verso, 1985), develop a logic of "hegemony" in which social movements become mere particular examples rather than bodies of theory-practice that might transfigure the fundamental logic, if carefully engaged. This problem is replicated in a different form in political liberalism, which normatively establishes the limits and basic modes of political society and then points to examples in civil society to show that, indeed, most political associational life is as it should be, fits within the limits of liberalism, nourishes a commitment to political liberal principles, and so forth. Robert Putnam's *Making Democracy Work: Civic Traditions in Modern Italy* (Princeton: Princeton University Press, 1993), and a significant portion of the "social capital" literature inspired by it, provides another case: A neo-Tocquevillean model of democracy is posited, followed by research into where, when, and how it works (or doesn't) to produce trust and cooperation in civil society and in effective representative institutions.

3. My claim is certainly not that this idea is an entirely new one—just that this project is too rarely and poorly pursued. In very different ways, writers like Harry Boyte, *Commonwealth: A Return to Citizen Politics* (New York: Harper and Row, 1989); Alain Touraine, *The Voice and the Eye: An Analysis of Social Movements* (Cambridge: Cambridge University Press, 1981); and Judith Butler, in many works, see "Competing Universalities," in Judith Butler, Ernesto Laclau, and Slavoj Žižek, *Contingency, Hegemony, Universality: Contemporary Dialogues on the Left* (London: Verso, 2000)—where she explicitly thematizes an approach to movements—have undertaken inquiries from which I have learned.

4. See, for example, Maurice Merleau-Ponty, *In Praise of Philosophy*, trans. J. Wild and J. Edie (Evanston, Ill.: Northwestern University Press, 1963); and Theodor Adorno, *Negative Dialectics*, trans. E. B. Ashton (New York: Continuum, 1973), especially the introduction.

5. Adorno, *Negative Dialectics*, 28.

6. My discussion of the IAF draws significantly from my participation for several years in an IAF organizing effort in Durham and from the growing literature on the IAF. Among the sources that inform my discussion: Mark R. Warren, *Dry Bones*

*Rattling: Community Building to Revitalize American Democracy* (Princeton: Princeton University Press, 2001); Rogers, *Cold Anger;* IAF, *Fifty Years Organizing for Change* (New York: Industrial Areas Foundation, 1990); Boyte, *Commonwealth;* William Greider, *Who Will Tell the People? The Betrayal of American Democracy* (New York: Simon and Schuster, 1992), chapter 10; Samuel G. Freedman, *Upon This Rock: The Miracles of a Black Church* (New York: HarperCollins, 1993); Edward Chambers, *Organizing for Family and Congregation* (New York: Industrial Areas Foundation, 1978).

7. For example, Michael J. Sandel, *Democracy's Discontents: America in Search of a Public Philosophy* (Cambridge, Mass.: Harvard University Press, 1996), 336–37. Robert N. Bellah et al., in *Habits of the Heart: Individualism and Commitment in American Life* (Berkeley and Los Angeles: University of California Press, 1985), provide a similar frame for interpreting this kind of democratic engagement. My own interpretation is, of course, not above the fray with these alternative interpretations; rather, it is a contestable effort to participate in forming directions of democratic theory and practice.

8. The vision and the strategic success are related: The formation of bridging relationships, or what Warren, in *Dry Bones Rattling,* calls "bridging social capital," forms the broad power base that enables IAF organizations to become important players in the political arena, and the formation of those relationships is greatly facilitated by the practices of receptivity discussed below.

9. This is one metaphor, democracy needs many.

10. Albert Hirschman, *Exit, Voice, and Loyalty: Responses to Decline in Firms, Organizations, and States* (Cambridge, Mass.: Harvard University Press, 1970).

11. Two prominent examples: Samuel Bowles and Herbert Gintis, *Democracy and Capitalism* (New York: Basic Books, 1986), and Mark E. Warren, *Democracy and Association* (Princeton: Princeton University Press, 2001).

12. Mark E. Warren, *Democracy and Association,* 103–4.

13. Hirschman, *Exit, Voice, and Loyalty,* 17.

14. My argument here, of course, is not that those who focus on voice either explicitly or entirely deny the role of receptivity in communication. Rather, my point is that this focus tends to steer our attention away from practices of receptivity in ways that *diminish* their visibility, distinctness, and importance in our accounts of the world and our theoretical formulations. Once again, it is instructive to read Hirschman, who recognizes the importance of organizations' listening and becoming more responsive to the voices of their members: He folds listening into his concern for voice. But more-horizontal receptivity is virtually absent in his analysis, both because of the paradigm that frames his inquiry and because the memberships and organizations with which he is concerned seem to appear to him to be devoid of power-laden and difficult differences such as race, class, gender, religion, sexuality, neighborhood, nationality, and the like. He argues that many organizations would have to become more responsive in order to enable voice. Yet the possibility that members and voices would have to *refashion themselves* through practices of difficult receptivity, or the possibility that organizations would have to develop these receptive practices in relation

to other organizations (across similarly power-saturated divides) with whom they would have to work both in order to discern and respond to intractable problems, undemocratic powers, and injustices and in order to pursue alternative democratic relationships and action—these possibilities are persistently marginalized in his work. I suspect that Mark E. Warren—who is keenly attentive to power relations, exclusion, and so forth—shares a certain inattentiveness to receptivity because of the voice-accented framework that guides his analysis. This framework marginalizes receptivity in his account of the tensions between deliberative commonness and difference (about which more below)—precisely where one might expect it to be more prominent. For another analysis of the absence of explicit discussions of listening in political theory, see Susan Bickford, *The Dissonance of Democracy: Listening, Conflict, and Citizenship* (Ithaca, N.Y.: Cornell University Press, 1996), chapter 1.

15. For example, Charles Tilly, *From Mobilization to Revolution* (Reading, Mass.: Addison-Wesley, 1978).

16. Jean Cohen and Andrew Arato, *Civil Society and Political Theory* (Cambridge: MIT Press, 1992), 505.

17. Richard Sennett, foreword to Touraine, *The Voice and the Eye*, xi.

18. For critical accounts of Habermas's weakness on questions of difference and receptivity, see my *Rethinking Generosity* and "Of Democracy, Discourse, and Dirt Virtue," *Political Theory* 28, no. 4 (August 2000): 540–64.

19. Cohen and Arato, *Civil Society and Political Theory*, 522.

20. Thus, speaking of the heart of feminist revolution from a position dramatically different from the one articulated by Cohen and Arato, Audre Lorde writes, "It is becoming always vigilant for the smallest opportunity to make a genuine change in established outgrown responses" (*Sister Outsider*, 141). White feminists who have attended to this fact tend to place listening and receptivity to difference prominently in their theoretical and historical accounts. See also my "Traditio: Feminists of Color and the Torn Virtues of Democratic Engagement," *Political Theory* 29, no. 4 (August 2001): 488–516.

21. Cohen and Arato, *Civil Society and Political Theory*, 522.

22. I am focusing here on what I take to be their *best*. IAF organizations also sometimes have problems in this regard, as I discuss at the end of the chapter.

23. The importance of open-ended listening—not organizing with a loud voice as if one knows what a "progressive platform" will be before encountering a diverse range of constituencies—is continually stressed by the IAF's southeast regional organizer, Gerald Taylor. And "how to listen to and affirm other people" figures high on the list of the democratic virtues and skills the IAF seeks to cultivate (along with "how to view and accept tension"), according to national IAF director Edward Chambers (*Organizing for Family and Congregation*, 21).

24. Rogers, *Cold Anger*, 59, 64. I think the expression "get out of yourself and under the skin of others" is important. It includes the kind of listening that Susan Bickford, drawing on Merleau-Ponty, insightfully discusses in *The Dissonance of Democracy*, where she writes, "In listening, I construct an 'auditory gestalt' in which I make myself the ground, the horizon, against which the other becomes the focused

on figure" (146). Yet it also evokes a more radical receptivity in which one (gradually, or suddenly to an important extent) experiences *others* (through their stories,
geographies, visceral expressivity) as the ground, experiences *their* horizon of experience and expectations, and experiences oneself as a figure upon their ground or
horizon. Listening to the other(s) might best be described as the stereophonic experience of the other that emerges *between* these two modalities of receptive attention.
In a world where oblivion is deeply inscribed in our corporeal responses to the world,
we may often do well to accent the more radical receptivity. Of course, we never *completely* experience "the other's horizon" or "the other as ground" (see, for example,
the work of Adorno and Merleau-Ponty, and also Iris Marion Young's "Asymmetrical Reciprocity: On Moral Respect, Wonder, and Enlarged Thought," in *Intersecting
Voices* [Princeton: Princeton University Press, 1997]). It is precisely a sense of the
nonidentity that pushes receptivity permanently to the forefront of the ethical, political, and epistemological project at hand. Yet listening, I am arguing, involves an endlessly incomplete, messy, and complicated shifting from my ground toward the
ground of the other(s) on which I/we figure. This shifting ought to be accented as an
essentially incompletable telos of our listening ethos. I discuss below in this chapter
the more radical receptivity in terms of the democratic table as a "ray of the world,"
drawing on Merleau-Ponty. For an extended account, see my *Self/Power/Other.*

25. Mark R. Warren, *Dry Bones Rattling,* 224.

26. Ibid.

27. See particularly, Rogers, *Cold Anger,* Mark R. Warren, *Dry Bones Rattling.*

28. On Baltimore's living-wage campaign, see David Harvey, *Spaces of Hope*
(Berkeley and Los Angeles: University of California Press, 2000), chapter 7. On the
Brooklyn campaign for affordable housing, see Freedman, *Upon This Rock.*

29. On gated geographies and oblivion, my discussion is informed by Kimberley
Curtis's profound account in *Our Sense of the Real: Aesthetic Experience and Arendtian Politics* (Ithaca, N.Y.: Cornell University Press, 1998.)

30. In this section I am drawing substantially upon my own experiences in IAF
organizing during the past few years. These traveling practices are a central part of
IAF bridge-building activity in cities throughout the United States, but to my knowledge they have not received sufficient attention. I draw the expression "traveling"
from Lugones, "Playfulness, 'World'-Travelling, and Loving Perception."

31. Here I am interpreting IAF traveling in a manner resonant with Michael Shapiro,
"Bowling Blind: Post Liberal Civil Society and the Worlds of Neo-Tocquevillean Social
Theory," *Theory and Event* 1, no. 1 (1997), http://muse.jhu.edu/journals/theory_and_
event/v001/1./shapiro.html. In relation to Shapiro, my chapter is an effort to read the
terrain often claimed by neo-Tocquevilleans in a manner that moves beyond some of
the problems and limits that Shapiro rightly identifies in Alexis de Tocqueville and
those who remain close to his thinking.

32. Here one might usefully consider Bruno Latour's understanding of democratic
activity as generated and oriented through assembled collectivities of human and nonhuman beings and things that interanimate one another. See Latour, *Pandora's Hope:
Essays on the Reality of Science Studies* (Cambridge, Mass.: Harvard University

Press, 1999). I am suggesting that different groups are significantly constituted in relation to their segmented portions of the world and that relationships between those from different segments are greatly aided by traveling to the built and lived worlds of other people's segments and by acquiring newly constitutive relationships with those segments.

33. See Mark R. Warren, *Dry Bones Rattling*, 85–88, on the IAF Southwest organizer seminars, which have met with over a hundred scholars in recent years. A similar project (in which I am involved), called the Third Reconstruction Institute, has recently been initiated in the Southeast between Durham IAF organizers and faculty at Duke University.

34. Hannah Arendt, *Lectures on Kant's Political Philosophy*, ed. Ronald Beiner (Chicago: University of Chicago Press, 1982), 43; Arendt's translation of Immanuel Kant, *Critique of Judgment*, part 1, section 40.

35. Arendt, *Lectures on Kant's Political Philosophy*, 40.

36. Ibid., 43.

37. Hannah Arendt, "Truth and Politics," in *Between Past and Future* (New York: Viking Press, 1968), 241.

38. Quoted in Ronald Beiner, "Hannah Arendt and Judging," in Arendt, *Lectures on Kant's Political Philosophy*.

39. Arendt's paraphrase of Kant, in *Lectures on Kant's Political Philosophy*, 44.

40. This critique is elaborated in my "Pluralization and Radical Democracy: Recent Developments in Critical Theory and Postmodernism," in *Political Science: The State of the Discipline,* ed. Ira Katznelson and Helen V. Milner (New York: Norton, 2002).

41. Jacques Derrida compellingly makes this claim in *Specters of Marx* and elsewhere.

42. This theme is elaborated in my *Self/Power/Other* and *Rethinking Generosity.* Among the more profound discussions are William Connolly, *Identity/Difference* (Ithaca, N.Y.: Cornell University Press, 1991), and Peter Euben, *The Tragedy of Political Theory* (Princeton: Princeton University Press, 1990).

43. On complementarities and tensions, see Mark E. Warren, *Democracy and Association;* William Connolly, *The Ethos of Pluralization* (Minneapolis: University of Minnesota Press, 1995); Iris Young, "Activist Challenges to Democracy," *Political Theory* 29, no. 5 (October 2001): 670–90; and my "Toward an Uncommon Commonwealth: Reflections on Boyte's Critique of Civil Society," *Good Society* 9, no. 2 (1999): 23–27.

44. Mark E. Warren, *Democracy and Association,* 171.

45. Ibid., 173.

46. Hannah Arendt, *The Human Condition* (Chicago: University of Chicago Press, 1958), 52–53.

47. Ibid.

48. My aim here is not to deliver democracy to a single image (for democracy needs many) but, rather, to rework this important and persistent one. The street, the rhizome, and the constitution are among several other vital and discordant images.

49. Mark E. Warren, *Democracy and Association,* 212.

50. Maurice Merleau-Ponty, *The Visible and the Invisible*, trans. Alphonso Lingus (Evanston, Ill.: Northwestern University Press, 1968), 218. For an extensive discussion, see my *Self/Power/Other.*

51. Arendt, *The Human Condition*, 52.

52. Mark R. Warren, *Dry Bones Rattling*, 171.

53. Even though, of course, these officials are elected by us, the relation between us and them is so often staged as their domain except on the day of election.

54. Hanna Pitkin, *The Concept of Representation* (Berkeley and Los Angeles: University of California Press, 1967), 1.

55. Ibid., 157.

56. This phrase comes from Gerald Taylor, speaking on the patience and long-term time horizons required for deep democratic transformation. Some indication of initial success in this regard is found in IAF organizations that have continued to grow stronger for more than three decades; third-generation participants; people wishing to be buried wearing their local IAF affiliate buttons.

57. Mark E. Warren, *Democracy and Association*, 176; and Mark R. Warren, *Dry Bones Rattling*, esp. chapters 4 and 5.

58. Mark E. Warren, *Democracy and Association*, 113–17.

59. Though in the reflective retreats between activists and academics, some of these issues are very directly engaged. And they sometimes emerge in organizing; see, for example, Mark E. Warren's discussion of race in *Dry Bones Rattling*, chapters 4 and 5.

## 8. Reconsidering the Politics of Education

This chapter was written in collaboration with Troy Dostert.

1. Stephen Macedo, "Liberal Civic Education and Religious Fundamentalism: The Case of God v. John Rawls?" *Ethics* 105 (1995): 468–96 (hereafter cited in the text as "Liberal Civic Education"), and *Diversity and Distrust: Civic Education in a Multicultural Democracy* (Cambridge, Mass.: Harvard University Press, 2000) (hereafter cited in the text as *Diversity and Distrust*); Gutmann and Thompson, *Democracy and Disagreement.*

2. Greenawalt, *Religious Convictions and Political Choice*, and *Private Consciences and Public Reasons* (New York: Oxford University Press, 1995); Connolly, *Why I Am Not a Secularist* and *The Ethos of Pluralization;* MacIntyre, *Whose Justice? Which Rationality?*

3. William Galston, *Liberal Pluralism: The Implications of Value Pluralism for Political Theory and Practice* (New York: Cambridge University Press, 2002). Hereafter cited in the text as *Liberal Pluralism.*

4. Galston uses the term "diversity state" in "Two Concepts of Liberalism," *Ethics* 105 (April 1995): 516–34. Hereafter cited in the text as "Two Concepts."

5. William Galston, *Liberal Purposes: Goods, Virtues, and Diversity in the Liberal State* (Cambridge: Cambridge University Press, 1991), 283–87.

6. Steven Bates, *Battleground: One Mother's Crusade, The Religious Right, and the Struggle for Our Schools* (New York: Henry Holt, 1993), 65–92, 120–52.

7. See my *Self/Power/Other* and *Rethinking Generosity.*

8. I do not draw Yoder into the orbit of receptive generosity—though perhaps one could—because I think he would mightily resist it. Others I have thrown together with this term would probably resist being drawn in as well, but perhaps not as strongly, and perhaps in ways that one can overlook given the specific aims of this section. At any rate, this delineation is shorthand, provisional, local, and pragmatically designed for the problems at hand. I am more concerned to emphasize Yoder's differences here because the issue at hand concerns Christian theology and politics.

9. The experimental and wild patience of radical reform efforts embraced by a politics of receptive generosity can be seen in part by the extent to which it proceeds significantly through "arts of the self" and "micro-politics" that work noncoercively on various registers of affect, perception, experience, and ideology to effect transformations. It moves *experimentally* in the formation of alternative practices: transfigured "families"; women's shelters; "sanctuary" as an alternative to nationalistic border practices; cooperatives; micro-practices of North-South fair trade; cinematic efforts to draw the bodily explicitly into political contestations concerning aging, nationality, assisted suicide, and sexuality; multiracial coalitions in urban areas experimenting with multidoctrinal discursive negotiations; practices of restorative justice; alternative practices of reverently caring for forests, rivers, and farmland; and so on.

Yet when what begin as minority sensibilities and practices effect widespread alterations in the perception, thoughts, and faiths of a variety of constituencies regarding gays and lesbians, punishment, borders, elements of doctrine in politics, nationalism, social heterogeneity, poverty and inequality, and the like, these sensibilities and practices have brought about and will frequently bring about laws and policies that alter the basic structure. This is a vital dimension of the more open democratic vision embraced here. Sometimes these changes will be justified in terms of (now expanded) widely shared secular principles. At other times they might be borne by a rhizomic network of disparate theological, secular, pagan, and postsecular discourses, none of which claims to possess the currency "shared and binding on all," yet each of which senses strange elements of resonance across lines of difference, resonance that affords alliances. Where the coalitions are deeper and more enduring, elements of a new and more common language may begin to emerge. Yet a politics of receptivity powerfully resists efforts to congeal and fortify this language as *the* uncontestable reason of the political core and its limit. It will strive to affirm spaces where differences that contest the new majority configuration (of which it is a part) can engage in experimentation with alternatives that resist its own encroachments and move in other directions. Clearly there will remain tragic encroachments that will require future radical reformations. A politics of receptive generosity does not deny that it is likely to engage in blindness and violence of its own. Yet it sees no political configuration that would escape or definitively minimize this. With Yoder, it responds to this predicament by engaging in practices that cultivate a readiness for reformation.

The experimentalism and wild patience of Yoder's radical reformation theology is evident in the church's approach toward the political sphere and its understanding of power more generally; the notion that the church's particular truths should be enforced coercively is antithetical to the very nature of the Good News. Once the church renounces the desire to rule, it can then assume an altogether different social and political stance, one with perhaps more expansive and creative possibilities. Rather than seeing its principal political responsibility as involving trying to govern the whole or to take part in "social engineering," it concerns itself with developing its distinctive practices and truths and presenting them, in embodied form, to the wider society. The church in this manner presents "signs" through which the "new world on the way" is revealed (*For the Nations*, 104; *Royal Priesthood*, 204; *For the Nations*, 50). Examples include the practice of radical peacefulness, as well as the egalitarian economic ethic embodied in the Eucharist, or the alternative means of conflict resolution made evident through the practice of dialogical discernment (*Royal Priesthood*, 359–73). The church can further exemplify this "minority ethic" by developing ad hoc "pilot programs" and social experiments that can seek to "meet previously unmet needs or to restore ministries which have collapsed" (*Priestly Kingdom*, 92). Importantly, these options do not exclude more conventional political strategies, which can involve tactical alliances with other communities on behalf of causes that Christians might share with those outside the church; Yoder argues against a facile church/world dualism that would limit Christians' political activity in the interests of maintaining the moral "purity" of the church (*Priestly Kingdom*, 164–66, 61–62). Indeed, holding political offices is a viable strategy for Christians, as long as the mode and substance of their participation is consistent with the "body politics" of Jesus — for example, pacifism, economic sharing, dialogical discernment, forgiveness — and resists what is at odds with it. What is essential is that the church must avoid seeking coercive power as a means of shortcutting the disciplined processes of discernment and engagement that are indispensable to its witness. Only when the church is faithful to its own practices and committed to approaching other communities receptively can its political activity be consistent with the Gospel.

10. Baier, "Justice and the Aims of Political Philosophy," 771–90.

11. Tully, *Strange Multiplicity*. See also Boaventura de Sousa Santos, *Toward a New Legal Common Sense: Law, Globalization, Emancipation* (London: Butterworths LexusNexus, 2002).

12. Bates, *Battleground*, 68; 65–92 generally.

13. Ibid., 117; 120–52 generally.

14. Nomi Maya Stolzenberg, "'He Drew a Circle That Shut Me Out': Assimilation, Indoctrination, and the Paradox of a Liberal Education," *Harvard Law Review* 106 (1993): 581–667, at 612–13.

15. Mark R. Warren, *Dry Bones Rattling*, 25–28. See also Mark E. Warren, *Democracy and Association*, for an insightful discussion of the relations between "politics of commonality" and "politics of difference."

16. Discussions with IAF southeastern regional lead organizer, Gerald Taylor.

17. John Stuart Mill, *On Representative Government*, ed. Currin V. Shields (New York: Liberal Arts, 1958), 234; Connolly, *Why I Am Not a Secularist*, 83–84.

# Index

Adorno, Theodor, 55
Alarcón, Norma, 197–98, 281n12
Alinsky, Saul, 215
Alterity. *See* Derrida, Jacques; Levinas,
  Emmanuel; Otherness
Anger: and feminist theory, 210–11;
  uses of, 212
Anzaldúa, Gloria, xiv, 65, 188–98,
  205; on anger, 210–11; on divided
  loyalties, 193; on tradition of
  migration, 191, 192
Aquinas, Thomas, 272n16. *See also*
  MacIntyre, Alasdair
Arato, Andrew, 218–19
Arendt, Hannah, 225–26
Audi, Robert, 266n6

Berlin, Isaiah, 14–15

Capitalism: and political liberalism, 33
Christianity, 240–49. *See also* Yoder,
  John Howard
Civil society, 213–14
Cohen, Jean, 218
Coles, Romand, 270n3, 273n3
Confidence trickster, 99–102
Cortes, Ernesto, 226
Cosmopolitanism. *See* Kuper, Andrew;
  Nussbaum, Martha; Waldron, Jeremy
Currency, 33, 36, 43, 44, 49–50; and col-
  onization, 44; and public reason, 43

Deliberation, xxviii
Democracy, 40, 49, 87, 214–16, 218,

219–21, 222–23, 228–35; and
democratic theory, 215; and listening,
216, 222–23; as tabling, 216, 228–
35; as *traditio*, 187; and voice, 218
Democratic theory, 185, 214, 215;
normative basis, 214. *See also*
Receptive generosity
Derrida, Jacques, xxiv–xxvi, 139,
140–66, 177–82; and democracy,
139, 159, 161–63, 166, 167; and
double contradictory responsibility,
153–62, 164; and difference, 155;
and ethics, 146; and Europe,
154–56, 158–61; and hospitality,
162; and Husserl, 140–53; and
otherness, 147–48, 150, 152, 156,
180–82; and responsibility, 147–48,
152, 156–57, 161, 176; and
tradition, 149, 151, 176
Difference, 155, 185, 188, 207, 261;
and liberalism, 188

Education, 240–45, 257–59; and
Christian fundamentalism, 240–45;
and political liberalism, 241–47;
and receptive generosity, 257–59
Ethics, 186, 198; and torn virtues, 198.
*See* Receptive generosity
Euben, Peter, 6

Feminists of color, 186, 187, 188–92,
202, 204, 210–12; and anger,
210–12; and liberalism, 202, 204;
and tradition, 186, 187

**Romand Coles** is professor of political theory at Duke University. He is the author of *Rethinking Generosity: Critical Theory and the Politics of Caritas* and *Self/Power/Other: Political Theory and Dialogical Ethics*.